EFFECTIVE STRATEGIES FOR TE

Effective Strategies for Teaching Reading

BERNARD L. HAYES
Editor

Utah State University

ALLYN AND BACON
Boston London Toronto Sydney Tokyo Singapore

Series Editor: Sean W. Wakely
Series Editorial Assistant: Carol L. Chernaik
Production Administrator: Annette Joseph
Production Coordinator: Holly Crawford
Editorial-Production Service: Ann Mohan, WordCrafters Editorial Services, Inc.
Manufacturing Buyer: Louise Richardson
Cover Administrator: Linda K. Dickinson
Cover Designer: Suzanne Harbison

A Division of Simon & Schuster, Inc.
160 Gould Street
Needham Heights, MA 02194

Library of Congress Cataloging-in-Publication Data

Effective strategies for teaching reading/editor, Bernard L. Hayes.
p. cm.
Includes bibliographical references and index.
ISBN 0-205-12646-4
1. Reading (Elementary) 2. Language arts (Elementary)
3. Interdisciplinary approach in education. 4. Reading teachers--Training of. I. Hayes, Bernard L.
LB1573.E34 1991
372.4'1—dc20 90-41978
CIP

Printed in the United States of America
10 9 8 7 6 5 4 3 2 1 95 94 93 92 91 90

Contents

PART FOUR: INCREASING POSITIVE ATTITUDES: READING AND THE AFFECTIVE DOMAIN 341

Preface

This book is designed to help present and future classroom teachers become more effective teachers of reading. The emphasis throughout is on what teachers do—and what they encourage students to do—that will enhance their ability and interest in reading. The basic premise of the book is that individual classroom teachers are responsible for the effectiveness of their reading programs. In order to provide children with effective programs, teachers need to be aware of the effective strategies available to them for teaching reading.

Effective Strategies for Teaching Reading is intended as a textbook for second courses in reading instruction for the elementary and intermediate grades. It would typically be used with third- or fourth-year undergraduates or returning master's level students who have had a general introductory class in reading instruction. However, the book could be used in an introductory course when used in conjunction with a basic developmental reading methods textbook or even in lieu of it when classroom activities, demonstrations, and lectures address topics that are covered by the basic textbook.

The book is organized into four parts. Part One presents suggestions for the development of reading skills and strategies that the effective teacher must help students acquire. The chapters in this part discuss the nature of reading and teaching, word identification, vocabulary, comprehension, study skills, content area reading, and the integration of reading and writing. Part Two contains information and procedures that the teacher can use to diagnose students' reading and writing strengths and weaknesses in order to make effective instructional decisions. Part Three discusses organizational and management concerns. It emphasizes methods of organizing the classroom for instruction, planning effective lessons, using basal readers effectively, meeting the needs of special students, and using parents and volunteers in the classroom reading program. Part Four describes important aspects of motivating students to read from a variety of materials both in school and at home.

Several features are provided to help readers make efficient use of the book. Introductions to the chapters and each of the four parts preview the information in each chapter and also relate one chapter to another. Each chapter also begins with several study questions that direct the reader's attention to important content. Summary, follow-up questions and activities, and additional readings conclude each chapter.

Acknowledgments

I am indebted to several people who helped make this book possible. First, I wish to thank the contributors for their efforts in translating their knowledge of literacy instruction into effective strategies for teaching reading:

Eunice N. Askov
The Pennsylvania State University

James F. Baumann
University of Georgia

Kay Camperell
Utah State University

Martha D. Collins
University of Akron

Nicholas P. Criscuolo
New Haven, Connecticut, Public Schools

Charles R. Duke
Clarion University

Jerome C. Harste
Indiana University

Joan E. Heimlich
University of Wisconsin—Whitewater

Beth Ann Herrmann
University of South Carolina

Winnie R. Huebsch
University of Wisconsin—Madison

Sharon Kossack
Florida International University

Stephen B. Kucer
University of Southern California

Susan D. Pittelman
University of Wisconsin—Madison

Peggy E. Ransom
Ball State University

D. Ray Reutzel
Brigham Young University

Richard J. Smith
University of Wisconsin—Madison

Linda L. Snyder
Franklin College

Dixie Lee Spiegel
University of North Carolina at Chapel Hill

Jennifer A. Stevenson
Highlights for Children, Inc.

William J. Strong
Utah State University.

In addition, my appreciation goes to Donna Alvermann, University of Georgia; Donna Emery, California State University—Northridge; Victoria Chou Hare, University of Illinois at Chicago Circle; George Hess, Kennesaw State College; and Leonie Rose, Central Michigan University, for their thoughtful and constructive suggestions during the review process. I would also like to acknowledge the editorial staff of Allyn and Bacon, particularly

Sean Wakely, for encouragement, guidance, and patience. I especially thank Ann Mohan for her care in editing the final manuscript. Most important, I thank my wife and children, Sandy, Amy, and Ross, for their support and understanding.

B.L.H.

PART ONE

Effective Teaching of the Reading Process

Part One deals with the development of reading skills and strategies that effective teachers must help students acquire. Activities for teaching writing also are given attention because of the clear and important relationship between reading and writing. Chapter 1 presents a brief overview of the purpose of this book as well as a discussion of the nature of reading and reading instruction and the importance of the effective teacher in the reading program. Chapter 2 offers suggestions for teaching students basic skills and strategies in word identification. Chapter 3 provides suggestions for expanding students' vocabulary. Chapters 4, 5, and 6 all address the complex task of teaching students to gain meaning from the various kinds of materials they read. Chapter 4 provides suggestions for teaching students to comprehend what they read; Chapter 5 provides strategies for helping students get the most from their reading by introducing study skills; and Chapter 6 describes the special strategies students need to cope with the reading demands in content area materials. Chapter 7 presents a clear discussion of the relationship between reading and writing and offers suggestions for integrating reading and writing in the reading program. Chapter 8 explains in detail further aspects of using writing to enhance students' reading growth.

1

The Effective Teaching of Reading

BERNARD L. HAYES

IN CHAPTER 1, Bernard Hayes provides an overview of the purpose of this textbook: to elucidate and emphasize selected aspects of teaching children to read. The book's intended audience is preservice teachers who have had only a basic introduction to reading instruction. It also provides an excellent update for experienced teachers who want to refresh their knowledge of reading instruction.

Hayes goes on to discuss the nature of reading and reading instruction. He suggests that, for the purpose of this book, reading is synonymous with comprehension, and he discusses factors that influence comprehension. He stresses the importance of teachers' forming their own definitions of reading so that the instructional approaches they present to children will not be fragmented or inconsistent.

Chapter 1 concludes with a discussion of the importance of the teacher in helping children learn to read. Hayes contends that it is the teacher who makes reading programs effective, and he lists characteristics of effective teachers.

STUDY QUESTIONS

1. What is the focus of this book?
2. How would you define reading?
3. What is the most important factor in teaching reading?
4. What are the characteristics of effective teachers?

Purpose of This Book

This book is designed to help you become an effective teacher of reading by planning learning experiences that will make a difference in the lives of students. One of our culture's most unfortunate misconceptions is that anyone can be a teacher. The truth is that being an effective teacher is difficult, especially when it comes to understanding the complexities of helping children acquire the literacy skills and strategies they need to cope with the demands of society.

To prepare you for this task, each chapter of the book deals with important aspects of teaching students to read, presenting current theoretical concerns and effective instructional applications. The book focuses on the elementary school and provides guidelines and suggestions that will help you make important decisions about how reading will be taught in your classroom. Because many teachers are expected to use a basal reading program in their classrooms, special attention is given to strategies and methods they can use to enrich these programs and make them more effective. The emphasis is on helping teachers organize and manage the realities and complexities of the classroom so that they can teach reading effectively with that most often employed and most maligned of instructional materials, the basal reader.

This book is intended to emphasize selected aspects of material usually covered in a basic introductory reading textbook and to further prepare you for the task of effectively teaching children to read. For those of you who are experienced teachers, the book will serve as an aid for reevaluating beliefs and reassessing reading practices.

What Is Reading?

This seemingly simple question is filled with complexity. Educators, psychologists, linguists, and others who are interested in the reading process have filled books with their efforts to define reading or develop models of the reading process. In many cases, these definitions or models are contradictory, each emphasizing a different component of the reading process. It would be counterproductive to present an extensive list of definitions here, because effective teachers must develop their own definitions of reading after they understand its components. However, a brief discussion of the major models of reading will be presented as background to help teachers arrive at their own definitions. Most models can be placed in one of three classes: bottom-up, top-down, or interactive.

Bottom-up Models

A bottom-up model of reading suggests that reading is basically a process of translating graphic symbols into speech during oral reading or inner speech during silent reading. The reader then uses previously acquired listening comprehension skills. A bottom-up model suggests that written language is subservient to oral language and that the only activity unique to reading is that of breaking the written code.

Lower-level processes such as sensory and perceptual processes are seen as taking place prior to, and perhaps not involving, higher-level or cognitive processes. According to this model, first the reader acquires graphic information such as letters and words from the printed page and then syntactic and semantic processing occurs. As a result of this sequence of activity, the printed material is understood. Reading comprehension is thought to be heavily dependent on rapid, accurate word recognition. Bottom-up theorists suggest that reading is controlled by textual input; the reader plays a relatively passive role in the process (Weaver & Resnick, 1979). Thus, the printed material provides more information than the reader does (Strange, 1980).

Some theorists apply bottom-up models to all levels of reading development. Others suggest that bottom-up models best describe the process of learning to read, but other models more accurately describe the activities of skilled readers.

The most often discussed examples of bottom-up models are those of Gough and Cosky (1977) and Laberge and Samuels (1985).

Top-down Models

In top-down models the reader's prior knowledge and cognitive and linguistic abilities are important factors in constructing meaning from the printed page. Top-down theorists suggest that before or shortly after any graphic input the reader develops predictions about the meaning of the printed page. These hypotheses are based on the reader's prior knowledge of the subject, the specific content of the material, and the ability to interpret the words in their grammatical functions. The reader relies on graphic clues only as needed. As the information is processed, the reader confirms, rejects, or refines predictions made about meaning. Thus, according to this model, the reader plays an active role and supplies more information regarding meaning than the printed page does.

An important contrast between bottom-up and top-down models is that top-down theorists believe that skilled readers go directly from print to meaning without first recoding print into speech.

Several top-down theorists contend that their models are more descriptive of skilled readers. However, Goodman and Goodman (1982) have suggested that beginning readers differ from skilled readers only in the lesser competence they have in the strategies needed for gaining meaning from the printed page. Two of the most widely cited top-down models are those of Goodman (1967) and Smith (1979).

Interactive Models

Interactive models are more than a compromise between bottom-up and top-down theories. In interactive models, different processes are thought to be responsible for providing information that is shared with other processes. As such, a hypothesis arrived at by means of top-down processing is directed by the results of bottom-up processing; the bottom-up processing is guided to a degree by the hypothesis imposed by top-down processing. The information obtained from each type of processing is combined to determine the most appropriate interpretation of the printed page. The different processes do not have equal influence in all interactive models, and there is no complete agreement as to which kind of processing initiates the reading process. Some interactive theorists believe that top-down and bottom-up processes occur almost simultaneously.

Rumelhart (1977) has developed the most widely cited interactive model, which suggests that, at least for skilled readers, top-down and bottom-up processing occurs simultaneously.

Your own definition of reading will continue to grow and change as new research evidence emerges. However, it is important to give careful thought to a definition of reading because you will be forced to develop an instructional program as soon as you enter the classroom. Since what children learn is influenced greatly by what teachers teach, if you have not given any thought to the question of what reading is your effectiveness will probably suffer from fragmented and inconsistent notions of the reading process.

A Definition of Reading

For the purpose of this book, reading is considered to be synonymous with comprehension. As such, reading involves both reconstructing an author's message and constructing one's own meaning using the print on the page. Within this definition, the context of the situation or the reader's purpose in reading will also influence meaning. This process of comprehension is interrelated with and supportive of the other communication processes: listening, speaking, writing, and thinking. According to Hittleman (1988),

> A reader's reconstruction of the ideas and information intended by an author is somewhat like a listener's reconstruction of ideas from a speaker's combinations of sounds. The reader, like the listener, may create meanings that are different from those intended by the author. What a reader understands from the reconstructed and constructed meanings depends on the reader's prior knowledge, prior experiences, and his or her maturity and proficiency in using language in various social contexts.
>
> Learning to read develops from a person's ability to understand and use both oral and written language in social situations; the ability to understand written language is an extension of the ability to communicate orally. Learning to read requires an understanding of the daily social functions of oral and written language. Learning to read requires the application of thinking strategies to ideas communicated in written form. Therefore, school programs for developing reading skills need to cultivate students' cognitive learning processes, oral language proficiency, and use of language in social contexts. (p. 2)

Not only is it important for effective teachers of reading to form a concept of what reading is, but also it is equally important for them to distinguish between the reading process and reading instruction. Weaver and Shonkoff (1978) addressed this point in their discussion of current research on reading:

> What actually is the nature of reading? . . . The research findings currently available do not provide conclusive information, and it may take a long time for

> these issues to be resolved and supported by the results of research. Reading educators do not have time to wait. Whatever view of reading is accurate, an equally pertinent question for educators as we see it is, How should reading be viewed so that its acquisition and development are facilitated? We think it is helpful to make the distinction between the reading process and effective teaching of reading. (p. 6)

If you accept the notion that reading is synonymous with comprehension, then there are two important facets of reading instruction that must be viewed realistically: decoding print into sound and decoding a graphic representative of language into meaning. This book takes the view that children's ability to recognize or decode printed word symbols is a necessary prerequisite for reading. However, the mere pronunciation of words is not reading; reading does not occur until this decoding process evokes meanings that the printed words in combination convey in oral language usage. As Hittleman (1988) pointed out, the meanings that are acquired from reading are highly related to "the reader's prior knowledge, prior experiences, and . . . maturity and proficiency in using language in various social contexts" (p. 2).

Importance of the Teacher

Since teaching reading is undoubtedly as complex as defining it, the teacher has emerged as a variable of considerable importance and attention in many reading research studies. Malmquist (1973) generally concluded that reading programs never rise above the quality of the instruction found in them.

The important influence of teachers on pupils' learning has been well documented for many years. Spache (1973) commented on the importance of the teacher after reviewing the results of the Cooperative Research Program in First-Grade Reading Instruction (1967), which attempted to compare several methods of reading instruction:

> Our reading research into the effectiveness of various instructional methods of classroom or remedial situations is often pointless. Such comparative research tends to ignore the fact that the dynamic practices of the teacher and the kinds of teacher–pupil interaction she promotes are the most important determinants of pupils' achievements. The collected results of the large-scale First Grade Reading Studies . . . strongly reaffirm this fact. Hardly any real differences in pupil achievement were found in comparisons among the half-dozen different approaches in carefully equated populations. Rather, in almost every study, achievement varied more from one teacher's classroom to the next than it varied according to the methods of materials employed. (pp. 43–44)

Goldbecker (1975) emphasized the assertion that the teacher is the critical part of the reading program when she stated that "the salient point remains that no reading program operates by itself. The teacher is still the single catalyst who can determine success or failure of a reading program, no matter where its emphasis lies" (p. 4). Tinker and McCullough (1975) maintained that experimental classes in experimental/control group comparative studies usually indicate great achievements in reading scores because they reflect the teacher's drive and enthusiasm during the experimental stage, regardless of the teacher's knowledge of specific reading skills. They concluded that the effective teacher is a greater factor in students' achievement than specific methods or materials.

What has not been a great concern until recently is what specific instructional behaviors effective teachers employ in order to have the greatest impact on students' learning. General qualities such as being enthusiastic and mentally and physically healthy and having a lot of drive are certainly important, but what specifically differentiates effective teachers of reading from those who are not as effective? Reading educators do not have all the answers to what sets effective teachers apart; however, they do know some of the characteristics of these teachers.

Characteristics of Effective Teachers

Recognition of the major role that teachers play in reading instruction has prompted many researchers to attempt to identify what characteristics are critical in effective teaching. Duffy and Roehler (1989) identified several of the more prominent characteristics.

First, they suggested that effective teachers view reading with regard to what students must learn rather than what tasks they must complete. The major goal is for students to be able to cope successfully with the real reading needs of literate people. Therefore, effective teachers do not provide instruction designed to get students to complete skill exercises correctly; rather, they strive to develop literate students who can read whatever is available to them.

Second, effective teachers have a broad view of reading. They see reading not as a skill or series of skills or even as a specific subject, but as a component of language in which the purpose is communication.

Third, effective teachers have clear ideas of the motivational importance of learning to read. They understand that, while it is important that students learn how to read, it is equally important that they *like* to read and that they read willingly in order to acquire information and enrich their lives.

Fourth, these teachers place importance on monitoring students' comprehension rather than emphasizing rote memory and correct answers. Rather than answering "You are correct," they choose to respond, "How did you arrive at that answer?"

Fifth, these teachers may use, but not depend on, a basal reader to direct their reading programs. They employ it as a tool, a guide, and a foundation, but not as an instructional imperative. Effective teachers may begin with a basal reader and enrich it according to the desired goals of their reading programs and students' reading needs.

Sixth, while teachers' guides that accompany basal readers do provide tasks, activities, and directions, effective teachers clearly understand that they rarely explain *how* to do a task successfully. As a result of this, effective teachers engage in task analysis of reading assignments to develop explicit instructions concerning how to complete the tasks.

Seventh, effective teachers understand the complex nature of teaching. They are not looking for a panacea. They understand that reading instruction is complex, that classrooms are complex, and that students and teachers are complex. They have accepted the fact that there can be no cure-all when so many complex factors interact. Because of this, effective teachers view themselves as continually refining their instructional skills, but they realize that they will never have "the answer."

Eighth, effective teachers realize that there is no perfect way to teach reading. They rarely do things exactly the same way from year to year. They are always thinking, changing, modifying, and innovating—constantly exploring for a means to enhance their instruction in reading.

Finally, effective teachers who are concerned with developing an educational program to foster student growth and development in the reading process realize that they must be readers themselves. They understand that to develop readers who are independent and self-reliant, who search for alternatives to problems, who realize that education does not occur just within classroom walls, who are comfortable and proficient in handling reading matter from a variety of sources, they *must* be able to do it themselves!

Teachers who play an effective role in the classroom are in control because they use their own professional knowledge rather than blindly following someone else's prescriptions. They are professionals who make their own decisions, not technicians who follow directions. They are teachers who recognize their own human and humane qualities and are continually working to fulfill their potential as effective teachers.

SUMMARY

The effective teaching of reading requires that teachers understand the nature of reading. They must understand that effective reading instruction means a constant emphasis on sense-making and comprehension. Such instruction demands much more than merely drilling children, asking them for correct answers, and following the suggestions offered in the teacher's manual. Effective teachers help students understand what reading is all about and how it works—what they are trying to accomplish when they read and how to monitor their understanding as they read.

This book offers suggestions that effective teachers can use to help students acquire the understanding and strategies needed to become good readers. However, you must remember that it is you, the teacher, who must use these suggestions in ways that best fit the realities and complexities of your particular situation. It is only then that you will be able to help students in your classroom learn to be strategic in making sense of what they read and use reading in their world outside of school.

FOLLOW-UP QUESTIONS AND ACTIVITIES

1. Discuss how a person's definition of reading will affect the practices that person will follow in teaching reading.
2. How would you react to the following statement? "Effective teachers are in control of what they teach."
3. What would you say to a teacher who thinks that the *best* way to teach reading is by using a particular reading program?
4. In your opinion, which of the characteristics of effective teachers discussed in this chapter are the most important? Provide a rationale for your choice.

ADDITIONAL READINGS

Duffy, G. G. (1982, December). *Context variables in reading teachers' effectiveness.* Paper presented at National Reading Conference, Clearwater Beach, FL.

Duffy, G. G., Roehler, L. R., & Putname, J. Putting the teacher in control: Basal reading textbooks and instructional decision making. *Elementary School Journal,* 87, 355-366.

Durkin, D. (1984). Is there a match between what elementary teachers do and what basal reader manuals recommend? *The Reading Teacher,* 37, 734-744.

Lehr, F. (1982). Teacher effectiveness research and reading instruction. *Language Arts,* 59, 883-887.

Shannon, P. (1987). Commercial reading materials, a technological ideology and the deskilling of teachers. *Elementary School Journal,* 87, 307-322.

Singer, H. (1978). Active comprehension: From answering to asking questions. *The Reading Teacher,* 31, 901-908.

Smith, F. (1985). *Reading without nonsense* (2nd ed.). New York: Teachers College Press.

Stern, P., & Shavelson, R. J. (1983). Reading teachers' judgments, plans, and decision making. *The Reading Teacher,* 37, 280-286.

REFERENCES

Bond, G. L., & Dykstra, R. (1967). The cooperative research program in first-grade reading instruction. *Reading Research Quarterly, 2,* 5–142.

Duffy, G. G., & Roehler, L. R. (1989). *Improving classroom reading instruction: A decision-making approach* (2nd ed.). New York: Random House.

Goldbecker, S. S. (1975). *Reading: Instructional approaches.* Washington, DC: National Education Association.

Goodman, K. S. (1967). Reading: A psycholinguistic guessing game. *Journal of the Reading Specialist, 6,* 125–135.

Goodman, K. S., & Goodman, Y. M. (1982, April). A whole-language comprehension-centered view of reading development. In L. Reed & S. Ward (Eds.), *Basic skill issues and choices: Approaches to basic skill instruction* (Vol. 2, pp. 125–134). St. Louis: Central Midwest Regional Education Laboratory.

Gough, P. B., & Cosky, M. J. (1977). One second of reading again. In N. Castellan et al. (Eds.), *Cognitive theory* (Vol. 2, pp. 271–288). Hillsdale, NJ: Erlbaum.

Hittleman, D. R. (1988). *Developmental reading, K–8: Teaching from a whole-language perspective* (3rd ed.). Columbus, OH: Merrill.

LaBerge, D., & Samuels, S. J. (1985). Toward a theory of automatic information processing in reading. In H. Singer & R. B. Ruddell (Eds.), *Theoretical models and processes of reading* (3rd ed., pp. 689–718). Newark, DE: International Reading Association.

Malmquist, E. (1973). Perspectives on reading research. In R. Karlin (Ed.), *Reading for all: Proceedings of the Fourth IRA World Congress on Reading* (pp. 142–155). Newark, DE: International Reading Association.

Rumelhart, D. E. (1977). Toward an interactive model of reading. In S. Dormick (Ed.), *Attention and performance* (Vol. 6, pp. 573–630). Hillsdale, NJ: Erlbaum.

Smith, F. (1979). Conflicting approaches to reading research and instruction. In L. Resnick & P. Weaver (Eds.), *Theory and practice of early reading* (Vol. 2, pp. 31–42). Hillsdale, NJ: Erlbaum.

Spache, G. D. (1973). Psychological and cultural factors in learning to read. In R. Karlin (Ed.), *Reading for all: Proceedings of the Fourth IRA World Congress on Reading* (pp. 43–50). Newark, DE: International Reading Association.

Strange, M. (1980). Instructional implications of a conceptual theory of reading comprehension. *The Reading Teacher, 33,* 391–397.

Tinker, M., & McCullough, Y. (1975). *Teaching elementary reading* (4th ed.). Englewood Cliffs, NJ: Prentice-Hall.

Weaver, P., & Shonkoff, F. (1978). *Research within reach.* St. Louis, MO: Research and Development Interpretations Services, Central Midwest Regional Education Laboratory.

Weaver, P., & Resnick, L. (1979). The theory and practice of early reading: An introduction. In L. Resnick and P. Weaver (Eds.), *Theory and practice in early reading* (Vol. 1, pp. 1–27). Hillsdale, NJ: Erlbaum.

2
Teaching Effective Word Identification Strategies

MARTHA D. COLLINS

THE ULTIMATE GOAL of effective reading instruction is to develop readers who can competently comprehend what they read. If this goal of a high level of comprehension is to be achieved, readers must be able to read individual words. It is clear that the ability to identify words is a necessary aspect of reading comprehension. However, effective teachers recognize that accurate recognition of words is only an aid to understanding and, by itself, is an insufficient goal of reading instruction.

In this chapter, Martha Collins discusses several word recognition strategies that readers can use to help them identify words. She provides a clear description of the value of four major areas of word identification: sight word identification (recognizing words instantly); phonic analysis (associating sounds and symbols); structural analysis (identifying words composed of a base word plus an inflectional ending or affix, compound words, or contractions); and contextual analysis (using other words in a sentence or passage [semantic cues] and the arrangement of words in a sentence [syntactic cues] to determine an unknown word). Collins presents a straightforward discussion of what each strategy involves and offers many suggestions for teaching children to apply the strategies.

STUDY QUESTIONS

1. Why is word identification so important in beginning reading instruction?
2. What areas of word identification need to be included in the reading curriculum?
3. How should teachers decide when various word identification strategies should be taught?
4. When do students need to begin to develop a sight vocabulary?
5. How does phonics instruction fit into word identification instruction?

What can teachers do to encourage their students to become effective word identifiers who use their ability to facilitate reading? This chapter is written to aid teachers in selecting for instruction word identification strategies that readers can use to recognize unfamiliar words quickly and independently in order to get meaning from print. The strategies are presented through discussions of four major areas of word identification: sight word identification, or the ability to recognize words instantly; phonic analysis, which involves analyzing words according to individual sounds; structural analysis, or the ability to decode words by units such as syllables or affixes; and contextual analysis, which uses surrounding words and ideas to determine the meaning of an unknown word. (See Figure 2.1 for a glossary of terms related to phonics.) Before these areas are discussed, consideration must be given to a broader issue—naturalistic learning of words (whole language) as related to skills instruction.

Learning to Recognize Words

The mother of a 3-year-old who comments that her child can read signs does indeed have a beginning reader. Using visual cues, colors, shapes, and other clues from the environment in which a word appears, the child says "Stop" upon seeing a red six-sided sign, and "McDonald's" when passing the Golden Arches. Children learn to read using a naturalistic process of making visual associations with print in the environment (Goodman & Goodman, 1963).

However, parents, teachers, and publishers do not always feel comfortable with children's incidentally learning to read through a natural process; thus, they continue to include structured word identification strategies in materials for reading instruction. This is especially true at the primary level.

Those responsible for reading instruction must realize that some children need this instruction, some need a little assistance in developing word identification strategies, and some seem to learn to read without instruction. However, even with children who seemed to have learned to read automatically at an early age, studies suggest that they had opportunities to develop letter/sound/word concepts and had been encouraged to respond when stories were read to them. In other words, it seems clear that some informal instruction was provided (Burns, 1986; Durkin, 1962; Plessas & Oakes, 1964; Price, 1976).

Since words are the foundation for reading, the decoding of these printed symbols must be included in reading instruction. Beginning reading is not an issue of whole language versus skills instruction; we must begin with the child's language and relate the learning of new words to the known language. Instruction in word identification strategies (i.e., sight word identification, phonics, structural analysis, and contextual analysis) is not going to fade from the reading curriculum, nor should it. Word identification strategies must be taught in ways that expand involvement with language in order to develop efficient readers. In her extensive review of the literature, Adams (1990) contended that the effective teacher need not remain trapped in the phonics versus teaching-for-meaning dilemma. She proposed that decoding ability can work together with a whole language or meaning emphasis approach to teaching reading.

Effective teachers understand that a good grasp of phonics does not equate to good reading and that good instruction does not rely *only* on a structured phonics program. Effective teachers do not throw instruction in

FIGURE 2.1 Glossary of Terms Related to Phonics

Blends: Blends consist of two or more letters or consonant phonemes that are blended when pronouncing a word. There are three major groups of blends: —*R* as the concluding letter (*br, cr, tr, str*); —*L* as the concluding letter (*fl, gl, bl, spl*); —*S* as the beginning letter (*sk, sm, sw, str*).

Consonant clusters: A term used to refer to consonant blends and digraphs.

Decoding: A term sometimes used as a synonym for phonics but generally thought to include more than sound-symbol relationships. Language cues and meaning are part of the decoding process.

Digraphs: Vowel and consonant digraphs exist when two letters result in one speech sound. Common examples include consonant digraphs such as *wh, th, sh,* and *ch* and vowel digraphs such as *al, oa, ea, ee,* and *ay*. A generalization frequently used with students is "When two vowels appear together in a syllable, the first usually represents the long sound and the second is silent." Clymer's (1963) research found this generalization to be useful only 45 percent of the time: however, teaching *oa, ee* with this generalization seems appropriate.

Diphthongs: Two adjacent vowels in which each contributes to the sound heard form a diphthong. Examples of diphthongs are *ou, ow, oi,* and *oy*.

Grapheme-phoneme relationship: A grapheme is a symbol used to represent the phoneme, which is the sound. There is not a one-to-one correspondence between the sounds and symbols in the English language.

Initial, medial, final consonant sounds: The sound represented by a consonant letter or letters at the beginning, in the middle, or at the end of a word or syllable. Letters do not always represent the same sound in words at these different positions. For example, *c* may represent /s/ in *city,* /k/ in *candy,* or /k/ in *mac,* or unite with *k* to represent /k/ in *quack* or with *h* to represent /sh/ in *machine.*

Pattern: A word or portion of a word used to make other words by changing the beginning or ending sounds. For example, *an* is a pattern used to develop a family of words including *pan, can, fan,* and *man.*

Phonic generalizations: Rules or principles that have been generalized about the decoding of sounds represented by certain letters or letter combinations. Some of these generalizations are presented in reading materials while others are developed by teachers as they give instruction in phonics. Studies have questioned the usefulness of some of these generalizations while finding others to be quite helpful (Clymer, 1963; Bailey, 1967; Emans, 1967; Collins, 1985). An example of a generalization that may be helpful is "When the letter *c* is followed by *o* or *a,* the sound of /k/ is likely to be heard."

Phonics instruction: An essential reading skill used in combination with other procedures to solve the pronunciation of a group of unknown letters in order to associate appropriate meaning with printed symbols.

Schwa: The sound of the vowel in an unstressed syllable as *climate* (cli ə m ə t). The Schwa is represented in the dictionary by the symbol (ə).

Silent letters: This term is used by some teachers to indicate that no sound is directly associated with a particular letter or grapheme. Many argue that there are no silent letters in relating sounds and symbols and that letters work together to represent various sounds. For example, in the word *have* the *h* represents /h/, the *a* and *e* work together to represent /a/, and the *v* represents /v/. The *e* is considered by some to be a "silent letter," or one that has no sound directly related. Silent letters may be used to relate to vowels as in the example just given or to consonants when they are double (*kitten*) or when letters are combined, as in *kn, wr, ck,* or *mb.*

word identification strategies out of the curriculum; they recognize its place in helping children learn to read for meaning. They understand that some readers develop their own system of decoding while others need instruction, and they are able to determine which students lack essential strategies. The remainder of this chapter provides information on incorporating word identification strategies into elementary school reading instruction.

Sight Word Identification

Sight words are words that a student recognizes instantly. Initially, these words are limited to the child's name, labels, and signs—words that are a part of the child's environment. In school, sight words may become the irregular words that are taught as a whole because they cannot be pronounced according to the rules presented for sound-symbol relationships. In addition to these, there is a small body of high-frequency words or service words that are used frequently in running print (i.e., *the, at, and, what, is*). These are contained in lists such as Dolch Basic Sight Words or Fry New Instant Words (see Figures 2.2 and 2.3).

FIGURE 2.2 The Dolch Basic Vocabulary of 220 Sight Words

Preprimer	*Primer*	*First Grade*	*Second Grade*	*Third Grade*
a	all	after	always	about
and	am	again	around	better
away	are	an	because	bring
big	at	any	been	carry
blue	ate	as	before	clean
can	be	ask	best	cut
come	black	by	both	done
down	brown	could	buy	draw
find	but	every	call	drink
for	came	fly	cold	eight
funny	cat	from	does	fall
go	did	give	don't	far
help	do	going	fast	full
here	four	has	first	got
I	get	had	five	grow
in	good	her	found	hold
is	have	him	gave	hot
it	he	his	goes	hurt
jump	into	how	green	if
little	like	just	its	keep
look	must	know	made	kind
make	new	let	many	laugh

(continued)

FIGURE 2.2 *Continued*

Preprimer	*Primer*	*First Grade*	*Second Grade*	*Third Grade*
me	no	live	off	light
my	now	may	or	long
not	on	of	pull	much
one	our	old	read	myself
play	out	once	right	never
red	please	open	sing	only
run	pretty	over	sit	own
said	ran	put	sleep	pick
see	ride	round	tell	seven
the	saw	some	their	shall
three	say	stop	these	show
to	she	take	those	six
two	so	thank	upon	small
up	soon	them	us	start
we	that	then	use	ten
where	there	think	very	today
yellow	they	walk	wash	together
you	this	were	which	try
	too	when	why	warm
	under		wish	
	want		work	
	was		would	
	well		write	
	went		your	
	what			
	white			
	who			
	will			
	with			
	yes			

As beginning readers learn these basic sight words and become more proficient readers, their sight word vocabulary increases. This expansion reflects students' automatic recognition of words they have been exposed to repeatedly and words they have an interest in learning, as well as the use of various word analysis techniques. Thus, sight word vocabulary is continually developing as the reader encounters new reading material. The development of strategies to facilitate the expansion of sight word knowledge leads to automaticity in word identification, and the reading process becomes more natural.

Richek (1977, 1978) found in her study of kindergarten students that the skills of letter recognition, visual discrimination, and digit span memory are significantly related to sight word learning. She also found that low-achieving

FIGURE 2.3 Fry New Instant Word List

FIRST HUNDRED	the	as	but	which	these	write	who
	of	with	not	she	so	go	oil
	and	his	what	do	some	see	now
	a	they	all	how	here	number	find
	to	I	were	their	would	no	long
	in	at	we	if	make	way	down
	is	be	when	will	like	could	day
	you	this	your	up	him	people	did
	that	have	can	other	into	my	get
	it	from	said	about	time	than	come
	he	or	there	out	has	first	made
	was	one	use	many	look	water	may
	for	had	an	then	two	been	part
	on	by	each	them	more	call	over
	are	word					
SECOND HUNDRED	new	after	before	also	even	us	house
	sound	thing	line	around	such	move	point
	take	our	right	form	because	try	page
	only	just	too	three	turn	kind	letter
	little	name	mean	small	here	hand	mother
	work	good	old	set	why	picture	answer
	know	sentence	any	put	ask	again	found
	place	man	same	end	went	change	study
	year	think	tell	does	men	off	still
	live	say	boy	another	read	play	learn
	me	great	follow	well	need	spell	should
	back	where	came	large	land	air	America
	give	help	want	must	different	away	world
	most	through	show	big	home	animal	high
	very	much					
THIRD HUNDRED	every	start	might	together	white	second	girl
	near	city	close	got	sea	late	sometimes
	add	earth	something	group	began	miss	mountain
	food	eye	seem	often	grow	idea	cut
	between	light	next	run	took	enough	young
	own	thought	hard	important	river	eat	talk
	below	head	open	until	four	face	soon
	country	under	example	children	carry	watch	list
	plant	story	begin	side	state	far	song
	last	saw	life	feet	once	Indian	leave
	school	left	always	car	book	real	family
	father	don't	those	mile	hear	almost	body
	keep	few	both	night	stop	let	music
	tree	while	paper	walk	without	above	color
	never	along					

Note: From E. Fry, (1977). *Elementary reading instruction.* New York: McGraw-Hill. Reprinted by permission of the author.

kindergarten students markedly preferred learning words by a sight method to learning by any other method.

Because words such as *the, which, could,* and *done* are abstract, having no specific meaning directly associated with them, children frequently have difficulty remembering them. To assist with visual discrimination of words that are similar in appearance, such as *what* and *that,* and to develop fluency in recognition of these basic words, teachers use flashcards or games such as Word Bingo to provide practice. These words can also be practiced using a VAKT (visual, auditory, kinesthetic, tactile) approach, in which children trace the letters of a word as they see and say the word. Of course the teacher would provide many opportunities for such words to be used in oral and written sentences, but developing a sight vocabulary involves much more than games and activities for practice. Teachers are also concerned with the selection of the words to be taught. Developing a sight vocabulary, especially as an initial vocabulary for the beginning reader, requires selection of words that are interesting and useful to the child to facilitate successful reading.

To select words that are interesting, the teacher looks first to those that represent something in the child's environment, usually nouns or adjectives. These are easier to remember than other types of words because they can be visualized by association with concrete objects. For example, words such as *dog, cat, sister, school, grandfather,* and *boy* are added to a child's reading vocabulary after only a few exposures, as compared to the weeks of repetition needed to remember *as, they,* and *them.*

Names of objects in the classroom are also of interest to children. Teachers sometimes label classroom objects to aid in the development of a sight vocabulary. While labeling helps children learn to recognize words, leaving labels on chairs, tables, desks, and doors for long periods of time decreases their usefulness because the labels tend to be forgotten and blend into the object. Thus, if the words are to be recognized in printed materials, labels should be changed often and teachers should call attention to them to help the children acknowledge their presence and realize their unique features.

Teachers who use the important words from children's spoken vocabulary via the language experience approach or experience charts to teach beginning reading expose their students to interesting and useful words in each lesson. This is an excellent strategy to develop sight vocabulary for beginning readers, and it continues to be a good way for intermediate-level readers to expand their vocabulary. Charts provide needed repetition and reinforcement by displaying the language and interests of the students. (Chapter 13 provides an in-depth discussion of the language experience approach.)

Interesting words also come from class discussions. *Computer* usually is not considered a word to be taught to beginning readers; however, when one of the students has a new computer or the class is learning to use the computer, it becomes an interesting and useful word that is easily incorporated into experience stories.

The Dolch Basic Sight Words are useful words that are often *not* of significant interest to beginning readers. As one preschooler complained to an overanxious parent, "Why do I care if t-h-e is *the?*" Many children have difficulty remembering these small words, which comprise 75% to 80% of their reading. Knowledge of these function words is essential for the reading of even the simplest sentences, but it is important to remember that, because sentence context is the natural way of seeing these words and provides meaning for them, they should always be taught in context (Adams & Huggins, 1985; Hudson & Haworth, 1983). Likewise, practice with function words should be done in context. If flashcards are used, the teacher should develop phrases or sentences for them and underline the appropriate word for emphasis. The word *that* looks less similar to *what* if used in "*That* is my red truck."

Useful words such as color words, numbers, and words found in written directions are also taught in context since this is how they appear in printed materials. Teachers may identify other useful words from basal readers, content books, or favorite library books as students begin to use common reading materials.

Discussions about each new word help students focus on the word, assist the teacher in clarifying misconceptions of meaning, and increase the possibility that the students will remember the word. An inductive teaching strategy can be used by giving the students a sentence containing an unfamiliar word that is underlined. The students are asked to pronounce and define the underlined word, with the teacher clarifying and raising questions to further their exploration and lead to an appropriate response. This strategy not only focuses attention on the word, to aid in adding it to the students' sight vocabulary, but also places emphasis on meaning.

Sight word instruction may involve teaching students to note cues that distinguish words. However, this strategy should be used with caution. Some instructional materials and teachers use colors (e.g., one word in red, another in blue, or long vowel sounds in red and short vowel sounds in blue) as cues to help students distinguish words. However, when the color is taken away students usually have the same difficulty with the word as they had in the beginning. This is not a realistic strategy for teaching sight words.

A more successful cue is configuration. Focusing on word shapes calls attention to unique features to aid students in distinguishing between two difficult words. An example of such an approach would look like this:

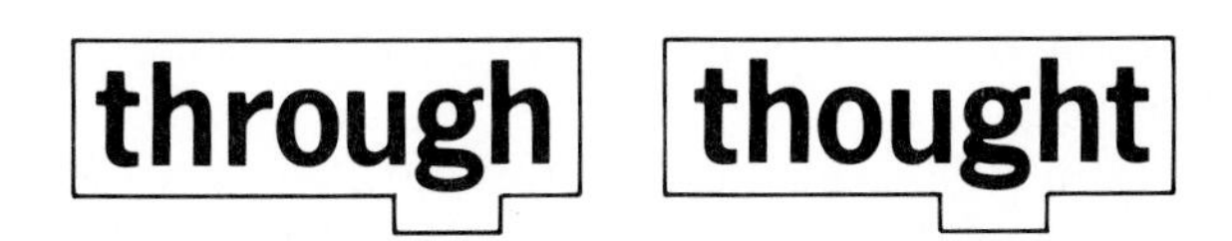

Word shape and word length are cues that are employed as "crutches" for troublesome words. These cues are not to be considered primary strategies for teaching sight words because many sight words do not have unique configurations.

Durkin (1987) has suggested that "a sizable sight vocabulary is one of the most important instructional outcomes in the beginning years" (p. 168). However, there is a question as to how much practice is needed to develop a sight vocabulary or for students to achieve automaticity (Samuels, 1976). It varies from student to student and from word to word. Other word identification strategies such as phonics, structural analysis, and contextual analysis are essential in expanding sight vocabulary and as aids in remembering words. Most children develop their own systems for discriminating and remembering words, using shape, meaning, length, context, beginning sounds, middle letters, or whatever else works for them. However, the best strategy for expanding and reinforcing a sight vocabulary is practice: *Read, read, read!*

Phonic Analysis

The one area of word identification that has received the most attention is phonic analysis, or the association of sounds and symbols. "Do you teach phonics?" "My child doesn't know his phonics." "Mary can't read because her second grade teacher didn't teach phonics." Such are the statements heard daily from parents who see phonic analysis as the major component of successful reading. Why does this belief exist? How does the teacher respond?

Until the mid-1800's, spelling and reading were taught simultaneously through the alphabet, syllables, and sounds. At that time the idea of teaching beginning reading through whole words was introduced in several reading textbooks, with the alphabet, sounds, and spelling presented later. Although phonics was frequently included as a separate component in the curriculum, more emphasis began to be placed on teaching words and sentences.

In the late 1800's, learning the alphabet and spelling words were only a small part of the reading curriculum. However, as students reached the upper grades unable to read words on sight, dissatisfaction was expressed. This resulted in a gradual rebirth of phonics in some curricula and a push for teaching whole words in others (Smith, 1964). With the publication of *Why Johnny Can't Read* (Flesch, 1955) and *Learning to Read: The Great Debate* (Chall, 1967), the importance of phonics was documented by those who believed it to be the most significant variable in learning to read. The latest wave of interest has grown from the following two recommendations in *Becoming a Nation of Readers* (Anderson, Hiebert, Scott, Wilkinson et al., 1984):

- Teachers of beginning reading should present well-designed phonics instruction.
- Reading primers should be interesting, comprehensive, and give children opportunities to apply phonics. (p. 118) Also, Adams's (1970) *Beginning to*

Read: Thinking and Learning About Print, which appears to support these recommendations, seems destined to press further attention on this important aspect of reading instruction.

One of the primary reasons for the continuing debate on phonics instruction relates to differing definitions. There are two approaches for teaching phonics—analytic and synthetic. Analytic phonics presents sounds in the context of words and encourages the student to generalize a sound from one word to another (e.g., /b/ is the sound heard at the beginning of *boy, ball, bat.* What sound is at the beginning of *book?*). Synthetic phonics instruction approaches phonics through isolated sounds. Students are taught that a sound represents a given letter (e.g., *b* says /b/).

Those who espouse the synthetic phonics approach believe that the analytic phonics approach does not teach students to sound out words but rather teaches them to memorize words as whole units. They do not view analytic phonics as a viable means of instruction. Proponents of analytic phonics, on the other hand, argue that synthetic phonics teaches students to sound words as though every letter represents a sound—an unrealistic way of identifying words in the English language. Whichever approach is used, however, some type of phonics instruction is contained in every basal reading series.

Just as the debate continues as to the proper emphasis to place on phonics in beginning reading, the issue of exactly what aspects of phonics to teach is also a concern to teachers. Each basal reading program is based on its own philosophy of phonics instruction. Some present phonics via an analytic approach while others present synthetic phonics. Some include phonics as part of the readiness or preprimer materials while others begin phonics in the first reader, with earlier materials emphasizing auditory and visual discrimination and sight words. One basal series begins to introduce all vowels at the preprimer or primer level, others introduce only one or two short vowel sounds, and still others present no vowel sounds until the first reader level.

Research provides no definitive sequence for teaching phonics. However, some specific sequence for phonic analysis should be followed during the first 2 or 3 years of school to provide the students with continuity of approach and instruction. The sequence a school elects to follow should represent the philosophies of the teachers within that school.

Beginning readers need a sight vocabulary to build confidence in their ability to read, with phonics initially taught by using the words that the children know and expanded to decoding unknown words. Not all students will learn or use phonics as prescribed by the teacher. *Phonic analysis should* not *be taught as an isolated skill; with the expectation that students will transfer the appropriate information when encountering an unknown word.* Direct instruction is required to show students how to use phonic analysis and what to do when phonics does not work. To provide this type of instruction, teachers must know phonics and how to impart appropriate information to the young reader. More in-depth information can be obtained from the numerous books available that focus on the subject of phonics instruction.

Phonics should be taught directly, through demonstration of how the strategy is used to decode a word. When new vocabulary words are introduced, a system of decoding them should be taught as well. Teachers can introduce the short vowel sounds as the new vocabulary is presented and show how consonant blends and vowel digraphs work together to make part of a new word that is completed by an *ing* ending (structural analysis). By using the new word in a sentence, they can show how contextual analysis is enhanced through the use of phonics. The learning of phonics should be a realistic experience. Generalizations can be taught, but those presented should be useful at least 75% of the time; that is, they should be used to decode three out of four unfamiliar words. Clymer (1963) identified 18 generalizations that met this criteria. In a replication of his study with more recent reading materials, Collins (1985) would suggest that the generalizations listed in Figure 2.4 are appropriate.

Teachers may approach phonics instruction in a variety of ways. *Deductive phonics instruction* moves from the general to the specific, or from a generalization to a specific word. For example, the generalization "Two or more consonants between vowels suggests that the first vowel represents the short sound" would first be presented directly in a deductive phonics lesson. This would be followed by a series of words that illustrate this generalization (e.g., *lesson, simple, success*). *Inductive phonics instruction* begins with analyzing words, followed by development of a generalization to describe the feature. For example, presented with the words *day, play, say,* and *away,* the students are helped to identify the similar parts and make the generalization that *ay* at the end of a word represents the /a/ sound.

Since each of these ways of teaching phonics has advantages, the teacher should move back and forth between the two so that phonic analysis is taught in a natural way. Inductive instruction helps students explore words to see how letter-sound relationships function and encourages them to analyze words and discover generalizations. However, inductive instruction is time consuming and does not always provide enough opportunities for students to discover needed generalizations. Thus, some deductive phonics instruction is also needed to teach generalizations that are useful in decoding.

Once direct instruction has been provided, students need many reinforcement activities that present them with words containing the various sounds studied. Of course, the best activity involves pleasure reading, but as beginning readers become involved with phonics they may become more comfortable with sound-symbol association activities. These are spelling activities in which the teacher presents a picture of a familiar object and asks for the first or last letter or encourages invented spelling that focuses on the new sound. Invented spelling encourages children to use their natural understanding about how writing works. Other effective activities include clipping

FIGURE 2.4 Generalizations Taught in Basal Reading Materials Grades 1–6

Generalization	*Percent of Utility*
Vowels	
–A vowel between two consonants in a word produces a short sound. The pattern CVC and CVCC produce the short V sound.	50
–Two or more consonants between vowels suggests that the first vowel represents the short sound.	95
–One vowel sound can be represented by many spellings.	100
–An e at the end of a word, and the only vowel in the word, represents the long e sound.	86
–In words with 2 or more syllables that end with the letter *y*, the *y* usually stands for the long e sound.	93
–Two vowel letters can stand for 1 vowel sound.	77
–If the letter *a* stands for the long vowel sound, the letter e at the end of the word is a marker to indicate that in these words the letter *a* stands for the long vowel sound.	99
–The letter *ai* and *ay* also represent the long *a* sound.	83
–When *o* is followed by a *w*, the *o* and the *w* together sometimes stand for the sound you hear in *flow* and *how*.	99
–The 2 letters *o* and *a* together stand for a single vowel sound.	100
–The 2 vowel letters *ea* usually stand for the sound of short e.	77
–The 2 vowel letters *oo* represent 1 sound in the middle or end of a word.	99
–The letter *r* following a vowel letter changes the vowel sound represented by that letter.	93
–Unstressed vowels usually have the schwa sound.	100
Consonants	
–Two letters in the English language can represent 1 sound.	100
–The *ch* spelling for *ch* may occur at the beginning, middle, or end but *tch* comes generally at the end of the word and the *t* in the middle of the word.	
ch for ch–beginning, middle, end	99
tch for ch–end	82
t for ch–middle	88
–The letter c can represent 2 sounds. The sound of *s* as in celery and *k* as in came.	98
–The letter *g* followed by e, *i*, or *y* usually stands for the sound heard in gem. When *g* is followed by *a*, *o*, or *u* it usually stands for The sound heard in game.	
g followed by e, i, or y	84
g followed by a, o, or u	90
–the letter *qu* represents the sound heard in quite.	94
–A consonant cluster is 2 or more consonant letters commonly blended.	95

(continued)

FIGURE 2.4 *Continued*

Generalization	*Percent of Utility*
–Digraphs consist of 2 letters that represent 1 sound.	91
–The *c* spelling and the *k* spelling for *k* may appear at the beginning, middle, or end of a word, while the *ck* may appear at the middle or end.	
c/k for ck–beginning, middle, end	100
ck for ck–middle, end	100
Syllabication	
–The number of vowel sounds in a word represent the number of syllables found in that word.	100
–A word with a vowel followed by 2 consonant letters and another vowel letter, the syllables are usually divided between the 2 consonants.	86
–A word has a vowel followed by a single consonant letter and another vowel letter is usually divided after the first vowel letter. The first vowel letter represents the long sound.	65
–When the second syllable of a word ends in *-le*, the word is divided between the vowel and the consonant preceding the *-le*.	33

Note: From Collins, M.D. (1985). *The utility of phonic generalizations: Past findings and present instruction.* Paper presented at the Annual Meeting of the College Reading Association, Pittsburgh, PA. Reprinted by permission of the author.

pictures of words containing the sound from magazines or circling words in the newspaper that contain the new sound. Language experience stories can relate to a topic that will facilitate the use of words with the appropriate sound-symbol correspondences. (One successful language experience exercise involves the use of chocolate chip cookies when studying the /ch/ sound.) Through the use of language experience, teachers can involve students in providing various sound-symbol correspondences as a word is written.

Phonics instruction can be complex. In fact, sometimes it becomes so complex that students decide that reading is too difficult for them! Because of this, phonics must be incorporated as an integral part of word identification instruction, the goal being to facilitate reading with ease. It is essential to remember that the goal of reading instruction is *not* to have students who know their sounds but to have students who use their knowledge of sound-symbol relationships to get meaning from print.

Structural Analysis

Identifying words involves more than recognizing words by sight or decoding individual sound-symbol correspondences. Consideration must be given to word parts (syllables, affixes, roots, contractions, compound words, etc.) to help students identify words using larger, more meaningful units (morphemes) rather than individual sounds (phonemes). Students involved in extensive phonics instruction, which focuses primarily on individual sounds, are handicapped when attempting to deal with these larger structural units.

Structural analysis is a natural process of expanding knowledge of words—both identification and meaning. As students learn to recognize base or root words either by sight or by phonic analysis, their word knowledge is expanded by looking at the word in other forms—with inflectional endings, prefixes, suffixes, or in compound form. For example, when students learn the sight word *jump*, the teacher may also choose to teach *jumps, jumping,* and *jumped* or the compound words *jumprope* and *jumpsuit*. Students begin to see how word parts affect the meaning of a word and learn that they can identify many words by knowing a base word and its various structural parts. This way of teaching structural analysis does not follow a specified sequence but relates to learning words as they are encountered in print.

However, the sequence of structural analysis skills in reading materials is presented in many different ways. One possible sequence is to present (1) inflectional endings, (2) compound words, (3) prefixes, (4) suffixes, and (5) contractions. Within each of these categories the subcomponents move from simple to complex, with the most frequently used prefixes taught first and less frequently used ones presented at higher levels. This type of organization provides some assurance that all areas will be addressed; however, teachers must make sure that words containing the component being taught are included in the reading material. A common and serious mistake in teachers' manuals is that structural analysis units are presented as isolated features to be learned, with no application provided in the reading text material for that lesson. Therefore, teachers are encouraged to monitor the introduction of structural analysis components carefully and to use opportunities to teach these strategies in conjunction with the introduction of new vocabulary contained in stories written or read by the students.

Syllabication is also a structural analysis strategy. However, research has questioned its usefulness in the reading process, finding that students employ syllabication principles more often in writing than in reading. (Writing strategies that can enhance reading instruction are discussed in Chapters 7 and 8.) One finding was that syllabication principles are of decreasing value above the elementary grades because of the increase in the number of exceptions (Courtney, 1960). Another study found that intensive instruction in syllabication did not improve the word attack or reading comprehension skills of second-graders, although the students could verbalize and apply the syllabication principles being taught (Canney & Schreiner, 1976–1977). In studying the use of syllabication during reading, Glass and Burton (1973) found that second- and fifth-graders looked at sound clusters rather than syllables and, if they used syllabication principles, they applied the principles *after* decoding the words.

Since knowledge of syllabication principles seems to have little effect on reading success, teachers should be prudent when teaching these principles when they are included in reading materials. Collins (1985) found that the principles of syllabication existed in at least three of five basal reading series reviewed. Three of the following four generalizations were also identified in Clymer's (1963) study of basal readers:

- The number of vowel sounds in a word represents the number of syllables found in that word. (Collins found 100% utility.) *Examples:* circumstance, thorough, journey.
- In a word that has a vowel followed by two consonant letters and another vowel letter, the syllables are usually divided between the two consonants. (Clymer found 72% utility; Collins found 86% utility.) *Examples:* dollar, wilderness. *Exceptions:* celebration, declaration.
- A word with a vowel followed by a single consonant letter and another vowel letter is usually divided after the first vowel letter. The first vowel letter represents the long sound. (Clymer found 44% utility; Collins found 65% utility.) *Examples:* isolate, evil. *Exceptions:* opera, amazement.
- When the second syllable of a word ends in *-le,* the word is divided between the vowel and the consonant preceding the *-le.* (Clymer found 97% utility; Collins found 33% utility.) *Examples:* table, maple. *Exceptions:* little, fumble.

While three of these principles were identified by Clymer (1963), only one was applicable 75% or more of the time in Collins's study. Collins's analysis suggests that only two of the generalizations may be appropriate to include in instruction on syllabication. This suggests that we are continuing to teach principles that were found to be questionable 25 years ago and that there is no justification for including them in the curriculum.

However, the other strategies of structural analysis do offer students a means of decoding print. Taught through application, these strategies can be helpful tools for facilitating reading.

Contextual Analysis

When students encounter unfamiliar words, many cues are needed to determine pronunciation. Phonic cues are used to determine the sounds in the word, structural cues are employed as word parts are studied, and surrounding words can be used as context cues. When other words in the sentence or passage are used to determine the pronunciation or meaning of a word, the process is called *contextual analysis.* Young children use picture cues as they read their picture books. As they progress into materials with more words and fewer pictures, students look for other means of decoding words not in their sight vocabulary. Better readers tend to look automatically at other words in the sentence for assistance (Schwartz & Stanovich, 1981); poorer readers are more likely to look at individual sounds in an attempt to analyze the word. Therefore, helping students learn to use context cues is an important instructional strategy.

Context cues commonly used as aids in word identification include titles or themes of a passage, syntactic cues, semantic cues, or a combination of several of these cues with structural or phonic cues. *Syntax* relates to the way words are arranged in a sentence; therefore, syntactic cues are used by noting the function of the unknown word in a sentence. For example, in the sentence

"Ben __________ his horse back to the barn,"

the unknown word tells how the horse got back to the barn and is a verb. Possible words that could be derived from the syntax include *led, walked, rode, trotted, chased, put,* and *pushed.* Thus, this syntactic cue must be combined with a phonetic cue

"Ben w__________ his horse back to the barn."

Using this cue, the reader decides that *walked* is a logical word that fits the pronunciation and meaning of this sentence.

Students who do not pay attention to syntax when reading will miscall words, using inappropriate words that make no sense in the sentence. Comprehension is adversely affected by such errors, and syntactic cues certainly will not be a strategy used by such readers. However, teachers can improve the use of syntactic cues by providing modified cloze sentences for instructional and reinforcement exercises.

Courtney __________ across the room to get her ball.

crawled slept swam wood

The __________ looked like a ball of white fur.

book came pot cat

By discussing with students the various options for completing a sentence, showing them how to think about words making sense in the context of the sentence, and helping them note other cues that may be useful, teachers can make exercises such as these worthwhile. However, such exercises are not beneficial when given as worksheets for independent seatwork without careful demonstration of their purpose.

Semantic cues often function jointly with syntactic cues, but they relate more directly to meaning. Whereas syntactic cues deal with the arrangement of words in the sentence, semantic cues depend on the other words in the sentence or adjoining sentences to assist in determining the meaning of the unknown word. In the following example, the meaning of the unknown word in the first sentence is easier to determine if a second sentence is read.

> Courtney ________ across the room to get her ball. She is a baby and cannot walk.

Here are some other examples of using semantic cues:

> My dog Clem is a ________ ________. He has long ears and very sad eyes. He is brown, black, and white.

> It was time for ________. Daddy was home from work, the meal was prepared, and everyone was hungry.

In the first example, students can employ several approaches to completing the blanks. After reading only the first sentence, they will initially think of descriptors such as *good dog, strange creature,* or *little puppy.* But after reading the next two sentences, most readers begin to think more specifically about the type of dog—German shepherd, little beagle, or maybe basset hound. As students begin to learn to use context cues, teachers should remember that in discussing examples such as these any words that fit the parts of speech and the meaning of the sentence are considered correct. Further aids such as phonic or structural cues can help students narrow their ideas down to the exact words to be identified. When words are suggested that fit the context of the sentence, the understanding of the idea is to be applauded.

As with other strategies used in word identification, direct instruction is also needed to teach contextual analysis. From the examples provided, teachers should note the importance of talking about the options for solution. Such discussions help students see a logic in using meaning and sentence structure to determine unknown words. Beginning with picture clues and moving to simple sentences that the students can complete with illustrations, the notion is established that print is associated with meaning and that visualization is involved in completing an idea. Word identification and meaning are presented as they should be—as interrelated components of the reading process.

Following direct instruction, teachers can move into providing sentences with unknown words and helping students use their listening and speaking vocabularies, along with their prior knowledge, to identify the words. Passages with missing words may become games in which groups of students work together to expand their reading vocabulary. All activities of this type suggest to the student that, as an unknown word is identified, the appropriateness of the word to the context must be acknowledged.

Contextual analysis is a word identification strategy as well as a way of determining meaning. Because of this dual function and because readers rely on this strategy more often as they become mature readers (Cohen & Faulkner, 1983; Simpson & Loriswick, 1983), contextual analysis *must* be included as part of the instructional program in reading at all levels, kindergarten through high school.

An Integrated Approach for Learners

As teachers work on word identification strategies with students, their goal should be to develop readers who use appropriate strategies as needed. One procedure that may facilitate such an integrated use of word identification strategies is as follows:

1. Look carefully at the word to see whether or not it is part of your sight vocabulary.
2. If not, look at the first letter or letters to see whether they help trigger a pronunciation for the word. This is used along with the context of the sentence.
3. Consider the kind of word that is to be identified. Is it the name of something? An action word? A describing word? Think of possible words of this type that begin with this sound.
4. Look at the vowels. How many vowels are in the word? In a short word, one vowel at the beginning of a word or between two consonants usually represents a short sound; one vowel at the end of a word usually represents a long sound; one vowel plus an *e* on the end of the word may have the long sound of the one vowel, and the *e* has no pronunciation.
5. Consider the ending sound. Blend the beginning sound, vowel sound(s), and ending sound to see whether you produce a word that makes sense in the context.
6. If not, try the other sound of the vowel. Blend the sounds again to see whether your new attempt makes sense in the context.
7. For longer words, identify the base word. Decode it using the previous steps. Look at the prefix or suffix or inflectional ending. What is the base word plus these structural components?
8. If you are unable to arrive at a pronunciation of the word and are reading alone, skip the pronunciation and continue to read for meaning. If you are reading aloud, ask the teacher for assistance. *Remember*: Every word does not have to be identified exactly; as

long as you understand what you are reading you are developing as a good reader.

SUMMARY

Word identification is a process to facilitate reading. While understanding must occur for the reading process to be fully activated, comprehension is facilitated when words are appropriately identified and the author's message is decoded as printed. Realizing that there are many strategies for identifying words, the teacher's role is to prepare students to use the strategy most suitable for each situation. Sight word identification provides for instant recognition of words, and, as the reader matures, sight word vocabulary grows. Phonic analysis allows the reader to associate sounds and symbols. This strategy works well for many one- and two-syllable words, but it must be combined with other strategies when more complex words are decoded.

Structural analysis assists in identifying words composed of a base word plus an inflectional ending or affix, compound words, or contractions. Many words can be identified by using phonic analysis to decode the base word and structural analysis to decode the other parts. Understanding of word meaning is enhanced when students consider the definitions of affixes as they apply structural analysis strategies for word identification. Another word identification strategy that works in concert with meaning is contextual analysis. Using other words in the sentence or passage (semantic cues) or the arrangement of words in the sentence (syntactic cues) to determine an unknown word requires that the reader attend to the meaning of all words, thereby increasing comprehension.

Word identification facilitates understanding but does not guarantee it. Some students read silently and understand very well, yet they are unable to read aloud because of word identification difficulty. These students should be encouraged to read silently. Teachers are responsible for communicating with parents that meaning is the goal of reading.

FOLLOW-UP QUESTIONS AND ACTIVITIES

1. As a primary grade teacher, how would you approach word identification instruction with a nonreader? With a student who has a small sight vocabulary? With a student who is reading above grade level?
2. A parent visits your class and asks whether or not you teach phonics. What would you say? If the parent asks to see you teach a phonics lesson, what might be observed?

3. Why is it necessary to help students develop a variety of word identification strategies? How can these strategies be developed and reinforced outside the class time designated for reading?
4. Observe reading instruction in several elementary school classrooms. How are word identification strategies taught? How are they developed at the upper elementary grade levels as compared to the primary level?

ADDITIONAL READINGS

Ceprano, M. A. (1981). A review of selected research on methods of teaching sight words. *The Reading Teacher, 35,* 314–322.

Cohn, M., & D'Allesandro, C. (1978). When is a decoding error not a decoding error? *The Reading Teacher, 32,* 341–344.

Durkin, D. (1984). Is there a match between what elementary teachers do and what basal reader manuals recommend? *The Reading Teacher, 37,* 734–744.

Dyson, A. H. (1984). N spell my grandmama: Fostering early thinking about print. *The Reading Teacher, 38,* 262–271.

Ehri, L. C. (1985). Movement into reading: Is the first sign of printed word learning visual or phonetic? *Reading Research Quarterly, 20,* 163–179.

Jewell, M. G., & Zintz, M. V. (1986). *Learning to read naturally.* Dubuque, IA: Kendall/Hunt.

Nagy, W. E., Herman, P. A., & Anderson, R. C. (1985). Learning words from context. *Reading Research Quarterly, 20,* 522–535.

Nicholson, T., & Hill, D. (1985). Good readers don't guess: Taking another look at the issue of whether children read words better in context or in isolation. *Reading Psychology, 6,* 181–198.

Sorenson, N. L. (1985). Basal reading vocabulary instruction: A critique and suggestions. *The Reading Teacher, 39,* 80–85.

REFERENCES

Adams, M. J. (1990). *Beginning to read: Thinking and learning about print.* Cambridge, MA: MIT Press.

Adams, M. J., & Huggins, A. W. F. (1985). The growth of children's sight vocabulary: A quick test with educational and theoretical implications. *Reading Research Quarterly, 20,* 262–281.

Anderson, R. C., Hiebert, E. H., Scott, J. A., Wilkinson, I. A. G., & members of the Commission on Reading. (1984). *Becoming a nation of readers: The report of the Commission on Reading* (Contract No. 400-83-0057). Washington, DC: National Institute of Education.

Bailey, M. H. (1967). The utility of phonic generalizations in grades one through six. *The Reading Teacher, 20,* 413–418.

Burns, J. M. (1986). *A study of experiences provided in the home environment associated with accelerated reading abilities as reported by parents of intellectually superior preschoolers.* Unpublished doctoral dissertation, Louisiana State University, Baton Rouge.

Canney, G., & Schreiner, R. (1976–1977). A study of the effectiveness of selected syllabication rules and phonogram patterns for word attack. *Reading Research Quarterly, 12,* 102–124.

Chall, J. S. (1967). *Learning to read: The great debate.* New York: McGraw-Hill.

Clymer, T. (1963). The utility of phonic generalizations in the primary grades. *The Reading Teacher, 16,* 252–258.

Cohen, G., & Faulkner, D. (1983). Word recognition: Age differences in contextual facilitation effects. *British Journal of Psychology, 74,* 239–251.

Collins, M. D. (1985, October). *Phonics generalizations: Past findings and present instruction.* Paper presented at the Annual Meeting of the College Reading Association, Pittsburgh, PA.

Courtney, B. L. (1960). Methods and materials for teaching word perception in grades 10–14. In H. M. Robinson (Ed.), *Sequential development of reading abilities* (pp. 42–46). Chicago: University of Chicago Press.

Durkin, D. (1962). An earlier start in reading? *The Elementary School Journal, 63,* 147–151.

Durkin, D. (1987). *Teaching young children to read* (4th ed.). Boston: Allyn and Bacon.

Emans, R. (1967). The utility of phonics generalizations above the primary grades. *The Reading Teacher, 20,* 419–425.

Flesch, R. F. (1955). *Why Johnny can't read and what you can do about it.* New York: Harper & Row.

Glass, G. G., & Burton, E. H. (1973). How do they decode? Verbalizations and observed behaviors of successful decoders. *The Reading Teacher, 26,* 645.

Goodman, Y. M., & Goodman, K. S. (1963). Spelling ability of a self-taught reader. *The Elementary School Journal, 64,* 149–154.

Hudson, J., & Haworth, J. (1983). Dimensions of word recognition. *Reading, 17,* 87–94.

Mason, J. M. (1967). Preschoolers concept of reading. *Reading Teacher, 21,* 130–132.

Plessas, G., & Oakes, C. R. (1964). Prereading experiences of selected early readers. *The Reading Teacher, 18,* 241–245.

Price, L. (1976). How thirty-seven gifted children learned to read. *The Reading Teacher, 30,* 44–49.

Richek, M. A. (1977–1978). Readiness skills that predict initial word learning using two different methods of instruction. *Reading Research Quarterly, 13,* 200–222.

Samuels, S. J. (1976). Automatic decoding and reading. *Language Arts, 53,* 323–325.

Schwartz, R. M., & Stanovich, K. E. (1981). Flexibility in the use of graphic and contextual information by good and poor readers. *Journal of Reading Behavior, 13,* 269.

Simpson, G. B., & Loriswick, T. C. (1983). The development of automatic and conscious components of contextual facilitation. *Child Development, 54,* 760–772.

Smith, N. B. (1964). *American reading instruction.* Newark, DE: International Reading Association.

3
Teaching Vocabulary

SUSAN D. PITTELMAN

JOAN E. HEIMLICH

CHAPTER 3 SUGGESTS techniques for teaching students to identify specific words and describes ways to help students develop generalizable and transferrable word identification skills. The focus is on helping children acquire a *meaning vocabulary*—knowledge of the meaning of specific words. Vocabulary knowledge is critical to reading comprehension because a child's meaning vocabulary connects the skills of word recognition and comprehension. In order for children to understand what they are reading, they must know the meaning of the words they encounter.

In this chapter, Susan Pittelman and Joan Heimlich discuss several prior-knowledge strategies for increasing a reader's meaning vocabulary. These strategies entail helping children learn new concepts (words) by relating them to those they already know. The authors recommend specific guidelines for using classification activities such as semantic mapping and semantic feature analysis as ways the effective teacher can help children learn new words and expand the meaning of many already known words by relating the two. The chapter concludes with six general principles for effective vocabulary instruction.

STUDY QUESTIONS

1. How is vocabulary knowledge related to reading comprehension?
2. Why should vocabulary instruction be integrated throughout the school day?
3. How can teachers increase and enrich students' schemata?
4. What approaches to vocabulary instruction have basal reading programs traditionally recommended?
5. What are semantic mapping and semantic feature analysis and how do they draw upon students' experiences?
6. What guidelines should be followed in planning vocabulary instruction?

The important thing about reading is you gotta understand the words.
Reading is easy,
Reading is fun,
Reading is hard sometime,
But the important thing about reading is you gotta understand the words.

Jon, Grade 3

This verse, written by a third-grade boy, was modeled after Margaret Wise Brown's *The Important Book* (1949). In this simple repeater verse, an 8-year-old child was able to capture the essence of what teachers and reading researchers have acknowledged for years: Vocabulary knowledge is critical to successful reading. As early as 1944, F. B. Davis, a pioneer in factor analytic studies of reading, found that word knowledge is the most important factor in reading comprehension. Current research continues to support the key role that vocabulary plays in the reading process (Barrett & Graves, 1981; Hayes & Tierney, 1982; Johnson, Toms-Bronowski, & Buss, 1983).

The Importance of Vocabulary in Reading Comprehension

It is not surprising that vocabulary knowledge, or knowledge of word meanings, is critical to reading comprehension. In order for children to understand what they are reading, they must know the meanings of the words they encounter. Children with limited vocabulary knowledge—especially those who have not learned techniques and strategies for inferring the meaning of unknown words—will experience difficulty comprehending both oral and written text.

The extent of a student's vocabulary can also be an indication of the level of previous information (or prior knowledge) he or she already has about a topic, which, in turn, affects comprehension. When readers are unfamiliar with the concepts represented by a word, it is difficult, if not impossible, for them to understand the author's meaning. While it is important that students master word identification strategies such as phonics, structural analysis, and contextual analysis to help them infer the meaning of an unknown word, teachers must also help them to develop their general vocabularies, thereby extending their conceptual bases.

The Role of Prior Knowledge in Vocabulary Development

Teachers traditionally have recognized the importance of the background knowledge students bring to the reading process. Most reading lessons begin with the teacher preteaching key vocabulary and providing necessary background information. It is only recently, however, that teachers and researchers alike have begun to clarify the relationship between prior knowledge and vocabulary and to appreciate the impact that a student's prior knowledge has on reading comprehension.

The concept of *prior knowledge,* the ideas already present in the mind, refers to the sum of an individual's life experiences and includes all the knowledge of the world that individual has acquired through life. As a result, it often is referred to as *world knowledge.* Other commonly used labels for this body of information are *background knowledge* and *experiential background.*

The important role that prior knowledge plays in reading comprehension highlights the importance of vocabulary in the comprehension process. According to schema theorists (Lindsay & Norman, 1977; Rumelhart, 1980), everything a person experiences or learns is stored in the brain in knowledge structures or categories called *schemata.* These schemata, which serve as frameworks for related concepts, are incomplete and are constantly being developed and revised. As new information is received, the schemata are restructured and fine tuned (Pearson & Spiro, 1982). For example, as a person reads about, sees pictures of, or visits the seashore, each experience adds to the schema for the concept of the seashore. Comprehension, therefore, is no longer viewed as simply deriving meaning from the printed page. Instead, comprehension is seen as an active process in which prior knowledge is used to create new knowledge (Adams & Bruce, 1980).

Research has shown that knowledge about a topic, particularly key vocabulary, is a better predictor of comprehension of a text than is any measure of reading ability or achievement (Johnston, 1984; Johnston & Pearson, 1982). Readers comprehend better when they can link what they are reading to something they already know. The skilled reader actively calls into play the knowledge and experience stored in his or her memory in response to the words on the printed page (Durkin, 1981). If new concepts are to be learned, they must be related to concepts already understood. A reader's prior knowledge, therefore, is a key factor in reading comprehension.

The Importance of Classification

Classification plays a key role in relating new knowledge to existing knowledge. We would be overwhelmed by the vastness of our world if we tried to relate to each new object or event in a unique way. When introduced to a new stimulus, therefore, we automatically try to identify it by relating it to something that is already familiar. We form categories or concepts to assimilate the new information, relating it to past experiences and prior knowledge. For example, although each budding plant in a garden may have a unique name, the common characteristics they all share enable us to refer to the plants by the same general term—*flower*—and to hold certain expectations about their general appearance.

To survive in this complex world, as well as to facilitate communication, we categorize information. We classify objects by comparing them to one another on the basis of our prior knowledge, noting how they are alike and how they are different. Because all of our experiences and our knowledge are stored in the brain in networks or categories, information is most accessible when strategies are applied that capitalize on these features. Classification activities, therefore, have been identified as being among the most important in any developmental vocabulary program (Johnson, 1984).

Development of Oral Vocabulary

From birth, children are immersed in a language environment in which the spoken word has purpose and function. Young children have numerous opportunities to practice and employ language, whether they are simply babbling in the crib or attempting to communicate with others. As a child continues to experience the world, siblings, playmates, and caring adults reinforce the child's attempts at language usage and serve as role models for language development. Up to the time most children start school, their entire lives are involved with experimenting and practicing spoken language in order to find labels for their experiences (vocabulary) and build meanings for words.

By the time most children come to school at the age of 6, they have developed an extensive listening and speaking vocabulary. Estimates of the size of this oral vocabulary range from 2,562, to 26,000 words (Anderson & Freebody, 1981). While many researchers believe the lower estimate is erroneous (Nagy & Anderson, 1982, 1984), it nonetheless represents an impressive number of words. These words express or symbolize children's life experiences during their early years. The majority have been internalized and will never be forgotten; some are frequently repeated common words, while others were learned through the personal experiences of the child.

Vocabulary Instruction in the Elementary School Curriculum

Vocabulary learning is a lifelong pursuit. When children begin formal schooling, the curriculum must be designed to ensure that schools fulfill their responsibility in the continual development of students' vocabularies. Vocabulary instruction at the elementary school level is most commonly associated with the basal reading program and content area instruction. While these two areas are of great importance, it is critical that teachers also allot time to general vocabulary development.

Traditionally, beginning reading instruction capitalizes on the words that are already a part of children's listening vocabularies. Primary-grade reading materials deal almost exclusively with words in students' oral vocabularies, with materials carefully controlled so that they do not seriously challenge the vocabulary knowledge of most young children. According to Nagy and Herman (1985), however, the reading vocabulary of the average child grows at a rate of 3,000 words per year between grades 3 and 12. It is therefore crucial that, as children progress through the grades, their vocabulary continues to expand so that they have the foundation they need to comprehend the many new words they will encounter.

In light of the impact that a student's vocabulary has on reading success, teachers must devote time to vocabulary development beyond that which is dictated by the teachers' manuals in most basal programs. Vocabulary development should be emphasized throughout the school day, not just in reading and language classes (Burns, Roe, & Ross, 1988). Johnson and Pearson, in *Teaching Reading Vocabulary* (1984), recommended that teachers set aside time each day outside the reading period for general vocabulary development. O'Rourke (1974) asserted that vocabulary instruction has typically been viewed in a narrow context and taught in an unstructured, incidental, or even accidental manner. He recommended that the elementary school curriculum include systematic strategies for vocabulary development beginning in kindergarten and continuing throughout the elementary and secondary school years. Unfortunately, however, teachers do not appear to be heeding this advice or giving sufficient emphasis to effective vocabulary development. Results of a survey administered to 359 elementary school teachers indicated that while teachers place a high priority on vocabulary instruction in both prereading and content area lessons, vocabulary instruction as a distinct area was not assigned a high priority. In fact, more than 50% of the teachers reported that they do not allocate any time to instruction for general vocabulary development (Johnson, Levin, & Pittelman, 1984).

Providing a Language Environment in the Classroom

Just as children have been immersed in oral language in the home, thereby learning new vocabulary in a natural and meaningful way, the classroom must continue to provide this type of nurturing atmosphere for language development. Teachers must provide an environment that is conducive to talking and listening, thus fostering an excitement about expression and an enthusiasm for words. The curriculum must do more than help, it must work to encourage children to continue to expand the large vocabulary base with which they come to school. Teachers need to provide opportunities for students to participate in many experiences, both real and vicarious, to help them develop word meanings and concepts. Students should have the opportunity to use and develop language in a variety of instructional situations, including reading, writing, speaking, and listening activities.

Words have meaning only when they can be linked to meaningful experiences. In fact, word meanings can be viewed as the products of experience, with vocabulary serving as a means by which this prior knowledge can be labeled. When they participate in new experiences, children expand their schemata. However, as Durkin (1989) has cautioned, potentially rich experiences may be wasted if key words do not receive explicit attention—before, during, and following the experiences. Numerous opportunities exist in the immediate school environment for providing meaningful experiences that can serve as springboards for vocabulary development. For example, the classroom pet, an unanticipated snowstorm, and a classroom visit by a fireman during Fire Safety Week are all experiences that offer opportunities for extensive vocabulary development.

Students should be surrounded with numerous examples of language, both written and oral. Important and interesting words should be posted on bulletin boards, with word concepts illustrated by pictures, cartoons, jokes, and headlines. A library of pupil-produced books should be part of the classroom reading materials, and individual vocabulary notebooks should be available to each child. Written notes should be used as an important means of teacher-student communication. Students should have the opportunity to participate in dramatic productions and to use a variety of materials, including films and filmstrips, with and without oral commentary.

Reading is a key activity through which children can expand both their vocabularies and the frameworks under which they associate new vocabulary with current knowledge. It is important for teachers to read to their students, as well as providing numerous opportunities for students to read themselves. Reading to students not only adds to their knowledge of words, but has many other benefits as well. It is an effective way of motivating children to want to learn to read. It also helps them develop the ability to process the language of literature, provides them with a sense of story or story structure, and expands their general knowledge and awareness of the world.

According to Nagy and Anderson (1982, 1984), a major factor in vocabulary acquisition after third grade is the amount of independent reading students do. Anderson and Freebody (1983) reported that by reading independently 25 minutes per school day, an average student in fifth grade would encounter tens of thousands of words per year that he or she did not know. For a student with a smaller than average vocabulary, the number of unfamiliar words would be even greater.

The importance of the teacher's role in creating a classroom environment that encourages language development cannot be overemphasized. The teacher serves as a role model for students. The interest and enthusiasm the teacher shows for words and for reading will greatly influence the attitude adopted by his or her students. Children learn language when they are talked with, listened to, and read to; their language flourishes when they are encouraged to read, experiment with language, and appreciate words.

Basal Vocabulary Instruction

Vocabulary instruction plays a key role in basal lessons. Typically, it is an integral part of both introducing a selection prior to its being read (prereading) and discussing a selection after it has been read (postreading). Basal reading vocabulary instruction generally refers to highlighting words from a basal selection to preteach in order to develop concepts and increase comprehension. It is clear that direct vocabulary instruction is important to the reading process. Spache and Spache (1977), for example, suggested that the first fundamental step in a basal reading lesson should be the introduction of new vocabulary. Teachers need to introduce students to words that are unfamiliar or are important to their understanding of the selection. According to Durkin (1989), "preparations for reading a basal selection are—or ought to be—a time for attending to new vocabulary" (p. 168). Smith and Johnson (1980) concurred, cautioning teachers to be sure to introduce vocabulary that is likely to be unfamiliar or misinterpreted.

Although directed vocabulary instruction is an important component of the reading program for all students, research has confirmed that vocabulary instruction can have an even greater impact on the reading performance of students who are poor readers. A study of fourth-grade students found that while high-ability readers encounter only 1 unknown word out of 100 in a typical instructional reading passage, low-ability readers encounter an unknown word once every 10 words (Gambrell, Wilson, & Gantt, 1981). It is clear that low-ability readers frequently encounter words they do not know. When students have difficulty understanding individual word meanings within connected discourse, reading comprehension is impaired. As Jon's simple verse stated, "The important thing about reading is you gotta understand the words."

The teachers' manuals that accompany basal series typically identify the words that should be taught for each selection. Words highlighted for instruction by the basal series most often are obtained from various lists that rate words according to how frequently they are used. These words generally are assumed to be in the children's listening and speaking vocabularies. Basal manuals also highlight words that are newly introduced in the series and are assumed to be unfamiliar. Students are then taught to use the word recognition skills of phonics, structural analysis, and contextual analysis to recognize, or, as Joan Nelson-Herber so aptly put it, "re-cognize" (1986, p. 627) these words. The manuals usually also suggest a repertoire of strategies, albeit a somewhat limited one, to introduce vocabulary words assumed to be unfamiliar to the children. In most basal lessons, the key words also are reviewed during the discussion and reinforced throughout the extension activities.

Methods for introducing new vocabulary commonly recommended by basal series include the definitional and contextual approaches. In the definitional approach, students learn definitions or synonyms for the highlighted key vocabulary words. The procedure usually involves some combination of looking up a definition, writing it down, using the word in a sentence, and then memorizing the definition. One of the problems with this approach is that many definitions are either inaccurate or inappropriate to the selection for which they are being used. Furthermore, even when a definition is accurate, it often does not contain sufficient information to allow a student to use the word correctly (Nagy, 1988).

The contextual approach to vocabulary instruction typically involves having the teacher write a sentence on the board that contains the key vocabulary word. The students are asked to derive the meaning of the new word from the meaning of the surrounding words in the sentence. The primary difficulty with this approach is that the sentence context rarely provides enough information for a student who does not already have some prior knowledge of the word. For example, given the sentence "Nancy felt awkward at the party because she was younger than everyone else," a child could easily assume that the author meant that Nancy felt "important" or "proud" instead of the author's intended meaning of "uncomfortable."

While it is recognized that learning key vocabulary words is important to comprehension, vocabulary in and of itself accounts for only 50% of a reader's comprehension ability. Comprehension is more than "knowing a lot of words" (May, 1990, p. 181). In order for comprehension to occur, vocabulary and schemata must interact. Consequently, instruction to improve reading comprehension must focus on both developing schemata and expanding vocabulary.

Vocabulary Instruction in the Content Areas

The primary purpose of instruction in the content areas is to teach subject-specific information. One of the major barriers to learning in the content areas, however, is that students constantly are confronted with new words and concepts that are outside of their personal frames of reference. Vocabulary development, therefore, plays a key role in content area instruction.

Vocabulary instruction in a content area should be designed to teach both the language and the concepts associated with the topic being studied. It is crucial that unfamiliar vocabulary be taught directly in every content area lesson in which the vocabulary load could affect a student's ability to comprehend the facts, concepts, and principles of the subject matter. New and difficult words must be taught *before* students are expected to recognize them in reading or use them in writing (Nelson-Herber, 1986).

Although extensive reading contributes to increased general vocabulary knowledge, direct vocabulary instruction usually is required in preparing students to read content material. Attention must be directed toward helping students identify and understand the words and terms, which, in turn, will assist them in comprehending the new information. The traditional approach to direct vocabulary instruction in the content areas, however, typically consists of directing students to define, memorize, and then use the new words in sentences (Vacca, Vacca, & Gove, 1987). The repertoire of activities teachers use to teach unknown vocabulary words is usually limited, and it often relies primarily on simple memorization of definitions. In order for a student to learn a word well enough to facilitate comprehension of related written material, the student must be able to link the new word to his or her own existing schemata. The instructional approaches used, therefore, must provide students with multiple opportunities to build both conceptual and contextual knowledge of the words and to relate this new knowledge to their own prior knowledge.

Two Semantic-Based Instructional Strategies

In this section, guidelines for using two successful, semantic-based vocabulary-building strategies are presented. These strategies, semantic mapping and semantic feature analysis, provide an alternative to the traditional vocabulary-building and prereading activities that are typically included in basal reading series. Both of these strategies, which draw their strength from the activation of children's prior knowledge bases, provide a way to organize and categorize both what students are learning about concepts and the words that name them. Organizing information in a meaningful way facilitates both comprehension and retention.

While these two strategies are not new, the value of semantic-based strategies has only recently been recognized as a result of an increased understanding of the important role that prior knowledge plays in the reading process. The strategies influence students to become active readers by triggering the brain to retrieve what is known about a topic and use this information in reading. This activation of prior knowledge is critical to reading comprehension. When a specific concept is activated, the entire memory structure for that concept is reawakened and becomes available to facilitate the comprehension process.

Semantic Mapping

Semantic maps, also referred to as *webs, semantic networks,* or *plot maps,* are graphic pictures that help students see how words are related to one another. (Chapter 7 also provides a discussion of plot mapping.) These maps help students connect or relate the conceptual meanings of new information to familiar information (prior knowledge). A major strength of the semantic mapping strategy, which capitalizes on the categorical nature of memory structure for individual words and words in context, is that it helps students to construct a model for organizing and integrating information.

Semantic mapping has been found to be a useful strategy in prior knowledge activation and assessment, general vocabulary building, pre- and postreading instruction, and study skill development (Heimlich & Pittelman, 1986). While the semantic mapping procedure may vary somewhat according to instructional objectives, the procedure generally begins with a brainstorming session in which students are asked to share words associated with the topic or the stimulus word. As the words are shared, the teacher maps (categorizes) them on the chalkboard. This mapping procedure provides students with an opportunity to actively engage in mental activity, thereby retrieving stored prior knowledge, and allows them to see a graphic representation of the concepts they are retrieving and/or learning. During the semantic mapping process, the topic word triggers the brain to retrieve information already stored in memory. When this information is activated, a link is made between past experiences and the topic being studied. Students have an opportunity to relate new concepts to their own background knowledge, thus "building bridges between the new and the known" (Pearson & Johnson, 1978, p. 24).

Discussion is a crucial part of all semantic mapping lessons in that it provides students the opportunity to verify and expand their own understanding of the concepts. Students learn the meanings and uses of new words, see familiar words in new ways, and view a graphic representation of the relationships among words. Discussion provides a way for students to share what they know and receive immediate feedback from their peers and the teacher on the words they suggest for addition to the classroom map. A completed semantic map provides the teacher with information about what the students already know and reveals anchor points upon which new concepts can be introduced.

During semantic mapping activities, the teacher is allowed to function as a facilitator rather than as a director. This less directive role encourages students to share in and direct their own learning. The altered teacher-student relationship inherent in the semantic mapping process might be one factor in the impact of semantic mapping as a strong motivational and brainstorming technique (Heimlich & Pittelman, 1986).

Semantic Mapping Procedure for General Vocabulary Development

Studies to evaluate the effectiveness of semantic mapping have supported its use as an effective strategy for general vocabulary development (Johnson, Toms-Bronowski, & Pittelman, 1982; Margosein, Pascarella, & Pflaum, 1982; Toms-Bronowski, 1983). It is simple to implement, and it can be adapted to meet a variety of specific instructional objectives.

The semantic map "Telephones," shown in Figure 3.1, was generated by a second-grade class during a general vocabulary lesson. The step-by-step procedure that follows provides a model for implementing a semantic mapping lesson for general vocabulary development. The procedure was adapted from the one suggested by Johnson and Pearson (1984).

Procedure

1. Choose a word or topic related to classroom work.
2. Write the word on a chalkboard, chart paper, or overhead transparency.

FIGURE 3.1 Classroom Semantic Map for "Telephones"

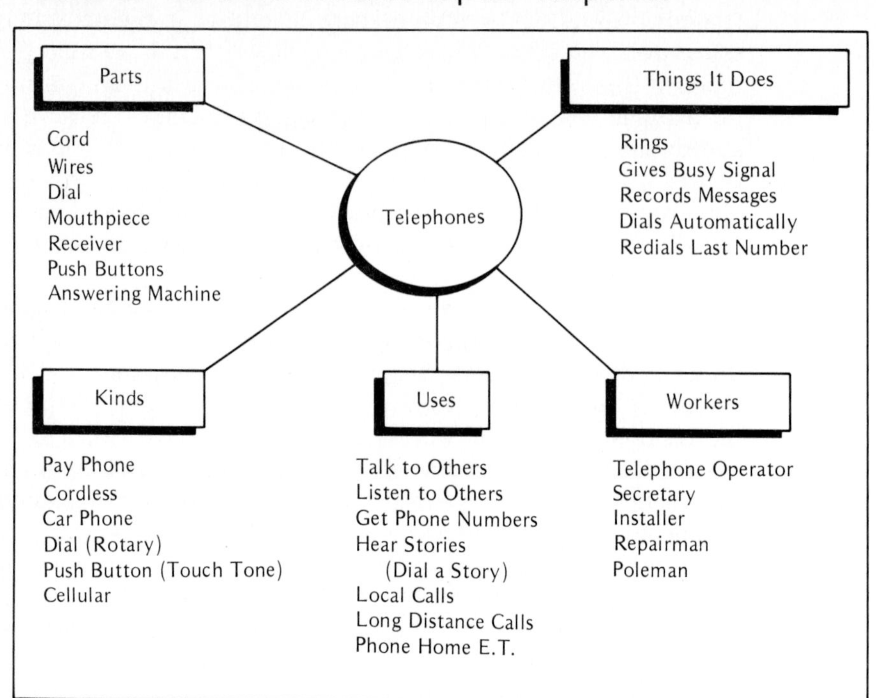

3. Ask the students to suggest the kinds of information they want to learn about the topic at hand. These headings can then be written on the map and will serve as a guide for generating related words. For example, for the topic "Telephones," the students suggested the following categories:

   Parts
   Things It Does
   Workers
   Uses
   Kinds

4. Encourage the students to generate as many words as possible that are related to the selected key word or topic. (Older students may be asked to write their words on a sheet of paper.)
5. Have the students share their words (or prepared lists) orally. As a word is suggested, write the word on the class map under the appropriate heading. Other headings may be added to the map as needed.
6. Conduct a class discussion of the topic, using the map as a guide. (Discussion of the map is a crucial part of the lesson.)

Note: Students could do further research on one or more of the subtopics. New information could then be added to the map. The procedure could be varied by postponing the discussion of categories until after the children have brainstormed a general list of words that relate to the topic. With this approach, category headings would be identified in Step 5, and Step 3 would be omitted.

Semantic Mapping as a Strategy for Pre- and Postreading

Semantic mapping also has been found to be an effective vocabulary-building strategy in pre- and postreading instruction, offering an alternative to the activities traditionally suggested in the teachers' manuals that accompany basal series. As an instructional method that precedes children's reading of a basal passage, semantic mapping can be used to activate students' prior knowledge and introduce key vocabulary words. This procedure helps students focus on relevant schema, thereby better preparing them to understand, assimilate, and evaluate the information in the material to be read. The maps serve to generate interest in the topic and help students become actively involved in constructing meaning from the written passage, thus enabling them to better understand the interrelated webs that authors create. Semantic mapping also provides the teacher with the opportunity to assess the students' prior knowledge, or schema availability, on the passage topic.

Class discussions using the semantic mapping procedure provide students with an opportunity to identify and integrate new information. These classroom interactions enable the teacher to identify what the students knew before they read the passage and what they learned from reading it. The final class discussion can serve as a comprehension check. At times in a prereading activity, it may be necessary to focus the majority of the discussion on only a few of the categories suggested by the students. By focusing the discussion, the teacher can direct the students' attention to specific words or categories on the map that best prepare them for reading the selection.

In the sample lesson that follows, students develop a semantic map of the story topic "Prairie Schooners" as part of a basal reading lesson (see Figure 3.2). The primary goals of the mapping experience are to activate the students' prior knowledge bases of the topic and to familiarize the students with the key vocabulary words the teacher has identified as being important to their comprehension of the passage. The map, which is a graphic representation of what the students know, provides a framework for their reading and instills in them a new confidence that they are already familiar with the topic and that it can be mastered. This may, in turn, be a key factor in motivating them to read the passage.

The procedure was used in a pre- and postreading vocabulary-building activity with a class of fourth-grade students. The students were reading "Prairie Schooner," a story about wagon trains in the old West, from a basal series. The students participated in semantic mapping both before and after

FIGURE 3.2 Classroom Semantic Map for "Prairie Schooners"

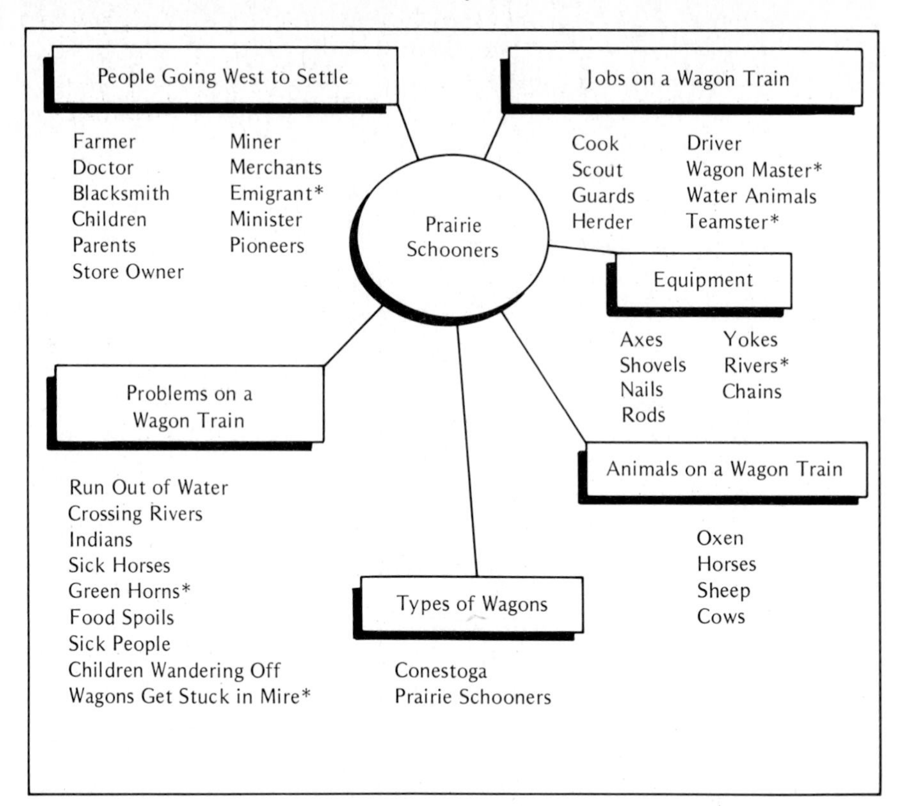

Note: Words with an asterisk are key vocabulary words that were introduced by the teacher.

reading the story in order to develop key vocabulary and enhance comprehension.

Procedure

1. Write the main topic of the story (in this case "Prairie Schooners") in the center of the chalkboard and draw a circle around the words.
2. Ask the students if they know what a *prairie schooner* is, and, if necessary, define it and explain that many of the pioneers who went west in wagon trains rode in prairie schooners.
3. Ask the students to think of words or ideas related to prairie schooners or to wagons on a wagon train.
4. List the students' suggestions on the chalkboard.
5. Discuss the words on the list, grouping them into categories. As you discuss each word, write it on the semantic map. The words should be entered on the map in clusters or categories.

6. After further discussion, ask the students to label each category on the map. If numerous categories were suggested by the students, it may be necessary at this point to focus the discussion on the categories that best prepare the students for reading the selection. At this time, any key vocabulary words that were not elicited from the students should be discussed and added to the map. (The vocabulary words may be either category labels or entries within a category.)
7. Direct the students to read the story. (The teachers' manuals often suggest a procedure.)
8. After the students have finished reading the story, ask them to share information they have learned about wagon trains. Add this new information to the map in the appropriate category. (Information that is added at this point can be written with chalk of another color to distinguish it from the entries that the students made before they read the passage.)
9. Discuss the information on the map, highlighting the key vocabulary words as well as any other important new concepts.

Semantic Feature Analysis

Like semantic mapping, semantic feature analysis (SFA) is a semantic-based instructional strategy for vocabulary development that capitalizes on the categorical manner in which information is stored in the brain. It focuses on the ways in which words in a category are alike and the ways in which they are different, fostering in students an ability to identify the relationships between and among concepts (Johnson & Pearson, 1984). Each word has characteristics or features that distinguish it from all of the other words in its category. These shades of meaning can be brought to light by the comparison process employed in semantic feature analysis. This activity is more appropriate for students at or above third grade.

In the semantic feature analysis procedure, students are involved in developing an analysis chart designed to illustrate that no two words have exactly the same meaning. A topic or category is selected, and words that relate to the topic are listed in a column at the left side of the chalkboard. Features or characteristics shared by some of the words in each column are written across the top of the chart, creating a grid. The words are compared, feature by feature; students put plus symbols and minus symbols in the grid to indicate whether or not the words in each column share the features listed along the top of the grid. The use of plus and minus symbols is recommended even though many features of a word are not truly dichotomous. In general, a plus sign indicates that a word usually or substantially possesses the feature designated in the grid. As students become more familiar with the procedures of semantic feature analysis and develop more sophisticated learning skills, a scale of numbers can be used in place of the pluses and minuses, with the numbers reflecting the relative degree of feature possession. (For example, a scale of 1 to 3 could be used, with 1 meaning *always*, 2 meaning *sometimes*, and 3 *never*.) During a prereading discussion, students may use a question mark to indicate that they do not know whether a word shares a specific feature. By the end of the semantic feature analysis lesson, students will have added new words and features to the grid and will have filled in the matrices. They will have discovered that, even with the most synonymous pairs of words, their patterns of pluses and minuses become different after enough semantic features have been considered.

In semantic feature analysis, vocabulary is presented in a logical, classified way. Grids display relationships among words, as well as the finer nuances within and among concepts. Students use the grids as vehicles to relate new vocabulary words to their own prior knowledge by showing how a new word is related to words that already are part of their cognitive domain.

Semantic feature analysis has been found to be effective for general vocabulary development, for basal instruction, and for refining and reinforcing vocabulary concepts in the content areas (Anders & Bos, 1986; Johnson, Toms-Bronowski, & Pittelman, 1982; Toms-Bronowski, 1983). Like semantic mapping, the semantic feature analysis procedure both activates prior knowledge and, through discussion, provides students with opportunities to relate new vocabulary to their own experiences.

Through semantic feature analysis, students improve their vocabulary and categorization skills and expand their content area vocabulary and concepts by building upon existing schemata. Semantic feature analysis also teaches semantic precision. The procedure impresses upon students the idea that no two words have exactly the same meaning and that *synonym* refers to *something like* rather than *the same as*.

As an example, as part of its study of oceanography, a third-grade class generated semantic feature analysis grids for the topics "Sea Animals" and "Underwater Plants." For each topic, the students developed an initial grid before they read a chapter in their science textbook. They refined the semantic grid after completing the assigned reading. Their grid on sea animals, which was developed as a prereading activity, is shown in Figure 3.3. The step-by-step procedure that follows provides a model for implementing a semantic feature analysis lesson such as this one. This basic procedure can also be adapted for general vocabulary lessons, as well as for basal lessons. Whether semantic feature analysis is used in a reading lesson or in a content area lesson, it is essential for the teacher to become thoroughly familiar with the assigned reading in order to be able to identify the key concepts presented in the passage.

Procedure

1. Select the concept or category to be analyzed (in this case, sea animals).

Sea Animals

Words	Teeth	Fins	Gills	Breathes Air	Man Eater	Swims	Pinches	Stings
Shark	+	+	+	—	+	+	—	?
Dolphin	+	+	—	+	—	+	—	—
Lobster	+	?	+	—	—	+	+	—
Sea Horse	—	+	?	?	—	+	—	—
Sea Snake	+	—	?	+	—	+	—	—
Eel	+	+	+	—	—	+	?	?

FIGURE 3.3 Classroom Prereading Semantic Feature Analysis Grid for "Sea Animals."

2. Along the left side of the chalkboard or predrawn grid, list two or three words that name concepts or objects related to the category. Try to select words that are already familiar to the students (e.g., shark, dolphin, lobster). Ask the students to suggest additional words that belong to this category, and list those as well.
3. Decide what features, traits, or characteristics are to be explored in the selected category. Write at least one of these features across the top of the matrix. Then ask the students to suggest additional features that at least one of the words possesses (e.g., teeth, fins, gills). Add these features to the top of the matrix. (As students become more familiar with semantic feature analysis, they will become more proficient at identifying features.) The more actively students are involved in the selection of categories, words, and features to be explored, the more effective the strategy will be.
4. Guide the students through the matrix, asking them to decide whether a particular sea animal listed along the left side of the matrix possesses each of the features listed across the top. Ask them to indicate whether each sea animal possesses the feature by writing a plus or a minus symbol in the space beside each word. If the children do not know whether an animal possesses a feature, direct them to write a question mark in the matrix and tell them that they can find the answer in their reading assignment.
5. Guide the students through the passage, encouraging them to look for missing information as well as additional words and features.
6. After the students have finished reading the passage, they are ready to expand the matrix to incorporate the new information. Help them replace the grid's question marks with pluses or minuses based on information in the textbook. Then ask them to suggest additional sea animals that share some of the features, as well as other features to be analyzed. (For example, the students might suggest *porpoise, jellyfish,* and *snail* for sea animals; *shell, sense of smell, sense of hearing,* and *lays eggs* for features.) As each new idea is suggested, add it to the grid.
7. Next ask the students to complete the remainder of the matrix by adding pluses and minuses. (You may have the students complete the grid independently or as a class.)
8. In class discussion, review the matrix, helping the students discover the similarities and differences among the listed animals. For example, which animals have gills? What animal does not have teeth? Help the students make generalizations as well as specific observations about the category items.
9. Ask the students how the words in the matrix are related to one another. Discuss the uniqueness of each word. If, at this point, some words still have identical patterns of pluses and minuses, encourage

the children to conduct additional research to identify features that would differentiate them. (For example, by adding the feature *beak* to the grid, students could differentiate between a dolphin and a porpoise.) Point out that even with the most synonymous pairs of words, the patterns will become different after enough semantic features have been included. Help the students realize that no two words have an identical pattern of pluses and minuses and, therefore, that no two words are identical in meaning.

Note: You may wish to duplicate a blank matrix so that each child can have one to complete and refer to during the discussion and reading.

The key to using semantic feature analysis for general vocabulary development is to begin with categories that are concrete and familiar to the students. As they become more comfortable with the procedure, it becomes possible to progress to more abstract categories. Suggested initial categories include weather, toys, sports, shelters, stores, pets, and planets. Advanced categories include emotions, government, battles, and measurement.

Uses of Semantic Mapping and Semantic Feature Analysis

Both semantic mapping and semantic feature analysis can be used in many different situations. Both approaches lend themselves especially well to instructional situations in which learning is facilitated by organizing or classifying information around a central concept or topic, and both provide students with graphic representations of how words and concepts are interrelated. Semantic mapping offers an opportunity to focus instruction on the hierarchical structuring of words within a category. The semantic feature analysis procedure, on the other hand, focuses on individual features and requires students to compare and contrast, thereby drawing distinctions between and among conceptually related words.

While the two strategies lend themselves to instructional situations in which the vocabulary words to be taught are related to a central concept or theme, semantic mapping and semantic feature analysis are also appropriate in prereading situations in which only a few of the key words highlighted by the basal manual relate to the theme of the story. According to Nagy (1988), there is no reason to limit instruction strictly to the vocabulary included in a given selection. Instead, additional words related to the theme should be included, as well as vocabulary from stories on similar themes that may be covered in the near future. (Nagy recommends the textbook glossary as a good source of words that are going to be introduced in other stories.)

General Guidelines for Vocabulary Instruction

While there is a general agreement that vocabulary instruction should be an important component of the school curriculum, research suggests that not all methods of instruction are equally effective (Carr & Wixson, 1986), nor is there a single best way to teach word meanings (Graves & Prenn, 1986). Different methods of teaching words are appropriate in different circumstances; vocabulary instruction needs to be tailored to the kind of word meanings to be learned as well as to the needs of the learners. Furthermore, there is concern that some of the procedures for vocabulary instruction suggested in commercially prepared basal reading programs may in fact detract from teachers' efforts to take advantage of the link between vocabulary learning and comprehension (Anderson & Freebody, 1981; Sorenson, 1985). Stauffer (1971) noted that teachers generally rely on the limited repertoire of vocabulary activities presented in the basal manuals when they could be creating their own.

According to Nagy (1988), two of the most common methods of vocabulary instruction—definitional approaches and contextual approaches—may not be nearly as effective as teachers suppose. While acknowledging that definitions do play a role in vocabulary instruction, he cautioned teachers that their substantial weaknesses and limitations must be recognized and corrected. Similarly, Nagy suggested that context as an instructional method in and of itself is comparatively ineffective in teaching new vocabulary. It is therefore extremely important that classroom teachers be able to evaluate instructional methods and, at the same time, be cognizant enough of options and alternatives that they are able to expand their own repertoire of vocabulary strategies. They need to be able to identify those activities that might be more useful for some students or more appropriate for certain types of reading.

Several principles should be considered in planning vocabulary instruction. While these principles are not absolute or all-inclusive, they do provide guidelines based on actual classroom practice and recent research on the relationship between vocabulary knowledge and reading comprehension.

Principle One: The instructional strategy should help students to relate new vocabulary to their own prior knowledge. Vocabulary must be introduced in such a way that existing knowledge is activated and new information is linked to that which is already known. Readers must be able to draw upon what they already know about a topic in order to relate it to what they are reading. Preparation for reading, therefore, must include activities that require students to mobilize existing information (schemata) so that they are able to relate it to what they are reading.

Principle Two: The instructional strategy should promote students' active involvement in learning new vocabulary. Encouraging students to discuss, generate, and apply the meanings of new vocabulary forces them to process a word's meaning more deeply. It also helps make students more word conscious, which in turn may motivate them to learn more vocabulary. Moreover, class discussions promote the active sharing of knowledge among students.

Principle Three: Vocabulary instruction should instill in students an understanding of words' meanings, relationships to other words, and appropriate contextual uses. Simple memorization of definitions is insufficient. As Nagy (1988) explained, research has shown that reading comprehension requires a high level of word knowledge—higher than the level achieved by many types of vocabulary instruction: "Only those methods that go beyond providing partial knowledge, producing in-depth knowledge of the words taught, will reliably increase readers' comprehension of text containing those words" (p. 3). Nagy urged teachers to augment traditional methods of instruction such as requiring students to memorize definitions with more intensive instruction aimed at producing richer, deeper word knowledge.

Rather than focusing on individual word meanings, instruction should emphasize the entire conceptual framework or schemata elicited by a word. Teaching words from a concept development approach places the emphasis on a word's place within the reader's established semantic repertoire, rather than limiting the meaning of the word to a particular sentence (Pearson, 1985). Students learn words more easily if they can incorporate them into their existing cognitive schemes (Ekwall-Shanker, 1988). Therefore, they must be given the opportunity to "make a word their own." Ownership of a word means that a child feels comfortable with a word and uses it with facility in daily language activities (Searfoss & Readence, 1989). In this way, the word's meaning becomes integrated into the student's own schemata, resulting in a deeper understanding of the word as well as a greater sensitivity to the various shades of meaning associated with it.

Principle Four: To be effective, vocabulary instruction must include multiple exposures to new vocabulary in contexts that require students to use the new words in meaningful ways. If word meanings are to be internalized, students must be directed to use the new words in a variety of situations throughout the school day. Activities that reinforce new vocabulary should parallel natural speaking, reading and writing; students should be required to process the meanings of new words, not merely to restate their definitions. To be successful, vocabulary instruction must provide students with multiple opportunities over an extended period of time to hear, speak, read, and write new words.

Principle Five: Vocabulary instruction must provide students with strategies they can use to decipher the meanings of unfamiliar words. It is assumed that a vocabulary program will include direct instruction in using the word identification strategies discussed in Chapter 2, such as contextual analysis, structural analysis, and phonics, so that a student will be able to draw upon them as needed. Students should also be taught to use such tools as the dictionary and the thesaurus.

Principle Six: Above all, the teacher must serve as a role model, demonstrating interest in and enthusiasm for vocabulary development. The classroom environment must foster an appreciation of language. As Deighton (1974) said, "A sense of excitement about words, a sense of wonder, and a feeling of pleasure—these are the essential ingredients in vocabulary development" (p. 59)

SUMMARY

Vocabulary instruction is more than directing students to look up and define words, memorize their definitions, and use them in sentences. It is more than a simple how-to procedure to be followed in introducing a story or chapter. Instead, effective vocabulary instruction draws upon existing schemata and lays the groundwork for future success.

To provide effective vocabulary instruction, teachers must employ substantive strategies that build upon children's word knowledge and expand their conceptual bases. Teachers must exert the effort and dedicate the time to ensure that students participate actively in a variety of meaningful experiences to introduce and reinforce new vocabulary. Finally, they must make vocabulary learning a priority and transmit this value to their students.

While offering students high-quality vocabulary instruction presents a professional challenge to the classroom teacher, it is one that is well worth undertaking.

FOLLOW-UP QUESTIONS AND ACTIVITIES

1. Select a chapter from a children's classic or a story from a basal textbook. Identify the key vocabulary words and concepts that a student would need in order to comprehend the selection. (If you use a story from a basal reader, compare your list to the key vocabulary words recommended in the manual.)

2. Create a simple semantic map on the topic "Sports." Include the categories "Names of Sports," "Equipment Used," and "Reasons for Sports," as well as two other categories. Develop the map by adding at least five entries to each category.
3. Independently complete the semantic feature analysis grid shown in Figure 3.4, using pluses and minuses. Then meet with other students in your class to share your responses. During the discussion, expand your grid to incorporate the words and features that were suggested.
4. Read a chapter or unit in either a science or social studies textbook. Select a topic and develop a semantic feature analysis grid that includes the key vocabulary and concepts presented in the chapter. (For example, if the unit were on weather you might develop a semantic feature analysis grid on the topic "Clouds.")
5. Choose a story from a basal manual and examine the activities suggested for introducing the key vocabulary words. Evaluate the activities in terms of the principles for vocabulary instruction that are presented in this chapter. If necessary, determine how you would restructure the lesson so that it meets the general guidelines for effective vocabulary instruction.

ADDITIONAL READINGS

Heimlich, J. E., & Pittelman, S. D. (1986). *Semantic mapping: Classroom applications.* Newark, DE: International Reading Association.

Johnson, D. D. (Ed.). (1986, April). Special issue on vocabulary. *Journal of Reading, 29.* Newark, DE: International Reading Association.

Johnson, D. D., & Pearson, P. D. (1984). *Teaching reading vocabulary* (2nd ed.). New York: Holt, Rinehart & Winston.

Klein, M. (1988). *Teaching vocabulary to improve reading comprehension.* Urbana-Champaign, IL: ERIC Clearinghouse on Reading and Communication Skills, National Council of Teachers of English and International Reading Association.

Moore, D. W., Readence, J. E., & Rickelman, R. J. (1989). *Prereading activities for context area reading and learning.* Newark, DE: International Reading Association.

REFERENCES

Adams, M., & Bruce, B. (1980). *Background knowledge and reading comprehension.* (Reading Education Report No. 13). Urbana: University of Illinois, Center for the Study of Reading.

Anders, P., & Bos, C. (1986). Semantic feature analysis: An interactive strategy for vocabulary development and text comprehension. *Journal of Reading, 29,* 610–616.

Anderson, R. C., & Freebody, P. (1981). Vocabulary knowledge. In J. Guthrie (Ed.),

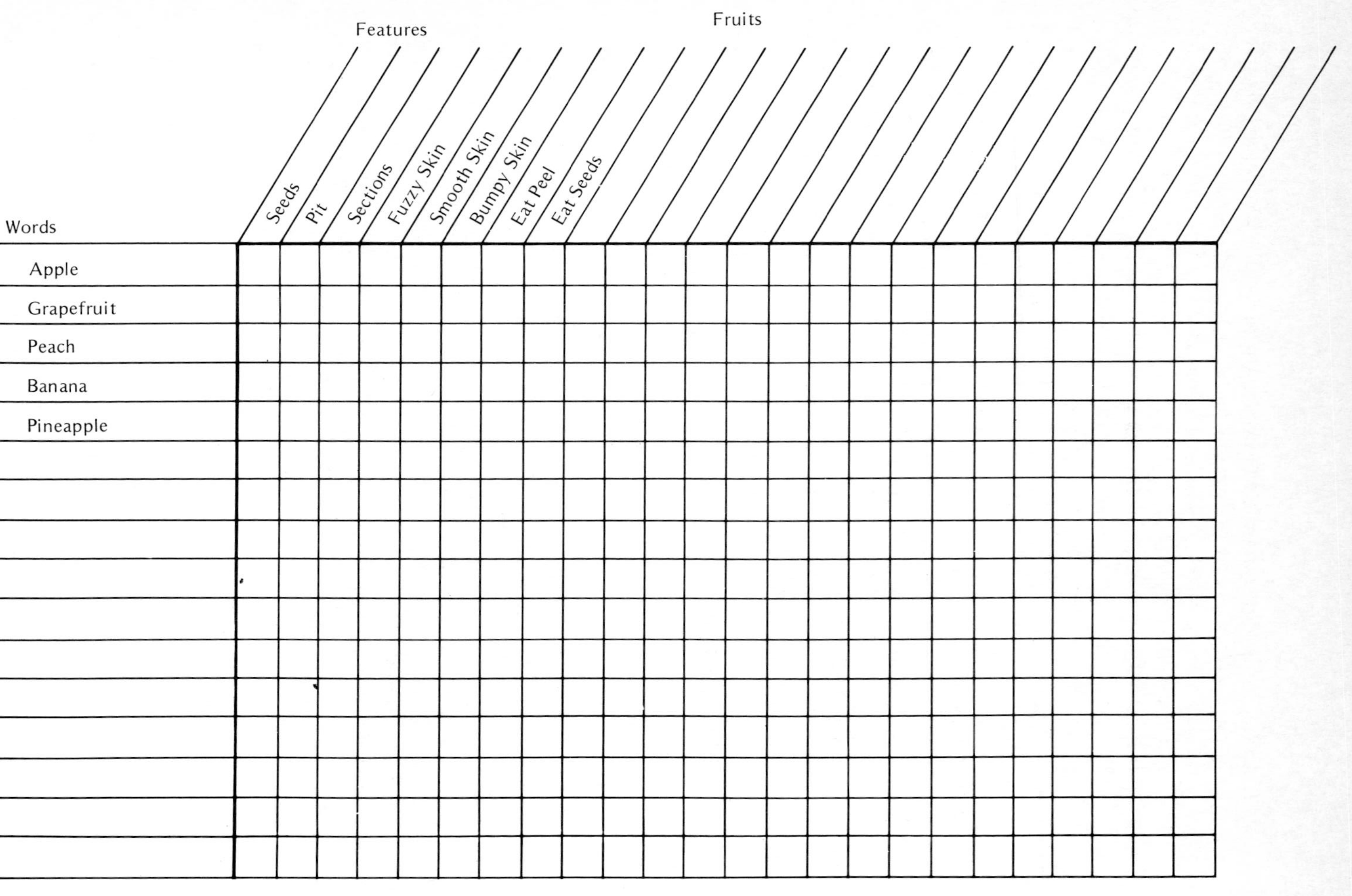

FIGURE 3.4 Blank Grid for Activity 3

Comprehension and teaching: Research reviews (pp. 77–117). Newark, DE: International Reading Association.

Anderson, R. C., & Freebody, P. (1983). Reading comprehension and the assessment and acquisition of word knowledge. In B. Hutson (Ed.), *Advances in reading language research* (pp. 231–256). Greenwich, CT: JAI Press.

Barrett, T. C., & Graves, M. F. (1981). A vocabulary program for junior high school remedial readers. *Journal of Reading, 245,* 146–150.

Brown, M. W. (1949). *The important book.* New York: Harper & Row.

Burns, C. P., Roe, B. D., & Ross, E. P. (1988). *Teaching reading in today's elementary schools.* Boston: Houghton Mifflin.

Carr, E., & Wixson, K. K. (1986). Guidelines for evaluating vocabulary instruction. *Journal of Reading, 29,* 588–595.

Davis, F. B. (1944). Fundamental factors of comprehension in reading. *Psychometrika, 9,* 185–197.

Deighton, L. C. (1974). *Vocabulary development in the classroom.* New York: Teachers College Press.

Durkin, D. (1981). What is the value of the new interest in reading comprehension? *Language Arts, 58,* 23–41.

Durkin, D. (1989). *Teaching them to read.* Boston: Allyn and Bacon.

Ekwall, E. E., & Shanker, J. L. (1988). *Diagnosis and remediation of the disabled reader.* Boston: Allyn and Bacon.

Gambrell, L. D., Wilson, R. M. & Gantt, W. N. (1981). Classroom observations of task-attending behaviors of good and poor readers. *Journal of Education Research, 74,* 400–404.

Graves, M. F., & Prenn, M. C. (1986). Costs and benefits of various methods of teaching vocabulary. *Journal of Reading, 29,* 596–602.

Hayes, D. A., & Tierney, R. J. (1982). Developing readers' knowledge through analogy. *Reading Research Quarterly, 17,* 256–280.

Heimlich, J. E., & Pittelman, S. D. (1986). *Semantic mapping: Classroom applications.* Newark, DE: International Reading Association.

Johnson, D. D. (1984). Expanding vocabulary through classification. In D. Johnson & J. Baumann (Eds.), *Reading instruction and the beginning teacher* (pp. 28–38). Minneapolis: Burgess.

Johnson, D. D., Levin, K. M., & Pittelman, S. D. (1984). *A field assessment of vocabulary instruction in the elementary school classroom.* (Program Report No. 84-3). Madison: University of Wisconsin, Wisconsin Center for Education Research.

Johnson, D. D., & Pearson, P. D. (1984). *Teaching reading vocabulary* (2nd ed.). New York: Holt, Rinehart & Winston.

Johnson, D. D., Toms-Bronowski, S., & Buss, R. (1983). Fundamental factors in reading comprehension revisited. In L. Gentile & M. Kamil (Eds.), *Reading research revisited* (pp. 247–255). Columbus, OH: Merrill.

Johnson, D. D., Toms-Bronowski, S., & Pittelman, S. D. (1982). *An investigation of the effectiveness of semantic mapping and semantic feature analysis with intermediate grade level students.* (Program Report 83-3). Madison: University of Wisconsin, Wisconsin Center for Education Research.

Johnston, P. (1984). Background knowledge and reading comprehension test bias. *Reading Research Quarterly, 19,* 219–239.

Johnston, P., & Pearson, P. D. (1982). Prior knowledge connectivity and the assessment of reading comprehension. (Technical Report No. 245). Urbana: University of Illinois.

Lindsay, P., & Norman, D. (1977). *Human information processing* (2nd ed.). New York: Academic Press.

Margosein, C. M., Pascarella, E. T., & Pflaum, S. W. (1982, April). The effects of instruction using semantic mapping on vocabulary and comprehension. Paper presented at the Annual Meeting of the American Educational Research Association, New York. (ED 217 390).

May, F. B. (1990). *Reading as communication* (3rd ed.). Columbus, OH: Merrill.

Nagy, W. E. (1988). *Teaching vocabulary to improve reading comprehension.* Urbana-Champaign, IL: ERIC Clearinghouse on Reading and Communication Skills, National Council of Teachers of English and International Reading Association.

Nagy, W. E., & Anderson, R. C. (1982). *The number of words in printed school English.* (Technical Report No. 253). Urbana: University of Illinois, Center for the Study of Reading.

Nagy, W. E., & Anderson, R. C. (1984). How many words are there in printed school English? *Reading Research Quarterly, 19,* 304–330.

Nagy, W. E., & Herman, P. A. (1985). Incidental vs. instructional approaches to increasing reading vocabulary. *Educational Perspectives, 23* (1), 16–21.

Nelson-Herber, J. (1986). Expanding and refining vocabulary in content areas. *Journal of Reading, 29,* 626–633.

O'Rourke, J. P. (1974). *Toward a science of vocabulary development.* The Hague: Mouton.

Pearson, P. D. (1985). Changing the face of reading comprehension instruction. *The Reading Teacher, 38,* 724–738.

Pearson, P. D., & Johnson, D. D. (1978). *Teaching reading comprehension.* New York: Holt, Rinehart & Winston.

Pearson, P. D., & Spiro, R. (1982). The new buzz word in reading is schemata. *Instructor, 91,* 46–48.

Rumelhart, D. E. (1980). Schemata: The building blocks of cognition. In R. J. Spiro, B. C. Bruce, & W. F. Brewer (Eds.), *Theoretical issues in reading comprehension* (pp. 38–58). Hillsdale, NJ: Erlbaum.

Searfoss, L., & Readence, J. (1989). *Helping children learn to read.* Englewood Cliffs, NJ: Prentice-Hall.

Smith, R. J., & Johnson, D. D. (1980). *Teaching children to read* (2nd ed.). Reading, MA: Addison-Wesley.

Sorenson, N. L. (1985). Basal reading vocabulary instruction: A critique and suggestions. *The Reading Teacher, 39,* 80–85.

Spache, G. D., & Spache, E. B. (1977). *Reading in the elementary school* (4th ed.). Boston: Allyn and Bacon.

Stahl, S. (1986). Three principles of effective vocabulary instruction. *Journal of Reading, 29,* 662–668.

Stauffer, R. G. (1971). Slave, puppet, or teacher? *The Reading Teacher, 25,* 24–29.

Toms-Bronowski, S. (1983). An investigation of the effectiveness of selected vocabulary teaching strategies with intermediate grade level students. *Dissertation Abstracts International, 44,* 1405A. (University Microfilms No. 83-16, 238)

Vacca, J. L., Vacca, R. T., & Gove, M. K. (1987). *Reading and learning to read.* Boston: Little, Brown.

4

Teaching Comprehension Strategies

JAMES F. BAUMANN

THE CHAPTERS IN Part One of this book, which deal with the effective teaching of the reading process, have progressed from an emphasis on decoding to an emphasis on meaning. Chapter 2 covered important aspects of word identification skills, while Chapter 3 discussed the development of meaning vocabulary. In this chapter, James Baumann focuses our attention on reading comprehension and presents comprehension strategies that effective teachers employ. He begins the chapter with a brief discussion of theoretical background that highlights several important principles of effective classroom instruction and six specific features of effective comprehension instruction.

Baumann then presents a detailed discussion of a What, Why, How, and When instructional model that incorporates these principles and features. He explains that the What step of the model requires the teacher to inform the students what reading strategy will be taught. In the Why step, the teacher tells the students why the comprehension strategy is important and how it will help them to be better readers. During the How step, the teacher directly teaches students how to use the comprehension strategy. The final stage, When, involves letting students know when the strategy should be employed. Baumann presents sample lessons that illustrate the use of the four-step model. These lessons provide a clear picture of how effective teachers can make use of the principles for teaching comprehension strategies to children.

The chapter concludes with guidelines to help teachers in deciding what comprehension strategies to teach their students.

STUDY QUESTIONS

1. What teacher behaviors and environmental conditions are associated with high levels of student learning?
2. What are the critical features of effective reading comprehension instruction?
3. How is a reading comprehension *skill* different from a comprehension *strategy?*
4. How might we use what is known about effective comprehension strategy instruction to design an instructional model that enables teachers to promote independent, strategic reading in their students?

Theoretical Background

Principles of Effective Classroom Instruction

Hundreds of research studies have been conducted to identify teacher behaviors and environmental conditions that are associated with high levels of student learning (e.g., see reviews by Baumann, 1984a; Brophy & Good, 1986; Rosenshine & Stevens, 1984). The research findings most relevant to reading comprehension instruction indicate the importance of

- teachers having a positive attitude about their own teaching abilities and their students' ability to learn;
- teachers being aware of the goals and objectives for their lessons and their ability to communicate these objectives to students;
- enough time in the school day being allocated for reading instruction;
- students being academically engaged or on task a high proportion of the time;
- a businesslike atmosphere in the classroom during academic activities;
- an environment in which teachers love and respect children and make them feel comfortable, important, and worthwhile;
- teachers skillfully managing the instructional time by being thoroughly prepared, administering instruction at a brisk pace, keeping transition time to a minimum, and being able to prevent misbehavior;
- teachers monitoring learning by checking students' understanding, providing corrective feedback, reteaching as needed, and insuring the completion of assigned work;
- and most importantly, teachers really teaching; that is, teachers showing, telling, modeling, demonstrating, explaining, *teaching* how various skills and processes function. (Baumann, 1987, pp. 16–17)

In other words, when teachers take the time to clearly, directly, and explicitly teach students reading comprehension skills, students tend to acquire these abilities. This common-sense notion of the effectiveness of teachers' actually teaching reading comprehension has been documented in several recent research studies (e.g., Baumann, 1984b, 1986a; Baumann, Jones, & Seifert-Kessell, 1988; Baumann, Seifert-Kessell, & Jones, 1987; see reviews by Pearson, 1985; Pearson & Gallagher, 1983; Winograd & Hare, 1988).

Critical Features of Effective Reading Comprehension Instruction

Building upon what has been learned about effective classroom instruction, several different comprehension instructional models have been proposed (e.g., Baumann, 1983, 1986b; Baumann & Ballard, 1987; Baumann & Schmitt, 1986; Baumann & Stevenson, 1986; Pearson & Leys, 1985). Even though these models differ in the number and labeling of steps, there are several characteristics of effective comprehension instruction common to most approaches. Among the most critical features are the following:

1. *Lesson introduction.* The teacher informs the students what skill will be taught, why it is important, and how its acquisition will make them better readers.
2. *Direct instruction.* The teacher explicitly teaches the students how the comprehension skill operates. This might involve the teacher's engaging in verbal explanation, description, modeling, or an oral think-aloud (the teacher relating the mental processes involved in applying the skill).
3. *Heuristics and visual displays.* The teacher provides the students a diagram, figure, logarithm, or series of steps that can be used when applying the skill independently.
4. *Constructive responses.* The teacher has the students compose or generate responses (orally or in writing), as opposed to giving them simple recognition tasks (e.g., multiple choice, matching). This requires students to discover concepts, think critically, and process text more deeply, which enhances their understanding.
5. *Transfer of responsibility.* The teacher assumes full responsibility for teaching and learning at the onset of instruction (explanation, modeling). Gradually the teacher transfers responsibility to the students through guided practice and has them assume full responsibility for strategy use in independent practice.
6. *Conditions for strategy use.* The teacher informs the students when the skill should be used, when it should not be used, and how to evaluate skill use (Winograd & Hare, 1988). This is what Paris, Lipson, and Wixson (1983) referred to as *conditional knowledge.*

Strategy Instruction, Not Skill Instruction

Up to now, the term *skill* has been used when referring to comprehension instruction, but the title of this chapter contains the word *strategy.* Often these terms are used interchangeably; however, some researchers (e.g., Paris et al., 1983) discriminate between them. Duffy and Roehler (1987, p. 415) defined a skill as an overlearned procedure for which the achievement of speed and accuracy is the goal. For example, a basal reader series might contain several skill lessons that require students to identify main ideas on worksheets that contain short, contrived passages.

In contrast, Duffy and Roehler (1987) argued that a strategy involves a learning plan to be used flexibly; that is, strategies are skills that are used intentionally, deliberately, and selectively in order to promote the understanding of text in natural reading situations. For example, the ability to identify main ideas will remain a skill unless students also know when they should call up this skill (e.g., when they become confused about the author's main points when reading a content textbook selection) and how to evaluate their use of the skill. Strategies involve skill use, but they include the added dimension of conditional knowledge; that is, strategic readers are not only *skillful* at comprehension processes such as determining an author's main ideas but also know why, how, and when a skill should be used. Therefore, the term *strategy* will be used from this point on to refer to instruction in a reading skill or process that includes the conditional knowledge necessary for independent skill use.

A Procedure for Teaching Comprehension Strategies

The Baumann and Schmitt (1986) What, Why, How, and When instructional model was developed to incorporate the general principles of effective classroom instruction and the six specific features of effective comprehension instruction noted previously. It consists of four steps.

Step 1: What. In the first step, the teacher informs the students what reading strategy will be taught. This might be a simple description or definition of the strategy or an example of its use.

Step 2: Why. In the second step, the teacher tells the students why the comprehension strategy is important and how its acquisition will help them become better readers. Collectively, steps 1 and 2 provide the students clearly stated instructional objectives so that there is no ambiguity about the purpose and nature of the ensuing instruction.

Step 3: How. The third step involves direct instruction in the strategy (Baumann, 1988). This might involve verbal explanation, modeling, or the use of an oral think-aloud. If appropriate, heuristics, visual displays, and constructive exercises are a part of this step. Responsibility for strategy use shifts gradually from the teacher to the students in step 3. Guided practice, which may include corrective feedback or reteaching, follows the direct instruction and teacher modeling. Complete student responsibility occurs when the teacher engages the pupils in independent practice of the strategy. The teacher may work with short, contrived texts initially, but ultimately natural reading selections from basal readers, content textbooks, or trade books should be used for application of the strategy. Depending on the complexity of the strategy that is being taught, step 3 may be completed in a single day or it may span several days.

Step 4: When. The final step involves the communication of conditional knowledge: when the strategy should be used (and not used) and how to evaluate and correct its use.

Sample Lessons

The following lessons present examples of the use of the four-step comprehension instructional model. Possible teacher wording is presented in quotation marks; annotations or comments are stated in brackets.

Note: It should be noted that the use of scripted lessons is *not* recommended; teachers need to react spontaneously to the ebb and flow of instruction, and scripts cannot account for all possible instructional contingencies (see Baumann, 1988). Teachers must plan thoroughly, but they must also be prepared to adapt instruction as it unfolds. Therefore, the reader should view the possible teacher wording in each sample lesson as a *transcript* of the lesson, not as a predetermined *script*.

Sample Lesson 1

Comprehension Strategy: Making inferences. This strategy involves teaching students to identify a set of basic inference types that they can then use to identify unstated but implied information in texts they read (inference categories taken from Johnson & Johnson, 1986, 1988).

Students: An average group of third-grade students.

Step 1: What. "When writers write, they give you lots of facts and ideas. But there are some ideas that they leave out. These are *unstated ideas.* It is your job as the reader to try to figure out what those unstated ideas are. Today we will learn how to look for and understand unstated ideas."

Step 2: Why. "Being able to figure out unstated ideas is important because writers leave out quite a bit of information, so you must be able to fill in these missing ideas. Then you will understand and enjoy stories better."

Step 3: How. "Listed on this chart are six different kinds of unstated information. [Teacher displays chart shown in Figure 4.1.] Let's look at the different kinds of things writers can leave out. Can someone read number 1? [Student reads example.] Good. Now, can you answer the question 'Who is Polly?' [Students respond.] Yes, Polly is a baseball player. So one kind of information that an author can leave out is information about *people:* who a

FIGURE 4.1 Instructional Chart Listing Six Inference Categories

UNSTATED IDEAS

1. PEOPLE OR ANIMALS

   Polly was up to bat. Her team was down by two runs. She swung at the pitch and hit a homer.

   Who is Polly?

   The farmer fed table scraps to the squealing animals. They rooted in the feeding trough with their noses and made snorting, oinking sounds as they ate.

   What are the animals?

2. PLACES

   Max took out his pencil and math paper when the teacher told the class to get to work.

   Where is Max?

3. THINGS

   Kristi pushed the roaring machine all over the lawn. When she was finished, the grass looked beautiful.

   What is the roaring machine?

4. TIME

   The bell rang, and Ms. Olson said, "All right, children. Go outside and play hard for 20 minutes, but be ready to take your spelling test when you come back inside."

   What time was it?

5. ACTIONS

   Jim took an end and let Nancy jump for a while. We all sang as she jumped. Nancy finally missed, and then she took an end.

   What were Nancy and Jim doing?

6. FEELINGS

   After his team lost the kickball game in gym class, Scott walked over to the bleachers, kicked them with his foot, and yelled, "darn."

   How was Scott feeling?

Note: Categories adapted from Johnson and Johnson (1986; 1988).

person is or what a person does." [Teacher works through the remaining categories on Figure 4.1 in a similar manner.]

"Now that we understand how writers leave things such as people, animals, and places unstated, let's think about what clues we can use to figure out unstated ideas. Look at this second chart. [Teacher displays the 'How to Figure Out Unstated Ideas' chart; see Figure 4.2.] It contains some steps we can use to figure out unstated ideas. The first step says to read and understand the facts. This means that you should first try to figure out what the *stated* ideas are—those that the writer has given you. For example, in the little story about Polly on the other chart, we first read to get the facts or stated ideas about Polly and what she was doing. Step 2 says that next you need to decide what the writer has left out. For the Polly story, we then recognized that the writer did not tell us who Polly was and what she was doing." [Teacher explains the remaining steps in the strategy in a similar fashion.]

"Let me show you how to use these steps. I will read this little story [the following text is displayed on the board or a chart] and tell you what I am thinking as I follow these steps and try to figure out the unstated ideas."

> Dr. Matthews said, "All right, Wendy, you can come in now."
> "Do I have to, Mom?" asked Wendy. "I don't want to."
> "It's all right, Wendy," said Dr. Matthews. "It won't hurt at all."

FIGURE 4.2 A Strategy for Inferring Unstated Information

HOW TO FIGURE OUT UNSTATED IDEAS

1. Read and understand the facts.
2. Decide what the writer has left out.
3. Figure out what the unstated ideas are.
   - Think about what you know about the story.
   - Look for clues in the story.
   - Make a guess about what the unstated ideas are.
4. Read on to check to see whether you were correct.
5. Go back to step 3 if you were wrong.

Note: Adapted from *Making Inferences* by Dale D. Johnson and Bonnie von Hoff Johnson of THE LEADERSHIP LETTERS, © 1988 by Silver, Burdett & Ginn Inc. Used with permission.

> Wendy walked in and sat down. Dr. Matthews said, "Open wide, please," and she inserted the instruments into Wendy's mouth. "Things look real good, Wendy. You must be brushing regularly."
>
> "Yes," said Wendy. "I brush after every meal."
>
> "That's great," said Dr. Matthews. "Now I am going to have Ms. Nelson do some cleaning, but don't worry; that won't hurt either. I will see you again in 6 months. Keep up the good work."

"Let's see, step 1 says that first I should read and understand the facts. All right, I'll begin by reading the first three lines of the story. [Teacher reads aloud the first three lines.] Well, here I learned that there is some kind of doctor, Dr. Matthews, and she or he is talking to someone named Wendy. Wendy's mother must also be there, because Wendy is talking to her. . . . " [Teacher continues paraphrasing the first three lines of the text.]

"Step 2 says that I should decide what the writer has left out. Let's see, we still don't know what kind of doctor Dr. Matthews is, and I suppose we should try to figure out who Wendy is, too. Therefore, I guess that I need to figure out unstated *people* like we did for Polly on the other chart. Also, I think we need to figure out *place,* since the writer does not tell us where this is happening. And we might want to think about Wendy's *feelings.*"

"Step 3 says to figure out these unstated ideas by thinking about what you know and by looking for clues in the story. There are many different kinds of doctors. For example, Dr. Matthews could be a medical doctor, an eye doctor, a dentist, or maybe even a veterinarian. I think Dr. Matthews is probably a dentist because he or she says it won't hurt, and some kids are afraid of going to the dentist because it might hurt. I bet that Wendy is Dr. Matthews's patient. If I am right about Wendy and Dr. Matthews, then the place is probably a dentist's office and Wendy is probably feeling afraid."

"Step 4 says to read on to check whether or not our guesses are correct. All right, I will read the next two lines. [Teacher reads text through ' . . . must be brushing regularly.'] It sure seems to me that Dr. Matthews is a dentist, that Wendy is a patient, and that this is taking place in Dr. Matthews's dental office. Clues that helped here were Wendy coming in and sitting down, Dr. Matthews saying, 'open wide' and looking in Wendy's mouth, and their talk about brushing. However, the writer now mentions "instruments," and they are unstated *things,* so I must try to figure out what those instruments are." [Teacher continues with the think-aloud procedure, modeling the use of the steps outlined in Figure 4.2.]

"Now it is your turn to try out these steps. Look at this other story I have. [Teacher presents the following text.] Read the first four lines of it to yourself. As you read do steps 1 and 2; that is, try to understand the facts and try to figure out what the writer has left out."

> Susan's father drove up to the speaker. They looked at the menu, and Dad asked Susan, "What do you want?"

"I think I'll have a cheeseburger, an order of fries, and an orange drink," answered Susan.

"OK," said Dad. Then he rolled down the window. From the speaker came the words, "May I take your order please?" Dad said, "Yes, we'll have two cheeseburgers, two orders of fries, one orange drink, and one coffee."

"How did you do? Were you able to figure out the facts and what the author left unstated? Who can tell us the facts? [Student is called upon and paraphrases the text that was read silently.] Good, now who can tell us what the writer has left out?" [Student responds that *people, place, time,* and *actions* are omitted. Teacher continues with guided practice of the remaining steps in Figure 4.2.]

"You have done a very good job on the story about going to a fast-food restaurant and using the drive-through window. Now I want you to practice using these steps on your own. Turn to pages 12 and 13 in your workbook. [Students find the exercise presented in Figure 4.3.] Here is an exercise for you to do on your own. As you do this exercise, look for examples of the six different kinds of things that writers sometimes leave out. Then use the five steps we learned about to help you figure out unstated ideas. Let's look at the directions on page 12. [Teacher reads directions aloud.] Do you understand what you must do?" [Teacher answers questions and then has the students complete the workbook pages on their own.]

[For additional independent practice and application in more natural reading situations, the teacher would engage the students in one or more of the following activities in subsequent review and application lessons:

- Have the students apply this skill when they read their next basal reader story.
- Have the students apply this skill when listening to a book the teacher is reading aloud to them.
- Have the students apply this skill when reading nonfiction selections from a content area textbook or an informational trade book.]

Step 4: When. "Before you begin your work paper, there are a few things I need to tell you about figuring out unstated ideas. First, try to figure out unstated ideas when you read stories and when you read informational books; writers will leave out ideas in both of these kinds of writing. However, look for more unstated *people, actions,* and *feelings* in stories and for more unstated *places, things,* and *times* in informational writing."

"Second, use the five steps when you become confused about what the writer is saying. Your confusion might be due to unstated ideas."

"Finally, figuring out unstated ideas will be easier when the topic about which you are reading is familiar to you. So when you are not very familiar

FIGURE 4.3 Commercial Exercise for Practicing Inferential Comprehension

Lesson 6 Unstated Information

Unstated information means that ideas are not right there in the story. To answer questions about unstated information, you must search for clues in the story. Sometimes you may have to use ideas that are not even in the story.

Read the story. Write an answer for each question.

Rachel was walking home from school. She saw a large puddle on the sidewalk. When Rachel got home, her mother made her put her wet shoes on the back porch.

1. How did Rachel get her shoes wet?

____

2. Where did the puddle come from?

____

Did you know the answers? Those answers were unstated information.

Hints: To answer questions about unstated information:
1. Search for clues in the story.
2. Use ideas only suggested in the story.

Read each story. Write an answer for each question.

Sarah's soccer team was in a tie. Sarah ran down the field fast. Kathy passed the ball to her. Sarah kicked it hard at the goal. The goalkeeper dived for the ball. When Sarah saw what happened, she jumped up and down. Her teammates shook her hand. The goalkeeper looked very sad.

3. Did the goalkeeper stop Sarah's kick? ______________________________

4. Why did Sarah jump up and down?

____

(12) Stated and unstated information

Note: From *Workbook C* of the GINN COMPREHENSION PROGRAM by James F. Baumann, © Copyright, 1986 by Ginn and Company. Used by permission of Silver, Burdett & Ginn Inc.

FIGURE 4.3 *Continued*

Danny had a lot of homework. He had math to do. He had spelling to do. He also had a book to read. Before supper, Danny watched TV. After supper, Danny played outside with his friend William. Danny was having so much fun, he did not check the time. At 8:00, Danny's father said, "Danny, it is time to come in and get ready for bed." Danny had a worried look on his face.

5. Why did Danny have a worried look on his face?

____

6. Did Danny get his homework done?__________ Why?______________

____

7. What do you think happened in school the next day?

____

Jane and Jack went for a walk in the woods. They were looking for berries. Jack said, "Look at this pretty orange berry. I never saw one like it before."

Jane said, "I would not eat those, Jack. You don't know what they are."

Jack ate a few of the orange berries. Later that night, Jack got a stomachache. Jane felt fine.

8. What made Jack sick?

____

9. Why did Jane say, "I would not eat those, Jack"?

____

Name ______________________________ 13

with the information in a story, you will need to work extra hard to figure out the unstated ideas."

Sample Lesson 2

Comprehension Strategy: Predicting and verifying. This strategy involves teaching students a modified version of the directed reading/thinking activity (Stauffer, 1969, 1975); that is, students are taught to make hypotheses about selection content, read to verify their hypotheses, and then revise the hypotheses or make new ones. Employing this strategy promotes active reading and enables students to engage in independent purpose-setting when reading.

Students: A low-average group of fifth-grade students.

Step 1: What. "Good readers make guesses or predictions when they read. For example, listen to this little story." [Teacher reads the following.]

> Max the dog likes to dig. He digs holes all over his back yard. Max also likes to bark at and chase squirrels. One day Max saw a gray squirrel eating a nut in the yard next door. Max wanted to chase it, but there was a strong fence all around his back yard.

"What do you think Max did? Make a prediction. [Students respond.] Yes, a good prediction would be that Max dug a hole under the fence and chased the squirrel. Today we will learn how to make predictions and how to read on to check or verify whether or not they were correct."

Step 2: Why. "Making predictions and verifying them is an important reading strategy because this will help you to think about what you are reading and look for ideas and information that the writer may tell you later in the story. When you make a prediction, it is like giving yourself a purpose to read—to check your prediction. This will help you become a more active reader and a better comprehender. Also, making predictions can be fun because you can then read to find out whether your guesses are correct."

Step 3: How. "There are four steps you can use to make and check a prediction. I have these written on this chart. [Teacher displays the 'How to Predict and Verify' chart; see Figure 4.4.] Step 1 says to read the story and think about what is happening. Step 2 says to predict what will happen in the story. There are four clues listed there under step 2. . . . " [Teacher explains the remaining steps in the strategy, elaborating and extending the information on the chart as required.]

"Open your *Ride the Sunrise* book (Clymer, Indrisano, Johnson, Pear-

FIGURE 4.4 A Strategy for Making and Verifying Predictions.

HOW TO PREDICT AND VERIFY

1. READ the story. Think about what is happening and what might happen next.
2. PREDICT what will happen in the story. To help you predict,
   - Use what you *know* about what's happening in the story.
   - Think about an important event in the story that might *cause* something else to happen.
   - Think about the *sequence* of events and what might happen next in that sequence.
   - Think about the *characters* in the story and how they might behave or what they might do next.
3. VERIFY your predictions. This means read on to see whether your guesses were correct.
4. CHANGE your predictions if necessary or MAKE NEW PREDICTIONS. Then read on to verify them.

HINT

You can make predictions about what will happen *NEXT* in a story (for example, in the next sentence or paragraph) or what will happen *AT THE END* of a story.

Note: Adapted from *Making Inferences* by Dale D. Johnson and Bonnie von Hoff Johnson of THE LEADERSHIP LETTERS, © 1988 by Silver, Burdett & Ginn Inc. Used with permission.

son, & Venezky, 1985) to page 162. This is the beginning of our next story, which is titled "The Tree People" by Shirley Nagel. [See Figure 4.5 for a reproduction of the first part of this selection.] Let me show you how to use these steps by reading the beginning of the story and making predictions as I read."

"Let's see, I think I will make a prediction right from the title of the story. I bet that this story is about people who live in trees. Maybe this takes place in a jungle where people have built tree houses to stay dry and away from dangerous animals. I'll read the first paragraph of the story to see whether I am on the right track." [Teacher reads first paragraph aloud.]

"I don't think this story is going to be about people living in trees. It

FIGURE 4.5 Portion of a Basal Reader Story Used to Teach a Predict/Verify Strategy. (From Clymer et al., *Ride the Sunrise,* Level 12 of the Ginn Reading Program, 1985, pp. 162, 163.)

THE TREE PEOPLE

by Shirley Nagel

1. Andy Lipkis has a nickname. He is called "Tree Boy" because he spends most of his time planting trees in the mountains of Southern California. Andy's unusual job began years earlier when he was at summer camp. A naturalist told Andy and his group what was happening in the forest because of smog.
2. "In twenty-five years the forest will be gone. This smog will have killed most of the trees. Nothing will be left but bare hills. You may be the last to enjoy this forest."
3. Andy couldn't believe it. But he looked down into the far-off valley below. He watched the yellow blanket of smog drifting up into the foothills. Maybe the naturalist was right.
4. "What can we do to stop the smog from killing the forest?" Andy asked.
5. "As long as there is smog, there's nothing we can do to stop the trees from dying," said the naturalist. "But there are some kinds of trees that will grow in spite of smog. We call them smog-tolerant trees."

Note: Adapted from TREE BOY, by Shirley Nagel.

takes place in Southern California, and I don't think anyone lives in trees there. Anyway, it said that Andy is called 'Tree Boy' because he spends a lot of time planting trees. So maybe he is one of several 'tree people' who do the same thing. I'll check on this prediction as I continue to read the story."

"What else have I learned so far? Well, Andy seems to be very concerned about the environment, so he plants a lot of trees. I guess he got interested in this when he went to camp some time ago. The last sentence of the paragraph says that the naturalist told the kids what was happening to the forest because of the smog. I wonder what the smog was doing to the trees. I know that trees take gas from the air in order to make food, so I predict that the smog was killing the trees because it interfered with their food-making. I better read the next paragraph to check on this prediction." [Teacher reads paragraph 2 aloud.]

"I was right about the smog killing the trees. However, it didn't explain yet how the smog killed the trees; maybe we will learn that later on in the story. My prediction about its interfering with food-making might be correct after all." [Teacher continues to model the predict/verify sequence as needed.]

"Now I want you to make some predictions. Do step 1. Read the next two paragraphs; then let's see whether there are any predictions you might want to make." [Students silently read paragraphs 3 and 4.]

"Let's try step 2. Does anyone have an idea for a prediction? [Students respond that they might predict what the naturalist said in response to Andy's question.] That's a good idea. How can we go about predicting what the naturalist said? Step 2 says you should use what you know about the topics—smog and trees in this case—and think about causes, sequences, and characters to help you predict. Try that out. Predict how the naturalist answered Andy's question." [Students suggest the following predictions, which the teacher writes on the board: (a) get people to cut down on pollution; (b) make laws to stop pollution from cars and factories; (c) put a chemical in the ground or spray it on the trees to protect them from the pollution; (d) plant trees that might not die from pollution.]

"Wow! You made lots of good predictions. Read paragraph 5 in the story to see whether any of your predictions are correct." [Teacher continues with guided practice of the four-step procedure until she is convinced that the students have grasped it.]

"You have done a great job making predictions and verifying them. Sometimes you were correct, sometimes you were not, but the important thing is that you were reading, thinking, and getting involved with the story. Now I would like you to read the rest of 'The Tree People' at your desk. As you continue reading, make more predictions and verify them. I want you to do this at least three more times in the story; that is, stop, make a prediction, and then read on to verify the prediction. Write down your predictions and your verifications on paper like this." [Teacher writes the assignment format shown in Figure 4.6 on the chalkboard.]

"Tomorrow, when we meet to discuss the story, we will look at your predictions and verifications." [For additional independent practice, the teacher could assign commercial activities such as that presented in Figure 4.7. In addition, the predict/verify procedure could be reviewed and applied

FIGURE 4.6 Assignment Format

Page: ________ I predict that ____________________

____

Page: ________ I checked my prediction and found that ________

____

FIGURE 4.7 Commercial Exercise for Practicing Prediction and Verification.

Lesson 56 Make a Prediction

Did you ever read a story and guess what would happen next? If you did, you made a **prediction.** Making predictions is a good way to help understand what you read. Being correct is not important. It is important, however, that you try to guess or predict what will happen. Then you can read to find out if your prediction was correct.

As you read the story "The Red Planet," you will be asked to make predictions or guesses. Make these predictions without looking ahead in the story. Then you can read on to see if your predictions were correct or not.

The Red Planet

Kim Evans walked along the path of her rose garden. Her husband, Sir Charles, walked beside her. Sir Charles spent his days riding horses, attending teas, and reading books. At night he and his assistant Allen spent long hours looking through his telescope. "You know, Kim," said Charles, "if my figures are correct, tonight will be the night I make my discovery."

Predict what kind of discovery Charles thinks he will make.

____

"Oh, yes, Charles," replied Kim, "I hope you discover your new planet tonight."
"Yes, yes," said Charles. "I will then become a famous astronomer. Then the name of Sir Charles Evans will be known to all!"

What kind of discovery was Charles hoping to make? ________________

____

"This morning as I was cleaning my telescope lens I decided to name the planet after you, Kim," said Charles. "What a fine name! KIM, a planet discovered by Sir Charles."
"Charles," interrupted Kim, "what has happened to your red sweater? Look at the tear in your sleeve. A piece is gone."

Predict if the torn sweater will be related to his discovery of a new planet. (You will not be able to check this prediction until the end of the story.)

____

____

(114) Prior knowledge/prediction

Note: From *Workbook E* of the GINN COMPREHENSION PROGRAM by James F. Baumann, © Copyright, 1986, by Ginn and Company. Used by permission of Silver, Burdett & Ginn Inc.

FIGURE 4.7 *Continued*

"Oh, I don't know about the sweater, Kim," said Charles. "Think of my discovery."

"Well, it's nearly time for tea," said Kim. "Do you care for biscuits or cake?"

"Oh, Kim," said Charles, "it doesn't matter!"

That evening, Charles set up the telescope. He waited for the sun to set. "Oh, I hope the weather is good tonight," said Charles.

Predict what kind of weather Charles hoped for.

___

"We need a clear, dry, cloudless night, Allen," said Charles. "Let's hope the weather stays clear. Then I will have a chance to make my discovery."

What kind of weather did Charles hope for? ___

___

After sunset, Charles sat in his observation seat at the bottom of the telescope. Instantly, he began talking to himself: "I can't believe it, Allen. This is impossible. What luck. It has happened!"

Predict what Charles was so excited about.

___

"I have made my discovery," cried Charles. "There it is, Planet Kim. It is a small, red planet."

What was Charles so excited about? ___

___

"Quick,"yelled Charles, "change the lens. Put on a stronger one."

Allen climbed up to the top of the telescope. "Sir Charles," he called, "you had better come here. Look at this lens. A speck of red wool is on the lens. I am afraid your discovery is a mistake."

Charles climbed to the top of the telescope. He looked at the speck of red wool. "Oh no," he cried. "My red Kim is no more than a speck of red wool." Charles was angry. "Where did this come from? Who is the fool who played this horrible trick on me?"

Where did the red speck come from? ___

___

Name ___

as an oral activity when the teacher reads aloud to the class for enjoyment. Finally, additional practice in the procedure could occur in subsequent basal reader selections and when content area materials such as science and social studies textbooks are being read.]

Step 4: When. "Making predictions and verifying them is something you should do just about all the time you are reading. This will help you do a better job thinking about and understanding what you read. It may even help you enjoy more of what you read. When you get really good at predicting and verifying, you will do this automatically without even thinking about it."

"Remember that you need to verify or check your predictions to see whether they are correct. It is all right for predictions to be wrong; just make certain that you recognize this and that you change your predictions or make new ones."

"Making predictions and verifying them is especially important when you are reading something particularly difficult. Then the predictions will give you a purpose for reading and help you get through the difficult material. Also, remember that you can make predictions both in stories and in informational writing such as your science and social studies textbooks."

Extensions

The preceding sample lessons demonstrate the use of the Baumann and Schmitt (1986) What, Why, How, and When model for teaching comprehension strategies. In addition to being used to design original or new comprehension lessons, the model can be adapted for use with instructional materials.

For example, it can be used to evaluate basal reader skill lessons (see Baumann, 1986b; Baumann & Schmitt, 1986). A teacher can then modify, embellish, or add elements of effective comprehension instruction to lessons determined to be inadequate or deficient.

Comprehension strategy lessons designed according to this model can also be coordinated with content area instruction. For example, a teacher could devise a lesson on how to identify or construct main ideas in expository writing according to this model and use a social studies textbook selection for application and independent practice.

Selecting Strategies for Instruction

How does a teacher determine which reading comprehension strategies to teach according to the What, Why, How, and When model in the first place? School district curricula and scope-and-sequence outlines for commercial reading programs (e.g., basal readers) may present 10 or 20 or more reading comprehension skills and strategies. Unfortunately, there is little evidence that the skills and strategies found within most skill hierarchies exist as distinct, discrete entities (e.g., Rosenshine, 1980). Even if they were discrete, it would be neither feasible nor practical to attempt to teach all of them in a comprehensive manner like the samples contained in this chapter. How, then, does a teacher determine which strategies to emphasize and teach intensively? Instead of recommending a specific list of skills or strategies that have no true empirical support and only reflect an opinion of what should be taught, what follows is a set of guidelines to help teachers make decisions about what to teach, how to teach it, and what not to teach.

Guideline 1: Teach strategies that pass the "reality test" According to P. David Pearson (personal communication, 1986), the reality test involves having teachers ask themselves (*before* instruction), "Why is this strategy important and how will its mastery help my students become skillful, independent readers?" If a teacher is unable to answer this question satisfactorily for a particular strategy, then the strategy is one that probably does not exist in reality and should be eliminated from instruction.

Guideline 2: Teach strategies, not skills Teach comprehension abilities that include conditional knowledge. A reading comprehension skill (e.g., inferring unstated main ideas) may pass the reality test, but it will remain a skill unless a teacher provides for students the conditional knowledge and extended application opportunities required for independent, intentional, strategic use of the skill.

Guideline 3: Emphasize comprehension processes, not products Comprehension products involve tasks or activities that come *after* reading and reflect memory for text, such as recalling the proper sequence, identifying cause-and-effect relationships, and the like. In contrast, comprehension processes involve the active, *ongoing* understanding of a text. Making inferences and checking them, predicting and verifying predictions, and recognizing comprehension breakdowns as they occur and then correcting them are examples of comprehension processes. Products are not inappropriate in and of themselves, but it is essential for students to acquire a repertoire of comprehension processes if they are to become self-directed, independent, strategic readers and learners.

Guideline 4: Collapse instruction for related strategies Often comprehension skills and strategies can be grouped or clustered together to make instruction more efficient. For example, teaching a general inference strategy may be more efficient and effective than teaching how to infer cause and effect, infer character traits, infer details, and the like as separate skills in separate lessons.

Guideline 5: Teach fewer things better When faced with numerous comprehension skills and strategies within a curriculum or scope and sequence, it is better to do fewer things well than many things not so well. Rely on guidelines 1 to 4 to help you select the comprehension processes you will emphasize in instruction, and then work on teaching them well.

In Chapters 13 and 14 you will see how these guidelines can be applied as the effective teacher plans reading instruction using basal reading programs.

SUMMARY

The perspective on comprehension instruction and the specific instructional model presented in this chapter can help teachers be more efficient and effective in their instruction. In addition, since the application of these procedures provides students with reading *strategies,* as opposed to reading *skills,* there is greater likelihood that they will exercise these reading abilities in a flexible, independent manner; that is, they will employ mature reading strategies when presented with natural texts and real-life reading tasks.

FOLLOW-UP QUESTIONS AND ACTIVITIES

1. Select a comprehension skill you have taught recently or one you are familiar with and see whether you can transform skill instruction into strategy instruction by applying the What, Why, How, and When approach.
2. In a basal reader teacher edition, identify a reading comprehension skill lesson and determine whether declarative, procedural, and conditional forms of knowledge are conveyed to students through the lesson. Then modify the skill lesson, relying on the principles presented in this chapter, so that the three forms of knowledge are conveyed.
3. Choose a content textbook (e.g., science, social studies) that you are currently using or one with which you are familiar. Identify a reading strategy that you could teach students to help them better understand and learn the information contained in that textbook (e.g., identifying and generating main ideas; summarizing; using text structures; reading and understanding graphic information). Then construct a lesson for that strategy that follows the What, Why, How, and When procedure and relies on the textbook for practice and application.

4. The What, Why, How, and When approach does not have universal application (Baumann, 1988); that is, there are some reading or language arts skills or processes for which using the model would not make sense. There also are some instructional tasks or situations that would not indicate its use. Think of some instructional tasks, texts, strategies, or purposes for which the four-step procedure should *not* be used. Then identify alternative teaching strategies or approaches that might be more effective (e.g., cooperative learning, discovery/independent learning).

ADDITIONAL READINGS

Irwin, J. W. (1986). *Teaching reading comprehension processes.* Englewood Cliffs, NJ: Prentice-Hall.

Irwin, J. W., & Baker, I. (1989). *Promoting active reading comprehension strategies: A resource book for teachers.* Englewood Cliffs, NJ: Prentice-Hall.

Klein, M. L. (1988). *Teaching reading comprehension and vocabulary: A guide for teachers.* Englewood Cliffs, NJ: Prentice-Hall.

McNeil, J. D. (1987). *Reading comprehension: New directions for classroom practice* (2nd ed.). Glenview, IL: Scott, Foresman.

Wilson, R. M., & Gambrell, L. B. (1988). *Reading comprehension in the elementary school: A teacher's practical guide.* Newton, MA: Allyn and Bacon.

Winograd, P. N., Wixson, K. K., & Lipson, M. Y. (Eds.). (1989). *Improving basal reading instruction.* New York: Teachers College Press.

REFERENCES

Baumann, J. F. (1983). A generic comprehension instructional strategy. *Reading World, 22,* 284–294.

Baumann, J. F. (1984a). Teacher and school effectiveness research: Implications for reading instruction. *Journal of Reading, 28,* 109–115.

Baumann, J. F. (1984b). The effectiveness of a direct instruction paradigm for teaching main idea comprehension. *Reading Research Quarterly, 20,* 95–115.

Baumann, J. F. (1986a). Teaching third-grade students to comprehend anaphoric relationships: The application of a direct instruction model. *Reading Research Quarterly, 21,* 70–90.

Baumann, J. F. (1986b). The direct instruction of main idea comprehension ability. In J. F. Baumann (Ed.), *Teaching main idea comprehension* (pp. 133–178). Newark, DE: International Reading Association.

Baumann, J. F. (1987). [Interview]. Reading comprehension instruction: The good, the bad, and the all-important teacher. *Wisconsin State Reading Association Journal, 31,* 15–22.

Baumann, J. F. (1988). Direct instruction reconsidered. *Journal of Reading, 31,* 712–718.

Baumann, J. F., & Ballard, P. Q. (1987). A two-step model for promoting independence in comprehension. *Journal of Reading, 30,* 608–612.

Baumann, J. F., Jones, L., & Seifert-Kessell, N. (1988, December). *Qualitative analyses in support of quantitative data: Portraits of fourth-grade students who participated in a metacomprehension training study.* Paper presented at the 38th Annual Meeting of the National Reading Conference, Tucson, AZ.

Baumann, J. F., & Schmitt, M. C. (1986). The what, why, how, and when of comprehension instruction. *The Reading Teacher, 39,* 640–646.

Baumann, J. F., Seifert-Kessell, N., & Jones L. (1987, December). *Effect of think aloud instruction on elementary students' ability to monitor their comprehension.* Paper presented at the 37th Annual Meeting of the National Reading Conference, St. Petersburg Beach, FL.

Baumann, J. F., & Stevenson, J. A. (1986). Teaching students to comprehend anaphoric relationships. In J. W. Irwin (Ed.), *Understanding and teaching cohesion comprehension* (pp. 95–123). Newark, DE: International Reading Association.

Brophy, J. E., & Good, T. L. (1986). Teacher behavior and student achievement. In M. C. Wittrock (Ed.), *Third handbook of research on teaching* (pp. 328–375). New York: Macmillan.

Clymer, T., Indrisano, R., Johnson, D. D., Pearson, P. D., & Venezky, R. L. (1985). *Ginn reading program.* Lexington, MA: Ginn & Co.

Duffy, G. G., & Roehler, L. F. (1987). Teaching reading skills as strategies. *The Reading Teacher, 40,* 414–418.

Johnson, D. D., & Johnson, B. V. H. (1986). Highlighting vocabulary in inferential comprehension instruction. *Journal of Reading, 29,* 622–625.

Johnson, D. D., & Johnson, B. V. H. (1988). *Making inferences.* (Leadership Letter). Needham Heights, MA: Silver, Burdett & Ginn.

Paris, S. G., Lipson, M. Y., & Wixson, K. K. (1983). Becoming a strategic reader. *Contemporary Educational Psychology, 8,* 293–316.

Pearson, P. D. (1985). Changing the face of reading comprehension instruction. *The Reading Teacher, 38,* 724–738.

Pearson, P. D., & Gallagher, M. C. (1983). The instruction of reading comprehension. *Contemporary Educational Psychology, 8,* 317–344.

Pearson, P. D., & Leys, M. (1985). "Teaching" comprehension. In T. L. Harris & E. J. Cooper (Eds.), *Reading, thinking, and concept development* (pp. 3–20). New York: The College Board.

Rosenshine, B. V. (1980). Skill hierarchies in reading comprehension. In R. J. Spiro, B. C. Bruce, & W. F. Brewer (Eds.), *Theoretical issues in reading comprehension* (pp. 535–554). Hillsdale, NJ: Erlbaum.

Rosenshine, B. V., & Stevens, R. (1984). Classroom instruction in reading. In P. D. Pearson (Ed.), *Handbook of reading research* (pp. 745–798). New York: Longman.

Stauffer, R. G. (1969). *Directing reading maturity as a cognitive process.* New York: Harper & Row.

Stauffer, R. G. (1975). *Teaching reading as a thinking process.* New York: Harper & Row.

Winograd, P. N., & Hare, V. C. (1988). Direct instruction of reading comprehension strategies: The role of teacher explanations. In E. Goetz, P. Alexander, & C. Weinstein (Eds.), *Learning and study strategies: Issues in assessment, instruction, and evaluation* (pp. 121–139). Hillsdale, NJ: Erlbaum.

5
Teaching Study Skills

EUNICE N. ASKOV

AS STUDENTS BEGIN to read from content area materials, the comprehension demands increase and at the same time they are expected to accept more responsibility for their own learning. The effective teacher can help children make this important transition from reliance on the teacher to self-reliance. In this chapter, Eunice Askov discusses the important learning-how-to-learn skills that will enable students to become self-reliant learners and readers. Askov contends that in today's Information Age it is essential to provide children with study skills if they are to cope successfully with the demands of education. She discusses how teachers can help their students develop study skills through teacher-directed activities such as study guides. After a discussion of guidelines in the development and use of study guides in general, she presents suggestions for the use of category guides and pattern guides, as well as common questions for alternative material guides.

Askov cautions that, while study guides enable the teacher to provide direct guidance, students must also learn how to learn independently. She offers suggestions for teaching students four aspects of study skills—taking tests, organizing study material, taking notes, and outlining and mapping—that are important for readers in attaining independence in learning.

The chapter concludes with a discussion of how effective teachers can help students develop techniques for independent study that will allow them to apply study skills in their own reading outside of class.

STUDY QUESTIONS

1. What are study skills? Why are they important?
2. What are some kinds of study guides?
3. Why is it important for the teacher's objectives for instruction, learning strategies, and test questions to be parallel?
4. How are study guides and notetaking similar? How are they different?
5. How can the teacher help students learn independently?

Study skills are the important learning-how-to-learn skills that enable students to become independent learners both in and out of school. The need for students to learn study skills seems greater now than ever before. No longer can it be enough to learn dates and facts about a content area. With knowledge about the world increasing every day, students can learn and remember only a few important facts. They need to learn the skills that make retrieval of dates and facts possible. Modern public libraries no longer rely on a card catalog, for example. To locate a particular book, we now can quickly consult a microfiche reader to find out the call numbers of the book. When we want to research a particular topic, we can use a computer search to locate information related to the topic. The ERIC (Educational Resources Information Center) system, for example, has indexed published and nonpublished articles, paper presentations, symposia, and reports by descriptors that enable us to call up these sources, providing bibliographic information as well as abstracts.

With the modern technology available to students, instruction in the skills of locating and using information from all sources becomes increasingly important. Unfortunately, in the past, content area instruction tended to focus on memorization of facts that were quickly forgotten after the final examination. Even today, too little attention is being given to instruction in the skills that enable students to retrieve information when it is needed. Chapter 6 will offer suggestions for helping students read more effectively for understanding.

Some evidence exists that teachers themselves have not mastered some of the study skills (Askov, Kamm, & Klumb, 1977). Furthermore, students who have not been taught study skills do not seem to pick them up on their own during their elementary and secondary school careers (Askov, Kamm, Klumb, & Barnette, 1980). If teachers are not familiar with the skills, they either do not teach them or else do a poor job (Kamm, White, & Morrison, 1977).

Because study skills include such varied skills as reading maps and graphs, locating information in a library, and using specialized references such as an almanac or atlas, it is difficult to give more than cursory treatment to this important area. A book entitled *Study Skills in the Content Areas* (Askov & Kamm, 1982) is recommended for further reading on this subject. To ensure their own mastery of study skills, readers may wish to work through the activities presented in that book in addition to reading this chapter, which focuses only on the teaching of study skills. Many of even the most sophisticated study skills should be taught at the elementary level in simplified forms with appropriate content area reading material.

Teachers can help students develop study skills through teacher-directed activities such as study guides, but they must also teach them how to apply study skills independently when reading materials both inside and outside of class. The continuum that follows illustrates the progression from teacher-directed to student-directed learning:

Directed Reading Activity → Study Guides → Study Skills → Independent Study Techniques

The directed reading activity and a directed reading/thinking activity are presented elsewhere in this book. Chapters 6 and 13 give particular attention to these activities, whereas this chapter focuses on study guides, study skills, and independent study techniques.

Study Guides

Some study guides are intended for use as students read. Others are to be used following the reading. The teacher must be sure that students understand the intended procedure. Variety is important because it can prevent student apathy and ensure that students use the guides and because different types of guides are more effective than others, depending on the purpose for their use. Several types of study guides are described in this chapter.

Creating a Study Guide

The first step in creating a study guide is to carefully analyze your objectives in assigning the reading material. What do you want the students to learn from reading the material? Do you expect all students to attain equal mastery of all the objectives? In other words, can you realistically expect similar comprehension of the material by all students?

For the best readers, you may intend the assigned reading material as a general introduction to a topic and plan to have them pursue more reading on the topic afterwards. With the average readers, you may use the reading material as the major resource for their study of the topic. A study guide may help to guide their comprehension. Poor readers need more assistance in reading the selection than the average and very able readers do. Much of the conceptual background—the content about which they are reading—may have to be filled in through sources other than reading, such as films, audiotapes, and class discussion. Your expectation for these readers is to have them grasp the main ideas from the reading selection.

Having determined the objectives for reading the material for each ability level, the next step is to analyze the text to determine what types of assistance might be most effective for the different types of readers. Since you have various options, including numerous types of study guides, it is important to study the reading selection to see whether any pattern or organization exists that the readers must detect to comprehend the selection. This step is particularly important for underachieving readers.

Also consider the levels of thinking that you want to promote. The level of thinking is usually encouraged by the kinds of questions you ask. If the objective in reading a selection is to learn factual information, literally stated, about a subject in the text, then literal-level reading comprehension is appropriate. Questions about facts and clearly stated main ideas encourage literal comprehension. If you want students to be able to make inferences beyond what is stated, then study guide questions should encourage inferential thinking by probing beyond what is specifically stated in the text. If you want students to be able to make critical or evaluative judgments (e.g., comparing two accounts of the same event in history), then the study guide should include questions to promote critical thinking. Teachers should try to include all three levels of questioning in study guides if their objectives and evaluation include these levels of thinking. Barrett's *Taxonomy of Reading Comprehension* (1972), based on Bloom's *Taxonomy of Educational Objectives* (1956), suggests some questions that are appropriate for each level.

After creating the guide, again check it against your objectives for reading. Also check it against the evaluation to be used at the completion of study of the topic. You should be able to see a clear correspondence between objectives, study guide, and evaluation. For example, if the objectives emphasize understanding of the main ideas, then the study guide and evaluation should similarly stress the main ideas of the material.

You can give advance organizers (Ausubel, 1968) (e.g., the study questions at the beginning of this chapter) to students before they read, to alert them to what is important in an assignment. Advance organizers can effectively promote reading comprehension when they appropriately reflect the instructor's objectives and evaluation. Study guides are types of advance organizers that help the reader—especially the underachieving reader—sort out what is to be learned from a reading selection.

Guide for Underachieving Readers

This study guide is intended for poor readers who are unable to read a textbook without help. The guide, in fact, tells them what to read and what not to read. Most content area textbooks contain descriptive details that embellish the main ideas. Poor readers usually get lost in the details, "unable to see the forest for the trees." This type of guide enables students to read a textbook that is actually at their frustration level. Figure 5.1 gives an example of a study guide that directs poor readers in what they should read while they are working on an assigned reading selection.

FIGURE 5.1 Sample from a Study Guide for Underachieving Readers

1. Read the last paragraph. This summarizes the selection.
2. Read paragraph 1. Write the main idea:
3. Skip paragraph 2.
4. Read the first sentence of paragraph 3. How does this help you understand the main idea in the first paragraph?

Having students write, summarizing in their own words as required by the study guide shown in Figure 5.1, is an effective way to enhance reading comprehension. In fact, most study guides should require students to write, since reading and writing are closely related (Dupuis, Lee, Badiali, & Askov, 1989). Poor readers may need help in learning to summarize information; Chapter 6 offers suggestions for such help.

Category Guide

Another type of study guide, one that can be used with all readers, requires them to organize information by filling in a chart. This type of guide is particularly useful for children who do not actively read for meaning. The guide forces them to think about the material.

First, the students read the material, which contains descriptive details. Upon completion of the reading selection, they fill in a chart requiring categorization of information. Figure 5.2 shows an example of a guide intended to accompany a social studies textbook. The textbook material describes the development of transportation systems in early America. Recording important details in the correct category helps the students remember them. This type of guide is also useful if students are reading a variety of materials on the same topics. They know what types of information they must seek from either assigned materials or library research.

Common Set of Questions for Alternative Materials

A related type of guide that is useful with alternative materials is simply a common set of questions to guide students in their reading. To accommodate differences in reading abilities, you may sometimes assign different reading

FIGURE 5.2 Category Guide

Transportation	Origin	Destination	Purpose	Date
Railroad				
Ships				
Overland				

materials of various difficulty levels on the same topic of study. Rather than creating a separate study guide for each set of materials, provide a common set of questions for the students to answer as they read, regardless of the materials they are using.

Similarly, you might allow a choice of topics and reading materials within a unit of study. Guide the students in matching reading materials to their reading abilities. If sixth-graders are researching life in different countries of their choice, for example, you can give them a common set of guide questions for studying each country. Questions can pertain to such topics as transportation, food, shelter, and trade products. One question might be "Describe the major industries in your country; why did these develop?". Regardless of which reading materials they are using, the students can search for answers to that question. The common set of questions taps the main ideas, guiding the students to grasp the important concepts of the unit of study.

Pattern Guide

Pattern guides (Estes & Vaughn, 1978) can help teach students to recognize patterns found in reading selections, such as patterns of cause and effect or comparison and contrast. (Chapter 6 provides a discussion of other common patterns.) The teacher can alert students to the organization of the text through a pattern guide. The example in Figure 5.3 is based on a science book about planets. Note that the teacher states previously learned facts about the earth; the students are required to extract from their science text what is similar or different about Mercury.

Benefits of Using Study Guides

As stated in the beginning of this chapter, providing variety in study guides is important to avoid tedium and serve the purpose of instruction, as well as to direct students to specific features of the text. When the same type of guide is used repeatedly, students tend to ignore it or else copy the answer from another student simply to get it finished. A bit of humor throughout helps lighten the task. Since you know your students better than a textbook publisher, you can tailor your guides to their interests and needs in ways that questions at the end of a textbook chapter cannot. Look at textbook questions and exercises carefully; often they require either rote recall or such high-level inferential and creative thinking that even the teacher is unsure of the desired answer! You can incorporate the textbook questions that *do* seem valuable into a study guide that includes items of your own devising.

Study guides help students in two important ways. First, through using

FIGURE 5.3 Pattern Guide

The Planets

There are many planets in our solar system. As you read, you will be learning some interesting facts about the planets. You will be learning some things that make the planets alike and some things that make them different.

The first planet that you are going to read about is Mercury. You will be comparing facts about Mercury with facts about Earth. See if you can find out how these two planets are alike and how they are different.

Below are two lists. List A tells you some interesting facts about Earth. Read these to yourself. Now you will need to complete List B. Fill in the facts about Mercury that match the facts about Earth using your science book. Number 1 has been done to help you. Read pages 3–10 to find out about Mercury.

A	B
1. Earth is the third planet from the sun.	1. Mercury is the first planet. It is planet nearest the sun.
2. The earth is 93 million miles from the sun.	2.
3. The earth is a medium-sized planet.	3.
4. It takes the earth 365 days to revolve or go around the sun.	4.
5. It takes the earth 24 hours to rotate or spin around one time.	5.
6. The earth gets just enough heat from the sun to let us stay alive.	6.
7. The coldest temperatures on the earth get down to 125 degrees below zero. If the earth were further from the sun, everything would freeze!	7.
8. The earth's surface has many different coverings. It has mountains, valleys, lakes and oceans.	8.

Note: Prepared by Sarah D. Weidler, State College, PA, Area School District, from *Meeting the Challenge: Corrective Reading Instruction in the Classroom* (p. 223) by E. N. Askov & W. Otto, 1985. Columbus OH: Charles E. Merrill. Reprinted by permission of Sarah D. Weidler.

study guides students learn study skills that foster independent learning. Second, study guides enhance comprehension of the content materials, enabling students to learn new information through reading, thus acquiring important background knowledge that aids further learning.

Study Skills

All readers need to know study skills in order to succeed academically in content area subjects, especially as they enter junior high school. Unfortunately, without guidance in reading and without important study skills, many underachieving readers do not make it through high school. This waste of human resources can be reduced significantly if teachers find appropriate alternative materials, offer guidance in reading, and teach the basic study skills.

Study skills are the important learning-how-to-learn skills. They enable a person to continue learning independently after completing school. They enhance school learning by making reading and study more efficient and effective.

Study skills are especially important for students who are having difficulty learning how to read. These skills help students improve their reading comprehension and retain what they have read. Askov and Kamm (1982) recommended that study skills be taught as part of content area studies to ensure transfer of the skills to realistic reading tasks. Incorporating study skills instruction into content area studies also helps students learn the content subject.

Four study skills that are particularly useful for all readers are discussed here. Coverage of additional study skills may be found in Askov and Kamm (1982).

Test-Taking Skills

Test taking is important for all students, regardless of reading abilities. Not only the teacher, but also the students should be able to see the correspondence, shown in Figure 5.4, between objectives for instruction, instructional processes, and test questions. Students should understand what they are expected to learn and how they will be evaluated. Instruction in test-taking skills helps this process.

Teachers should objectively examine their test questions to see whether the questions accurately reflect the instructional objectives and learning strategies employed. For example, a science unit for elementary school children may present information on the forms of matter (solids, liquids, gases) and on how physical changes occur. The objectives for instruc-

FIGURE 5.4 Flowchart for Analyzing Instruction

Objectives for Instruction ⟶ Learning Strategies (Study Guides/Study Skills) ⟶ Test Questions

tion may include knowledge of this information and application of the knowledge in children's lives. Learning strategies may include reading textbook materials with a study guide plus classroom demonstrations of physical changes (e.g., changing cake batter into cake by baking). Test questions should appropriately assess understanding of this information and application in the children's lives. If test questions require students to know material that has not been taught, they are not appropriate.

Test questions should also assess the type of reading that has been required. If a study guide has stressed only the main ideas found in reading materials, assessing comprehension of details would not be appropriate. On the other hand, some teachers like to give a "thought question" on a test that requires students to make inferences beyond the materials studied. This is appropriate if it has been included in the objectives for instruction and encouraged by instruction.

Once you have determined this correspondence between objectives, learning strategies, and test questions, the next step is to make sure that this correspondence is communicated to students. Be sure to inform students what the objectives for instruction are as well as the importance of these objectives to their lives. Unless students understand the objectives and see their relevance before study begins, only the very able students, motivated by other factors, will learn the material (Anderson & Armbruster, 1982).

One teacher, before beginning a unit of instruction in social studies, shows his objectives for instruction and his unit test questions to all students. He points out how the test questions measure mastery of his objectives. Although students have no further access to the test questions during study, they have a better idea of what the teacher considers important in the unit. They understand whether he is interested primarily in their learning main ideas or whether details, such as names and dates, are also important. They also see what type of test will be given—multiple choice, completion, essay, or a combination.

The advantage of such a procedure is that the students learn how to prepare for different types of examinations. If they receive no guidance, they may spend study time learning only factual details, while the test may require that they grasp main ideas and concepts. This procedure will help students learn how to cope with a variety of test types and study appropriately.

Another advantage of the approach is that it keeps a teacher honest, so to speak. If you wait until the night before the test date to dash off some quick test items, your test may not accurately reflect your objectives for instruction and what you have been stressing in instruction.

Another approach to teaching test-taking skills is to encourage students to work in small groups to analyze test items after an examination. The procedure is as follows:

1. After the examinations are scored, assign the students to small groups to analyze the test content.

2. Put the objectives for instruction on the chalkboard with the numbers of the test items that relate to each objective.
3. Have the students discuss each item, telling why a particular answer is correct or incorrect.

Be sure to include in each group at least one child who did well on the examination and can talk about his or her choices if necessary. (This role is sometimes good for gifted children, who may need leadership experience.) This activity will prevent students from getting tests back without understanding or giving any thought to the questions they could not answer.

Through analysis of test items, you are laying the foundation for later work on test-taking skills. As students learn how you construct tests to measure particular objectives for instruction, they also learn to study to prepare for those types of tests. When they are in high school, they can learn more sophisticated test-taking skills such as analyzing multiple-choice items for distractors. Underachieving readers particularly benefit from test-item analysis because their study is often inefficient and ineffective. Because they do not know how to read appropriately, they also do not know how to study appropriately for a test. Unfortunately, by the time they reach junior or senior high school, many have simply given up because their past efforts have not been successful.

The following study skills will not only help students prepare for tests but also enable them to learn content concepts more easily and independently.

Organization of Study Material

Most elementary school students have trouble organizing notes and other papers. Usually desks, book bags, and textbooks are crammed with assorted papers with no apparent order.

Because students need to take notes in class, the first step may be to provide them with composition books for each content area. If the school budget does not permit this expenditure, another alternative is to require students to purchase either a ring binder notebook with dividers or separate spiral-bound notebooks for each subject. Make it clear to the students that they should do all notetaking in these notebooks, not on loose sheets of paper. They should leave the notebooks at school and use them for no other purpose.

Some teachers have found daily or weekly assignment sheets to be helpful. The usual weekly assignments in spelling, reading, social studies, writing, and so forth are listed in the left column, with the days of the week listed across the top of the page as column heads. Vertical and horizontal lines are drawn to create boxes. The students enter the dates that various assignments are due. When a student has organizational problems, the assignment sheet becomes a communication device between teacher and parents so that progress can be monitored at home.

Students should also be informed of the realities of middle school or junior high school—that late assignments lose points and lost assignments receive no points. As students mature, they assume responsibility for their own assignment sheets and are able to handle long-range assignments with only interim progress checks by the teacher. These activities not only have value in later grades, but also have immediate value to students in helping them organize their efforts in school.

Notetaking

Content area materials for first- and second-grade students are often written in the narrative form so children can understand them more easily. By third grade, however, most children are expected to read expository content materials. Many children have difficulty at this point for two reasons. First, they can no longer rely on the familiar story organization; expository organization is characterized by presentation of main ideas with supporting details. Second, the content may not be as familiar as in the narrative stories. In fact, one purpose of content reading materials is to introduce new information. Vocabulary terms become increasingly harder as familiar background concepts are extended and new concepts are introduced. Students must learn to take notes to deal with the new information and the unfamiliar method of presentation. Chapter 6 provides an in-depth discussion of the differences between narrative materials and expository reading materials.

As discussed earlier, the study guide requires a form of notetaking when used with younger children. The teacher, however, is directing the students to the important aspects of the material. One way to construct study guide questions is by rewording the headings used in the material. Because teachers sometimes use this strategy in developing study guides, students learn to read the headings to help them identify the main ideas. Therefore, teaching the use of study guides is a good way to begin teaching notetaking.

As students become accustomed to study guides, they need opportunities for independent notetaking. They need to make a transition from dependence on the teacher to their own ability to focus on the important information in a text. You can help students by alerting them to what is important for them to remember from the material and modeling how you might make notes of this important material. If not guided, they may try to write down everything or they may record very little. A teacher's directions, while not as explicit as study guide questions, help students learn to pick out what is important in the materials.

Eventually, students must take notes independently. At that point, they must have the purpose for their notetaking clearly in mind. They must know whether they are reading the material to prepare for a test, to pursue a research project, or to achieve some other end. You can help by establishing the purpose for reading.

Students' notes should reflect that purpose. If you have directed them to read for the main ideas, then their notes should contain the main ideas of the content materials. Again, this is something that you can model. As a part of teaching notetaking, check students' notes to see whether they have recorded the type of information that you have modeled.

Students should learn to use notecards to prepare for a research project. You might require that a certain number of notecards be filled out in response to specified questions about the subject to be researched. One fifth-grade teacher helped a student devise three questions about Charles Lindbergh to be used as a guide to notetaking in an individual research project. The questions related to Lindbergh's contributions to aviation, his role in World War II, and the circumstances of his child's kidnapping. The student was to gather information from the research only about these questions. Different aspects of each question were to be recorded on separate notecards. In preparing an outline for the research report, the student was then expected to organize the notecards first by the questions and then by the topics under each question.

Students should be required to paraphrase the text in taking notes. Simply writing down an author's words does not help a student remember the material well. Rewording forces the student to think about meaning. The active thought process or depth of processing aids comprehension (Anderson & Armbruster, 1982, p. 229).

Having students write a summary of assigned material is another way to check their ability to grasp main ideas (Dupuis, Lee, Badiali, & Askov, 1989). Encourage them to create summaries *in their own words* in addition to taking notes. The summary expresses only the main ideas; notes, on the other hand, may express both main ideas and important details. Chapter 8 provides additional suggestions for helping students enhance their understanding of information with the use of written learning logs.

Outlining and Mapping

Outlining while reading is a specialized form of notetaking. The objectives in teaching outlining are to help students see relationships while reading and to help them learn to organize their own ideas in preparing a written or oral report. Outlining is probably more useful for the second purpose. Nevertheless, teachers often use outlining of reading material to teach students the process of outlining. In other words, the first step is to learn how to outline written material; the next step is to create an outline of one's own ideas to present to others.

Students can learn to outline material in the middle elementary grades by completing partial outlines. You can provide the main headings and some supporting details, requiring students to fill in most of the subheadings that represent the important details. Chapter 14 also offers important ideas related to teaching students specific reading strategies that you will find helpful in teaching study skills. Figure 5.5 presents an example of a partial outline given to third-graders studying bees from written material and observation of a hive.

There is no need to be overly concerned about formal outlining in notetaking. In formal outlining each heading and subheading should be presented in the same form class, or part of speech. While formal outlining may be of some value in teaching logical thinking and organization, it does not seem necessary when outlining is used as a form of notetaking.

Outlining shows the logical relationships when main ideas and supporting details are clearly presented. A variation of the semantic mapping procedure, discussed in Chapter 3, may be more effective in illustrating relationships when the organization does not consist of main ideas and supporting details. Mapping is a visual representation of the relationships in a passage. Since it can be quite complicated and time-consuming to try to show all relationships within a passage, we recommend using mapping only when a visual representation is particularly helpful in understanding the meaning of a passage. If the intent of a passage is to describe a concept or idea, then mapping can show the relationship of descriptive characteristics to that concept.

In mapping we usually place the main idea in the center, with relationships to other concepts represented visually. For example, the characteristics

FIGURE 5.5 Partial Outline

Bees

1. Types
    - A. Queen
    - B.
    - C.
2. Home
3. Food
4. Movement
5. Reasons for raising bees
    - A.
    - B.
    - C. Pollination

FIGURE 5.6 Mapping

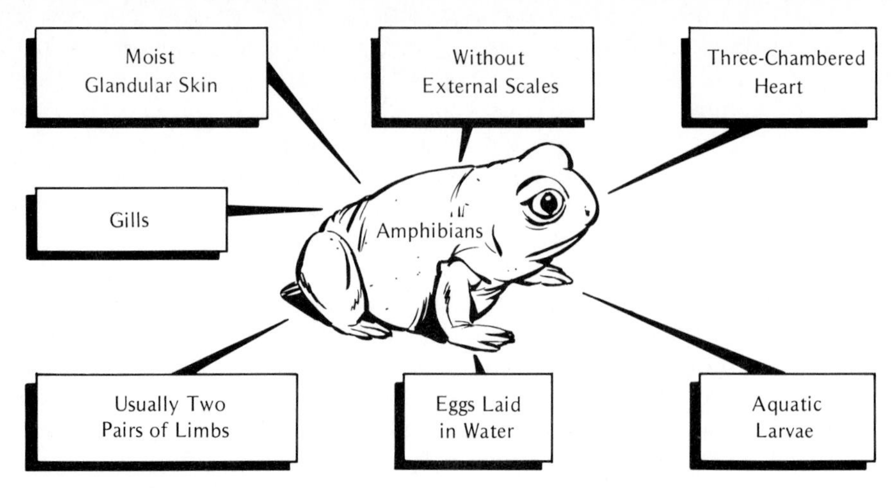

Note: Eunice N. Askov and Karlyn Kamm, from *STUDY SKILLS IN THE CONTENT AREAS.*

of amphibians are represented in Figure 5.6; the visual depiction helps students see relationships and thereby aids retention. Many different representations of the same material are possible. Encourage student creativity in devising visual representations of important material. Students remember the material better not only because they have a visual representation in mind but also because they must spend time and effort thinking about the relationships expressed in order to be able to portray them in a map. Because mapping requires considerable time and effort, it ought to be used only for significant passages, those developing important concepts for the content area study. Sometimes a map can help readers visualize and understand relationships that otherwise are too abstract to be grasped immediately.

Instruction in outlining and mapping should include the following steps. First, the teacher identifies significant content that is important for the students to remember. Next, the teacher decides what method of instruction is most appropriate. Then the teacher and students together work through the process of identifying the main idea and important details. Finally, the students apply the study technique in pairs or small groups, with the teacher available for assistance. Once the students are comfortable with the method of study, they can use it independently.

Independent Study

The treatment of study guides and study skills has been included to emphasize the importance of moving students toward independence in learning. Unfortunately, many underachieving readers, because they are unable to read the materials appropriate for their grade level, tend to become dependent upon their teachers, parents, and other students. As a result, they lack confidence in their abilities to function independently. Unless they have access to appropriate materials so that they can have successful learning experiences, their dependence upon others may become a major problem in itself. Because students cannot always depend on having their teacher's guidance, they need to learn how to guide their own reading to achieve good comprehension, as they ultimately will have to do in the upper grades and once they are out of school.

The earliest and probably most widely known technique for independent study is SQ3R (Robinson, 1961), which is an abbreviation for Survey, Question, Read, Recite, and Review. Others, such as PQRST (Preview, Question, Read, State, and Test) (Spache, 1963), are variations on the original SQ3R. REAP (Read, Encode, Annotate, and Ponder) (Eanet & Manzo, 1976), on the other hand, uses writing as a means to enhance reading comprehension as the students retell the selection, which they condense into a summary. ConStruct (Vaughn, 1982; 1984) employs multiple readings for different purposes; the outcome is the construction of a graphic overview during and following each reading. Vaughn and Estes (1986) described a variety of study techniques to be used before, during, and after reading. Similar formulas have been devised to prompt students to remember steps in the studying process. The acronyms are relatively unimportant; what *is* important is teaching students the process, which applies to short selections or whole books. The following list explains the steps involved in the independent study technique.

Surveying, or previewing, the material: The student quickly reads through the major headings as well as the introductory and summary paragraphs to get an overview of the selection. In a book, this involves reading the table of contents and prefatory material, which explain the purpose of the book and its intended audience. In this step the material may be deemed acceptable or rejected as inappropriate for the reader's intended purpose. This survey process is essentially the same as skimming.

Formulating questions: Based on the survey, the reader formulates questions that he or she expects the reading material to answer. The reader may do this by converting headings or chapter titles into question format. (For example, a question for this section heading might be, "What independent study techniques aid reading comprehension?") The reader should write down questions, leaving space for answers. Some texts may include pre- or postquestions covering the material that the student may use to direct reading.

Reading the material: Now the student is able to read purposefully because of the questions set forth. It is easier to grasp the main ideas and see the relative importance of supporting details.

Answering questions: The student writes answers to the questions set down in the second step, also jotting down other important details. If the questions have identified the main ideas of a selection (and using major headings and subheadings as an aid in forming questions should help the student do this), then, in essence, answering them becomes similar to the process of outlining. The reader should write notes in his or her own words to ensure that they are meaningful.

Studying: At a later point, the student should review the notes to recall the main ideas and important details. Because the student has gone through the process of actively reading the material—by formulating and answering questions—the notes should be meaningful. In fact, rereading notes should be more meaningful than reading the material itself.

Teach these steps using content area reading material. First, demonstrate the steps with a reading assignment in class. Next, assign the students to groups (including at least one able reader in each group) and have each group go through the steps of independent study in writing. Finally, ask the students to turn in as an assignment the written steps of independent study. Periodically require these written steps throughout the school year for reading assignments that are not accompanied by a study guide. This will reinforce the students' learning of this technique.

Students usually do not readily accept the extra work involved in using independent study techniques. Passively reading and rereading material is easier than actively trying to anticipate what the author is saying. Therefore, you must require them to formulate and answer questions. You must check the answers, as you would a study guide, until the process becomes truly independent. Effective independent study habits may indeed be the most important learning that students can take away from content area study.

One caution, suggested by Anderson and Armbruster (1982), is in order. Sometimes a student's questions tend to be trivial if the textbook headings do not adequately state the main idea of the section. For example, if a heading in a social studies textbook were labeled "The Louisiana Purchase," a student might convert that heading to "What was the Louisiana Purchase?" While an answer stating the date, extent of territory purchases, and the amount of money paid might be appropriate in some instances, the important point may actually be the impact that the Louisiana Purchase had on the eventual development of the United States. Therefore, students should be aware that a heading may not always form the best question; the material may very likely go beyond the scope suggested by the heading. Chapter 7 provides additional suggestions for teaching children to use text aids effectively.

SUMMARY

Various types of study guides help students comprehend content area textbooks. Your choice of a study guide depends upon the organization of the text and your purpose for the reader. While study guides enable you to provide direct guidance, students also need to learn how to learn independently. Study skills are taught as part of the content area studies to help students achieve independent learning. Four aspects of study skills—taking tests, organizing study material, taking notes, and outlining and mapping—are particularly useful to underachieving readers in attaining more independence in learning. Techniques for independent study help students apply study skills in their own reading outside of class. The goal is to teach the lifelong learning skills that enable students to continue learning in later school years and adulthood.

FOLLOW-UP QUESTIONS AND ACTIVITIES

1. Using a unit from a content area textbook, list your objectives for instruction; then create a test to measure mastery of those objectives.
2. Using the same unit as in question 1, design the following to enhance the reading comprehension of poor readers:
   a. a category study guide,
   b. a guide for using alternative materials in addition to the textbook,
   c. a pattern guide.
3. Create a partial outline for students to complete as they read a section of a content area textbook.
4. Select a section of a content area textbook that describes a concept. Create a mapping exercise for students to complete as they read that section.
5. Create a lesson plan for teaching SQ3R to fourth-graders. Select an appropriate selection from a content area textbook for that purpose.

ADDITIONAL READINGS

Askov, E. N., & Kamm, K. (1982). *Study skills in the content areas.* Boston: Allyn and Bacon.

Dupuis, M. M., Lee, J. W., Badiali, B. J., & Askov, E. N. (1989). *Teaching reading and writing in the content areas.* Chicago: Scott, Foresman.

Estes, T. H., & Vaughn, J. L. (1985). *Reading and learning in the content classroom: Diagnostic and instructional settings* (2nd ed.). Boston: Allyn and Bacon.

Herber, H. L. (1978). *Teaching reading in content areas* (2nd ed.). Englewood Cliffs, NJ: Prentice-Hall.

Paris, S. G. (1986). Teaching children to guide their reading and learning. In T. Raphael (Ed.), *Contexts of school-based literacy* (pp. 115–130). New York: Random House.

Vacca, R. T., & Vacca, J. L. (1989). *Content area reading* (3rd ed.). Glenview, IL: Scott, Foresman.

Vaughn, J. L., & Estes, T. H. (1986). *Reading and reasoning beyond the primary grades.* Boston: Allyn and Bacon.

REFERENCES

Anderson, T. H., & Armbruster, B. (1982). Reader and text-studying strategies. In W. Otto & S. White (Eds.), *Reading expository material* (pp. 219–239). New York: Academic Press.

Askov, E. N., & Kamm, K. (1982). *Study skills in the content areas.* Boston: Allyn and Bacon.

Askov, E. N., Kamm, K., & Klumb, R. (1977). Study skill mastery among elementary school teachers. *The Reading Teacher, 30,* 484–488.

Askov, E. N., Kamm, K., Klumb, R., & Barnette, J. J. (1980). Study skill mastery: Comparison between teachers and students on selected skills. In M. L. Kamil & A. J. Moe (Eds.), *Perspectives in reading research and instruction: Twenty-ninth yearbook of the National Reading Conference* (pp. 207–212). Washington, DC: The National Reading Conference.

Ausubel, D. (1968). *Educational psychology: A cognitive view.* New York: Holt, Rinehart & Winston.

Barrett, T. C. (1972). Taxonomy of reading comprehension. *Reading 360 Monograph.* Lexington, MA: Ginn.

Bloom, B. S. (Ed.). (1956). *Taxonomy of educational objectives. Handbook I: Cognitive domain.* New York: David McKay.

Dupuis, M. M., Lee, J. W., Badiali, B. J., & Askov, E. N. (1989). *Teaching reading and writing in the content areas.* Chicago: Scott, Foresman.

Eanet, M., & Manzo, A. V. (1976). REAP: A strategy for improving reading/writing/study skills. *Journal of Reading, 19,* 647–652.

Estes, T. H., & Vaughn, J. L. (1978). *Reading and learning in the content classroom.* Boston: Allyn and Bacon.

Kamm, K., White, S., & Morrison, B. A. (1977). *A report of the procedures used in the implementation of an objective-based reading program in 15 schools.* (Working Paper 246). Madison: Wisconsin Research and Development Center for Cognitive Learning.

Robinson, F. P. (1961). *Effective study* (rev. ed.). New York: Harper & Row.

Spache, G. (1963). *Toward better reading.* Champaign, IL: Garrard.

Vaughn, J. L. (1982). Use the construct procedure to foster active reading and learning. *Journal of Reading, 25,* 412–422.

Vaughn, J. L. (1984). Concept structuring: The technique and empirical evidence. In S. D. Holley & D. F. Dansereau (Eds.), *Spatial learning strategies* (pp. 127–147). New York: Academic Press.

Vaughn, J. L., & Estes, T. H. (1986). *Reading and reasoning beyond the primary grades.* Boston: Allyn and Bacon.

6

Teaching Reading in Content Area Materials

KAY CAMPERELL

CHAPTER 5 DISCUSSED ways to help prepare students to cope with content area materials. However, effective teachers recognize their instructional responsibility to guide students in reading materials in science, social studies, and other content areas. In this chapter, Kay Camperell describes some basic approaches for guiding student learning from content area materials. She starts the chapter by presenting a clear picture of how content materials are different from basal reading materials. Such factors as background knowledge, purpose for reading, and the ability to identify various organizational structures all change appreciably as readers move from basal reading series into content area materials. Camperell suggests that basal readers provide but one kind of reading instruction. She contends that the instruction students receive in content areas and the strategies they learn for reading content area text are equally important if we are to produce competent readers.

In the second part of the chapter she presents three instructional approaches for guiding student learning from content area texts. Two of these approaches are variations of traditional reading lesson formats, the directed reading lesson and directed reading/thinking lessons. The third approach is reciprocal teaching. Camperell discusses the adaptations that teachers must make in these approaches to allow them to be flexible enough to meet the demands of various subject areas as well as the needs of their students.

STUDY QUESTIONS

1. What factors influence students' ability to understand and remember information they read.?
2. How does comprehension instruction with content area texts differ from comprehension instruction with basal readers?
3. Why do students have to develop new strategies for reading content area texts?
4. How do text structures influence student comprehension?
5. How do directed reading lessons and directed reading/thinking activities differ with content area material?
6. What are the procedures for conducting a reciprocal teaching lesson?

A consistent theme in the educational literature is that reading instruction should help students learn how to read books in all subject matter areas. This theme was reemphasized in the recent *Report of the Commission on Reading* (Anderson, Hiebert, Scott, & Wilkinson, 1985). According to the authors of this report, the best way to ensure that young readers extend their beginning skills is via instruction that helps them understand and learn from content area materials.

Thousands of hours are devoted to reading instruction in the elementary grades. Most of that instruction, however, centers around basal materials. Unfortunately, many teachers and administrators have become convinced that these materials provide a total school reading program, assuming that no additional reading instruction is needed. Results of research on comprehension and learning (Stein, 1983; Van Dijk & Kintsch, 1983) undermine such assumptions for several reasons. First, what people of any age comprehend depends on the degree of background knowledge they have about the topic of a text prior to reading it. Even highly educated individuals will have difficulty understanding a text if they have limited prior knowledge about its topic. Second, a reader's purpose also influences the process. Given the same text but different purposes for reading, what people remember varies with their purpose. Directions to recall, summarize, list, or compare result in different outcomes. Finally, readers' ability to identify and adhere to the organizational structure of texts varies according to their familiarity with those structures. Most elementary school students are not familiar with the organizational structures in content area materials (Garner, 1987), and they need to be taught how to identify and use them to aid comprehension and learning.

Such findings reveal that it is impossible for any basal series to provide a comprehensive school reading program. The materials in basal readers and textbooks differ in (a) content area, (b) the purposes for which they are read, and (c) the writing patterns in which they are organized. Basal readers furnish one source for reading instruction. But an equally important, if not more important, source is the *instruction* students receive in subject matter domains and in strategies for reading content area texts. Helping students develop knowledge in various content areas is a crucial element of reading instruction in that the subject matter knowledge students acquire as they progress through school has a pervasive influence on their growth in reading beyond the primary grades (Beck & Carpenter, 1986; Bisanz & Voss, 1981; Bransford, Sherwood, Vye, & Reiser, 1986; Glaser, 1984).

Both knowledge of particular subjects and reading ability develop over long periods of time. This development begins in the elementary grades, when much information is new to students. Most knowledge is conveyed to students in textbooks, and we expect them to acquire it through reading. Yet, if the research findings (Durkin, 1978–1979) are accurate, students rarely receive explicit instruction in ways to understand and learn from content area materials. We do not expect students to learn how to read by themselves, and we should not expect them to learn how to read to learn from textbooks by themselves.

Differences Between Basal Materials and Content Area Materials

The aim of basal reading instruction is to help students learn how to read. Passages are selected for basal readers because the content appeals to students of a certain age or because the passages afford opportunities for students to practice specific reading skills. Typically, the passages are written in story form and convey information about ways people resolve personal conflicts and overcome problems in dealing with other people and events in life. Or, the stories are about myths, legends, and historical events and personalities that are part of the cultural knowledge and social values we want members of our society to share (Stein, 1983). The stories are intended to be entertaining to students and represent familiar situations or ones that students can easily relate to. Most important, the stories are designed to provide students with successful and enjoyable reading experiences.

Students are supposed to remember how to employ particular reading strategies from story to story, but they are not expected to remember the content of most stories (i.e., particular characters, events or themes) over extended periods of time. As students progress through these books, they are expected to apply increasingly sophisticated reading strategies. The content of the material is of secondary importance. Students are tested on their ability to employ strategies rather than on their ability to remember and apply story-specific information.

Practice in reading story material is an important instructional goal because it helps students develop a schema for reading and remembering narrative material (Mandler, 1984). This schema is the foundation on which they learn to deal with more complex literary texts and narrative forms. Nevertheless, just because students develop strategies for comprehending narratives does not ensure that they will develop strategies for learning from expository texts (Meyer, 1985). To read these texts, students must acquire new knowledge as well as new strategies for extracting, understanding, and remembering that knowledge.

The aim of content area reading instruction is to help students read to learn about a variety of knowledge domains. Ideas and the relationships among ideas in specific disciplines drive this type of instruction (Herber & Nelson, 1984). Textbooks are used to impart subject matter knowledge, and they are organized into chapters written in expository forms. Information in these books is cumulative, and students should remember the information they read from chapter to chapter.

Textbooks are designed to transmit to students information about history and mathematics as well as information about the physical, social, and biological world in which they live. This information is more difficult for students to understand because it may have little to do with their prior knowledge and personal experience. For instance, students probably do not know much about atoms, cells, fractions, different cultures, or various systems of government before they learn about them in school. None have personally experienced most of the events that they read about in history. Nevertheless, they are expected to gain such knowledge in schools, and textbooks are one tool to help them do so.

Expository texts are vehicles for knowledge acquisition (Kintsch, 1982). Complex vocabulary, sentence structures, and writing patterns cannot be avoided if these books are to inform students about ideas that are new to them. Students cannot learn about photosynthesis, for example, without encountering the word *photosynthesis,* and that process cannot be explained without expressing some complicated and abstract relationships. The chart shown in Figure 6.1 contains a representative sample of vocabulary from three content areas.

Teaching students strategies or schemata for identifying the expository structures in textbooks is an important goal of content area reading instruction. Any given expository structure may exist at a sentence, paragraph, or passage level, depending on the communicative purpose of the writer. These structures help people connect ideas by indicating to them the superordinate/subordinate and logical relationships among ideas in a text. While there are some common patterns referred to in the literature (e.g., cause/effect, comparison, sequence), the particular organizational patterns that occur in expository texts can differ markedly. Some passages are organized in cause/effect patterns, some in comparison/contrast patterns, and others in explanatory patterns.

FIGURE 6.1 Examples of Content Area Vocabulary

Vocabulary Chart

Social Studies	*Science*	*Mathematics*
town	energy	sum
city	mammal	more
country	solar system	less
community	orbit	add
mayor	gravity	subtract
government	nerves	denominator
coastal	molecules	product
Constitution	carbon dioxide	angle
longitude	protoplasm	parallelogram
representation	neutron	congruent

These differences exist because of differences in writers' purposes as well as differences within and among subject matter disciplines. Biologists, historians, mathematicians, and geographers vary in how they organize and communicate ideas in their respective fields (Voss & Bisanz, 1985; Wixon & Peters, 1987). Even within the same passage, differences occur as writers connect ideas in cause/effect, explanatory, and definitional patterns depending on what they are trying to convey (e.g., a reason, an explanation, or a definition). This means that students need guidance in identifying and using these structures when they encounter them in each content area. The organizational patterns in a text establish how ideas fit together and how students are to organize the ideas in their minds as they read.

Most chapters in textbooks consist of (a) introductory paragraphs, which signal to readers either their purpose for reading or important ideas in the chapter; (b) the body of the text, which should be organized in a predominant pattern; (c) transitional paragraphs, which indicate a change in the flow of ideas or introduce new ideas; and (d) enumeration, discussion, or summary paragraphs, which indicate the conclusion of the reading selection. Cause/effect, enumeration, compare/contrast, and sequence patterns commonly appear in content area texts at the elementary school level.

Cause/effect patterns describe how facts, concepts, or events (causes) result in or bring about other facts, concepts, or events (effects). Words such as *if . . . then, as a result of, because, so, therefore,* and *so that* frequently signal this pattern. The following paragraph illustrates a cause/effect pattern in which the pattern is not explicitly signaled:

> The sun gives off great amounts of energy. It travels in all directions and strikes all of the planets in the solar system. Planets near the sun get much energy. These planets are very hot. Planets far away from the sun get less energy. These planets are cold.

Enumeration patterns connect objects, ideas, materials, elements, forces, and the like with shared characteristics or functions under a common heading. A *type of, one kind . . . another kind,* or *the three most important groups, for instance, an example,* and so forth signal an enumeration pattern. The following paragraph illustrates this pattern:

> Some of the gases in the air are called "rare gases" because they are found in very small amounts. The six kinds of rare gases are helium, neon, argon, krypton, xenon, and radon. These gases rarely combine with other materials.

In compare/contrast patterns, similarities and/or differences among related ideas, concepts, and events are described. Words such as *but, on the other hand, however, although,* and *yet* signal a contrast, whereas words such as *similarly, as well as, either . . . or,* and *not only . . . but also* signal a comparison. The following paragraph illustrates this pattern:

From California, the lumbermen moved north to Washington and Oregon. At first, the lumber from the northern forests was used only along the West Coast. It cost too much to send the lumber to eastern cities because it had to be shipped by boat around South America. When the Panama Canal opened in 1914, the trip to the East became shorter and cut the cost of transportation.

Students need to learn how to identify and use these structures because they provide students with expectations for guiding comprehension and a foundation for learning basic study skills such as outlining, mapping, and summarizing. Moreover, the more unfamiliar the material is to students or the lower their reading ability, the more important it is for the structure of a passage to be clear to them and for the relationships to be explicitly signaled for them. Without sufficient knowledge or skill, students will be unable to infer which ideas are important or how the ideas are related. Chapter 7 offers instructional activities in reading and writing that will help students become familiar with a variety of text structures.

Approaches to Content Area Reading Lessons

Most students in the elementary grades are unfamiliar with both the information and the expository structures in content area materials. Therefore, these materials should not be used without careful teacher guidance. No predetermined list of skills or information can aid teachers in deciding what to teach in a content area reading lesson. Each lesson may vary according to students' background knowledge and the organizational structure of the text. Fortunately, however, the lesson formats commonly employed with content area materials are simply adaptations of those followed in a typical basal reading lesson. In this section, three of these adaptations are described.

The Directed Reading Lesson

The directed reading lesson (DRL), sometimes called the directed reading activity (DRA) format, is one of the most widely used approaches for organizing instruction with basal materials (Harris & Sipay, 1989). It will be discussed in further detail in Chapter 13 as it relates to basal reading instruction. The DRL is a structured lesson plan that involves three phases: a presentation phase, a guided reading phase, and a response phase. Most basal manuals provide teachers with a variety of instructional activities to choose from for each lesson phase. However, such may not be the case with the teachers' editions that accompany subject matter texts. Thus, since more preparation may be required in planning content area reading lessons, the discussion of this approach has been divided into four phases: planning, presentation, guided reading, and response.

The Planning Phase

The particular instructional activities employed in each phase of a DRL should be based on an examination of the text and an awareness of students' background knowledge. Findings from numerous studies (Anderson & Armbruster, 1986) indicate that the way a text is written greatly influences what students are able to understand and remember. Teachers need to be able to distinguish well-written texts from poorly written texts so that they can assist students in overcoming obstacles in reading assignments. Teachers also need to know how to identify the organizational structures that occur in expository materials, such as those discussed previously, because most strategies taught will stem from the writing pattern that exists in lesson material. Excellent discussions of these techniques are presented by Anderson and Armbruster (1984, 1986) and by many writers of content area reading methods texts.

Regardless of how well written a text is, students can still fail to understand it if they lack the appropriate background knowledge. As previously noted, the most powerful determinant of what students gain from reading is what they know about a topic prior to reading. When planning a content area reading lesson, therefore, teachers must establish how familiar or unfamiliar the topic is to their students. This information shapes the instructional activities a teacher uses in the presentation phase of a lesson. The more students know about a topic, the less preteaching is needed; the less they know, the more preteaching is needed.

A variety of informal techniques such as pretests and discussions can be used to gauge students' familiarity with a topic. Langer (1981) has developed a discussion approach in which student responses to words, phrases, or pictures are classified according to how much assistance they will need prior to reading. She calls this a Prereading Plan (PreP). To begin PreP, the teacher examines the text to identify three to five key concepts. Words, phrases, or pictures are then presented to students to introduce the concepts. For each concept, the teacher asks the following questions:

> "Tell me anything that comes to mind when you hear the word (*nerves*)?"
> "What made you think of (*being nervous*)?"
> "Based on our discussion, have you any new ideas about (*nerves*)?"

Student responses should be written on the board, an overhead transparency, or chart paper. All responses to the first question should be accepted, and the teacher should encourage students to think of as many ideas as possible. The second question should help students listen to each other, reflect on what they know, and elaborate on one another's responses. The discussion should be like a conversation students might have with their friends. From this conversation, the teacher can determine whether or not the students' responses are related to information in the text. With the third question, the teacher helps students reformulate what they know about a topic and refine their initial responses.

Student responses are classified into three categories: much knowledge, some knowledge, and little knowledge. Langer has found that these categories are good predictors of how much students are able to recall from specific passages (Langer & Purcell-Gates, 1985). Students who are able to give definitions, analogies, superordinate concepts (e.g., "Nerves are part of the nervous system"), or links to other concepts (e.g., "They connect the brain and the spinal cord") have *much prior knowledge.* These students can probably comprehend the text without very much assistance. Students who give examples or characteristics of the topic (e.g., "Nerves have branches") have *some prior knowledge.* They will need concept instruction prior to reading and guidance during reading because they may have difficulty understanding relationships among ideas or connecting ideas to what they already know. Finally, students who respond with low-level associations or irrelevant first-hand experiences (e.g., "My mom says I get on her nerves") probably have *little prior knowledge* about the topic. These students will need a great deal of concept instruction prior to reading.

The Presentation Phase

There are four instructional goals in the presentation phase of a lesson: activating or developing background knowledge, introducing key vocabulary, activating or developing knowledge about organizational structure, and establishing a purpose for reading. In practice, activities to accomplish these goals merge and overlap. Activating or developing prior knowledge is the most important goal in this phase because it sets the stage for understanding by helping students construct a mental framework for reading.

Activating and developing knowledge For topics that are familiar to students, focused discussions and reviews assist them in activating background knowledge. Even with very easy material, students often fail to use what they know to make sense out of what they read. This is especially true of young readers who have insufficient experience or insufficient subject matter knowledge to build their own connections between prior knowledge and new information. Discussions and reviews should guide students to link new ideas to old ones by having them recall experiences, stories from basal reading lessons, events from popular television shows, or information learned in previous chapters. Teachers should direct discussions so that the ideas the students activate are matched to information in the text.

Much of teaching students how to read and learn from subject matter texts involves helping them confine their interpretations to the information in the text. What students perceive as important is greatly influenced by their prior knowledge, and students who overrely on personal knowledge can misinterpret what they read. Writers of most content area books have an intended interpretation they want students to achieve, and the prereading discussion should gear students toward that interpretation. Prior to reading, therefore, students should be made aware of how information in a text will relate to what they already know, yet go beyond their current level of understanding.

With unfamiliar topics, much more instruction is needed to help students develop the appropriate background knowledge. Explanations, demonstrations, and guided practice commonly are used to teach new concepts and skills in mathematics before students are expected to deal with textbooks, but seldom is such instruction provided before students read in other content areas. Without sufficient background knowledge, however, any text is just a string of unrelated and disconnected words to students. Films, demonstrations, discussions, and/or explanations should precede the reading of all content materials. These activities prepare students to distinguish main ideas from details and determine the relationships among ideas.

Experiments and demonstrations prior to reading are crucial for helping students understand many physical science concepts. Students cannot form concepts about such things as magnetic fields, barometric pressure, inertia, or condensation or, at earlier grades, simpler concepts such as plant growth, without concrete experiences with and explanations about these phenomena. This suggests that many of the experiments and learning activities recommended in science textbooks should precede rather than follow an assigned chapter. The text, in this case, is not the primary means for students to acquire science concepts but a means for them to elaborate, refine, and check their understanding of those concepts.

Introducing Vocabulary The second goal to be accomplished in the presentation phase is to introduce new vocabulary. This may occur naturally as teachers help students activate and/or develop prior knowledge. Students cannot be introduced to all the unfamiliar words they might encounter in a subject matter text, but it is essential that the terms that represent major concepts be explained.

Presentation of new vocabulary in a content lesson involves more than assisting students in word pronunciation or memorizing definitions. The presentation should engage students in using definitions to classify examples and nonexamples of new concepts. Definitions then serve as tools for guiding students to attend to examples, and the examples help them clarify the meaning of definitions. Presenting definitions alone will not suffice, since the meanings of definitions become clear to students only as they use them to identify and classify other information. Memorizing that a spruce tree is a type of evergreen, for instance, will do students little good if they cannot recognize a spruce tree when they see one.

Introducing students to key vocabulary may also include showing them how superordinate and subordinate concepts are related to each other. Structured overviews (Vacca & Vacca, 1989) and matrix charts (Jones, 1985) are effective techniques for explaining these relationships. These are simple diagrams that depict key ideas and the connections among ideas in a graphic form. Figure 6.2 is an example of a structured overview that could be used to

FIGURE 6.2 Example of a Structured Overview of a Chapter on Rocks and a Chapter on the Senses

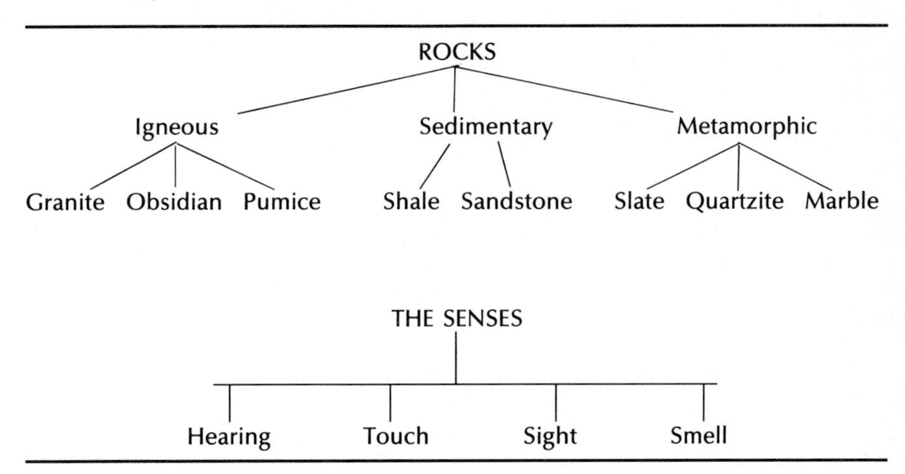

introduce students to a chapter about classes of rocks, and Figure 6.3 is an example of a matrix chart that could be used to introduce the same chapter.

To create these diagrams, all a teacher has to do is to examine the text to identify key concepts and supporting details and arrange the concepts in some type of hierarchical order that displays the superordinate, subordinate, and coordinate relationships among the terms on the diagram. In Figure 6.2, for example, "Rocks" is the superordinate concept in the chapter, the classes of rocks (igneous, sedimentary, and metamorphic) are coordinate concepts, and the specific rocks are the subordinate concepts. The diagrams can be presented to students on the board, a handout, or an overhead transparency. The teacher would then use them to explain key terms and relationships among the terms to students. Chapter 3 of this text provides additional suggestions that will be useful in helping students develop vocabulary knowledge.

FIGURE 6.3 Example of a Matrix Chart of a Chapter on Rocks

TYPES	*HOW FORMED*	*CHARACTERISTICS*	*EXAMPLES*
Igneous			
Sedimentary			
Metamorphic			

Introducing Organizational Structure The third goal of the presentation phase is to familiarize students with the organizational structure of the text. If students are already familiar with a pattern, then a brief review can alert them to look for it. If students are not familiar with the pattern, then direct instruction is needed. As previously noted, students' ability to detect and follow the organizational patterns in content area materials aids them in understanding how ideas are related and, therefore, helps them organize the ideas in their minds as they read.

To assist students in identifying the organizational structure of an assignment, have them read only the title, introductory statements, headings, and summaries from a chapter. Words that signal the author's pattern, such as *first, next,* or *as a result,* should be pointed out and explained. Structured overviews, matrix charts, or traditional outlines can be employed to introduce new vocabulary to students and explain to them the organizational structure of a text. Words that signal these patterns should be incorporated into the diagrams to ensure that students see how the ideas are connected.

Establishing Purposes for Reading The final goal of the presentation phase is to establish for the class a precise purpose for reading. That purpose will shape what students attend to and guide them in reading strategically. The purpose should be written on the board and stated in a way that students are informed about how they will use the information. Statements such as "After reading you should be able to compare/contrast why the North and South fought the Civil War," "After reading you should be able to explain how plants produce chlorophyll," or "After reading you should be able to classify rocks into three groups" provide explicit purposes for reading. These types of statements specify for students (a) what information to search for as they read, (b) what they will be expected to talk about in a discussion, and (c) what information they are accountable for knowing.

The Guided Reading Phase

In most instances the presentation phase of a lesson should provide sufficient guidance so that students can read an assignment silently and comprehend it. However, if students are unfamiliar with a topic, the text is poorly written, or students are not familiar with an organizational pattern, then more support is needed. Under any of these circumstances, the teacher can create a reading guide or pattern guide, as discussed in Chapter 5, to help students achieve their purpose for reading. Properly constructed, reading guides can help students maintain their purpose for reading, attend to important ideas, adhere to the writer's organizational pattern, and encode information so that it is integrated and organized in their minds.

Properly designed guides should help students make appropriate inferences, connect related ideas that occur in different parts of a text, follow the organizational pattern, or learn basic study skills. Improperly designed guides interfere with comprehension. Such guides include too many questions, emphasize details, or lead students to overrely on personal knowledge. Pattern guides, incomplete outlines, and matrix charts (Vacca & Vacca, 1989) are preferable to lists of detailed questions because students have to read entire segments of text before responding. The matrix chart shown in Figure 6.3 could serve as a guide if students were required to complete the cells in the chart as they read.

Pattern guides, outlines, and matrices also provide students with a plan for organizing information for study purposes. These guides lay a foundation for teaching study strategies because they model for students ways to organize information as they read. During the response phase, the teacher can use them to teach students how to reformulate ideas into their own words and how to reduce ideas for study purposes.

Guides are not ends in themselves. They are a means to help students accomplish their purpose for reading or acquire study strategies. Both teachers and students should maintain this perspective, or the guides will become busywork. Students will approach them with the goal of completing an activity rather than with the goal of using the guides to assist them in learning.

The Response Phase

There are two major goals of the response phase. The first is to determine whether or not the purpose for reading was achieved; the other is to engage students in deeply processing the information so that it will be remembered. One way to begin the response phase is with a discussion in which the teacher asks questions to determine whether students can distinguish major from minor points, describe relationships among ideas, and explain key terminology. Obviously, if a reading guide was assigned, the discussion can center around how accurately students have completed the guide. The aim of the initial discussion should be to establish whether or not students have understood the information or reteaching and/or rereading are needed.

Oral reading may be required in which students read segments of the text to support and justify their responses. Oral reading can be used also to focus on sections that students have misinterpreted. Explanations and leading questions should assist students in revising their initial interpretations. This means that errors must be made public in the response phase so that students feel free to make mistakes and receive correction. Guides should be checked, but not graded. Students should perceive the correction of guides as an opportunity to verify their understanding or as occasion to ask for help. Assigning grades to guides makes them into tests, not vehicles to foster learning.

The second goal of the response phase is to encourage in-depth processing so that students integrate the newly acquired information with prior knowledge and personal experience. The aim is for students to be able to *use* new ideas, not just remember them. Once the teacher is satisfied that students have comprehended the key ideas from a selection, application questions or activities in which students use the information to classify, explain, or make predictions about other ideas should be employed.

Until students can use information, a teacher cannot be sure that they have truly comprehended it. Thus, in-depth processing activities should assist students in discovering how the information they have read helps them understand and explain other events and phenomena. Writing activities also are suited for this phase (Jones, 1985), because they engage students in reformulating ideas into their own words and in organizing information to generate answers to questions, summaries, or short essays. Chapters 7 and 8 offer excellent suggestions for using writing to enhance reading.

The Directed Reading/Thinking Activity

Directed reading lesson formats are perhaps the most traditional method for guiding reading with basal materials. Some basal series, however, adopt a variation of this format called a directed reading/thinking activity (DRTA). A DRTA differs from a DRL in that students are more actively involved in making decisions as they read and there is more interaction between the students and teacher. The DRTA is an excellent bridge between basal reading lessons and content area reading lessons because the teacher and students construct the meaning of the text together.

The DRTA was developed by Stauffer (1969) to engage students actively in thinking about what they read. With basal material, the lesson is conducted in two phases. In the first phase, students generate predictions about information in a story, read to confirm or disconfirm their predictions, then evaluate and/or revise their initial predictions using information from the story to support their responses. The story is divided into sections, and students make predictions, read, and support their responses for each section of the story. Specific reading skills are taught in the second phase of the lesson.

Only slight modifications are required to adapt this format for content area lessons. Usually the information in content area material is unfamiliar to students, and they cannot make fruitful predictions. Thus, three phases should be incorporated into a DRTA with subject matter texts. In the first phase, the teacher needs to develop the appropriate background knowledge and introduce new or technical vocabulary. The particular activities used would be similar to those employed in the presentation phase of a DRL, except that the teacher should *not* establish for students a purpose for reading. A major goal of a DRTA is to teach students to generate their own purposes for reading.

Once students have some familiarity with new concepts, the teacher initiates the second phase of the lesson. In this phase, the teacher has students read the title of a chapter, examine any pictures or graphic aids in the first section or page of the chapter, and generate several predictions about the information they think will be discussed in the text. Student predictions should be written on the board. Students then silently read the first section, searching for information to confirm or disconfirm their predictions. After reading, the teacher guides a discussion by asking questions such as "Were your predictions correct? Why?" and "What do you think now? Why?" Students should evaluate and support their predictions with information from the text. If their predictions were not supported, they should revise them and justify their revisions with information they read. New predictions are made for the next segment, and students again examine headings, pictures, or graphic aids to make predictions. As students proceed through the chapter, the same predict-read-support cycle continues until the chapter is completed. Direct strategy training is provided in the third phase. After reading the chapter, skill lessons can focus on teaching students how to read maps, charts, or graphs or they can focus on teaching students how to identify main ideas, draw conclusions, and so forth.

The DRTA is an excellent way to teach students to identify and follow an author's organizational structure. During the prediction phase, teachers can direct students to use features in the text that indicate the writer's pattern. Students then base their predictions on such features as headings and topic sentences. Gradually, students will learn that these features in their textbooks assist them in understanding because they reveal how ideas are organized.

This lesson format also is well suited for classes in which students vary in reading ability. As students read a chapter section by section, poor readers can make predictions on shorter segments of text before confirming or disconfirming them, whereas students with more ability can read longer segments. In this way, teachers can tailor the predict-read-support cycle to meet the needs of different learners. Moreover, all students have an opportunity to acquire subject matter knowledge in these lessons because of the frequent discussions that precede and follow silent reading.

Reciprocal Teaching

Reciprocal teaching is an adaptation of the DRTA developed by Palinscar and Brown (1984, 1985). Like the DRTA, reciprocal teaching enables teachers to use the same text with readers of different ability levels while varying the instructional support students receive. Reciprocal teaching lessons are a highly interactive yet structured approach for teaching students how to read and learn from content area material. The approach is more structured than a DRTA because the goal of reciprocal teaching is to provide students with a supportive context for reading in which they learn *when, how,* and *why* to use four specific strategies: predicting, questioning, clarifying, and summarizing. These are strategies that successful readers engage in spontaneously, and they foster both comprehension and comprehension monitoring.

Prior to initiating a reciprocal teaching lesson, the teacher needs to be sure that students have some ability to seek clarification in everyday situations (e.g., "Why do birds fly?" "Why do I have to do it this way?") as well as some skill in generating questions from sentences and identifying explicitly stated main ideas in short paragraphs. Students without these basic skills must develop some proficiency with them before they can participate successfully in reciprocal lessons.

When first introducing students to reciprocal lessons, the teacher has to do most of the work. Each strategy is modeled or demonstrated by the teacher before students employ it. To begin a lesson, the teacher makes a prediction that establishes a purpose for reading and activates background knowledge or knowledge of text structure (e.g., "The title of this chapter is 'The Solar System.' I would expect a chapter with this title to be about the sun and its planets.").

After students read the first paragraph silently, the teacher creates a question that is typical of questions that teachers ask on tests (e.g., "Which planets are the hot planets?") and models for students how disorganized text and unfamiliar vocabulary or difficult concepts interrupt comprehension (e.g., "What does 'radiant energy' mean?"). The teacher should also model fix-up strategies students can use, such as rereading or asking for help when they encounter interruptions.

Finally, the teacher models a summary statement (e.g., "The hot planets are Mercury and Venus. Mercury is hot because it is closest to the sun. Venus is hot because it is the next closest planet to the sun."). The summary should state only the most important information in the paragraph, and it should serve as a self-test of comprehension. Students learn in reciprocal lessons that if they cannot summarize what they have read in their own words then they have not understood it. As the teacher models these strategies, students can answer questions and elaborate on the teacher's summaries, predictions, and demands for clarification. Gradually, as students become familiar with the strategies and lesson format, they take turns assuming the role of the teacher. The teacher then serves as a mediator who tells students when they are doing well, elicits more information from them, or returns to modeling when needed.

Palinscar and Brown (1985) suggested the following format for reciprocal lessons with content area material. To begin the lesson, write the title of a chapter on the board and have the students predict three things they will learn from the chapter. Discuss the predictions, relating them to content previously covered, then direct the students to read the first paragraph silently. For each text segment, the students write a brief summary, one question they would expect to see on a test, and one idea or word they found difficult to understand. All students should complete these activities, even if they are not expert comprehenders. Discussion follows each text segment. In it, the students should share their summaries, ask one another questions, and clarify for one another words or ideas that were not clear. The students should justify, explain, or elaborate on their own and each other's responses.

When disagreements occur, the students should reread the text and continue the discussion until a consensus is reached. Without consensus, they may not proceed to the next segment. After the chapter is completed, a test can be constructed by selecting items from the best of the student questions. The students can be given credit by writing their names next to their questions on the test.

Palinscar and Brown (1984, 1985) suggested that this approach is effective for the following reasons:

1. Teacher modeling makes the strategies overt, explicit, and concrete.
2. Strategies are modeled in appropriate contexts, not as isolated skills.
3. Discussion focuses on both text content area and students' understanding of the usefulness of the strategies.
4. Feedback can be tailored to the ability level of each student.
5. Students learn to become responsible for comprehending what they read.

Having to explain and defend their responses or teach each other pushes students to evaluate, integrate, and elaborate on the knowledge they gain from reading (Brown, Armbruster, & Baker, 1986). This approach, therefore, ensures that students acquire subject matter knowledge as well as strategies for extracting, understanding, and remembering that knowledge. Additional information on this effective teaching procedure is provided in Chapter 14.

SUMMARY

The DRA, DRTA, and reciprocal teaching lessons are effective approaches for guiding student learning from content area materials. Provision is made for developing prior knowledge, teaching text structure, guiding reading, and checking to ensure that students comprehend and learn new ideas. The approaches are flexible, and teachers can develop lessons to meet the demands of various subject areas as well as the needs of their students.

FOLLOW-UP QUESTIONS AND ACTIVITIES

1. Examine one chapter on the same topic in three different textbooks for the same grade level. Determine (a) the organizational pattern of the passages and (b) how well the writers explicitly signal the relationships among ideas for students. Rate the effectiveness of the chapters for communicating new ideas to students.

2. Select a chapter from a content area text and create a structured overview for it. Use the overview for a lesson in which students are supposed to recall the most important information.
3. Examine the second or third chapter in a science, mathematics, or social studies text for students at the same grade level. Write down all the technical vocabulary students are expected to gain from the chapter and the manner in which the vocabulary is explained to students. How often are abstract or difficult terms presented without adequate explanations for students? How could you compensate for those inadequacies?
4. Conduct a directed reading/thinking activity with a chapter from a content area text. How did the lesson differ from (a) recommendations provided in the teacher's manual and (b) the way in which you typically conduct lessons in that content area?
5. Examine a chapter from a content area text and develop (a) two or three application questions and (b) a writing assignment.

ADDITIONAL READINGS

Estes, T. H., & Vaughn, J. L. (1985). *Reading and learning in the content-area classroom.* Boston: Allyn and Bacon.

Herber, H. L. (1978). *Teaching reading in content areas.* Englewood Cliffs, NJ: Prentice-Hall.

Jones, B. F., Palinscar, A. S., Ogle, D. S., & Carr, E. G. (Eds.). (1987). *Strategic teaching and learning: Cognitive instruction in the content areas.* Alexandria, VA: Association for Supervision and Curriculum Development.

Readence, J. E., Bean, T. W., & Baldwin, R. S. (1985). *Content-area reading: An integrated approach.* Dubuque, IA: Kendall-Hunt.

Singer, H., & Donlan, T. (1985). *Reading and learning from text.* Hillsdale, NJ: Erlbaum.

Vacca, R. T., & Vacca, J. (1989). *Content-area reading.* Glenview, IL: Scott, Foresman.

REFERENCES

Anderson, R. C., Hiebert, E. H., Scott, J. A., & Wilkinson, I. A. (1985). *Becoming a nation of readers: The report of the Commission on Reading.* Washington, DC: National Institute of Education.

Anderson, T. H., & Armbruster, B. B. (1984). Content area textbooks. In R. C. Anderson, J. Osborn, & R. J. Tierney (Eds.), *Learning to read in American schools* (pp. 193–226). Hillsdale, NJ: Erlbaum.

Anderson, T. J., & Armbruster, B. B. (1986). Readable textbooks, or, selecting a textbook is not like buying a pair of shoes. In J. Orasanu (Ed.), *Reading comprehension: From research to practice* (pp. 161–162). Hillsdale, NJ: Erlbaum.

Beck, J. L., & Carpenter, P. A. (1986). Cognitive approaches to understanding reading: Implications for instructional practice. *American Psychologist, 41,* 1098–1105.

Bisanz, G. L., & Voss, J. F. (1981). Sources of knowledge in reading comprehension: Development and expertise in a content domain. In A. M. Lesgold & C. A. Perfetti (Eds.), *Interactive processes in reading* (pp. 215–239). Hillsdale, NJ: Erlbaum.

Bransford, J., Sherwood, R., Vye, N., & Rieser, J. (1986). Teaching, thinking, and problem-solving: Research foundations. *American Psychologist, 41,* 1078–1089.

Brown, A. L., Armbruster, B. B., & Baker, L. (1986). The role of metacognition in reading and studying. In J. Orasanu (Ed.), *Reading comprehension: From research to practice* (pp. 49–76). Hillsdale, NJ: Erlbaum.

Durkin, D. (1978–1979). What classroom observations reveal about reading comprehension instruction. *Reading Research Quarterly, 14,* 481–533.

Garner, R. (1987). Strategies for reading and studying expository text. *Educational Psychologist, 22,* 299–312.

Glaser, R. (1984). Education and thinking: The role of knowledge. *American Psychologist, 39,* 93–104.

Harris, A. J., & Sipay, J. R. (1989). *How to increase reading ability.* New York: Longman.

Herber, H. L., & Nelson, J. (1984). Planning the reading program. In A. Purves & O. Niles (Eds.), *Becoming readers in a complex society* (pp. 174–208). Chicago, IL: The University of Chicago Press.

Jones, B. F. (1985). Response instruction. In T. L. Harris & E. J. Cooper (Eds.), *Reading, thinking and concept development* (pp. 105–113). New York: College Board.

Kintsch, W. (1982). Text representations. In W. Otto & W. White (Eds.), *Reading expository materials* (pp. 87–101). New York: Academic Press.

Langer, J. A. (1981). From theory to practice: A prereading plan. *Journal of Reading, 25,* 152–156.

Langer, J. A., & Purcell-Gates, V. (1985). Knowledge and comprehension: Helping students use what they know. In T. L. Harris & E. I. Cooper (Eds.), *Reading, thinking and concept development* (pp. 53–70). New York: College Board.

Mandler, J. M. (1984). *Stories, scripts and scenes: Aspects of schema theory.* Hillsdale, NJ: Erlbaum.

Meyer, B. F. J. (1985). Prose analysis: Purposes, procedures and problems. In B. K. Britton & J. B. Black (Eds.), *Understanding expository texts* (pp. 11–64). Hillsdale, NJ: Erlbaum.

Palinscar, A. S., & Brown, A. L. (1984). Reciprocal teaching of comprehension fostering and monitoring activities. *Cognition and Instruction, 12,* 117–175.

Palinscar, A. S., & Brown, A. L. (1985). Reciprocal teaching: Activities to promote "Reading with your mind." In T. L. Harris & E. I. Cooper (Eds.), *Reading, thinking and concept development* (pp. 147–158). New York: College Board.

Stauffer, R. (1969). *Teaching reading as a thinking process.* New York: Harper & Row.

Stein, N. L. (1983). On the goals, functions, and knowledge of reading and writing. *Contemporary Educational Psychology, 8,* 261–292.

Vacca, R. T., & Vacca, J. (1989). *Content area reading.* Glenview, IL: Scott, Foresman.

van Dijk, T., & Kintsch, W. (1983). *Strategies for discourse comprehension.* New York: Academic Press.

Voss, J. F., & Bisanz, G. L. (1985). Knowledge and the processing of narrative and expository texts. In B. K. Britton & J. B. Black (Eds.), *Understanding expository texts* (pp. 173–198). Hillsdale, NJ: Erlbaum.

Wixon, K. K., & Peters, C. W. (1987). Comprehension assessment: Implementing an interactive view of reading. *Educational Psychologist, 22,* 333–356.

7

The Reading and Writing Connection: Counterpart Strategy Lessons

STEPHEN B. KUCER   JEROME C. HARSTE

In this chapter, the relationship between reading and writing is discussed. Stephen Kucer and Jerome Harste present an overview of why reading and writing instruction should be viewed as complementary processes and integrated into the literacy curriculum. They explain that the supportive relationship between reading and writing is both cognitive and developmental in nature. They contend that while they are not identical processes, reading and writing have a number of significant similarities. These similarities involve important processes in both reading and writing and are associated with meaning-based activities associated with the generation, integration, and revision of ideas.

Numerous classroom activities for integrating reading and writing are presented. Kucer and Harste caution that if instructional activities are to help students see the cognitive connections between the two processes their relationship must be demonstrated or highlighted by the teacher. They have termed these activities *counterpart strategy lessons.* In these lessons, the way in which literacy is used in the reading activity parallels or is a counterpart to the way in which literacy is used in the writing activity. The lessons can be used with a wide range of students. Each group of lessons highlights cognitive activities common to both reading and writing.

STUDY QUESTIONS

1. In what ways are reading and writing currently regarded as similar and supportive processes?
2. How do counterpart strategy lessons build upon the cognitive connections between reading and writing?
3. What counterpart strategies can be used to help children use text structures as they read and write?
4. What counterpart strategies can be used to help children generate and organize chunks of meaning as they read and write?
5. What counterpart strategies can be used to help children find conceptual relationships between major and minor ideas as they read and write?

Traditionally, reading and writing have been taught as separate subjects within the elementary school curriculum. This separation of reading from writing reflects the belief that the two literacy processes have little in common. Reading has been viewed by some as an act of *decoding*—a process by which the individual moves from print to sound to meaning. The reader's task is to abstract or pick up meaning from the printed page through the use of various word attack skills. The reader converts the print into oral language, "listens" to the language, and obtains meaning. The result of this interaction between reader and print is comprehension and an increase in the individual's knowledge. (See Figure 7.1)

Writing, on the other hand, is seen as an act of *encoding*—a process by which the individual moves from meaning to sound to print. The writer's task is to generate meaning, which is then translated into print. Simply put, the writer thinks about what is to be expressed and then "says it" through print. In contrast to the reader, who uses reading as a source to learn, the writer simply writes what is already known. The writer does not write to discover new meanings or generate new thoughts; rather, writing is used to communicate existing ideas. Because the writer is thought to be the source or creator of meaning, he or she is perceived as being more active and making more use of cognitive resources than the reader. In a sense, this view holds that writing involves more thinking than reading does. Finally, in contrast to reading, writing is seen as context dependent. That is, the writer is influenced by purpose and audience when interacting with print. Traditionally, reading has not usually been considered to be influenced by such factors. It is this view of reading and writing that has caused them to be separated and isolated from each other within the elementary curriculum.

Currently, the relationship between reading and writing is being reexamined. During the past several years, research has found a clear and supportive relationship between the two processes (Boutwell, 1983; Flood & Lapp, 1987; Kucer, 1985, 1987; Shanklin, 1982; Squire, 1983; Tierney & Pearson, 1983). This reciprocal relationship is cognitive as well as developmental in nature.

Cognitively, we know that language users make use of a number of

FIGURE 7.1 Reading and Writing as Opposite Processes

Reading	*Writing*
Decoding	Encoding
Passive	Active
Less Use of Cognitive Resources	More Use of Cognitive Resources
Easier Than Writing	Harder Than Reading
Meaning-abstracting	Meaning-generating
Building Background Knowledge	Expressing Background Knowledge
Context-independent	Context-dependent

common processes when engaged in reading or writing. As reflected in Figure 7.2, both readers and writers are involved in an active search for meaning when interacting with print. This search requires the use of background knowledge from which meaning can be generated and structured. The reader is no longer viewed as passively abstracting meaning from the page, but, like the writer, as actively constructing meaning based on prior knowledge and the print being processed.

This generation of meaning is guided by the language user's purpose for reading or writing. We do not engage in reading or writing simply for its own sake, but rather because it meets a personal or social need. Reading and writing help the individual accomplish something, learn something, or influence someone. Stated another way, reading and writing are influenced by the context or environment in which they take place.

As well as using existing knowledge, reading and writing can lead to the building of knowledge. Just as the language user reads to gain new information, the language user can write in order to discover new ideas or relationships. Writing is more than simply putting down on paper what is already known; it also may require the writer to synthesize and integrate existing background knowledge in new or novel ways. Writing helps the individual reflect on what is already known and then go on to discover new information.

In both reading and writing, revision—rereading, rewriting, or rethinking—is a natural part of the process. Because language users predict upcoming meanings, they frequently need to revise their predictions when meaning is lost; that is, when their predictions do not make sense in light of what is being read or written. As language users discover new information through reading or writing, they must continually evaluate and frequently revise previous meanings so that they fit with current meanings. Therefore, rather than being linear, word-by-word processes, both reading and writing require the language user to shuttle back and forth between past and present meanings.

These cognitive connections between reading and writing have a direct

FIGURE 7.2 Reading and Writing as Common Processes

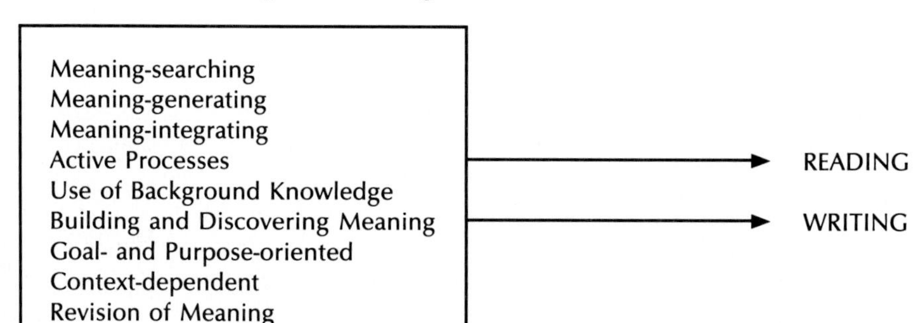

FIGURE 7.3 Common Literacy Data Pool

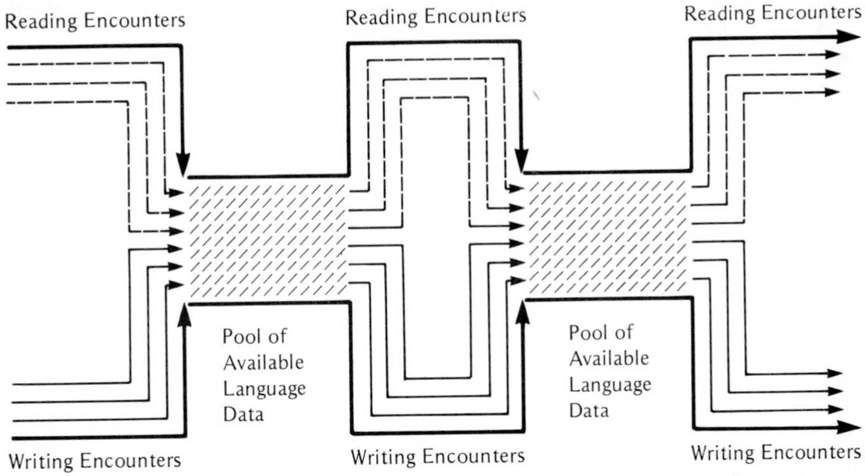

Note: Adapted from Harste, J., Woodward, V., & Burke, C. (1984). *Language stories and literacy lessons.* Portsmouth, NH: Heinemann.

influence on development. Developmentally, we know that growth in one process often supports growth in the other process (DeFord, 1981; Eckhoff, 1983; Harste, Woodward, & Burke, 1984; Newkirk, 1982). As illustrated in Figure 7.3, cognitive discoveries that the child makes about how the reading or writing process operates feed into a common pool of knowledge and can be used to support development in the other process. Contributions to this pool of knowledge from reading can be used in writing, and contributions from writing can be used in reading. For example, the discovery that writing involves the integration of meaning into an organized whole sets up expectations by the child that meanings generated through reading should also form an organized whole.

In summary, the processes of reading and writing, while certainly not identical, do have a number of significant similarities. These similarities are essentially meaning-based in nature and involve the generation, integration, and revision of ideas.

Classroom Activities for Integrating Reading and Writing

The cognitive and developmental connections between reading and writing have direct implications for literacy instruction in elementary school classrooms. Because reading and writing share common processes, and because advances in one process frequently promote advances in the other, the literacy curriculum should integrate reading and writing instruction as fully as possible. Such integration should move beyond simply having students write about what they read or read about what they write, although these are useful activities. Rather, instructional activities should be implemented that help students perceive the cognitive connections between the two processes. Kucer and Rhodes (1986) have termed such activities "counterpart strategy lessons" (p. 186). In counterpart lessons, the way in which literacy is used in the reading activity parallels or is a counterpart to the way in which it is used in the writing activity. Both activities require the student to utilize processes that are common to reading and writing. Such lessons help students fine-tune their use of one process with information they have learned when engaged in the other process.

It is necessary to help students see the links between reading and writing through the use of counterpart lessons because such connections may otherwise go unnoticed. However, in counterpart lessons students are not simply told what the connections are, nor are they left to discover them on their own. Instead, the connections are demonstrated to or highlighted for the learners (Smith, 1981a, 1981b). Through such demonstrations and modeling by the teacher, students become sensitive to the reading/writing connection being highlighted and learn to utilize the connection in subsequent reading and writing.

The remainder of the chapter presents a number of counterpart strategy lessons that can be used with a wide range of students. The lessons (See Figure 7.4) are grouped around the following six cognitive processes that are common to both reading and writing: Readers and writers seek text structure; use text aids; chunk meaning; search for patterns that connect; reflect upon and revise their meanings; and take ownership of text through authorship. Strategy lessons for each of the six cognitive processes are presented by (a) stating the focus of the lesson; (b) listing the materials and supplies needed for teaching; (c) discussing the teaching procedures to be used; and (d) introducing instructional variations that might be used as follow-up.

Seeking Text Structure

This group of strategy lessons highlights the fact that texts are organized. Effective readers and writers make use of their knowledge of various text structures or organizational patterns to generate and structure meaning when interacting with print. (Chapter 6 provides a discussion of different ways texts are organized.)

Strategy Lesson: Text Sets

This lesson helps the learner use various organizational patterns when reading.

FIGURE 7.4 Overview of Common Literacy Concepts and Corresponding Counterpart Strategy Lessons

Concept	*Lessons*
Seeking Text Structure	Text Sets Structured Stories
Using Text Aids	Previewing Aiding the Text
Chunking Text Meanings	Card Strategy Schema Stories Text Construction Semantic Mapping
Searching for Patterns That Connect	Card Sort Idea Expansion
Reflecting and Revising	Say Something Tell Me Reader Selected Miscues Help Me Ask Me
Taking Ownership through Authorship	Synonym Substitution Say It Again

Materials

1. Several stories with common organizational patterns, such as repeatable or cumulative episodes, or compare/contrast, cause/effect, pro/con, or problem/solution patterns. "The Three Little Pigs" and "The Three Billy Goats Gruff" are two stories that share a common pattern. Figure 7.5 lists the similarities in these two texts. When first introducing this lesson, it is important to make the common pattern in the texts fairly evident.
2. Blackboard and chalk.

Teaching Procedures

1. Give the students the stories to read with instructions to look for all of the ways in which the two stories are similar. If students are just beginning to read or have reading difficulties, the stories might be read to them, you can read one and have the students read the other, or the stories can be read in small groups.
2. After the students have finished reading, ask them to discuss all of the ways in which the stories are similar. Questions to begin the discussion might include the following: "What was the same about

FIGURE 7.5 Similarities between "The Three Little Pigs" and "The Three Billy Goats Gruff"

Similarities	*Three Little Pigs*	*Three Billy Goats Gruff*
Three main characters:	Three pigs	Three goats
Villain:	Wolf	Troll
Repeatable episodes:	Each pig builds a house.	Two goats are bothered by the troll.
	The wolf blows a house down.	Two goats tell the troll to wait for the bigger brother.
The villain is outwitted:	The pigs boil water and tell the wolf to come down the chimney.	The biggest goat butts the troll with his horns.

these two stories?" "What information did you find in both of the stories?" "What are the similarities in the way these stories were written?" List all similarities discussed on the board.

3. Once all the students' thoughts about how the texts are similar have been elicited, ask the students to identify which of the similarities are of major significance and why. Circle these similarities. At this point in the lesson, you can also inquire as to whether the students have read or heard other stories that are similar in nature. Give the students the opportunity to share these stories.

Variations

In the example discussed here, the lesson involves the comparison of two texts. The lesson may also have the students compare three or more texts. If there are a number of stories with similar characteristics, such as folk tales or fables, the entire class may read one story and then read various others in small groups. These groups can then share their stories with the entire class.

Rather than using stories with similar structures, different versions of the same story can be read. For example, there are a number of versions of "The Three Little Pigs" that the students can read and then compare and contrast. The use of text sets need not be limited to narratives; exposition or informational pieces can be used as well. While narratives typically use a time sequence to structure events, informational pieces introduce students to such structures as compare/contrast or pro/con points of view.

Strategy Lesson: Structured Stories

This lesson helps the learner to use various organizational patterns when writing.

Materials

1. Text sets that the students have read and compared.
2. Pencils and paper.

Teaching Procedures

1. After the students have completed the comparison of two stories with similar organizational patterns, inform them that they are going to write a third story to accompany the set of texts.
2. Working with the children as a group, brainstorm possible alternatives for the significant similarities between the two stories read for the "Text Sets" lesson. Record these alternatives on the board. For example, major similarities between the "Three Little Pigs" and the "Three Billy Goats Gruff" include the use of animals, three main characters, the existence of a villain, and repeatable episodes. Possible alternatives for the main characters might be the use of various animals, birds, insects, or even humans. Repeatable episodes might involve the building of different types of structures or journeys to a variety of locations. The point here is to have the children generate alternative meanings that can be structured in a pattern similar to that of the two stories read.
3. Once ideas have been shared, the children should be told that they are to write their own stories using some of the ideas listed on the board. While each story will be unique, they should all contain an organizational pattern similar to that found in the "Text Sets" lesson.
4. After the stories have been written, allow the children to share them and have the class discuss the similarities between each story and the "Text Sets" lesson.

Variations

When first introducing this strategy, or for children who are experiencing difficulty with the writing process, it may be a good idea to have the structured story written as a group. When instructed in this manner, the children identify which alternatives listed on the board are to be used in the story. Then, as you scribe what is dictated, various children are asked to create a part of the story orally.

A second alternative is to have the students write their stories in small groups. In this case, one child in each group is appointed to record the story as it is dictated.

Using Text Aids

In these lessons, students learn to recognize and use text aids such as titles, subtitles, graphs, charts, or pictures to chunk meanings as they read and write. Text aids help writers organize and more fully express their ideas; they help readers better understand the writer's ideas and organization.

Strategy Lesson: Previewing

This lesson helps the learner use various text aids to predict and understand the writer's ideas.

Materials

1. An expository piece of writing that contains a variety of text aids such as titles, subtitles, graphs, charts, or pictures. Chapters from social science, health, or science textbooks or articles from resources such as Scholastic's *Weekly Reader* contain appropriate expository material.
2. Blackboard and chalk.

Teaching Procedures

1. Give each student a copy of the text to be read. Inform the class that they will be given several minutes to quickly look through the material to find out what the entire text will be about. However, tell the students that they will not have enough time to read the text word for word.

   The amount of time given for previewing will vary, depending on the length of the material and the reading proficiency of the students. Care should be taken so that the students will have ample time to read the text aids but not enough time to read the body of the piece.
2. Tell the class the amount of time they will have for previewing, and let them begin. Stop the previewing when the time is up.
3. On the blackboard, make two columns. The first column is labeled "Predictions"; the second is labeled "Parts of the text used." Ask the students to share what they think the text will be about based on their previewing of the material. List this information under the first column.

4. Ask the students what parts of the text they read in the limited amount of time given to them. These text aids are listed in the second column. At this point in the lesson, you will want to discuss the use of text aids and how they help readers and writers predict and organize—or *chunk*—meanings. Such a discussion might include the following questions: "Why do you think the writer put pictures, graphs, and subheadings in the article you just read?" "How does the use of pictures, graphs, and subheadings help the writer?" "How does the use of pictures, graphs, and subheadings help the reader?" "How did they help you?"
5. Using their predictions as a guide, the students then read the material in its entirety. As they read, they consider which of their predictions are accurate. In most cases, predictions will be general enough so that they will be correct. However, the students should be told that the purpose of this activity is to help them use text aids to make guesses about what they will read, not necessarily to always be correct in their predictions.
6. After reading, bring the students together and ask them to discuss the material and which of their predictions were accurate.

Variations

The students are given only the text aids to preview. Take the expository piece of material and cut out all of the text aids. Then arrange and glue the text aids onto white paper in the same format as in the original material. (See Figure 7.6.) At this point, there are two instructional options. Overhead transparencies can be made of the modified text or copies can be made for each student. If overhead transparencies are made, simply display each page of the modified text on the screen and ask the students to make predictions about the content to be found under each text aid. These predictions are written directly on the transparency, and, as previously discussed, the purpose of text aids is explored. Then give the students copies of the original material to read and discuss the accuracy of their predictions.

If copies of the modified material are made for each student, tell the students to look at the text aids and then write what information they think they will find below each text aid. This may be done individually or in small groups. These predictions are shared with the class, and the original text is read and discussed.

Strategy Lesson: Aiding the Text

This lesson helps the learner generate text aids around major ideas or key concepts.

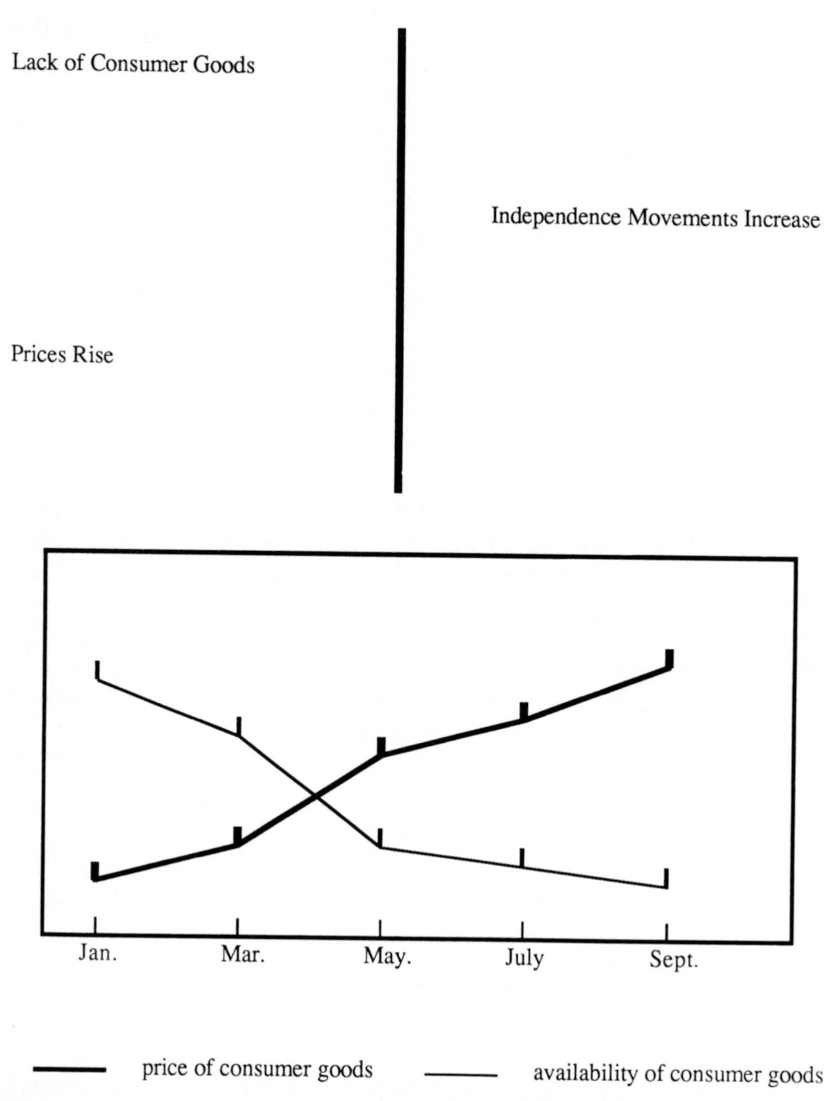

FIGURE 7.6 Sample of Material for Aiding the Text

Prerequisites and Materials

1. Experience with the "Previewing" lesson.
2. A piece of expository material containing text aids such as titles, subtitles, summaries, graphs, charts, and pictures. Chapters from social science, health, or science textbooks or articles from resources such as Scholastic's *Weekly Reader* contain appropriate expository material.
3. The same piece of expository material, which has been typed with all text aids deleted.
4. White paper, scissors, glue, and crayons or colored markers.

Teaching Procedures

1. Review with the students what they know about text aids; that is, what they are (list the various kinds on the board) and how they help the writer and the reader organize and predict meaning.
2. Give the students a copy of the expository material to read. After they have finished reading, tell them that all text aids have been removed and that they are to put text aids back in. The students should be encouraged to use as many different kinds of text aids as possible.
3. Working either individually or in small groups, the student(s) decide what kind of text aids will be put into the text and where they will be put. These text aids are then created using the white paper and crayons or markers provided.
4. After the text aids have been generated, the students cut apart the article at each point where a text aid is to be inserted. They then reconstruct the article by pasting the text aids and the segments of the article on blank sheets of paper.
5. Allow the students to share their "new" article, discussing where and why text aids were added.
6. Compare and contrast the various text aids that were created and their placement in the article, and discuss their effectiveness.
7. Give the students the original article with the text aids included. Have them compare and contrast their own use and placement of text aids with the original. It should be stressed, however, that the purpose of this lesson is not to replicate the author's use of text aids. Text aids can be used in a variety of ways, and the focus of the lesson is on helping students use them effectively. Therefore, students should not be given the original article if they are likely to see their own versions as wrong.

Variations

Rather than using a published piece of material, drafts of student expository writing can be used. Working independently or in small groups, the students generate text aids for their drafts. Each student then revises his or her piece of writing, putting text aids in where appropriate. Chapter 8 offers helpful suggestions for aiding students in the revision process.

Chunking Text Meanings

In reading and writing, the language user must generate and organize chunks of meaning or major ideas. These chunks of meaning help the language user link ideas together so that they form an organized whole.

Strategy Lesson: Card Strategy

This lesson helps the learner generate and organize chunks of meaning when writing.

Materials

1. Notecards or paper scraps.
2. Writing paper and pencils.

Teaching Procedures

1. Give the students three or four notecards (or paper scraps), and ask them to jot down three or four potential writing topics, each on a separate card. If you have assigned a general topic, the students can generate specific topics related to it or they may choose their own topics.

   While topic generation is taking place, the students should be encouraged to share ideas. This will often lead to the discovery of other writing topics and provide added support to students who have difficulty identifying potential topics.
2. After the students have generated topics, they select the topic card about which they would most like to write and put the other cards into individual envelopes for future use.
3. After the students have selected their topics, they consider the major ideas related to them. These major ideas are also written on notecards, one idea per card. Encourage the students to generate as many ideas as possible to demonstrate to them the variety of ideas that are available during writing. Such encouragement frequently results in the discovery of ideas that had not been considered previously. Take care not to specify the unit of language to be put on the cards. A sentence, clause or phrase, or word will be recorded depending on the student and the meaning to be captured. The language used simply serves as a place holder for chunks of meaning.

During the generation of major idea cards, the students should again be provided with an opportunity to share ideas. This can be done most easily in small groups.

4. After the students have shared their cards, they select the ideas they think they want to use in their writing. Cards not used should be set aside. However, tell the students that they are free to make any changes in their cards (e.g., add, reject, modify) at any time.
5. After the major ideas have been selected, the students organize the cards in a meaningful order, laying the idea cards in front of themselves, beneath the topic card, and in the order decided upon.
6. At this point in the lesson, the students pick up their sequenced cards and shuffle them. After shuffling, each student exchanges cards with a partner, who reads them and arranges them in a meaningful order. The partner then explains the order to the cards' author and gives reasons. The author takes back his or her own cards and puts them in the original order, also explaining the reasons for the order. If the students will benefit from experiencing a variety of possible idea organizations, this procedure can be repeated with other partners.

   The shuffling part of this lesson is especially beneficial because it encourages students to use the cards only as a guide during their writing. They understand that the order can be changed as needed. Also, students frequently are amazed that their ideas can be structured in a variety of ways and still make sense. The shuffling of the cards builds flexibility in the writing process and gives students access to a variety of options.
7. Using their cards as a guide, the students write their texts. It should be noted, however, that the cards serve only as a source of potential meaning; students are free to use them in any way they choose. A one-to-one correspondence between the cards produced and the actual written text should not be expected. The cards should not be used as a restraint or as a rigid outline. As students write, they will frequently discover new ideas to include in their texts.

Variations

You may want to engage younger students or students who will have difficulty understanding the basic steps in the lesson in a language experience activity using the strategy. In this version, the entire class will write one text. Simply ask the class to brainstorm possible writing topics and list these on the chalkboard or overhead.

After the class has agreed on one topic, ask for major ideas related to it. Once again, record the ideas. After major ideas have been listed, the class decides which ideas should be in the text and the order of their presentation. Then ask individual students to dictate orally the text for each major idea selected, and write it on the blackboard or an overhead transparency. By presenting the lesson in this manner, you can be sure that the students clearly understand the procedures before they are asked to engage in the activity independently.

Strategy Lesson: Schema Stories

This lesson helps the learner organize chunks of meaning when reading.

Materials

A short narrative or expository text should be located that the students have not previously read and that is well within their proficiency to read. At least until students have become accustomed to this strategy, the text should have some structural similarity to others they have read, the concepts should be easily understood, and the text should not be too lengthy. The text should also be a complete one—a whole story or an entire expository piece about a particular concept. Fables often serve as suitable short narratives, and resources such as Scholastic's *Weekly Reader* contain appropriate expository texts.

Teaching Procedures

1. The text should be cut into natural language units—paragraphs, titles, subtitles, morals, or whatever is appropriate to the text. The units should be arranged in a random order on a sheet of paper and photocopied. This procedure eliminates the possibility that students will put the text together by means of paper-cut cues. After photocopying, the copies are once again cut into separate text units. Each text, cut into its units, can be stored in an ordinary envelope.
2. In small groups, students are given a single envelope containing all the text units and told that they should think about and discuss the text as a puzzle that needs to be put together so it makes sense.
3. Before the students begin working, they consider or talk about their ideas about how to proceed with the task. They should be helped to understand that it is useful to read all of the text units before beginning in order to get a feel for what the text is about. This is similar to getting a feel for the whole of a puzzle by looking at the picture on the box before trying to put the pieces together. If expository material is being used, the students may want to group together similar units of text such as pictures, subtitles, or paragraphs. This is analogous to sorting puzzle pieces by color and/or by whether the pieces are or are not border pieces before putting the

puzzle together. Before the students begin sequencing the text, each group should designate a member to make a list of the reasons used to decide the order of the text units.

4. As each group finishes the task, its members look over the shoulders of a nearby group to see whether that group structured the text units in the same way. If the groups' organizations are different, they discuss the differences with a focus on whether the texts make sense as structured. As with the "Card Strategy," this lesson can also help students realize that meanings can frequently be organized in a variety of ways.
5. In a class discussion, the groups share both their solutions and the cues used in arranging the textual units. In case of disagreement, the groups share the reasons for their decisions. A group may decide to change the order of the text pieces on the basis of an argument made by another group.
6. Students may be provided with the original text once they have constructed their own textual organization. However, this should only be done if students fully understand that the purpose of this activity is not to find the "right" answer. When students construct textual sequences different from that of the author, it is because meanings may be structured in a variety of ways or because the cues provided by the author were not salient enough for the readers. If the latter is the reason, the students can discuss what the author might have done to provide more supportive textual cues for the reader; that is, how the text could be revised.

Variations

Rather than having the students work in small groups, the lesson can be taught to the entire class. Give a different segment of the text to a student or a small group of students. Each segment is shared with the entire class. Then ask, "Who has the first piece of the story or article and why?" "Who has the second piece of the story and why?" Continue in this fashion until the entire text has been assembled. In case of disputes, the class attempts to reach a consensus as to which segment comes next. However, you will want to emphasize the idea that there might be various ways in which the text can be put together.

Because various text forms employ unique text meanings and organizational patterns, it is a good idea to present students with various text structures to organize. The relationships among units of meaning in expository texts, for example, are different from the relationships in narrative texts, and both are different from those found in the Yellow Pages of a telephone directory.

Strategy Lesson: Text Construction

This lesson helps the learner organize chunks of meaning when writing.

Prerequisites and Materials

1. Experience with "Schema Stories."
2. Student writing in draft form.
3. Scissors, writing paper, and pencils.

Teaching Procedures

1. Discuss with the students their experience with schema stories and the idea that texts can frequently be ordered in a number of different ways. Schema stories are stories based on students' understanding or knowledge of how stories are organized.
2. Ask the students to cut their drafts apart by paragraphs or any chunk of meaning that is appropriate and then to shuffle the segments.
3. Pair the students and have them exchange their segments with their partners. Each student then becomes the "author" of the segments and puts them into a meaningful order.
4. Each author then presents and discusses the order with his or her partner.
5. The segments are returned to the original author and put into their original order. The order is also presented and discussed. Students then evaluate which organization was more effective and why.
6. Repeat this procedure as many times as you feel are necessary and useful.
7. Revise the organization of the texts as needed.

Strategy Lesson: Plot Mapping

This lesson helps the learner generate and organize chunks of meaning when reading.

Materials

1. A short expository text. Articles with text aids such as subheadings, charts, or graphs are especially good.
2. White drawing paper.
3. Crayons or colored markers.
4. A map of a geographical landmass such as a city, state, country, or island. This map should be large enough for all students to see, or copies should be given to each student.
5. A blackboard.

Teaching Procedures

1. On the blackboard, make two columns. Label the first column "Purposes That Maps Serve" and the second column "Ways in Which Map Makers Show These Purposes."
2. Have the students look at the geographical map. Ask the students to discuss why maps are made or what purposes maps serve. A key purpose that should be discussed is that maps show relationships among things—in this case, among geographical locations. List the purposes discussed in the left-hand column.
3. Next, discuss with the students the ways in which a map maker shows or illustrates geographical locations through the use of color, line, shape, or spacing. List these in the right-hand column.
4. Discuss with the students the idea that not all geographical locations are usually shown on a map. For example, a state map would not include small streams or every street. Only locations that are significant and relevant are included on the map.
5. Tell the students that they are going to construct a map of their own. This map, however, will not illustrate geographical locations and their relationship to other locations. Rather, it will show relationships among major ideas within an article. Remind them that just as map makers choose only major things to represent in their maps, they as readers should only select ideas that are of major importance. If the students have experienced the "Card Strategy" lesson, relate the generation of major ideas before they wrote to the location of major ideas in the article they will read.
6. Give the students the article to read, and tell them to list the major ideas they find.
7. Give the students pieces of white drawing paper and a variety of crayons or colored markers. Students are then to construct maps using the major ideas found in the article. They construct their maps and indicate relationships among concepts using any of the ways discussed in class concerning how map makers express relationships (i.e., color, line, shape, or spacing).
8. Give the students the opportunity to share their maps, discussing in particular the major ideas used and how and why they were related to one another.
9. After the maps have been shared, have the students discuss how the various maps were similar or different and why.

Variations

When first introducing this activity to the students, you might want to construct your own plot map of an article that the students have already read. This demonstration is useful in helping students conceptualize the idea of mapping something they read. In addition, the students can generate plot maps in small groups.

If the students have experienced the "Card Strategy" lesson, you can ask them to generate and organize the major idea cards that the author might have used to write the text.

This activity can be used as a writing activity as well. Students generate a plot map of something they have written and then exchange their writing with a partner. Each student maps the partner's text and shares the map, explaining what major ideas were used and why they were related as they were on the map. The author of the text shares his or her map, also explaining what major concepts were used and why they were related as they were on the map. Finally, the two maps are compared and contrasted.

Chapters 3 and 5 contain additional suggestions for mapping in the sections on semantic mapping, which may also be used as variations of this strategy lesson.

Searching for Patterns That Connect

In both reading and writing, the language user must attempt to find conceptual relationships among the minor ideas generated. In turn, each group of related minor ideas forms a major idea or chunk of meaning.

Strategy Lesson: Card Sort

This strategy lesson helps the learner chunk minor ideas into a major idea.

Materials

1. A blackboard.
2. Paragraphs about a particular theme or topic that have been taken from a variety of sources such as trade books, magazines, newspapers, or textbooks. This particular activity works well at the end of a thematic unit or a unit from social studies or science. If the lesson is taught as a concluding activity, the sources from which the paragraphs are taken can represent various readings the students have encountered in the theme.
3. Each paragraph is typed on a notecard and given a different number. Photocopy several copies of each paragraph and put them into envelopes, with each envelope containing one copy of each paragraph photocopied.

Teaching Procedures

1. Assign the students to small groups, and provide each group with an envelope containing all of the paragraphs.
2. Tell the students that they are to sort the cards into piles. All of the cards in each pile should be related to one another in some manner. Encourage the students to read all of the paragraphs before beginning in order to get a feel for the categories that are possible.
3. Before the sorting begins, ask each group to generate a list of possible sorting categories. Assign one student in each group the task of recording the categories.
4. After the possible categories have been generated, the students in each group review their categories and select those they want to use for sorting the cards.
5. Based on the categories selected, the students sort their cards. Inform them that as the cards are sorted new categories may emerge or existing categories may appear to be inappropriate. This is to be expected, and categories can be generated or rejected as needed. The purpose of generating categories before the sorting begins is simply to help students see the range of ways in which the cards might be related.
6. After all groups have finished, record the categories and their corresponding card numbers on the board for each group. Give each group the opportunity to share the reasons for its categories and why the cards were placed where they were.

Strategy Lesson: Idea Expansion

This strategy lesson helps the learner generate minor ideas when writing.

Materials

1. Student writing in draft form.
2. Notecards or paper scraps.

Teaching Procedures

1. Ask the students to read through their drafts and identify one or two parts that need to be developed more fully. This can be done in groups of three or four, with group members helping each writer identify parts in need of expansion.
2. After several parts have been identified, students brainstorm ideas that relate to each part to be expanded. Each idea is recorded on a separate notecard. Allow each author to share the ideas with the

group, and encourage group members to discuss which ideas should and should not be put into the text.

3. After sharing their ideas, the students choose the ideas they want to develop more fully in the selected parts of their texts. These ideas are placed in the order in which the students will write about them.
4. The students revise their texts, expanding those sections for which additional ideas have been generated.

Reflecting upon and Revising Meanings

Revision is at the heart of all reading and writing. Revision, or re-seeing, requires that the language user reflect upon and respond to what is being read or written.

Strategy Lesson: Say Something

This strategy lesson helps the learner reflect upon and respond to what is being read.

Materials

A short narrative or expository text is located. When the "Say Something" strategy is first introduced, select a text that can be read in one session. The text selected should be of particular interest to the students so that it will be likely to elicit response. Throughout the text, place dots and number them. Place the dots at points where you anticipate that the students might have something to say.

Teaching Procedures

1. Give the students copies of the text containing the numbered dots. Tell the students that they are to read silently up to the first dot in the text. After all students have finished reading, ask them to say something about what they have just read.
2. Encourage the students to respond in ways that move beyond simple summaries and to generate evaluative, inferential, appreciative, and questioning responses. Connections to previous experiences the students have had are also valued responses. Initially, what the students say and ask may be limited, but this rapidly changes. Soon they will move beyond a simple restatement of what was read and into more personal responses.
3. Give the students time to read and respond to each section of the text.

Variations

Rather than having the students respond to the entire class, they can be assigned to small groups or pairs. Responses can be written rather than oral, with students recording them in a reader response notebook for later sharing. Finally, the students can select the points at which responses will be generated. In this version, the students place dots and corresponding numbers in the text where they want to respond, and then they respond in a notebook. If writing in the text is not possible, they write the idea to which they want to respond in a notebook and then write their responses.

Strategy Lesson: Tell Me

This strategy lesson helps the learner use peers to reflect upon and respond to what has been written.

Prerequisites and Materials

1. Experience with the "Say Something" strategy.
2. Student writing in draft form.

Teaching Procedures

1. Discuss with the students their experience with the "Say Something" strategy. Explore the idea that the writer of the text to which they responded most likely had friends respond to drafts of the text. Such responses help the writer become aware of what parts of the text need to be revised. Tell the students that they are going to use a similar procedure to help them revise something they have written.
2. Ask the students to put dots in their drafts at points where reader feedback is desired. After the dots are placed, the students read their drafts aloud to small groups or to partners, stopping at each dot. The members of the group or the partners then respond orally to what has been read.
3. After the procedure has been repeated a number of times, the students revise their drafts based on the responses given.

Variations

As with the "Say Something" strategy, a number of alternatives are possible with this lesson. Responses can be written rather than oral, and drafts can be read silently by the responder rather than orally by the author. Finally, rather than having the author place the dots, the reader can select the points at which to respond. Responses are written on notebook paper and given to the author at the end of the lesson. These written responses then serve as the basis for revision of the drafts.

Strategy Lesson: Reader-Selected Miscues (Adapted from Watson, 1980)

This strategy lesson helps the learner reflect upon the meanings generated during reading and revise them when meaning is lost.

Materials

1. A short narrative or expository text containing words, ideas, or relationships that will cause the students difficulty.
2. Paper and pencils.

Teaching Procedures

1. Discuss with the students the fact that all readers frequently encounter things they have difficulty reading or understanding. Emphasize the idea that while lack of understanding may be due to not knowing a word, often it is due to not understanding the ideas or relationships that the author is trying to convey.
2. Give the students the text to read, telling them that they will probably encounter things in this text that they will have difficulty reading or understanding. When students encounter these things, they underline them. If it is not possible to underline in the text, they can record them on a piece of paper.
3. After the reading has been completed, gather the students together as a group. Ask them to review the problems they underlined and put a check by those that are most important. This gives you the opportunity to discuss the idea that not all problems in reading or understanding are of equal significance and that some of them can simply be ignored without disrupting the overall meaning of the text.
4. After the most important problems with the text have been selected, give various students the opportunity to share them. For each problem shared, discuss together with the class strategies the reader might use to solve the problem. These strategies would include rereading portions of the text preceding the problem, reading portions of the text following the problem, or substituting one or several words for the problematic word(s).
5. If a lack of understanding of certain ideas or concepts—rather than word identification—is the problem, engage the students in a discussion about the ideas or concepts. Give various students the oppor-

tunity to share how they understood the concept and to supply information from the text supporting such an understanding.

Variations

Once students become comfortable with this lesson, they can begin applying it to their free reading or reading in such subject fields as science and social science.

Strategy Lesson: Help Me

This strategy lesson helps the learner use peers to revise meaning in writing.

Materials

Student writing in draft form.

Teaching Procedures

1. Ask the students to silently read the drafts of their papers and identify several problems with which they would like help.
2. Put the students into small groups. In the group, each student reads aloud his or her paper and then discusses the problem(s) with which help is needed. Other members of the group suggest ways in which they think the problem(s) could be solved.
3. Have the students revise their drafts based on the suggestions provided.

Strategy Lesson: Ask Me (Adapted from Bouffler, 1980)

This strategy lesson helps the learner use peers to revise meaning in writing.

Materials

Student writing in draft form.

Teaching Procedures

1. Put the students into small groups. In the group, each student reads his or her draft orally.
2. After the draft has been shared, each member of the group is responsible for asking the writer at least one question about the text that has just been read. These questions can be shared orally or be written on notecards.
3. The writer responds to the question.

4. Have the students revise their texts as necessary based on the questions asked.

Variations

It is important with younger or less proficient writers that the drafts be read aloud so that the group focuses on meaning rather than on such conventions as penmanship, spelling, or punctuation. Once the meaning focus has been established, the drafts can be read by the members of the group and questions written on notecards or scraps of paper. Chapter 8 provides additional suggestions for helping children work together in revision activities in reading and writing.

Taking Ownership through Authorship

Reading and writing involve the ability to draw upon and use one's own language when interacting with print.

Strategy Lesson: Synonym Substitution (Adapted from Goodman & Burke, 1980)

This strategy lesson helps the learner use his or her own language when reading.

Materials

1. A short narrative or expository text.
2. A blackboard and/or overhead projector.

Teaching Procedures

1. Throughout the text selected, underline and number words, phrases, or clauses that can easily be replaced with synonyms. These points should be selected carefully so that the reader will be able to make use of previous context to first read what is underlined and then generate synonymous language. Copies of the text with its underlined portions should be given to each student, or the text can be shown on an overhead projector.
2. After they have read the text silently, tell the students that they will be reading aloud a text in which some things have been underlined. When they come to these underlined portions, they are to replace them with language that means the same thing (synonyms).
3. Begin reading the text aloud. Read along as part of the group so as to maintain the pace, but do not supply synonyms. Rather, pause at the

underlined portions and allow the students to generate their own synonyms.
4. After the entire text has been read, write the numeral 1 on the board, to correspond to the first numbered word or phrase, and ask the students to share all of their synonyms. Record these substitutions on the board. Write the numeral 2 on the board, share and record substitutions, and so forth.
5. Discuss with the students the idea that authors can convey their meanings using a variety of language. Changing the language, therefore, does not necessarily change the meaning of what is written. Similarly, readers frequently change the language when reading but still get the same meaning.
6. Have the students read the text out loud a final time, with each student selecting his or her favorite substitutions from the lists on the board.

Variations

Rather than reading the text aloud as a class, students can generate substitutions in small groups. For each underlined portion of the text, the group generates as many alternatives as possible. One member of the group is selected to record the alternatives. After all groups have finished, have each group share its synonyms.

Strategy Lesson: Say It Again

This strategy lesson helps the student discover that meaning can be expressed in various linguistic forms.

Materials

1. Student writing in draft form.
2. Writing paper and pencils.

Teaching Procedures

1. Discuss with the students their experience with the "Synonym Substitution" strategy and the idea that meaning can be expressed using a variety of language.
2. Ask the students to read their written drafts silently and underline and number any use of language that does not adequately express what they want to say.
3. Put the students into small groups. Each author shares his or her text and indicates where language needs to be changed. Members of

the group provide possible substitutions, which the author records on a piece of paper.

4. Have students revise their drafts based on the substitutions provided.

SUMMARY

The brain is not compartmentalized; it does not have one part that handles reading and a separate part that handles writing. Historically, when reading and writing were viewed as unrelated cognitive activities, it made sense that we designed school curricula that separated the two processes. However, we now know better. From the perspective of what the mind does, reading and writing bear much in common. We know, for example, that both readers and writers seek text structure, use text aids, chunk meaning, search for patterns that connect, revise their meanings, and take ownership of text through authorship. Given these insights, it follows that school curricula must change.

The function of curriculum is to give perspective. It is not good enough if the teacher is the only one who understands why a language activity is important and how it relates to becoming a more successful reader and writer. Curriculum must be made visible to students as well as teachers. The strategy lessons presented in this chapter highlight key cognitive processes in reading and writing. When juxtaposed in classrooms, counterpart strategy instruction demonstrates what we currently know about the integrative power of reading and writing.

FOLLOW-UP QUESTIONS AND ACTIVITIES

1. In this chapter, six cognitive connections between reading and writing were discussed. After reflecting on your own reading and writing behavior, generate additional cognitive connections between the two processes.
2. Select one of the reading/writing connections you generated in the previous question or one of the connections discussed in this chapter, and construct several counterpart strategy lessons.
3. Locate additional reading or writing lessons, and construct counterpart lessons for them.

ADDITIONAL READINGS

Harste, J., Short, K., & Burke, C. (1988). *Creating classrooms for authors: The reading-writing connection.* Portsmouth, NH: Heinemann.

Jensen, J. (Ed.). (1984). *Composing and comprehending.* Urbana, IL: National Council of Teachers of English.

Kucer, S., & Rhodes, L. (1986). Counterpart strategies: Fine tuning language with language. *The Reading Teacher, 40,* 186–193.

Mason, J. (1989). *Reading and writing connections.* Newton, MA: Allyn and Bacon.

Petersen, B. (Ed.). (1986). *Convergences: Transactions in reading and writing.* Urbana, IL: National Council of Teachers of English.

Rowe, D., & Harste, J. (1986). Reading and writing in a system of knowing. In M. Sampson (Ed.), *The pursuit of literacy: Early reading and writing* (pp. 126–144). Dubuque, IA: Kendall/Hunt.

REFERENCES

Bouffler, C. (1980). *Ask me.* Unpublished manuscript. Bloomington: Indiana University.

Boutwell, M. (1983). Reading and writing processes: A reciprocal agreement. *Language Arts, 60,* 723–730.

DeFord, D. (1981). Literacy: Reading, writing, and other essentials. *Language Arts, 58,* 652–658.

Eckhoff, B. (1983). How reading affects children's writing. *Language Arts, 60,* 607–616.

Flood, J., & Lapp, D. (1987). Reading and writing relations: Assumptions and directions. In J. Squire (Ed.), *The dynamics of language learning: Research in the language arts* (pp. 9–27). Urbana, IL: National Conference on Research in English and ERIC Clearinghouse on Reading and Communication Skills.

Goodman, Y., & Burke, C. (1980). *Reading strategies: Focus on comprehension.* New York: Holt, Rinehart & Winston.

Harste, J., Woodward, V., & Burke, C. (1984). *Language stories and literacy lessons.* Portsmouth, NH: Heinemann.

Kucer, S. (1985). The making of meaning: Reading and writing as parallel processes. *Written Communication, 2,* 317–336.

Kucer, S. (1987). The cognitive base of reading and writing. In J. Squire (Ed.), *The dynamics of language learning: Research in the language arts* (pp. 27–51). Urbana, IL: National Conference on Research in English and ERIC Clearinghouse on Reading and Communication Skills.

Kucer, S., & Rhodes, L. (1986). Counterpart strategies: Fine tuning language with language. *The Reading Teacher, 40,* 186–193.

Newkirk, T. (1982). Young writers as critical readers. *Language Arts, 59,* 451–457.

Shanklin, N. (1982). *Relating reading and writing: Developing a transactional model of the writing processes* (Monographs in Language and Reading Studies). Bloomington: Indiana University.

Smith, F. (1981a). Demonstrations, engagement and sensitivity: A revised approach to language learning. *Language Arts, 58,* 103–112.

Smith, F. (1981b). Demonstrations, engagement and sensitivity: The choice between people and programs. *Language Arts, 58,* 634–642.

Squire, J. (1983). Composing and comprehending: Two sides of the same basic process. *Language Arts, 60,* 581–589.

Tierney, R., & Pearson, P. D. (1983). Toward a composing model of reading. *Language Arts, 60,* 658–680.

Watson, D. (1980). Reader selected miscues. In B. Farr & D. Strickler (Eds.), *Reading comprehension: An instructional videotape series (Resource guide)* (pp. 65–70). Bloomington: Indiana University.

8
Writing Strategies That Enhance Reading

WILLIAM J. STRONG

IN CHAPTER 7, Kucer and Harste introduced the rationale for integrating reading and writing instruction and presented instructional activities to aid teachers in implementing a literacy curriculum. In this chapter, William Strong presents additional strategies for teachers to use to help students use writing as a tool for learning. Strong discusses what effective teachers must consider if they are to keep the idea of writing to learn in perspective. He contends that writing-to-learn activities demand that we avoid the role of judge, examiner, or language guardian. He states that writing to learn means *engaging in* learning, not proving one's learning to a grade-dispensing authority. He goes on to present several activities that teach basic writing skills, such as dictation, sentence combining, and fact sheets, which are designed to help students acquire some degree of fluency.

However, Strong cautions that while cleverly devised exercises may develop certain skills, they are still not real writing. With real writing, we figure out something to say and how to say it. He suggests that writing is a tool for learning and that writing journals and learning logs presents opportunities for students to really write. He also provides suggestions to help teachers use peer response groups and conferences. He concludes the chapter with a discussion of successful programs that use writing activities as an aid to reading.

STUDY QUESTIONS

1. What do we mean by the phrase "writing to learn?"
2. Why should teachers not correct writing-to-learn activities?
3. How can we use writing to develop skills of reading and thinking?
4. When and how should we use response groups and conferences?
5. How does increased attention to writing affect comprehension?

During the Dark Ages of reading and writing instruction, many well-intentioned teachers learned to distrust their own best instincts. The profession encouraged them to think of reading and writing separately and to delay writing until their students had acquired certain "basics"—knowledge of phonics rules, good handwriting, correct spelling, skills of punctuation, and so on. The role of writing in helping children internalize the conventions of print was virtually ignored. Error in children's writing, like sin for the Puritans, was viewed as a corrupting influence.

Unfortunately, many of today's curricula are still guided by a Dark Ages philosophy of instruction. In a survey of language arts textbooks, for example, Graves (1978) found that over 70% of the activities dealt with punctuation, grammar, spelling, editing, and proofreading, all taught in isolation; he therefore concluded that "most writing instruction isn't instruction at all" (p. 59). Other studies of classroom practice have confirmed that what often passes for instruction in reading and writing is an endless stream of nonsense worksheets, with purple ink fading like the interests of students (Durkin, 1978; Goodlad, 1984; Rosenshine & Berliner, 1978).

It does not have to be that way. In Chapter 7, Stephen Kucer and Jerome Harste make the case for integrating reading and writing rather than separating them. Kucer and Harste argue that both reading and writing are active, *constructive* processes—ways of making the world known to ourselves. According to this view, one now shared by growing numbers of classroom teachers, reading and writing are different sides of a coin called *meaning*. And it is meanings that accumulate in our cognitive bank accounts as we make our way through the world and engage in productive schooling.

This chapter asserts that writing should *not* be delayed in the elementary schooling of children. Indeed, making meaning on paper can and should be a vital part of the curriculum from preschool forward. Also, writing should *not* be taught one skill at a time, with emphasis on exercises, worksheets, meaningless copying, and red-pencil correction. Rather, instruction should capitalize on the child's need to share and communicate with others. When writing becomes a functional part of the curriculum, students acquire its skills without the groans so often elicited by dreary, skill-based approaches.

This chapter examines writing strategies that put attention where it belongs—on making *sense* rather than nonsense. To accomplish this aim, the chapter is divided into five parts: (1) the concept of writing to learn in perspective; (2) writing activities that enhance reading; (3) writing as a tool for learning; (4) activities for teaching the writing process; and (5) research on reading/writing relationships. The chapter does not deal with the language experience approach to beginning reading—a topic in itself—but rather with ways to use writing in content area learning.

Writing to Learn in Perspective

Generally, we think of talking and writing as ways to communicate. Equally important and much less obvious, however, is the fact that we use language to figure out the world and explain it to ourselves. For ample evidence, listen to the barrage of questions asked by any normal preschooler and the way the child rehearses learnings orally, sometimes while playing with toys or drifting off to sleep. In other words, whenever we use talk or writing for *learning*—as opposed to communication—the main audience is ourselves, not somebody else.

We need to remember that although writing is "frozen talk," it differs from speech. A typical conversation disappears at the moment of utterance, whereas writing remains. Talk uses gestures and intonation, whereas writing depends on textual cues. In speech, the context is shared by speaker and listener and the speaker usually gets abundant feedback—nods, frowns, yawns, and verbal responses—about intended meanings. In writing, however, context must be created, and the writer may get little, if any, feedback from readers. All of these differences help to explain why a transcript of conversation is often barely intelligible as a written document. They also suggest that writing builds upon a foundation in oral language but goes beyond talk in its cognitive demands.

Both of these points anchor the main idea of this chapter, namely, that writing-to-learn activities demand that teachers avoid the role of judge, examiner, or language guardian. Writing to learn means *engaging in* learning, not merely jumping academic hoops to achieve a grade or move on to another assignment. Given the bottom-line purpose of writing-to-learn activities, the most helpful attitude for us as teachers is one of support—acknowledging student effort, answering questions, and giving friendly encouragement.

On occasion, of course, it *is* important to respond fully and thoughtfully to a student's best efforts, providing helpful, constructive feedback as outlined by Charles Duke in Chapter 11. However, for purposes of writing to learn, students should do much more writing than we have the time or inclination to read, and we should control our impulses to deal with spelling, punctuation, or other skills. Such restraint does not mean we are "soft" on skills. Indeed, skill-focused teaching can be fully integrated into the writing process activities discussed later in this chapter.

The point is that fluency and thinking should be the guiding purposes as we use writing to enhance learning. Why? Because little genuine involvement in writing occurs when students are fearful about putting their ideas down on paper. More specifically, students need to be fluent on a scribal level (handwriting), on a syntactic level (making and transcribing sentences), and on an ideational level (generating connected discourse). We choke off the development of fluency in writing-to-learn activities when we focus on usage, punctuation, and spelling.

So much for general context. Let us now deal with reading/writing relationships—more specifically, how writing serves as a tool for learning whenever we read. Think about your own experiences with notetaking and expressive writing (for example, writing to a close friend to discuss a personal problem) as you consider the following points.

First of all, writing is important in reading instruction because it is thought made visible, a way of monitoring our own mental activity. Whenever we summarize, analyze, or argue with an author, we see our comprehension taking shape phrase by phrase. In other words, writing mirrors cerebral activity and helps us see for ourselves what we know and do not know so that we can clear up our own confusion. Or, as E. M. Forster is reported to have said, "How can I know what I think 'til I see what I say?"

Writing also enhances reading because it helps us *use* the words, sentence patterns, and concepts that we encounter in text, making them our own. Put another way, writing helps us connect what we already know to whatever it is we are trying to learn. Writing is an excellent comprehension activity because it helps us focus our thinking and rehearse concepts. Through such rehearsal, we naturally link main ideas with details and organize our knowledge for better retention. Such linkage is essential for long-term learning.

Finally, writing to learn helps us make new discoveries for ourselves and eventually share those thoughts with others. Writers often report that the act of writing somehow leads to unexpected discoveries and connections—the "Aha!" experience in which insights occur suddenly and surprisingly. One reason for this is that writing forces us to slow down, to sustain sentence after sentence in a connected way. Writing is a highly demanding reading activity because the writer must simultaneously play two roles—composer and reader/responder.

In summary, then, writing represents a real advance in the evolution of our brains, and children speak the truth when they tell us that "writing is hard." Because writing gives us *feedback* on our own thinking, it helps us build readiness for reading as well as monitor our own understanding of text. And because writing can be read, analyzed, and reshaped, it tends to hone our thinking, making it more precise, more integrated, more fully articulate.

Writing Activities That Enhance Reading

To help students make the transition from talk to writing without resorting to worksheet activities, many teachers use brief *dictation exercises* for work on basic writing skills. The content for dictation should center on a self-contained passage, the concepts of which relate to what students are currently reading. In a science context, here is such a dictation exercise on caterpillars:

> A butterfly's eggs hatch in a few days (or even a few hours) into caterpillars. This is called the larvae stage. Because of their big appetites, these caterpillars can do great damage. They often strip leaves down to bare ribs in only a few days.

In a health unit, for younger students a short dictation might deal with one of the four food groups; older students might transcribe the health effects of a single vitamin. In social studies, a dictation might deal with democratic freedoms or some other topic related to class reading.

In dictating a passage, read it through once as a paragraph unit. Then read it sentence by sentence, allowing time for writing. Then read the paragraph a third time, asking students to check their writing as you read. After the dictation, students should compare their transcription with the passage in its original form, either projected on an overhead transparency or photocopied. All differences in spelling, punctuation, and phrasing are noted and checked by students. (Dictation activities can also be done in pairs, with students taking turns reading orally.)

Far from being mere busywork, this type of activity does much to teach certain basics of writing and reading. For one thing, it teaches students to hold sentences in short-term memory, a physiological prerequisite to composing and comprehending. For another, it helps children attend to form, see connections between speech and writing, and concentrate on handwriting. Finally, dictation helps students develop a feel for the structure of text—for example, the signals and cues that tie main ideas to specific details. Judiciously used, dictation works as well today as it did over 2,000 years ago when Greek and Roman teachers first used it.

Another activity, one that teaches content as well as reading and writing skills, is called *sentence combining* (SC). A typical SC exercise consists of short sentences that have been organized narratively or thematically. The task for students is to combine related clusters of sentences into more complex and readable prose. As with dictation, the content of SC exercises should be tied to real classroom content.

Because SC exercises seem like puzzles or games to students, they have become a popular way to enhance reading skills. Instead of merely transcribing sentences, students must interact with them, transforming them to produce coherent meanings. Moreover, SC exercises can often be used as writing starters or springboards, with students using their own ideas to extend the exercise. Here is a sample exercise that deals with butterflies and caterpillars:

1.1 The butterfly has a life cycle.
1.2 The cycle occurs in four stages.

2.1 A female first lays her eggs.
2.2 These eggs number 100 or more.
2.3 They are on the underside of leaves.

3.1 These eggs hatch into larvae.
3.2 The larvae are wiggling.
3.3 The larvae are called *caterpillars.*

4.1 Caterpillars grow fast.
4.2 The caterpillars are wormlike.
4.3 They eat leaves from bushes.
4.4 They eat leaves from trees.

5.1 They store up fat.
5.2 The fat is for their sleep.
5.3 Their sleep is long.

6.1 This sleep is called a "metamorphosis."
6.2 It changes their form.
6.3 The change is from caterpillar.
6.4 The change is to butterfly.

In this exercise, each cluster can be combined to create a more complex sentence. The point of such an activity is to help students explore different ways of saying the same thing and then to choose clear, effective sentences for transcription. Like dictation, SC helps to develop short-term memory and focus attention on the relationships between spoken and written language. Unlike dictation, however, SC demands interaction and problem solving. There are many right answers for good SC exercises just as there are many correct interpretations in text comprehension.

When you create SC exercises for your own classroom, you break sentences down into their kernel (or underlying) structures. The first task is to find a passage in material that you intend to introduce to the class. Here, for example, is a passage from the opening pages of *The Slave Dancer* by Paula Fox (1978), a winner of the Newbery Medal:

> The night air was clear. The air was faintly scented with the aroma of flowers which grew in such profusion inside the walled gardens that belonged to the rich families in our neighborhood. Often I had climbed those walls and peered through the black iron grillework into the great rooms of their houses or looked down into the gardens where, among the beds of flowers, a stone hut had been piled up to shelter the house slaves. (p. 11)

The next task is to "decombine" sentences into their underlying kernel structures. The process is illustrated in the following passage:

> The night air was clear. The air was faintly scented. There was an aroma. The aroma was flowers. They grew in such profusion. They grew inside the gardens. The gardens had walls. The gardens belonged to the rich families. The families lived in our neighborhood. Often I had climbed those walls. I had peered through the grillework. The grillework was black. The grillework was iron. I had peered into the great rooms. The rooms were in their houses. I looked down into the gardens. A stone hut had been piled up there. The hut was to shelter the house slaves.

With the exercise completed, you might invite your students to combine sentences so that the exercise passage sounds better. Students will quickly see that they can delete unnecessary words and rearrange sentence parts to make the description flow. Put the class into small groups to share and compare solutions to the exercise. As a final step, share the author's original passage.

Many students enjoy matching wits with professional writers. The point is that the author's version is one among *many* possibilities. While in no sense is it the "right" answer, it *is* a version that students can learn from, just as they learn from each other. Thus, students are learning about reading and writing simultaneously.

Such a writing activity serves as an excellent prereading motivator. When you introduce stories or books in this way, you will find that students are often eager to know more about the original text. Two or three well-chosen exercises from the same text can create real interest and anticipation. In addition, many students seem to read more carefully after having worked closely with an author's "decombined" sentences.

The fact that SC enhances syntactic fluency is now well established in educational research (Strong, 1986). Moreover, when used at the right time and in the right way, SC seems to improve the quality of student writing. Finally, some studies even indicate that SC improves reading comprehension directly, although the findings in this area are by no means clear at present (Combs, 1977).

A third teacher-directed writing activity that enhances reading is the *fact sheet*. Fact sheets are much like dictation and sentence combining in that they require students to transcribe and transform given information. Typically, fact sheets emerge from class discussions about reading that students have done.

For example, students might work in teams to research information about unit topics. As a research group, students could make lists of key facts, item by item. After fact sheets are set up, students combine related facts into sentences and then arrange those sentences into paragraphs. Here is a typical fact sheet on whales:

Fact Sheet: Whales

are among the most intelligent animals
have no ears
use sound signals to communicate
use sound signals to navigate
are the largest living creatures
strain plankton from the seawater
are mammals
can sometimes be found in fresh water
have voices
may become extinct
have teeth
eat fish
have fishlike bodies
have paddleshaped flippers
range in size from the porpoise to the blue whale
can hold their breath for up to two hours

are insulated by a layer of blubber, or fat
are aquatic animals
have lungs, not gills
have horizontal tail fins, unlike fish
are different from fish
have thick, smooth skin
can dive to depths of 4,800 feet
do not see very well
range from 4 feet to 100 feet in length
are social animals
may weigh as much as 150 tons
cannot smell
have nose openings, or blow holes, atop their heads
are hunted for oils in their bodies
live in all the world's oceans (Strong, 1986, p. 41)

Depending on grade level, practice with fact sheets can be set up as a series of challenges. For example, fourth graders of differing ability might work with the following challenges:

1. Use 5 facts in no more than 4 sentences.
2. Use 10 facts in no more than 6 sentences.
3. Use 15 facts in no more than 8 sentences.
4. Use 20 facts in no more than 10 sentences.
5. Use 25 facts in no more than 12 sentences.

So far, we have discussed three types of skill-building activities, all of which help students acquire some degree of fluency. But it is important to remember that however cleverly devised such exercises may be, they are not real writing. With real writing, we figure out something to say and how to say it.

This caveat brings us to a popular, virtually no-fail way to use writing as a tool for improved comprehension. The technique is known as the *writing journal* or *learning log.*

Writing as a Tool for Learning

With learning logs, students write expressively (i.e., using their own voices, not trying to please the teacher) about whatever topic is being introduced, reviewed, or discussed. This is writing done strictly for the sake of learning, not writing that is graded or corrected by the teacher.

In other words, log entries are a way of thinking on paper about subject matter (and reading) in a variety of situations: (a) at the beginning of class or when a new unit is being introduced; (b) during class when the teacher needs to focus attention or raise questions; and (c) at the end of class or at the close of a unit of study when it is important to consolidate, summarize, and evaluate.

With a question log, for example, students write personal questions about a topic being studied. Students are encouraged to ask whatever *they* would like to know. Here is a typical entry from Lynda Chittenden's class of fourth- and fifth-graders who participated in a year-long program of reading and writing about whales:

> I'd like to know how a whale is related to a porpoise. When does a whale come to the breeding ground, when does it leave and where does it live after? Also a whale at Marineland had two kids and they both died. I want to know if she has a problem. How does a whale find a mate? What is the whale with the horn? What is the horn for? (Chittenden, 1982, p. 36)

On the other hand, a reflection log invites students to make sense of their reading, class discussion, or other experiences. Students are encouraged to use their real voices in making sense of their classroom activities. Here a student from Chittenden's class reflects on a field trip to Marineland:

> What I learned about marine mammals is: baby whales, when they are born, they do not have any teeth. I never knew killer whales could be so big. I never knew dolphins were so intelligent. I never knew sea lions could be so huge in a small amount of time and I never knew that a female sea lion could be so much like a male guarding his property. (Chittenden, 1982, p. 40)

Ungraded log entries of this kind provide evidence of a student's ability to observe, generalize, and inquire. They also suggest the student's level of involvement. In Chittenden's class, students used their logs to clarify and deepen their knowledge about whales. They eventually wrote and published their own book, *Our Friends in the Waters.*

Different reading situations will prompt different assignments for learning logs. But whether you ask students to raise personal questions, reflect, summarize, or make judgments in their logs, stress the idea of being honest. Tell children that their thinking matters. Talk about "heroes" and "heroines" of thinking. Emphasize how much you value people who think for themselves about their reading.

You can encourage involvement by emphasizing the *fun* of learning logs—the reader's chance to talk back to an author, a classmate, the teacher, or even himself or herself. As you share logs in class or read them for insight into students' reading processes, praise students for using their heads. Respect differing viewpoints. Encourage creativity and personal engagement in learning. Be positive in any marginal responses, and *never make corrections*. If you correct or grade learning logs, you will quickly ruin the activity.

Properly introduced and used, expressive writing of this kind is fun for students. In fact, many elementary school teachers report that their students come to regard log time as a favorite activity in the school day. No gimmicks or story starters are required. The key is to be genuinely interested in what the students write about their reading.

One format for logs that has worked well in many classrooms is the dialogue journal (Berthoff, 1981). Students work either with 8 1/2- by 11-inch sheets of paper divided into two columns or with spiral-bound notebooks with left- and right-facing pages. The class should be taught how to take traditional notes from their reading on the left side and "make meanings" about their notes on the right side. The left side provides an objective record of key points; the right side is where students think about and comment on what they have read. These comments can be memories, questions, or thoughts about the significance of the reading.

Whatever strategy you use, remember that log entries provide material for discussion: "How many of us agree with Jason's idea? That was interesting, wasn't it? Are there other interpretations of the reading? Okay, Jenny, let's hear your log entry." As you allow students to share their writing-to-learn log entries in an attentive environment, invite productive discussion and rereadings of the text that support your content objectives.

Logs can also help students process information in creative, personal formats such as stories, poems, and plays. Although the content of such writing may come from a science textbook, its literary *form* is what is being read and enjoyed in language arts—in this case, a play. The example that follows is an illustration used by Jane Hansen (1987) in her wise and useful book, *When Writers Read.* The student text is drawn from Margaret Kolbjornsen's fifth-grade class, which was working on blood circulation.

A Day at School by Jacob Michaels

Character list
Chub: white blood cell
Carrier: red blood cell
Clot: platelet
Ms. Hearty
Mr. Stomach

One day Ms. Hearty said to her class, "Today we'll tell Mr. Stomach what we want to be when we grow up. Chub, you go first."

"I want to be a policeman and kill those nasty germs."

Carrier said, "I want to be a mailman and bring food and oxygen to all the other cells with my friend Blood."

"I want to be a repairman and fix all the cuts," said Clot.

Then Ms. Hearty said, "Very good. Class dismissed." (Hansen, 1987, p. 147)

Besides rehearsing learning, logs help students verbalize their unvoiced questions. Students are often quite willing to ask questions on paper that they would hesitate to ask aloud in class. Once questions have been written in logs—and once the sharing of logs becomes a regular part of class routines—students become more confident about disclosing what their difficulties are in processing information.

Learning logs can be used in all curriculum areas. If students write expressively about how to do long division—explaining the steps to a younger audience—the process is likely to be more fully internalized. If students write letters from a figure from history, that person is sure to come alive. If students imaginatively "become" various foods and write about nutritional value, a routine health unit suddenly becomes fun. Such assignments help to *personalize* learning.

Here is a helpful, generic list of writing-to-learn strategies. Try these ideas when designing units of instruction or planning day-to-day lessons.

1. *Diagnosis.* Find out what children already know (and don't know) about a topic: "Tomorrow we start a new unit on ______________. Write down whatever you already know about ______________."
2. *Notetaking.* Help the class gather information by taking notes and making notes about subject matter: "Draw a line down the center of your paper. On the left side, take notes on the important ideas you read in this chapter. On the right side, make a personal note about each recorded note. In other words, react to, rephrase, respond to, question, or associate the ideas with something you know."
3. *Prediction.* Encourage students to predict what will happen next in the text: "Now that you have read about ______________, what do you need to know next? What do you think will come next in the chapter?"
4. *Summarizing.* Invite youngsters to paraphrase, translate, or rephrase the text: "There are 10 sections in this chapter. After receiving a number from one to 10, put that section of the chapter in your own words. Tomorrow we will share what we learned."
5. *Freewriting.* Help children associate images, events, ideas, or personal experience with subject matter: "When you think of the Declaration of Independence, what do you see: images, events, ideas, or even a personal experience that reminds you of that time in our history?"
6. *Definition.* Assist students in defining concepts or ideas about subject matter: "In your own words, define the terms in bold print found in the second section of this chapter."
7. *Evaluation.* Promote reactions or responses to texts or discussions. "Take the last 5 minutes of class to write down the most important ideas for you in our discussion."
8. *Application.* Assign the class to create problems to be solved with

subject matter: "Make up a word problem for a real-life situation that requires the use of fractions."

9. *Personalizing.* Encourage children to apply the subject matter to their own lives: "After reading about the moon, tell what you think it would be like to visit it."
10. *Recording.* Ask youngsters to narrate their observations and reactions: "Tell what happened on the field trip and your personal reactions at various points."
11. *Questioning.* Invite questions about what the text or discussion means or how the parts of the topic relate: "List at least three things in Chapter 12 that aren't clear to you. Or write down two questions you would like to ask the author."
12. *Dialogue.* Have students talk on paper with the teacher or another student about a topic or idea: "Choose a friend and write your understanding of (and your questions about) using quotation marks."
13. *Imagination.* Assign children to invent a role (or language) that characterizes the subject matter or person under study: "Write Lincoln's diary entry the night before he wrote the Gettysburg address to show what he was thinking about."
14. *Analysis.* Help the class analyze a topic or their reactions to it: "List the images you see in this poem and try to figure out how they relate to one another."

Judy Self (1987) has provided other strategies that you will find helpful in planning your lessons.

Let us consider for a moment how learning logs might be adapted to out-of-class reading assignments. Instead of assigning traditional book reports, invite students to go *inside* their books in imaginative ways. In their logs, for example, students might describe an experience they have had that was like one in the book. They might pretend that they are a character whose task it is to introduce other characters. They might make up five interview questions (with answers) for the main character. They might pretend they are the book's author and explain why they chose the book's title. They might create a book jacket to sell the book to other readers.

Learning-log tasks of this kind engage students. For example, in keeping diaries for animal characters in E. B. White's *Charlotte's Web* (1952), students assume a "voice" and find themselves making *predictions* about what happens next in the book. Their reading (or listening) is enhanced because their emotional involvement is heightened.

As an aid to reading comprehension, then, ungraded writing-to-learn activities help children develop *fluency* in written expression. It is a central tenet of modern writing instruction that before children can make progress with the technical skills of writing, they must have frequent occasion to use language functionally and purposefully. Writing-to-learn activities such as those described here provide the foundation for closer study of writing in the upper grades.

Activities for Teaching the Writing Process

We have seen that writing-to-learn activities help students personalize and integrate their reading experiences. The companion approach is one that emphasizes writing as a process. With this approach, students often draw upon learning logs as source material. However, their ultimate aim is to communicate with a broader audience in more public and conventional ways such as stories, essays, reports, or poems.

Central to the idea of writing as a process is the concept of children working together in small groups. This is because children in small groups provide real, live, responding audiences for one another. Working in groups helps children see that what is clear to them may not always be clear to others. Constructive response provides content suggestions and encouragement for making changes. And finally, peer response takes pressure off the teacher to be the sole judge and arbiter of writing quality.

To help students work productively in small groups, begin by emphasizing positive comments. Over a period of several days or even weeks, ask the class to focus on short pieces of text from reading assignments, the local newspaper, or class writing folders. Volunteer your own work for these sessions, and you will find that children soon follow suit. After a selection is read aloud, have students write down one or two things they liked about the piece. In your own modeling, try to point to specific features of the text that made it effective: vivid images, use of dialogue, interesting facts, and so on.

As these sessions evolve, ask students to raise questions they have about a piece. Encourage them to point out specifically where they had trouble following the text. Direct them to summarize the message of the writing in a single sentence. Question them about the purpose and audience for the writing. Have them point to words that "don't sound quite right." Ask them to make suggestions on how a piece might be rearranged. Practice writing lead sentences for text that opens slowly. Such training does much to develop skills of critical reading; equally important, it helps students help one another—and themselves—when writing. Through such modeling, you develop a reading/writing connection.

Before students work in peer response groups, be sure to model the process and discuss guidelines for response. Response groups of four work best when each writer prepares photocopies or carbon copies of a draft. If this is not possible in your classroom, you can put students in groups of three, with the writer in the center and responders sitting to each side, following the text as it is read aloud. The following guidelines have worked well with many students in elementary school:

How to Get Feedback on Writing

1. Read your work aloud twice.
2. Don't defend your work.
3. Take notes on what others tell you.
4. Ask questions to clarify what others say.
5. Thank people for their comments.
6. Never apologize for the piece you are going to read.

How to Give Feedback on Writing

1. Listen for the overall effect in the first reading.
2. Make notes and comments during the second reading.
3. Tell what you liked best about the writing.
4. Identify a place in the writing that may need work.
5. Comment on content and organization first, then mechanics.
6. Be specific by pointing to places on the actual page.

Move around the room as groups work. Be alert to problems such as insensitive criticism or misbehavior, and reinforce students for responding effectively to the work of others. You may want responders to write out their responses before amplifying them orally. Typically, this is more important at the beginning stages of response groups than later on. Skilled teachers set time limits for group work (10 minutes per paper) and conclude response group sessions by asking writers to draft their plans for revising.

Try to develop checklists in advance for your response groups and conferences. Say, for example, that your class has been reading fables and has begun writing them. Working with the class, you might spend some time developing a list of general features (or criteria) for fables, as in the following example:

Writing a Fable

1. The characters are animals with human qualities.
2. The story has some kind of problem or conflict.
3. The story is told to make a point (moral).
4. The moral comes at the end of the fable.
5. The animals may talk to one another in the fable.
6. The fable is usually short (one page or so) and fun to read.

With such a checklist made public, you would have a good framework for prewriting and response group activities. In prewriting discussions, students could list animals and conflicts that might form the basis for narrative; then they could think about the moral they wanted to teach. Oral storytelling or creative dramatics might follow, with students working from notes and trying out their ideas on classmates.

After written drafts had been developed, students could use the six criteria to evaluate their work. Each element in the checklist might be followed by a three-point rating scale, with 3 designating *excellent,* 2 designating *good,* and 1 designating *work on this.* The checklist would form a "scaffold" for thinking, helping students to read their own fables (and the fables of others) more carefully. As a result of close, thoughtful reading and time allocated for revision, some well-crafted fables—the kind of work that students are excited to share—could be expected.

To help children think analytically, teachers in the Writing Project at the University of California-Irvine have developed frameworks for prewriting (Olson, 1984). In a typical unit, children write persuasive letters with certain explicit elements such as those shown in the following list and develop reasons in support of their arguments.

Writing a Persuasive Letter

1. Clearly state what you want and why.
2. Use a tone suited to your audience.
3. Predict three possible objections your audience might have.
4. Meet those objections with logical arguments.
5. Follow the standard letter form of greeting, body, and closing.

As students learn to work with such elements in writing, they become better able to understand them in their reading.

To teach writing as a process, you might take children through a modeling activity, one designed to teach certain writing and thinking skills. For example, on the blackboard you might set up a four-part framework for thinking as part of a class brainstorming activity. *Who* would designate *audience*; *What* would designate the *desired goal*; *Objections against* would designate *possible reactions of the audience*; and *Arguments for* would designate *reasoning of the persuader.*

Role playing could easily become part of this prewriting activity, with pairs of students trying on two roles. On lined paper, one student writes: "Mom, would you let me take three friends to Farrells for my birthday?" The partner responds, "No, it's too expensive." Papers are passed back and forth as students rehearse both objections and arguments. After this activity, the chart could be filled in, using the contributions of the entire class. Such a framework could later be used independently by children as they each develop persuasive letters on their own topics.

Another aspect of prewriting instruction is written models. For the assignment just described, you might have students analyze a model, both to teach letter format and to analyze tone or judge effectiveness. Note that the following model states what is wanted and why, gives three possible objections, argues persuasively against those objections, and provides a closing summary:

Dear Mom,

This year I would like to have my birthday party at Farrells with three of my best friends. I've always wanted to go to Farrells because they sing "Happy Birthday" and play the big drum if you tell them it's your birthday.

I know that you probably will think it will be too expensive, but it really won't be because I will pay for my friends' ice cream with my allowance. You won't need to give me any extra money because my ice cream will be free just because it's my birthday. That's why everyone likes to go to Farrells on their birthday.

You might not know where there is a Farrells and be worried about driving with kids in the car. Guess what? There is a Farrells just two blocks from school. We could walk and meet you there.

I hope you will think about my idea and say "yes." The only thing I really want for my birthday is to have a party at Farrells. Please let me know what you decide.

Love,

Molly

Reading such a model would help students think more carefully about their own approaches to persuasive letter writing.

Conferencing regularly with children on pieces they have decided to revise provides a context for content suggestions and for work on individual skills. It is through conferences that you can collaborate with students rather than judge them. As noted earlier, Charles Duke deals with the subject of conferencing in Chapter 11.

To make conferences work, try to adapt open-ended questions such as these to your grade level: What do you like best about this piece so far? Where are you having trouble? What are your goals for this piece? Who is the audience? Why did you make these changes? How would you like me to help you today? What changes have you made so far in this piece? Which skill will you practice next? For in-depth discussions on the conference approach, refer to *Writing: Teachers and Children at Work* by Donald Graves (1983), *The Art of Teaching Writing* by Lucy Calkins (1986), or *In the Middle* by Nancie Atwell (1987).

Through good conferences, students come to see that printed text permits us to rework and revise our ideas until we get the meanings right. Also, because text exists apart from us, it may have many audiences, including ourselves, and many purposes. When writing is used to communicate to a broader, public audience, a writer must think about the needs and purposes of the readers being addressed. Conferencing helps children understand that writing is a kind of conversation in which the writer plays two roles—speaker *and* listener. Emphasize that although one can read without writing, it is impossible to write without reading.

Process approaches to writing inevitably point toward publication—putting work in final form and sharing it with others. Many elementary school teachers develop an Author's Corner where work is made public and celebrated. In the Author's Corner, the writer reads aloud while the class listens and finally applauds. Then the writer's book is made part of the classroom library for the school year.

As children develop feelings of pride about their experiences in the Author's Corner, they become part of what Frank Smith has called a "Literacy Club" (1988, p. 214). They develop a personal commitment to reading, writing, and thinking. And that, of course, is a goal we all seek as teachers.

Research on Reading/Writing Relationships

"It sounds good in theory," you may be thinking to yourself, "but do writing-to-learn and writing-as-process activities really pay off in terms of measurable improvements in reading comprehension?"

Paula Fleming, who used writing in a reading improvement program with second- and fourth-graders at Petersborough Elementary School in New Hampshire, gives one answer to that question. Meeting with students for four 1-hour sessions each week for a year, Fleming introduced a program of daily writing. About 40 to 60 minutes each week were devoted to oral reading by the teacher; students then discussed specific elements that made a selection interesting or effective.

The writing program was open-ended, with students invited to work on self-sponsored topics and then conference with their teacher. Children worked in small groups to get feedback when they decided to publish a piece for the class and school library. Other forms of publication included radio broadcasts, gifts, bulletin boards, letters home, newspapers, and public readings for adult and peer audiences.

While strict experimental control conditions were not observed, the results were impressive. On an individually administered reading test, The Diagnostic Reading Scales (1981), the average gain in oral reading was 16 months for second-graders and 32.7 months for fourth-graders. The average gain in silent reading was 19.7 months for second-graders and 13.7 months for fourth-graders (Fleming, 1982). Needless to say, both teachers and parents were very pleased.

What about other studies? In a comprehensive review of research on reading/writing relationships, Sandra Stotsky concluded that

> almost all studies that used writing activities or exercises specifically to improve reading comprehension or retention of information in instructional materials found significant gains. Depending on the length and type of study, the gains

varied from better recall of specific material read to improved scores on standardized reading tests or achievement tests in academic subjects. (1983, p. 636)

SUMMARY

In a world of gimmicks, skillbuilders, and quick-fix solutions to problems of literacy, writing seems to work. Used intelligently, it helps children read and learn. Neglecting to use writing as a tool for learning—or subverting its potential with overly fussy standards for learning-log activities—would mean returning to the Dark Ages of literacy instruction.

FOLLOW-UP QUESTIONS AND ACTIVITIES

1. This chapter may have stirred memories of positive or negative school experiences. Did any of your teachers use writing as a tool for learning? Did any of them use writing to discipline the class? How do your present attitudes toward writing grow out of your school experiences? Discuss.
2. Without rereading, jot down several key words, phrases, or ideas from this chapter. Now, using words or phrases from your list, develop a paragraph that summarizes the chapter in your own words. Reorder items in the list and add your own thoughts as you write.
3. Swap paragraphs with a friend and read what he or she has written. Find what you regard as the best or most interesting line in your friend's paragraph. Underline it. Then write in the margin why you like this line or find it interesting. Mention what the line made you think of as a reader. Give the paragraph back to the author.
4. Read what your friend has written about your writing. How do the comments *feel* to you? Do they cause you to think more about the chapter? Discuss your reactions to these comments with your friend. How do these comments compare with ones you received on other school papers? So what?

ADDITIONAL READINGS

Graves, D. (1983). *Writing: Teachers and children at work.* Portsmouth, NH: Heinemann.

Hansen, J. (1987). *When writers read.* Portsmouth, NH: Heinemann.

Klein, M. L. (1985). *The development of writing in children: Pre-K through grade 8.* Englewood Cliffs, NJ: Prentice-Hall.
Mason, J. (1989). *Reading and writing connections.* Newton, MA: Allyn and Bacon.
Watson, D. J. (1987). *Ideas and insights: Language arts in the elementary school.* Urbana, IL: National Council of Teachers of English.

REFERENCES

Atwell, N. (1987). *In the Middle: Writing, reading, and learning with adolescents.* Portsmouth, NH: Heinemann.
Berthoff, A. (1981). *The making of meaning.* Upper Montclair, NJ: Boynton/Cook.
Calkins, L. M. (1986). *The art of teaching writing.* Portsmouth, NH: Heinemann.
Chittenden, L. (1982). What if all the whales are gone before we become friends? In M. Barr, P. D'Arcy, & M. K. Healy (Eds.), *What's going on: Language/learning episodes in British and American classrooms* (pp. 36–51). Upper Montclair, NJ: Boynton/Cook.
Combs, W. E. (1977). Sentence-combining practice aids reading comprehension. *Journal of Reading, 21,* 18–24.
Diagnostic Reading Scales. (1981). Monterey, CA: CTB/McGraw-Hill.
Durkin, D. (1978). What classroom observations reveal about reading comprehension instruction. *Reading Research Quarterly, 10,* 481–533.
Fleming, P. (1982). The write way to read. In T. Newkirk & N. Atwell (Eds.), *Understanding writing: Ways of observing, learning and teaching* (pp. 93–100). Chelmsford, MA: Northeast Regional Exchange.
Fox, P. (1978). *The slave dancer.* New York: Dell.
Goodlad, J. (1984). *A place called school.* New York: McGraw-Hill.
Graves, D. (1978). *A two-year case study observing the effects of primary children's composing, spelling, and motor behaviors during the writing process.* Unpublished proposal submitted to the National Institute of Education.
Graves, D. (1983). *Writing: Teachers and children at work.* Portsmouth, NH: Heinemann.
Hansen, J. (1987). *When writers read.* Portsmouth, NH: Heinemann.
Olson, C. B. (1984). *Thinking/writing units.* Unpublished curriculum materials developed at the Writing Project, University of California-Irvine.
Rosenshine, B., & Berliner, D. (1978). Academic engaged time. *British Journal of Teacher Education, 4,* 3–16.
Self, J. (1987). The picture of writing to learn. In J. Self (Ed.), *Plain talk about learning and writing across the curriculum* (pp. 16–17). Richmond, VA: Virginia Department of Education.
Smith, F. (1988). *Understanding reading* (4th ed.). Hillsdale, NJ: Erlbaum.
Strong, W. (1986). *Creative approaches to sentence combining.* Urbana, IL: National Council of Teachers of English and The ERIC Clearinghouse on Reading and Communication Skills.
Stotsky, S. (1983). Research on reading/writing relationships: A synthesis and suggested directions. *Language Arts, 60,* 627–642.
White, E. B. (1952). *Charlotte's web.* New York: Harper & Row.

PART TWO

Effective Evaluation and Diagnosis and Reading Instruction

Part Two looks at issues of how to assess individual students' reading and writing ability intelligently and efficiently so that effective teachers can provide appropriate instruction for them. Chapter 9 looks at how teachers can use informal reading inventories, cloze tests, observations, and other informal measures to determine children's instructional needs. Chapter 10 discusses how to interpret standardized reading test scores correctly. Recognizing the importance of writing and its relationship to reading instruction, Chapter 11 concludes Part Two with a discussion of guidelines for effective evaluation of the writing process.

9

Informal Measures of Reading

PEGGY E. RANSOM LINDA L. SNYDER

IN CHAPTER 9, Peggy Ransom and Linda Snyder discuss informal measures of reading ability. Informal measures are different from the formal measures to be discussed in Chapter 10. The assessment measures presented in this chapter are not standardized, and they do not include formal procedures for administration and scoring. Teachers will usually focus on the number and kind of correct and incorrect responses a student makes on these tests. In many cases, these tests may be constructed by teachers rather than by commercial test publishers.

Ransom and Snyder present an overview of five different means for informally measuring reading: the informal reading inventory, the cloze test, focused observation, work samples, and teacher-made diagnostic tests. They remind us that informal measures are essential for effective instruction. They form the basis of sound instructional decisions that effective teachers must make daily by aiding them in matching students with appropriate materials and by focusing on specific, rather than global, aspects of reading.

STUDY QUESTIONS

1. How can you identify a student's independent, instructional, and frustration reading levels?
2. When teaching, how can you record the miscues made by students when they are reading?
3. How are a cloze test and an informal inventory alike? How are they different?
4. What is meant by *focused observations* for an individual student?
5. What are the values of informal measures?

When used in combination, and in addition to more formal measures, informal measures can provide a wealth of useful information about student performance. The term *informal* means that the instruments used are not standardized, norm-referenced tests; that is, they do not have formal procedures for administration and scoring and do not report scores in percentiles or stanines to compare one student to a normative population. Informal tests are usually constructed by teachers, although some are produced commercially, and they may be given throughout the year to individuals or groups for specific instructional purposes and for continuous evaluation (Vacca, Vacca, & Gove, 1987).

Value of Informal Measures

Aid in Instructional Decision Making

Although many fine commercial reading tests are available, teachers often make their best professional judgments through careful, structured observations of pupils and use of informal procedures they make up themselves (Ransom & Patty, 1984). Any reading assessment, along with a teacher's professional judgment, should lead to informed instructional decisions. Two of the major areas in which informal measures may assist in instructional decision making are (1) determining students' instructional reading levels so that they are assigned to basal readers or content textbooks of appropriate difficulty and (2) identifying specific reading skill strengths and weaknesses so corrective instruction can be provided whenever necessary.

Graded paragraphs—reading selections determined to be at certain reading levels—might be used to estimate the reading levels of students when they transfer from school to school or at the beginning of the school year. Also, checking the match between students' reading levels and content area textbooks will point out the need to make adjustments in assignments or select alternate materials. The following simple rule of thumb can help children select trade books at their independent level: If a child misses five or more words on a page, the chances are that the book is too difficult. Children can be taught to practice this quick check when selecting books for recreational reading.

Validity and Reliability

The more behavior samples a teacher collects, the more likely the assessment is to be reliable. Informal assessments are often more valid measures than standardized reading tests because they employ a wide variety of procedures to assess reading performance over a number of different occasions (Farr & Carey, 1986). Teachers need to check not only students' knowledge of specific aspects of the reading process but also their functional ability to apply their reading skills to various tasks. In addition to monitoring the development of basic reading skills, teachers can also pick up a great deal of information about students' attitudes toward reading, their reading interests, their levels of concentration and perseverance, and other important areas by conducting informal assessments.

Availability

Informal measures are always available, since teachers can construct tests or employ procedures as needs arise. Of course, the quality of the informal measures will depend on the teacher's competency in selecting, designing, implementing, and evaluating them (Lapp & Flood, 1983). Informal measures are readily available for collecting usable information every day.

Informal Measures and Procedures

Informal Reading Inventories

One popular informal diagnostic instrument that is effective and easily obtained or constructed is the informal reading inventory (IRI). Generally, an inventory consists of a series of graded word lists, graded passages, and comprehension questions. Its purpose is to determine how students interact with print when reading orally or silently and to help place students in materials of appropriate difficulty.

Although IRIs are designed to be administered individually, they may also be adapted and used as silent group reading tests for purposes of screening or initial placement when other information is not available. The questions must be rewritten in a multiple-choice format and duplicated for each student, along with a copy of the reading selections, before an inventory can be used for group assessment.

IRI is useful in determining a student's independent, instructional, and frustration levels, commonly called *functional reading levels*. The independent level is considered to be the level at which a student can read successfully with little or no assistance, while the instructional level is the one at which students can learn with the teacher's guidance. The frustration level is to be avoided at all times, because students cannot be expected to read and learn from materials that frustrate them. If a student misses one out of every ten words and is unable to answer at least three out of four comprehension questions over a short selection, then reading material at that level is clearly too difficult.

Constructing an IRI

Although commercial inventories are available, teachers should know how to construct their own using selections from a basal reading series. This is accomplished through the following steps:

1. Duplicate passages of 100 to 200 words from each level of the graded basals.
2. Randomly select 10 to 20 words from each passage and put in list form.
3. Develop at least five comprehension questions for each passage. Include questions of various types such as vocabulary, main idea, details, cause/effect, and sequence. Avoid questions that could be answered without reading, those that would require a simple yes or no response, or those that demand excessive recall of detail. Be sure

to include higher-level thinking ability questions as well as literal questions.

4. When it comes time to administer an IRI, approach the task in a positive manner by explaining to students the purpose for the assessment. Students should understand that the assessment will provide information to help them succeed in reading.

Administering an Oral IRI

Although exact procedures are provided in published inventory manuals, the following steps are commonly recommended and can be used with teacher-made IRIs. Teachers who have not administered several inventories before should tape record the oral reading. This will enable them to go back and check their skill in coding.

1. Start with the graded word lists and proceed until a student misses five or more words in one list. Code incorrect responses for later analysis.
2. Have the student begin reading the graded paragraphs at the highest level of the word lists at which he or she scored 100%. Code any word recognition errors as the student reads. (If graded word lists are not used, begin paragraph reading two grade levels below the student's grade placement.)

Oral reading errors may also be called *miscues,* since both terms describe a difference between what a student reads and what is printed on the page. Although the teacher will not count all of these in scoring to determine a student's reading level, all errors or miscues the student makes while reading orally should be recorded. (See examples in Figure 9.1.)
The following coding system may be used:

1. *Omission:* Circle the omitted word or words.
2. *Substitution:* Write the substituted word above the one missed.
3. *Insertion:* Use a caret and write the inserted word.
4. *Help:* Write "H" and supply the needed word if the student pauses for more than 5 seconds.
5. *Mispronunciation:* Record the incorrect response above the word missed.
6. *Reversal:* Mark over and under reversed letters and words.
7. *Repetition:* Draw a wavy line under repeated words.
8. *Correction:* Write "C" next to self-corrections.

Scoring and Analysis

Determining Reading Levels Only the first five miscues listed should be counted to determine reading levels. Later, the teacher should analyze all

FIGURE 9.1 Coded Miscues on an IRI

How Teacher Marks Miscues	Explanation of Miscues
Not Really a Nut	(Count Only Numbered Miscues When Scoring)
It may come as a surprise, but a	
peanut is not really a nut at all. It	
looks like a nut, and it tastes like a nut,	1. insertion
but it is really the seed of a plant which	
belongs to the pea family. After a	
peanut plant attains a certain height,	2. substituted attaches
shoots from the stem grow longer and	3. insertion
longer. Eventually they bend downward	4. pronounced word for student (omitted -ward)
and push into the earth. Underground,	
a shell develops and encloses each seed,	5. substituted includes
or peanut. That's why people in some	(repeated phrase)
other countries call the peanut a ground-	
nut.	
Roasted peanuts are a popular and	6. omitted words
nutritious snack, and they are also made	7. Help—pronounced word for student
into peanut butter, candy, and other	
foods. In addition, parts of peanuts are	(Self-correction)
used to make some cosmetics, plastics,	
soap, and explosives.	8. mispronunciation
The nut that is not a nut is a very	(insertion—meaning not changed)
interesting and useful plant!	Reversal

miscues—including repetitions and self-corrections—to make some judgments about the quality or significance of the miscues.

Although slightly different percentages have been suggested by various educators, Table 9.1 contains commonly used criteria to help teachers determine estimated reading levels from an informal reading inventory. Of course, the reader's background knowledge and interest in the topic must also be considered in interpreting scores and making judgments about reading levels.

TABLE 9.1 Informal Reading Inventory Criteria

Level	*Word Recognition (%)*	*Comprehension (%)*
Independent	99	90
Instructional	90	75
Frustration	Below 90	Below 75

Analyzing Miscues According to Goodman (1973), students do not make random errors. Instead, they use many clues in their attempts to construct meaning from the printed page. Grapho-phonic (letters and sounds), semantic (meaning vocabulary), and syntactic (grammar, word order) clues are used in combination during effective reading. By analyzing the kinds of miscues made by students, teachers can gain valuable insights into their knowledge of language and the strategies they use while reading. In particular, it is important to note *self-corrections* (which show that the student is monitoring his or her reading and is using available clues); *substitutions* (which give an indication of the graphic and phonic clues the student uses, indicating comprehension monitoring if meaning is intact or lack of comprehension monitoring if meaning is affected); and *help* (which shows that the student lacks confidence to try, has inadequate sight vocabulary or decoding strategies, or is unable to make predictions while reading).

Charting miscues according to grapho-phonic, semantic, or syntactic categories will provide the teacher with evidence of the reader's strengths and offer direction for future instruction.

Assessment of Listening Levels

In addition to determining the three functional reading levels, it is a good idea to get a general idea of the student's listening level or potential for reading growth. This provides an indication of how well the child may be able to read if word recognition problems are removed. Such an assessment can be made by reading increasingly difficult graded passages from the IRI to the student and recording his or her responses to comprehension questions. The highest passage at which the student scores at least 75% is the student's listening level. Of course, a listening test would yield only a measure of comprehension, not word recognition skills.

Cloze Tests

A cloze test is another informal means of assessing a student's reading comprehension. The word *cloze* is derived from the principle of closure from Gestalt psychology, and it describes the human tendency to complete a familiar but unfinished pattern. Originally developed by Wilson Taylor in 1953, cloze tests have been widely used to assess the difficulty, or readability level, of a book, to informally measure students' reading comprehension, and as an instructional strategy for comprehension. When it is used as an informal diagnostic measure of reading, the cloze test has several advantages:

1. It is relatively easy to construct, administer, and score.
2. It may be administered to a group.
3. It provides a good measure of students' ability to use contextual clues.
4. Research findings (Bormuth, 1967; DeSanti, 1986) and validity for children over age 8 are impressive.

In a cloze test, words are systematically deleted and replaced with blanks of equal length. The reader's task is to supply the deleted words, using available semantic and syntactic clues along with background knowledge. Correctly replacing deleted words is considered to be an indication of global comprehension. Although commercial tests are available (DeSanti, 1986), cloze tests are easily constructed from basal readers or content texts. Figure 9.2 shows an excerpt from a cloze passage.

Constructing the Cloze Test

The following steps can be used to develop a cloze passage for informal assessment:

1. Select a reading passage of approximately 275 words from material that students have not yet read.
2. Leave the first sentence intact. From the second sentence, randomly select one of the first 5 words. Delete every 5th word thereafter, until 50 deletions have been made. Leave at least one intact sentence at the end of the passage. (For students below grade 4, a deletion system of very 10th word is often recommended.)
3. Make an underlined blank 15 to 20 spaces long for each word deleted. Numbering the blanks is optional.

Administering the Cloze Test

Because students may be unfamiliar with cloze tasks, the following steps are suggested:

1. Explain to the students that they are to try to supply the words that have been deleted. Work through some examples and discuss the necessary thinking processes. Tell the students that spelling errors

FIGURE 9.2 Excerpt from a Cloze Passage, with Answers

Directions: Predict and write a word in each blank that would make sense in the sentences below.

BUSY BEES

All summer long bees are very busy. They fly (1) ________ one flower to another, (2) ________ nectar that they carry (3) ________ to their hives. From (4) ________ nectar, they make honey (5) ________ they store in their (6) ________. This stored honey provides (7) ________ for the bees.

People (8) ________ to eat honey, too. (9) ________ many people raise bees (10) ________ sell the honey the (11) ________ make. But beekeepers leave (12) ________ in the hive for (13) ________ bees to eat during (14) ________ winter. They take the rest and sell it.

Answers to Cloze Passage

1. from
2. gathering
3. back
4. this
5. which
6. hives
7. food
8. like
9. Today
10. and
11. bees
12. enough
13. the
14. the

will not be counted as long as the word is recognizable and that this will not count toward a grade.

2. Suggest that the students read through the entire passage quickly before writing any words. Then they should read it again, this time supplying words for the blanks.
3. Allow the students ample time to complete the cloze passage. This is a challenging task.

Scoring and Interpreting the Cloze Test

Follow these guidelines to score and interpret a cloze test:

1. Count only exact replacements as correct. (You may want to analyze responses later and consider synonyms that might be appropriate, but score only exact replacements when using a cloze test for assessment.)
2. Multiply the number of correct responses (out of 50 possible) by 2 to arrive at a percentage-correct score.
3. Determine approximate reading levels from the percentage of correct responses and record on a sheet of paper the names of students whose scores are within each range. (See Figure 9.3.)
4. You now have from one to three instructional groups to form the basis for differentiated assignments.

The cloze test yields reading levels that are comparable to those from an informal reading inventory. The following guidelines are suggested for interpreting scores:

FIGURE 9.3 Example of Cloze Performance Record

CLOZE PERFORMANCE RECORD

Date ______ Teacher ________________ Period ______

Below 40%	*Between 40% and 60%*	*Above 60%*
Billy	Sam	Randolf
Jennifer	Mike	Juan
Paula	Elaine	Bernie
	Joe	Janelle
	Mary	
	Paul	

Independent Level: A score of 60% or higher indicates that students should be able to read the material with little difficulty and with little guidance. More challenging materials may be appropriate for some of these students.

Instructional Level: A score of 40% to 60% represents the level at which students can be expected to read with guidance and instruction.

Frustration Level: A score below 40% indicates that the material will probably be too difficult for the student. Unless you can provide a great deal of guidance, you should look for materials written at a lower level for students in this group.

Used in combination with other informal measures, the cloze test can be a valuable diagnostic tool.

Observation Procedures

In addition to measures such as informal reading inventories and cloze tests, teacher observations are an important means of gathering information about students' reading. Observations may range from noticing a typical or unusual behavior, to keeping systematic anecdotal records or checklists, to holding personal conferences or interviews with students. Observation plays a powerful role in helping teachers make decisions about how to guide children's development in reading and language. Harris and Smith (1986) have stressed that observation is the single most important element in an evaluation program.

On a daily basis, teachers have countless opportunities to appraise the needs and progress of learners. Teachers' observations can also help to synthesize and confirm what they have found out through other formal and informal measures. Observation may give clues to students' interests, attitudes, and skills. However, since it is impossible to observe everything that happens in the classroom, teachers must decide what to observe about students' reading and language usage. In other words, focused observations are the most beneficial. Taking time to record observations facilitates the job of diagnosing students' strengths, weaknesses, and needs so that the teacher can guide their reading growth more effectively. Being alert to the way students respond to instruction and adapting plans when necessary are important ingredients of effective teaching.

Observing Reading

Interest inventories such as the ones discussed in Chapter 17 or questions such as the following may provide clues to students' attitudes and interests in reading:

- Do you read in your spare time?
- What types of material do you choose?
- Are you interested in books read aloud in class?
- What kind of book do you like to read?
- Which ones do not appeal to you?
- Do you spend money on books?
- Do you borrow books regularly for pleasure reading?

Observations of oral and silent reading behaviors offer additional clues for instructional needs. Excessive head movements, finger pointing along with word-by-word reading, inappropriate rate, inability to maintain attention, and visible signs of tension are often indications that a student finds it difficult to cope with the reading materials or with the situation in general. Likewise, a child who holds a book closer or farther than the normal 12- to 18-inch distance may need to be referred for a vision check.

Although oral reading is often emphasized for beginning readers, the transition to silent reading takes place gradually, over a period of time. Frequent lip movements or vocalization beyond the transition time may suggest that the material is too difficult. This has important implications for instruction.

Likewise, observations during oral reading may signal the need to employ additional measures. Numerous omissions, additions, or substitutions; lack of fluency; or failure to use context may be noted for later checking. Responses to comprehension questions during a directed reading lesson may reveal strengths or weaknesses in predicting, determining main ideas, locating or recalling details, inferring characters' feelings, understanding cause and effect, and essential vocabulary. One way to record these errors is to keep a list of students being instructed in material being used during the day. When a student makes an error, it should be written down with the date. At the end of the day, it becomes apparent that certain students are having the same reading problems. These students are then grouped for additional instruction. Other examples are found later in this chapter under the heading "Recording Observations."

Observing Writing

Topics students write about can provide insight into their interests and experiences. Teachers also can gain valuable insights and information about students' sense of language and vocabulary, as well as the mechanics they use, by observing them as they write. It is said that the more one reads the better one can write; however, as discussed in Chapters 7 and 8, writing can also help students become better readers. Teachers should have students write daily and watch for letter formation, capital letters and punctuation, and sentence structure. Lesson plans can then be developed around what is needed. For instance, if a student in first grade writes "Me sees it," it signals a lack of oral language ability. The student needs to have time to talk with other peers and have the chance to hear books read before the teacher tries to correct the writing. The student does not sense the more mature use of language and needs time for growth.

Older students' writing should provide the teacher with information about the students' sense of the structure of stories and reports, as well as their ability to use different styles of written language. The teacher can read a story to students and then have them write the story. What they leave out is an indication of what they found unimportant or did not understand or remember. It also reveals their knowledge of letters, sounds, and grammar (Mason & Au, 1990). Additional suggestions in this area are offered in Chapter 11.

Recording Observations

Unless teachers use focusing to determine what they are going to observe and develop some recording systems, their observations may be lost in the midst of daily responsibilities.

However, over a period of time, focused observations for an individual or a group can accumulate into a revealing and informative record of learning to read (Vacca et al., 1987). Several practical suggestions for recording observations follow.

Anecdotal Notes

Journals, charts, index cards, memos, or notebooks can help teachers keep observation notes in order and safeguard against the limitations of memory. Keeping an index card for each child is one simple but useful procedure. Memos in the form of a chart are another practical way of keeping anecdotal notes. They can be used in an ongoing, continuous manner to record student activities or behaviors that may be influencing their learning. Figure 9.4 gives an example of a reading observation memo.

Checklists

A more expedient alternative to notes, which are time-consuming, is a checklist that is prepared in chart form. A checklist differs from an observation memo in that it consists of categories that have been identified for specific purposes. The teacher chooses individual items to selectively guide observations. Figures 9.5 and 9.6 are examples of checklists that show how particular groups of students are interacting with a text during a reading lesson. Checklists can help teachers analyze such things as the appropriateness of grouping, students' skills in responding to certain types of questions, or their knowledge of sounds or structural elements of words. They may also point out the need for additional instruction for particular students.

FIGURE 9.4 Reading Observation Memo Form

Observation Memos — Reading

Grade ________ Teacher ______________________ Group ________

NAME	DATE	BEHAVIOR	DATE	BEHAVIOR	DATE	BEHAVIOR
PEGGY	2/14	FREQUENTLY ASKS FOR HELP WITH WORDS	2/26	APPEARS TO NOW ATTEMPT TO UNLOCK NEW WORDS	3/1	DOING WORKSHEETS INDEPENDENTLY
SUSAN	2/14	HAS PROBLEMS USING CONTEXT CLUES	2/27	STILL HESITATES TO USE CONTEXT CLUES	3/1	WORKBOOK - NEEDS HELP FROM OTHERS TO COMPLETE
GEORGE	2/18	READS WELL ORALLY - DOES NOT UNDERSTAND	2/20	SUMMARIZED WELL AFTER SILENT READING	2/27	MUCH BETTER ANSWERING QUESTIONS AFTER READING
LINDA	2/18	VOCABULARY NEEDS IMPROVEMENT	2/20	ATTACKING NEW WORDS WITH SEVERAL APPROACHES	3/2	RECEIVED 98% ON VOCAB. TEST
TIM	2/20	EXTREMELY SHY READING ALOUD	3/1	VOLUNTEERED TO READ ORALLY	3/6	ASKED TO READ A STORY TO THE CLASS

Conducting Student Interviews

A student interview, or a conference between the teacher and individual students, may provide valuable insights about what students think and how they feel about reading, classroom instruction, and themselves as learners.

FIGURE 9.5 Reading Checklist

Reading Group ______________ Grade ________ Date ________

	Name of Lesson	Vocab.	Predict	Summary	Cause-Effect	Sequence	Details
SUSAN	CHILDREN PLAY	X		X		X	X
PEGGY	"		X		X	X	X
GEORGE	"	X		X	X		
LINDA	"	X	X		X	X	
TIM	"	X	X	X	X	X	X

Through interviews, the teacher may develop a better understanding of students' reading interests and attitudes, how they perceive their strengths and weaknesses, and the awareness they have about processes related to language learning.

Questions asked of students can help teachers gain knowledge that will result in improved reading instruction. For instance, if a teacher wanted to know more about certain students and how they perceived reading, he or she might consider asking questions such as the following.

- How did you learn to read? Tell me about it.
- What do you like to read if you get to choose? (If nothing, why not?)
- If you read all by yourself and come to a word you don't know, what do you do?
- What do you do when a person is reading out loud and says a word incorrectly?
- Should the teacher teach you all the new words before you read a story? Why or why not?
- Who do you think is an excellent reader? Why?
- What is reading?

FIGURE 9.6 Reading Skills Checklist

Teacher ______________ Grade ______ Period ______

Name	SUSAN				PEGGY				GEORGE	LINDA	TIM
Date	2/14	2/17	3/10	3/22	2/14	2/17	3/10	3/22			
PREDICTING	X		X	X				X			
SUMMARIZING	X	X		X		X	X				
VOCABULARY		X		X	X			X			
RECALLS DETAILS	X		X	X		X		X			
RELATES EXPERIENCES	X		X		X	X					

Interviews provide a rich source of information. When coupled with observations during teaching, interviews strengthen information from other informal measures of student performance. Moreover, interviews may reveal information that cannot be gleaned from more traditional means of testing (Vacca et al., 1987).

Collecting Work Samples

Analyzing samples of a student's work over a period of time can also be extremely helpful in evaluating that learner informally. Patterns of errors can be detected easily, and progress can also be documented. Teachers might want to collect samples of writing in broad skill areas such as comprehension or word recognition, or in more specific areas, depending on the grade level and the particular situation. One of the simplest ways to collect work samples is to keep a folder for each student. Samples might be collected from each student in the class on a regular basis, or, at other times, the teacher might save a paper that provides particularly important documentation for an individual student. Work samples are also beneficial in communicating students' progress or problems to parents and the school principal.

For instance, Billy has trouble in reading for comprehension, so in his folder the teacher keeps her observations and samples of his work that indicate how Billy has not comprehended the material. She also keeps written work by Billy providing examples of how he has asked questions about a story and given the answers. (This indicates whether or not Billy can ask more than detail questions and also displays his writing skills.) The teacher now has information to share with Billy's parents regarding his difficulty in comprehending what he reads. With these concrete examples, the teacher can help the parents understand why they should not only read to Billy at home, having him answer questions or tell about the story, but also have Billy read to them.

At times school principals visit classrooms for observation or supervision. When they meet with teachers concerning student progress, the folders just described will be most helpful. Also, when a parent calls the principal about their child's reading, the teacher has examples of the student's work in the folder (a good reference).

Teacher-Made Diagnostic Tests

In addition to other informal measures, teachers can construct short tests to pinpoint specific skill strengths and weaknesses. These might be administered to a small group as pretests before a particular unit of study, or they might be used to verify teacher observations during reading lessons or after analyzing miscues on an informal reading inventory.

Informal diagnostic tests provide the information needed to plan appropriate reading activities for individuals or small groups of students. Since they are not normed, or standardized, they offer no comparisons. The sole purpose of teacher-made diagnostic tests is to aid teachers in making judgments as they plan instruction. Figure 9.7 gives examples of the kinds of informal subtests needed to accomplish the goals of a reading program.

SUMMARY

Informal measures of reading are essential for effective instruction. Unlike formal, standardized tests that compare one student to a normative population, informal measures provide continuous and valuable information about a student's reading skills and habits, as well as interests and attitudes. They form the basis of sound instructional decisions on a daily basis by helping teachers match students with appropriate materials and by focusing on specific rather than global aspects of reading.

Informal reading inventories, cloze tests, focused observation and re-

FIGURE 9.7 Teacher-Made Skills Tests

Name ______________________________ Date ______________

Directions: Draw a ring around the prefixes and suffixes

subway	backward	scoreless	disagree
underestimate	cupful	misspell	replay
unzip	friendship	neighborhood	readable

Name ______________________________ Date ______________

Directions: Draw a ring around the words in each row that have the same vowel sound.

1. straight	stare	pray	braid	cap	plate
2. hope	cot	coat	choke	long	short
3. bite	city	night	fly	slide	grin
4. sweet	heap	grieve	bread	well	treat

cording of information, analysis of work samples, and teacher-made diagnostic tests are some of the informal measures discussed here. However, there is no end to the number of means teachers can devise to informally assess students' reading skills and abilities. Every moment of the school day offers opportunities for informal observation and assessment of students' reading to provide the information on which more effective instruction can be based.

FOLLOW-UP QUESTIONS AND ACTIVITIES

1. Administer an informal reading inventory to a student. Determine independent, instructional, and frustration levels, and then analyze miscues. What information would be useful in planning instruction for this student?
2. Construct a cloze passage, following the suggested guidelines. Have a classmate do the same, and then exchange tests. See how well you are

able to resupply deleted words. Were you challenged? Try this again with material at a higher reading level.

3. Make an observation chart for a classroom. Observe the teaching of a reading lesson and record your observations. Discuss these with the classroom teacher.
4. Develop short skills tests for several areas of reading. Examples might include prefixes, homographs, blends, or use of context. If possible, try these with students.
5. Describe informal ways to assess students' progress in learning to read.
6. How does a teacher use informal measures? Ask a teacher to explain the uses of informal measures in the classroom. If possible, invite a teacher to class to share his or her ideas.

ADDITIONAL READINGS

For more information on IRIs:

Burns, P. C., & Burns, B. D. (1988). *Informal reading assessment.* Chicago: Rand McNally.

DeSanti, R. J. (1986). The DeSanti Cloze Reading Inventory. Newton, MA: Allyn and Bacon.

Ekwall, E. (1985). Ekwall Reading Inventory (2nd ed.). Newton, MA: Allyn and Bacon.

Johns, J. L. (1988). Basic Reading Inventory (4th ed.). Dubuque, IA: Kendall/Hunt.

For more information about informal measures:

Baumann, J. S., & Johnson, D. D. (1984). *Reading instruction and the beginning teacher.* Minneapolis: Burgess.

Burns, P. C., Roe, B. D., & Ross, E. P. (1988). *Teaching reading in today's elementary schools.* Boston: Houghton-Mifflin.

Durkin, D. (1989). *Teaching them to read* (5th ed.). Newton, MA: Allyn and Bacon.

Mason, J. M., & Au, K. H. (1990). *Reading instruction for today.* Glenview, IL: Scott, Foresman.

Vacca, J. L., Vacca, R. T., & Gove, M. K. (1987). *Reading and learning to read.* Boston: Little, Brown.

REFERENCES

Bormuth, J. R. (1967). Comparable cloze and multiple-choice test comprehension scores. *Journal of Reading, 10,* 291–299.

DeSanti, R. J. (1986). The DeSanti cloze reading inventory. Newton, MA: Allyn and Bacon.

Farr, R., & Carey, R. F. (1986). *Reading: What can be measured.* (2nd ed.). Newark, DE: International Reading Association.

Goodman, K. S. (1973). *Miscue analysis: Application to reading instruction.* Urbana, IL: National Council of Teachers of English.

Harris, L. A., & Smith, C. B. (1986). *Reading instruction: Diagnostic teaching in the classroom* (4th ed.). New York: Macmillan.

Lapp, D., & Flood, J. (1983). *Teaching reading to every child* (2nd ed.). New York: Macmillan.

Mason, J. M., & Au, K. H. (1990). *Reading instruction for today.* Glenview, IL: Scott, Foresman.

Ransom, P. E., & Patty, D. (1984). Informal diagnosis of reading abilities. In J. F. Baumann & D. D. Johnson (Eds.), *Reading instruction and the beginning teacher* (pp. 122–141). Minneapolis: Burgess.

Vacca, J. L., Vacca, R. T., & Gove, M. K. (1987). *Reading and learning to read.* Boston: Little, Brown.

10

Standardized Reading Tests and Reading Instruction

JENNIFER A. STEVENSON

THE USE OF standardized, norm-referenced tests is almost universal, and there appears to be little chance that their use will lessen in years to come. Given this situation, it is imperative that effective teachers be knowledgeable regarding how to interpret the scores from these tests. In Chapter 10, Jennifer Stevenson defines what standardized tests are and compares and contrasts the three scores most often used to report students' performance on these tests: grade equivalency, percentile, and stanine scores. For each of these scores, she discusses how norms are constructed and how the scores are correctly interpreted. This chapter contains important information that effective teachers must understand if they are to use the results of standardized tests in ways that are in their own best interest and that of their students.

STUDY QUESTIONS

1. What are standardized reading tests, and how are they different from other kinds of tests?
2. Why do educators administer standardized reading tests?
3. What are three kinds of scores typically obtained from standardized reading tests?
4. What are some problems inherent in the use of standardized reading tests?
5. How can the results obtained from standardized reading tests best be used in making instructional decisions?

Standardized tests are widely used in various instructional settings. This chapter describes standardized tests in general and, in particular, shows how these tests can be used appropriately to assess students' reading ability.

Definition and Purpose of Standardized Tests

As opposed to the informal measures and tests discussed in the previous chapter, a standardized test is any test for which there are uniform, prescribed procedures for administration and scoring. The test manual pre-

Portions of this chapter were adapted with permission from James F. Baumann and Jennifer A. Stevenson (1982), "Understanding Standardized Reading Achievement Test Scores." *The Reading Teacher*, 35, 648–654.

scribes specific directions to be given to the students; there is a prescribed time allotted for the total test and for each subtest; and the scoring is completed according to exact procedures. Many people are probably familiar with some of these tests from their own elementary school days: the Metropolitan Achievement Test, the Iowa Tests of Basic Skills, and the Stanford Achievement Test, for example, are standardized tests. All of them are formal, published tests and all contain a battery of achievement tests that are generally administered annually. Most of these tests assess major subject areas such as reading, mathematics, and science; within subject areas, they assess some core components such as—in reading, for example—vocabulary and comprehension.

The standardized tests discussed in this chapter are also norm-referenced, which is not the case with all standardized tests. A *norm-referenced test* is one that compares students to each other. It may compare the achievement of one student to the achievement of another or to the achievement of a large group, or it may compare the average achievement of two groups. In any case, a norm-referenced test discriminates between students (individuals or groups) in order to determine the relative status of the students being compared.

A look at the procedures used to construct the norms for standardized norm-referenced tests can help clarify the nature of these assessment instruments. Once a test intended to be used as a norm-referenced test is constructed, it is administered to large numbers of typical groups of students at various grade levels across the country. The scores of these large groups are then used to determine the norms for the test—that is, for example, to determine the typical score of an average third-grader on the vocabulary subtest of the reading achievement test battery. Based on the performance of the norm population, sets of statistics—or norms—are developed so that the performance of future test takers can be compared to the norm group. In other words, the norms enable a teacher to determine how a student's performance compares to the local, state, or national average, depending on the norming population. The test contains items of varying difficulty (easy to hard) so that the performance of various students is spread out and the resulting scores will clearly discriminate among those who are good, average, and poor.

Remember that a norm-referenced test reports the *relative* performance of students—how well Alex, for example, performed compared to Rita, or how well Alex performed compared to the national average for all third-graders. This kind of information can be contrasted with the kind of information provided by criterion-referenced tests. A *criterion-referenced test* would show how Alex's performance compared to the desired standard or level of performance. For example, if, on a vocabulary test of 100 items, students are required to read 90% of the words correctly to demonstrate mastery, the student would be compared to this specific standard and not to another student's performance. Thus, a criterion-referenced test shows how well a student performs in relation to a standard of performance; a norm-referenced test shows how well a student performs in relation to norms based on the performance of large numbers of students.

Standardized norm-referenced tests, then, are formal, published tests that have uniform procedures for administration and scoring. They permit comparisons among students by comparing individual or group performance to that of a local, state, or national norm group. One more point is important in a definition of standardized norm-referenced achievement tests. These tests provide general achievement information; they are not diagnostic. A standardized norm-referenced reading achievement test, for example, might include three subtests: vocabulary, word recognition, and comprehension. Each of these subtests has a limited number of items, and therefore student performance in each area is merely sampled, not comprehensively tested. Thus, scores provide survey information about student achievement. In addition, although specific skill areas may be tested quickly, student performance within these areas is not noted within the scores.

For example, a reading comprehension subtest may include questions that require students to discern the main idea or identify specific details, but the resulting scores do not designate performance in these particular areas. Nor should they; the items are too limited to provide a diagnosis of particular skills. What *is* appropriate to garner from performance on a standardized test is a global assessment of general areas of strength or weakness—for example, a general score of reading comprehension. More detailed and lengthy assessments than those contained within a standardized test are needed to diagnose student abilities in particular areas.

Scores of Standardized Reading Achievement Tests

A variety of derived scores can be obtained from standardized reading achievement tests. A derived score is a converted raw score, which is merely the number correct on the test. Three kinds of derived scores will be discussed here: grade-equivalent scores, percentile scores, and stanine scores. An understanding of each kind of score will enable teachers to use it appropriately in an instructional situation.

Grade-Equivalent Scores

Grade-equivalent scores (often called *GE* or *grade-level scores*) are perhaps the most widely used and also perhaps the most misinterpreted and misused. In fact, in 1982 the International Reading Association published a resolution on the misuse of grade-equivalent scores. The resolution urged "those who administer standardized reading tests [to] abandon the practice of using grade equivalents to report performance" and also urged "test publishers . . . to eliminate grade equivalents from their tests" ("Misuse," 1982, p. 464).

In order to understand the problem of misuse of grade-equivalent scores, it is important to understand how these scores are constructed and what, if any, is their proper use. Grade-equivalent scores provide information about students' reading achievement in relation to other students at various grade levels. A GE score consists of two digits separated by a decimal point (e.g., 3.1). The first digit designates the grade level, and the second digit designates the month in school. For example, if Alex's GE score is 3.1 on the vocabulary test, then he performed at a level that has been designated as average for students who have completed 1 month of the third grade. The month digit ranges from 0 to 9 and corresponds to September through June; thus, Alex's score corresponds to that of an average third-grader during the month of October. A score of 5.3 would correspond to that of an average fifth-grader during the month of December (a fifth-grader who has completed 3 months of school).

If Alex's grade-equivalent score is 5.3 on a third-grade vocabulary test, should he then be placed in fifth-grade reading materials? Probably not. In order to understand why not—and also what may be the danger of using GE scores—it is necessary to understand how the norms for these scores are constructed. The procedure used is this: Once the tests have been constructed, test publishers administer each battery of tests to large groups of students at several grade levels. For example, the test designed for third-grade vocabulary is administered locally, statewide, or nationally to large groups of third-graders and also to large groups of second- and fourth-graders, who are representative of the type of students who might take the test later. If this is done in September (the 0 month), then the mean (average) raw score of all third-graders who took the test is designated as 3.0, the mean raw score of all second-graders who took the same test is designated as 2.0, and the mean raw score of all fourth-graders who took the same test as 4.0. Figure 10.1 provides an example of raw score means converted into grade-equivalent scores; raw scores of 17, 25, and 31 are converted to grade-level scores of 2.0, 3.0, and 4.0.

Figure 10.1 also shows raw score means below and above 17 and 31, as well as grade-equivalent scores below and above 2.0 and 4.0. Does this mean that the third-grade vocabulary test was administered to large groups of students in grades other than second through fourth (e.g., to students in kindergarten through grade 7)? Ideally the procedure would have been followed, but, because of cost, it probably was not. Instead of administering tests to norming groups at many grade levels and at each month of the school year, thus establishing precise, month-by-month mean raw scores and corresponding grade-equivalent scores, tests makers determine many of these correspondences by interpolation and extrapolation.

Interpolation is a procedure in which the difference in raw scores obtained from the norm groups (who were tested in just one particular month of the school year) is divided into tenths and the in-between grade-equivalent scores are determined by being plotted against this curve. For example, in Figure 10.1, a raw score of 22 can be converted to a grade-equivalent score of

FIGURE 10.1 Example of Interpolated and Extrapolated Grade-Equivalent Scores

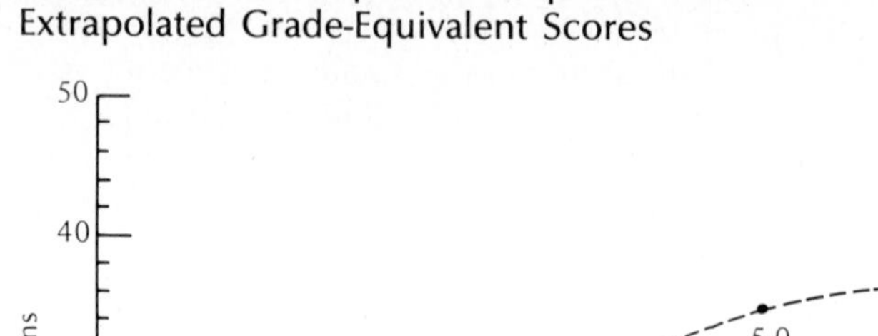

2.6 (as noted by the dotted line), and a raw score of 30 can be converted to 3.8. Interpolation, then, is used to designate the in-between scores within the grades tested in the norming population.

Extrapolation is a procedure used to obtain grade-equivalent scores outside of the range of grades included in the norming population. Extrapolation is a method of projecting the average performance of students at those grade levels which were tested to the average performance of students at those grade levels which were not tested. The interpolated curve is extended, and correspondences are thereby designated for grades at either end of the scale. Thus, as shown in Figure 10.1, a raw score of 10 can be converted to a grade-equivalent score of 1.2, and a raw score of 36 can be converted to a grade-equivalent score of 5.4.

Since both interpolated and extrapolated scores are based on best guesses rather than on proven correspondences, they are suspect. Extrapolated scores are especially suspect, since no students within the designated corresponding grade levels were tested at all and the scores are based on mathematical projections rather than actual test results. In the case of extrapolated scores, the best interpretation of very high or very low scores is simply that they are high or low; specific grade-level designations may well be wrong.

Finally, one additional problem with interpolation is that through this procedure the growth of 1 year is divided into 10 equal segments, thereby assuming that growth throughout the year occurs at an equal rate.

This probably is not the case, as teachers will note by comparing student progress in October with that in December or progress in February with that in May.

A second problem with grade-equivalent scores is that no comparisons can be made properly across subtests. For example, it is inappropriate to conclude that one student's scores of 3.6 on the third-grade vocabulary subtest and 3.6 on the third-grade comprehension subtest indicate equal performance. Nor does a score of 7.7 on the third-grade vocabulary test necessarily indicate better performance than a score of 7.2 on the third-grade comprehension subtest. Such paradoxes can result from the processes of interpolation and extrapolation, and they occur more frequently with very low or very high grade-equivalent scores. Therefore, comparisons of these kinds of scores should be made only within subtests (Alex's score on vocabulary may be compared with Rita's score on vocabulary) and never between subtests (Alex's scores on the two subtests of vocabulary and comprehension should not be compared).

A third, and perhaps most critical, problem with grade-equivalent scores is their frequent misinterpretation. For example, if Alex's score on the third-grade vocabulary subtest is 5.4, one might interpret this result to mean that Alex should be placed in fifth-grade reading materials. Such an interpretation is inappropriate for at least two reasons. First, the raw score designated on the third-grade vocabulary test as being equivalent to the average performance of a fifth-grader after the fourth month of school (5.4) was probably a guess; it was probably extrapolated from the scores of the second-, third-, and fourth-graders who took the test. A second and more important reason is that those norm-group students who took the test read vocabulary words that were appropriate for the third-grade test; they were not asked to read words appropriate for a fifth-grade test. Although a score of 5.4 indicates a very good knowledge of third-grade reading vocabulary, it does not show that Alex is ready for the full content of fifth-grade vocabulary words and a fifth-grade reading curriculum. The test did not include fifth-grade materials, and therefore it is inappropriate to conclude that Alex is "reading at a fifth-grade level."

Another frequent misinterpretation of grade-equivalent scores is that they represent a standard of performance—that is, for example, that all third-graders should be reading at the level designated as average for the third grade. In fact, it would be impossible for all students in a normal population to be reading "at or above grade level." Remember that a score of 3.0 is the grade equivalent that corresponds to the mean (average) raw score of many third-graders across the country who took a given standardized test. Averages are usually derived from some scores that are low, some that are high, and some that are in the middle. Therefore, it is to be expected that, within a given class, many scores will cluster around the mean but many will also be above and below. In fact, by definition, a mean score is that score above which half of the scores fall and below which half of the scores fall. Therefore, if test norms are up to date and are representative of the students who took the test, many students within a typical group should be expected to fall both above and below their grade-level designations.

After considering the many problems inherent in the construction and interpretation of grade-equivalent scores, the obvious question arises: Why are they used at all? The major appeal of grade-equivalent scores is that they are an easy, concrete referent for comparing students' performance. In the cases in which scores fall within a grade level or two of a student's actual grade placement, they are probably fairly accurate. However, given their potential problems, it is probably best not to use grade-equivalent scores at all.

Percentile Scores

While grade equivalency norms are determined by testing students at several grade levels, percentile score norms for reading achievement tests are determined by noting the performance of students within just one grade. Third-grade norms, for example, are developed by testing only third-graders. What is similar about GE and percentile scores is that, as with all standardized norm-referenced test scores, students are compared to one another (rather than to some desired level of performance); the scores show the relative status of the students tested.

A percentile score compares a student to the norming population and indicates how many students in that group scored better than the particular student in question and how many scored at a lower level. For example, if Alex's percentile score on the third-grade vocabulary test is 85, his score indicates that 15% of the students in the third-grade norm group scored higher than Alex on the vocabulary test and 85% scored lower. Thus, the relative status of Alex's score in relation to a representative group of other third-grade students' scores is identified.

A note on the construction of percentile scores may be helpful here. After the norm group has taken a test, all of the raw scores are plotted on a frequency diagram. This distribution usually leads to a bell-shaped curve, as shown in Figure 10.2. Percentile scores are based on percentages and can range from 1 to 99, with 50 being the middle (median) score. Scores are constructed by segmenting the raw score distribution into hundredths.

Percentile scores have at least two good features. They are straightforward and easily interpretable, and they can be readily compared across subtests. A percentile score of 85, for example, has the same construction and meaning in the context of a vocabulary test, a word identification test, or a social studies test. In each case, the relative status of the score is that it is above 85% of the scores of the norm group and below 15%.

One possible problem with the interpretation of percentile scores occurs because these scores are not equally spaced across the 1 to 99 range. Instead, they tend to cluster in the middle around the 50th percentile. The

FIGURE 10.2 The Construction of Percentile Norms

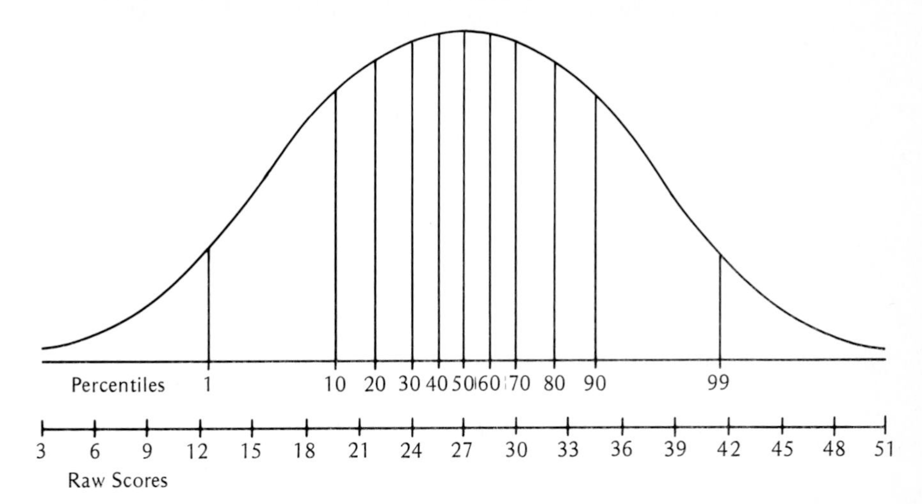

uneven distribution occurs because the relationship between percentile units and corresponding raw score points is not constant. For example, consider the difference between the percentile scores of 50 and 55 and compare that to the difference between the percentile scores of 90 and 95. In the latter case, the actual raw score point difference that separates the two percentile scores is greater than that in the former case. Thus, the percentile point difference between 90 and 95 is more noteworthy than that between 50 and 55, since the difference there indicates more correct answers on the test.

There is another potential problem with percentile scores. They appear to be very precise, but, because of the built-in error attendant to all achievement tests, they may not be precise. Thus, Alex's percentile score of 85 on the third-grade vocabulary test may not really be different from his percentile score of 81 last year on the second-grade vocabulary test. A four-point percentile difference, in most instances, would not be educationally significant.

Standard Scores and Stanine Scores

Standard scores are a third type of score commonly reported for standardized norm-referenced reading achievement tests. As with GE and percentile scores, a standard score compares the performance of one student or a group of students to the performance of other students. Of the three kinds of scores, standard scores are the most straightforward and the easiest to interpret.

Standard scores, or stanine scores (stanines are one type of standard score), are like percentile scores in several ways. They show the relative performance of students within just one grade level, they generally follow a normal bell-shaped curve distribution, and they range from 1 to 99 (standard scores) or 1 to 9 (stanine scores). What is different and helpful about standard scores is that the relationship between standard score units and corresponding raw score points remains constant. Thus, the differences between standard scores have the same meaning (in terms of raw score points) wherever their position on the scale.

Stanine scores are frequently reported for reading achievement tests. The word *stanine* comes from "standard nine-point scale." Stanine scores are single digits ranging from 1 to 9. The stanine 5 surrounds the 50th percentile, showing average performance. Stanines 1, 2, 3, and 4 show relatively poor performance, while stanines 6, 7, 8, and 9 show increasingly good performance.

A correspondence between stanine scores and raw scores is shown in Figure 10.3. The same raw score data as was shown in Figure 10.2 has been used here, but, except for the first and ninth stanines, all stanines are of equal size. This is because a stanine score is, in fact, a form of converted percentile score in which the tendency for clustering around the middle is eliminated by using a standard measure of spread (the standard deviation) and basing increments upon it. What these mathematical calculations mean is that raw scores and stanines are equated, and thus differences between stanines have the same meaning wherever their position on the scale. What also occurs is that there are different percentages of scores within each stanine. Figure 10.3 shows, for example, that 20% of the scores fall within the fifth stanine and only 7% within either the second or eighth stanines.

Stanine scores have several helpful features. Like percentile scores,

FIGURE 10.3 The Construction of Stanine Norms

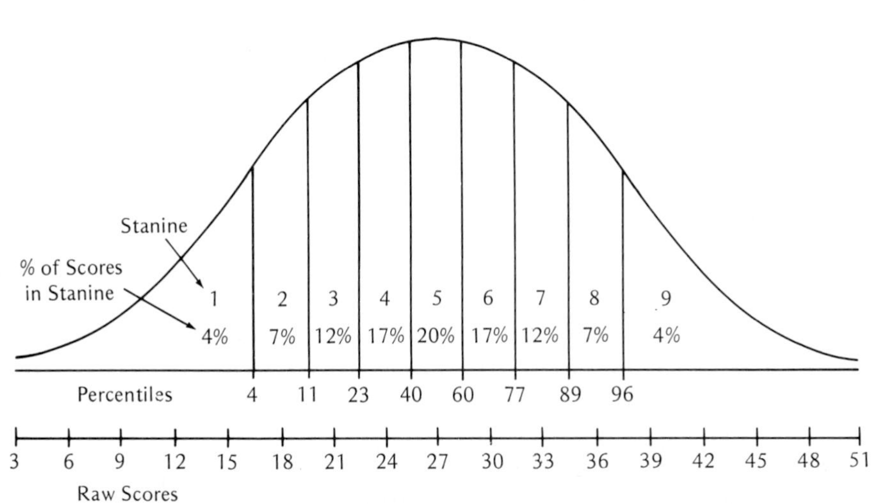

they are easily interpretable and they can be directly compared across subtests. In addition, stanine scores are evenly spaced across the raw score distribution, so that a difference of one stanine, for example, has the same meaning at any point on the scale.

Because stanines have only nine units, they are rather gross measures. Alex's vocabulary score, if reported as a stanine, would be the seventh stanine—a range of 77 to 89 in percentile scores. Some standard scores, other than stanines, are reported as two or three digits, with ranges of 1 to 99 or 1 to 999; in those cases, more precise information is provided.

Standardized Reading Tests: Some Caveats

Standardized, norm-referenced reading achievement tests have a number of problems that have been described often in the literature (Farr & Carey, 1986; Hopkins & Stanley, 1981; Mehrens & Lehmann, 1984; Schreiner, 1979; Thorndike & Hagen, 1977). Teachers need to be well aware of the weaknesses inherent within these assessment instruments so that they can use them wisely. Almost every teacher will encounter instructional situations in which standardized tests are a required form of assessment and will be asked to discuss student scores with parents or with other teachers. Thus, some caveats regarding standardized tests follow.

The problems associated with standardized tests can be grouped in three areas: (1) problems inherent in the tests themselves; (2) problems inherent in the test situation and administration of the test; and (3) problems inherent in the interpretation and use of the scores.

Problems inherent in the tests themselves are, unfortunately, legion. For example, standardized tests have been faulted for ethnic bias (Is the content more appropriate for white middle class students than for those of other cultural or ethnic backgrounds?); for reliability (How consistent would the results be if the test were taken more than once?); for validity (Are the test items actually measuring reading-processing behaviors, or are they measuring something else, such as test-wiseness?); for question/passage independency (Can test comprehension questions be answered without having read the preceding test comprehension passage?); and for employing limited methods to assess skills (Does a student's performance on a multiple-choice, main-idea comprehension item indicate how well the student could discern a main idea without attendant choices?). Another criticism of standardized tests that has been noted increasingly in the literature during the past several years has to do with the gap between the content of instruction and the content of assessment.

As Squire (1987) and Valencia and Pearson (1987) noted, recent research has provided educators with new information about reading processes and learning to read. This research is being translated into new classroom practices and materials, so that the content of instruction now more frequently promotes process-oriented learning, activation and use of prior knowledge during reading, and students' active response to what is read. Unfortunately, however, the content of assessment (and particularly of standardized tests) continues to promote product-oriented learning; the mastery of small, disparate skills; and an assembly-line approach to reading. Thus, the content of instruction and the content of standardized assessments differ, and it becomes increasingly difficult to use the results of these assessments to make wise decisions regarding instruction. It should be noted that there are now efforts under way to construct standardized achievement tests that are attentive to these concerns. Educators in Michigan, Illinois, and elsewhere, working with current views and understandings of the reading process and instruction, have recently developed new reading assessment instruments. For example, statewide assessments in Michigan now measure and report reading in a more holistic manner than in the past (Wixson, Peters, Weber, & Roeber, 1987).

A second set of problems associated with standardized tests are problems inherent in the testing situation and test administration. Standardized tests are formal; they are large-group situations; they are timed; they reward guessing; they are generally administered only once a year; they may or may not include sufficient and clear directions; and so on. Any of these characteristics of standardized test situations and administration may affect student performance, and thus the scores may reflect something other than reading ability. That is, the scores may more truly distinguish students who are comfortable in such test situations from those who are not than they distinguish students who read well from those who do not.

A third set of problems are those associated with the interpretation and use of scores. Many of these were described in the discussion of grade-equivalent, percentile, and standard scores. They include problems such as using grade-equivalent scores to determine placement in classroom reading materials; believing scores to be precise rather than gross indicators of achievement; comparing scores inappropriately across subtests; or using subtest score information diagnostically.

Certainly, the use of standardized test scores to place students in reading groups, to make decisions about student promotion, or to judge the quality of specific teachers or schools is problematic. Also problematic is another use—administering a battery of standardized tests each year and then simply filing the results away. The purpose of any assessment should be to lead to instructional decisions; therefore, if the information gained from an assessment cannot or will not be used, the test should not be administered at all.

Given the many problems associated with standardized reading achievement tests—problems in the makeup of the tests, in the test situation, or in the interpretation and use of scores—are there *any* appropriate ways to use the scores? There are several, and this chapter concludes with some recommendations.

Recommended Uses of Standardized Tests

Standardized norm-referenced tests, as currently constructed, will probably be with us for some time to come. They are widely used in schools today; teachers are required to administer them in reading and other subject areas and to make use of the results. Test results can be used and interpreted wisely in the following ways: (1) as a gross, global measure of reading achievement; (2) as a screening device; and (3) in conjunction with other measures of reading progress.

Actually, these three recommended uses form a continuum. Standardized tests are intended to be gross, rather than detailed, indicators of achievement; they are survey instruments. If the results are viewed in this fashion, they can be used as a screening device. Teachers can note those students who seem to do well and those who seem to have problems as indicated by this broad-brush, survey information. After that, a look at the scores in conjunction with other assessment information can be helpful; that is, standardized survey test results can indicate a need for more detailed observation and analysis.

For example, if a student scores below grade level on a standardized test at the beginning of the year and has also been placed in a below-grade-level reading group based on the previous year's performance, then it behooves the teacher to take a closer look at what is causing the problem—that is, to begin detailed diagnosis. Alternatively, a student may score very well on a standardized test, perhaps well above grade level. In that situation, too, a teacher needs to look at other information. To determine whether or not the student should be placed in an advanced reading program and materials, a teacher should use the standardized test information as a first clue and then move beyond into a more detailed analysis of reading progress.

As discussed in Chapter 9, there are a number of ways in which teachers can gather a more detailed analysis of reading progress. They can informally note individual students' daily work in a regular classroom situation; they can administer individual or group informal reading inventories; they can give teacher-made or commercial criterion-referenced tests; and so on.

Let us look at an example of how standardized test information can be used in conjunction with other information to provide a valid analysis of reading progress and plan wisely for instruction. Iona, a third-grade student, was tested in September and obtained a standard score of 35 on the reading vocabulary subtest and 39 on the reading comprehension subtest. Mrs. Jung, Iona's third-grade teacher, noted that the second-grade teacher had recommended Iona's placement this fall in third-grade reading materials. Mrs. Jung also noted that the standardized test information showed a possible problem with Iona's ability to learn well at a third-grade reading level.

An appropriate procedure for Mrs. Jung to follow at this point would be to gather other assessment information. First, Mrs. Jung might recall Iona's behavior during the administration of the standardized test. Poor attitude or concentration might have caused a poor performance, and thus Iona's scores on the test might not reflect her real abilities. Second, Mrs. Jung could note how well Iona is reading in the third-grade material in which she has been placed. Then, since it is early in the school year and perhaps too soon to judge Iona's in-class performance well, a more detailed analysis of Iona's progress and proper placement should be obtained. Through the administration of an informal reading inventory, Mrs. Jung or a reading specialist could assess Iona's ability to read first-, second-, and third-grade reading materials and could diagnose Iona's word identification and comprehension strengths and weaknesses. Finally, Mrs. Jung might wish to consider another test score—Iona's score on an IQ or aptitude test, if available.

When all of this information was combined, Mrs. Jung could look at and plan appropriately for instruction. In this case, five indices showed that Iona would learn well in third-grade reading materials and one did not. The informal reading inventory showed Iona to be capable of reading third-grade materials, as did Mrs. Jung's in-class observation and the previous teacher's report and recommendation. Two additional indices supported this conclusion: Iona's IQ score showed her aptitude to be fairly high, and Mrs. Jung had noted that Iona was having a bad day at the time of the administration of the standardized test. In this case, then, the one index that was an initial clue to possible problems—Iona's scores on the standardized test—proved to be invalid.

Certainly, in another case poor scores on a standardized test might be confirmed by other analyses. In that case, a different but also appropriate instructional decision would be made: placement and instruction in lower-level reading materials. Finally, it should be noted that, in this case, the results of an informal reading inventory not only showed that Iona should be placed in third-grade materials, but also identified areas of strength and weakness so that instruction in the third-grade materials could proceed expeditiously.

SUMMARY

Three different kinds of scores commonly reported for standardized norm-referenced reading tests have been described here. All have certain advantages and disadvantages. Most recommended for general use are percentile scores and stanine or standard scores. Grade-equivalent scores are not recommended for general use, in part because of the technical problems associated with them, but also—the most critical point—because of problems with their proper interpretation.

As noted throughout this chapter, a critical point regarding the use of survey test results is that they be used not alone, but in concert with a variety of other assessment and diagnostic information. Using a variety of information—from gross indicators such as formal survey tests to very specific notations such as daily informal observations—teachers can plan wisely for future instruction.

That is the final important point. Assessments should lead to instructional decisions; otherwise they have no purpose. Standardized test results, when viewed as a gross, global measure of achievement, interpreted properly, and used together with other diagnostic information, can lead to wise instructional decisions.

FOLLOW-UP QUESTIONS AND ACTIVITIES

1. Three kinds of scores that are typically obtained from standardized reading tests have been described in this chapter. Of these, which type of score is most readily interpretable, and why?
2. Lee, a student in your fourth-grade class, obtained a grade equivalent score of 7.1 on the reading comprehension subtest of a standardized test administered in September. Lee's parents insist that he be placed in seventh-grade reading materials. How would you respond?
3. Within the same fourth-grade class, about half of the students scored at or above the 50th percentile on the reading comprehension subtest of the standardized test administered in September and about half of the students scored below the 50th percentile. Your principal has asked that you aim to improve the reading performance of students in your class so that at least two-thirds of the students score above the 50th percentile when the test is administered again the following May. How would you respond?
4. Devise three student profiles using hypothetical scores from the reading comprehension subtest of a standardized test. For the first profile, devise three hypothetical scores—grade equivalent, percentile, and stanine—that indicate at-grade-level performance for a fifth-grade student taking the test in May. For the second profile, devise three hypothetical scores—grade equivalent, percentile, and stanine—that indicate above-grade-level performance for a fifth-grade student taking the test in May. Finally, follow the same procedure so that the three scores all indicate below-grade-level performance.

ADDITIONAL READINGS

Anderson, R. C., Hiebert, E. H., Scott, J. A., & Wilkinson, I. A. G. (1985). *Becoming a nation of readers: The report of the Commission on Reading.* Washington, DC: National Institute of Education.

Farr, R., & Carey, R. F. (1986). *Reading: What can be measured?* (2nd ed.). Newark, DE: International Reading Association.

Meier, D. (1981, Fall). Why reading tests don't measure reading. *Dissent*, 457–466.

Pumfrey, P. D. (1985). *Reading: Tests and assessment techniques* (2nd ed.). London: Hodder and Stoughton.

Schreiner, R. (Ed.). (1979). *Reading tests and teachers: A practical guide.* Newark, DE: International Reading Association.

Standardized testing: Problem or solution? (1987). *National Center on Effective Secondary Schools Newsletter,* 2 (2). Madison, WI: University of Wisconsin.

Venezky, R. L. (1974). *Testing in reading: Assessment and instructional decision making.* Urbana, IL: National Council of Teachers of English.

Wigdor, A. K., & Garner, W. R. (Eds.). (1982). *Ability testing: Uses, consequences and controversies.* Washington, DC: National Academy Press.

Ysseldyke, J. E., & Marston, D. (1982). A critical analysis of standardized reading tests. *School Psychology Review, 11,* 259–266.

REFERENCES

Farr, R., & Carey, R. F. (1986). *Reading: What can be measured?* (2nd ed.). Newark, DE: International Reading Association.

Hopkins, K. D., & Stanley, J. C. (1981). *Educational and psychological measurement and evaluation* (6th ed.). Englewood Cliffs, NJ: Prentice-Hall.

Iowa Tests of Basic Skills. (1982). Chicago: Riverside Publishing.

Mehrens, W. A., & Lehmann, I. J. (1984). *Measurement and evaluation in education and psychology* (3rd ed.). New York: Holt, Rinehart & Winston.

Metropolitan Achievement Test. (1985). San Antonio, TX: The Psychological Corporation.

Misuse of grade equivalents. (1982). *The Reading Teacher,* 35(4), 464.

Schreiner, R. (Ed.). (1979). *Reading tests and teachers: A practical guide.* Newark, DE: International Reading Association.

Squire, J. R. (1987). Introduction: A special issue on the state of assessment in reading. *The Reading Teacher,* 40(8), 724–725.

Stanford Achievement Test. (1988). San Antonio, TX: The Psychological Corporation.

Thorndike, R. L., & Hagen, E. (1977). *Measurement and evaluation in psychology and education* (4th ed.). New York: Wiley.

Valencia, S., & Pearson, P. D. (1987). Reading assessment: Time for a change. *The Reading Teacher,* 40(8), 726–732.

Wixson, K. K., Peters, C. W., Weber, E. M., & Roeber, E. D. (1987). New directions in statewide reading assessment. *The Reading Teacher,* 40(8), 749–754.

11

Evaluating the Writing Process

CHARLES R. DUKE

SEVERAL CHAPTERS IN Part One of this book stressed the relationship of writing to reading instruction and offered suggestions for helping students develop writing skills and for integrating reading and writing instruction. In this chapter, Charles Duke suggests that if we are to use writing effectively in our reading program we must have a plan of evaluation and feedback for students that promotes the development of literary skills. He states that students who have papers returned with comments such as "good" or "well done" scribbled hastily in red ink have a right to feel cheated: They have received no signals that the teacher has interacted with their texts on a personal level the way we know readers do when reading regular texts.

Duke suggests that teachers need to provide both formative evaluation (the kind that helps writers refine their work) and summative evaluation (the kind that says something about the finished product) if they are to be effective in helping students learn to communicate and relate to written ideas. He offers specific examples of how both types of evaluation can be built into writing activities and provide necessary evaluative information about performance both during and after the writing process without detracting from important instructional time.

STUDY QUESTIONS

1. What effect do teacher responses have on students' attitudes toward writing?
2. What are effective ways of responding to student writing?
3. How do we recognize growth in student writing?
4. How can students accept responsibility for responding to each other's writing?
5. How can a system of evaluation be established for a writing program?

Mark looked at the paper, studying the red marks carefully, turning the paper sideways to continue reading the comments and symbols. He looked up to where his teacher was busily distributing papers to other students. Then he looked down at his paper, sighed, and stuck it between some pages in his social studies book. Later that day he approached his teacher during a lull in the classroom activity. "Mr. Lewis, why do you keep writing 'frog' all over my papers?"

Mr. Lewis glanced down at Mark in puzzlement. "What do you mean, Mark? I can't remember writing 'frog' on your papers!"

"Well, sir, like right here on this paper you passed back today; see, right there."

Mr. Lewis looked at the place on the page marked by a stubby forefinger. He frowned and said, "But, Mark, that's not 'frog,' that's 'frag,' for fragment; you know, not a sentence. You have a real problem with sentence fragments in all of your papers."

Previous chapters have discussed the importance of including writing activities in the reading program. However, to include such activities without providing students with effective feedback that will allow them to gain a better understanding of the writing process would be to limit the value that writing has for reading. Scenarios such as this one are played out in many classrooms, but many students do not have the courage Mark has even to raise such a question with their teachers. How long might Mark have gone on thinking he had some mysterious frog disease in his writing had he not asked the question? Dilemmas such as this simply underscore the significance of communicating clearly and effectively with students when responding to their writing. Whether it be over the matter of handwriting—and clarification of symbols—or in more extended discussion of how to improve a piece of writing, teachers must never underestimate the powerful effect any evaluation of writing can have on a student.

To use this power wisely, teachers need to understand what the term *evaluation* really means in the case of writing instruction. In one sense, and perhaps the most important, evaluation means to respond to a piece of writing much as we might respond to a work of art we see emerging from clay or on a canvas for the first time; we make comments, raise questions, and, if possible, engage the artist in a discussion about the work to be certain we understand the intent. This is *formative evaluation,* because it assists the writer in refining the message to be conveyed. For students, formative evaluation provides the support they need as they venture to communicate their messages to an audience.

Another, and perhaps more familiar, kind of evaluation is the response that comes at the end of a process. The finished product is judged, and a stamp of approval is placed upon it; in school settings, teachers resort to grades, percentiles, or other devices to place a quality and performance mark on the work. This is called *summative evaluation.* The standardized testing discussed in Chapter 10 could be placed in this category. While summative evaluation also has its purposes in the teaching of writing, the outcomes may be quite different from those of formative evaluation.

The integration of both kinds of evaluation into the writing process is not as difficult as it might first appear, for the overall purposes of such evaluation can be placed into three categories: evaluation of student needs, evaluation of program, and evaluation for the purpose of reporting to parents and students. This chapter shows how these categories, built into a writing program designed to enhance reading, provide the necessary evaluation information about performance both during and after the reading-writing process without robbing the student or teacher of instructional time.

Evaluating Student Needs

A teacher's judgment of student writing traditionally has been conveyed via grades, marking symbols, and occasional brief and often cryptic comments that more frequently than not leave students such as Mark puzzled and frustrated. Too often, in responding to student writing, teachers forge ahead without adequate knowledge of students' development and then are dismayed when little improvement occurs. Ironically, considering the amount of time spent correcting students' writing, teachers have, until recently, shown very little understanding of the writing process or recognition of where students are in their writing development.

But effective evaluation begins with diagnosis. No more important skill exists for assisting students in their writing development, yet it is the one skill that most educators feel least equipped to handle. Writing diagnosis comes under the label of formative evaluation. Peacock (1986) described this formative evaluation as "a systematic attempt on the teacher's part to identify strengths and weaknesses in a writer's script and to help the pupil to overcome selected difficulties" (p. 43). Such evaluation is not new. Effective teachers have always attempted to recognize signals from their students' behavior and work and use those signs as a means for congratulating students on achievement or for developing individualized instruction. However, effective application of formative evaluation to writing instruction requires some adjustments in our attitudes and perceptions.

Chapters 7 and 8 discussed how writing need not be reduced to drill or frustration exercises. A teacher's careful preparation and attentiveness to students' writing abilities and needs, along with a supportive environment, will go a long way toward showing students that writing is a productive learning activity. To understand how this can be accomplished, however, students need ample opportunities to ask questions, engage in brainstorming about topics, explore linkages between their reading and writing, and come to value their roles as authors in the writing process.

Providing students these opportunities and ensuring that they develop a sense of the accompanying responsibility for making choices about response are important steps toward developing an effective evaluation system in the classroom. Teachers also need to pay close attention to the signals in students' composing processes, helping them to refine their ideas without passing early—and often erroneous—judgments on what they are producing. The teacher's initial role in this process should be that of collaborator, not evaluator. The role of collaborator requires the teacher to approach the student's text as a reader, not an evaluator. Together, student and teacher work to make meaning in the early stages of a draft. A dialogue occurs between the writer and the reader, each checking to make sure that the other understands. Bissex (1980) offered a glimpse of how this collaborative approach works:

> When Paul asked me if POST OFISS was correct, I replied, "That's the way 'office' sounds but not the way it looks." I gave him credit for the part he got right while pointing out another aspect of written English. I might also have commended him for doubling the final s, a new feature in his spellings which showed differentiated representation of "s" depending on its position in the word. I might also have asked him to think of another letter that could represent the "s" sound and talked about the "e" marker after the "c." (p. 113)

Ruth (1987) suggested that "we should learn to read the text the child produces for its meanings rather than for its errors" (p. 759). But replacing the role of teacher as error-hunter with teacher as reader does not happen automatically. Teachers have to work to overcome old habits and develop new ways of looking at texts if they hope to be successful in communicating to students where they are in their writing development.

Responding as Interested Reader

The case of Mark, and particularly the response of his teacher, is not as isolated as some might believe. Jackson (1965) offered this example of a passage from a 9-year-old boy:

> My father is on the broad side and tall side. My father was a hard working man and he had a lot of money. He was not fat or thin . . . His age was about thirty years when he died, he had a good reputation, he is a married man. When he was in hospital I went to see him every Sunday afternoon. I asked him how he was going on, he told me he was getting a lot better . . . He likes doing woodwork, my father, for me, and he likes a little game of cards now and then . . . He chops the wood and saws the planks and he is a handsome man but he is dead. (p. 1)

What comment did the teacher make to the student about this piece? "Tenses, you keep mixing past and present." Students who have papers returned with such comments or even just "good" or "well done" scribbled hastily in red ink have a right to feel cheated. They are receiving no signals that the teacher has interacted with their texts on a personal level the way we know readers do when reading regular texts. Protherough (1983) suggested that "responding to students' writing really demands something of the openness that we bring to other texts, a willingness to be moved or interested or excited, a making of meaning by bringing something of ourselves to the words on the page" (p. 180).

Some teachers find it difficult to replace the objective stance with a more personal one, but the switch makes it possible for the teacher to send evaluative responses that encourage students to view their reading materials as pieces that merit a real reading. Contrast the teacher comments just cited with the following: "I like the way you bring me into the story; the smells and sounds help me get a better picture of the place." "How did you get from the garage to the attic so fast?" Such responses can be oral or written; it is the perspective rather than the method of delivery that is the key. In all cases, however, the alternative responses should incorporate the following criteria:

1. *Cultivate the personal tone.* "It took real courage, Janice, to write about this experience; I'm glad you shared it with us."
2. *Be selective.* Knowing where each student is developmentally makes it easier to select what ought to be worked on. Stress the major problem in the draft and leave the lesser problems for later drafts. For example, "Let's focus on finding really clear examples to use to show your reader what happened."
3. *Model self-review through questions.* For example, "How did you get that animal back in the cage?" "What color was the water?" Such questions suggest ways for students to develop their own critical review apparatus while also forcing them to make decisions consistent with their own view of the piece, not the reader's.
4. *Reinforce growth whenever possible.* Call the student's attention to achievements: "I can see you tried to use details this time." "I like the adventure because you give us a clear order for the events."
5. *Provide practical options for improvement.* Talk with the writer about what might be done to improve a piece. Again, questions are effective: "What would happen if you used this paragraph for the beginning?" "How could we find out exactly what the two people said?"

Remembering to convey a sense of the interested and supportive reader and basing the evaluation responses on where the student is in terms of his or her writing development will go a long way toward building the kind of classroom environment in which student writers are willing to share their understanding and responses to reading material or personal experiences. Writing in this environment becomes a dialogue in which writer and teacher converse about each piece, collaborating to make it work. Given this kind of support, students will risk more and develop faster.

Classroom Applications

The reality of dealing with classes of 35 or more students often discourages teachers from adopting a diagnostic evaluation approach. However, if teachers are willing to take the time they normally might use to mark students' papers in the traditional way and replace it with a management system that combines personal with oral, written, and peer response groups as discussed in Chapter 8, then students will receive more information about their writing and teachers will not be increasing their own time commitments substantially.

Conferences

In the elementary grades, particularly, a good case can be made for initiating a conversation with each student about a piece that has been produced. These conferences, or consultations, can provide formative evaluation during the actual writing process, often when students need it most. A few minutes spent conferring with a student can be much more productive than marking all the grammatical and spelling errors that could be found in the same amount of time. The overall purpose of such conferences is to assist students in saying what they know. For example, suppose that a student was writing the following and the teacher had a chance to respond at this early stage:

> One day Brent and me was going with his father in his truck. His father is a big man. We were going to the shop to get some tools but we had an accident. The truck went off the road. We turned over. I was scared. Brent broke his arm. His father was on crutches for three weeks. The end.

Such a student draft is not unusual, but it has little life, few details, and virtually no sense of audience or purpose. If the student handed this in, there might be resistance to revision; but if the teacher saw this draft as it emerged, a quick conference might make a difference in the final product.

A choice has to be made, however, about what kind of conference approach to use. For instance, the teacher could chat with the student briefly about accidents, swapping tales and hoping that exchanging details of the accident will help the student incorporate more detail into the account. Or the teacher might try to make some aspect of the accident come alive: "How did you feel as the truck went off the road?" "How did you get out of the truck?" Another choice would be to address the structure of the story, asking clarification about the sequence of the events or which details might not be important. Still another option would be to raise the question of audience and purpose: "I'm not sure why you're telling us about the accident" or "I'm having trouble seeing exactly where and how the accident took place. Can you help me there?"

When teachers consult with students on a one-to-one basis, they have to make quick decisions about what approach to use. Seldom is there the luxury of seeing a paper ahead of time. Instead, based on what is known about the student's stage of writing development, the teacher selects a focus for discussion that will help the student move ahead and enhance the piece of writing, but not leave the student frustrated because the teacher has asked for too much too soon. None of the approaches mentioned here is necessarily better than another, but with practice and attention to the developmental needs of students, teachers can make the right choices.

If class meetings are held in workshop format once or twice a week, the teacher can spend a good amount of time conferencing and reach most students at least once, if not more often. The key to successful conferencing, however, is the ability to diagnose, select an appropriate evaluation response that engages the student with the problem, and then move on.

Peer Response Groups

Teachers often believe that they are the only ones capable of evaluating students' papers. That this is not the case has been amply demonstrated (Calkins, 1986; Graves, 1983; Meeks, 1986). Although they do not possess the same level of expertise as their teachers, students do have a fine sense of what works and what does not work in a piece of writing. As readers, they can provide useful evaluative responses to authors, particularly at early stages of the writing process, which will relieve the teacher of considerable work. But other benefits come from the use of peer response in a classroom evaluation system. Students gain valuable experience in writing to audiences other than their teachers and having the benefit of direct feedback from those audiences. Lagana (1972) and others have found that improvement occurs in grammatical usage, organization, sentence revision, and critical thinking. Students who have frequent opportunities to examine each other's writing also can develop internal standards against which to measure their own progress.

Establishing peer response groups in the classroom requires some planning, but if the procedures are clear, most students adapt to the group work well and can be relied on to carry out their task (Meeks, 1986). However, students must be taught how to respond to writing. The personal, supportive approach recommended for teacher response is equally valid for peer response. To help students understand the response process, teachers should model it for the class as a whole, presenting it as a writing workshop. Suggestions for establishing peer response groups follow.

Modeling Responses Begin by selecting a sample of student writing, preferably one that has been written in response to an assignment students have just completed, but not necessarily by a student in the class. Provide copies or project the piece via a transparency. Then model a dialogue with the students, stressing the importance of providing as much useful response as possible. Questions such as the following may be helpful:

- What parts of this piece do you like best? Why?
- What would you like to know more about?

- What questions do you have for the author?
- What changes would you suggest to the author? Why?

Responses to the questions should always be keyed to the text. If students have difficulty expressing their feelings about the piece, be encouraging, asking them to point to a particular word or phrase that seems to be related; then ask other students to respond. During the entire discussion, emphasize the help they are providing to the author.

Eventually these class dialogues about selected pieces can serve another purpose. Two or three pieces selected for certain characteristics can be shared with the class for discussion. Take care in using such an approach that the pieces reflect strengths as well as problems common to a number of students in the class; then all can take part in the discussion and no one will need to feel singled out. These pieces can be placed on transparencies and projected for discussion or run off so each student has a copy. Talk about the pieces should focus on major aspects such as purpose, content, and audience, with stylistic or editorial matters kept to a minimum, at least in the initial sessions. Matters of correctness can be addressed when the students are ready to publish their pieces or have received sufficient response so they are ready to address specific issues. Mellon (1975) suggested that this kind of incidental teaching is far more effective than the traditional drill and practice, and it continues to provide a modeling of appropriate peer response.

Monitoring Group Responses After the response process has been modeled several times, have students work in pairs, exchanging papers and perhaps responding to just two questions:

- What parts of the piece do you like best?
- What would you like to know more about?

Students then can discuss their responses to each other's papers. When they are finished, encourage the whole class to talk about how they felt as they responded. The questions can be varied from session to session, depending on the maturity of the students and the nature of the writing assignment. Eventually, students should be encouraged to volunteer to have their papers reviewed by the class. Once this has happened, students will be ready to move into small response groups of three or four.

Specific criteria or questions, as suggested in Chapter 8, should be given to peer response groups as a basis for their evaluation. A response may be oral or written, but younger children work best with the oral response and at first should be asked to respond to no more than two questions. A basic procedure is for each author in a group to take a turn in reading his or her paper; the other members of the group respond, using the specific criteria that have been determined in advance. For instance, the group might be asked to answer such questions as "What examples do you like most in this piece?" and "What more information would you like the writer to give?" Older students, as they gain experience, can handle more questions and may even provide written commentary. The purposes for which the groups respond should vary so that they gain experience in looking at their own texts from a variety of perspectives.

Students do not learn appropriate response behavior in one lesson. A combination of modeling, monitoring, and whole-class discussion of the process will be necessary for a period of weeks. Occasionally, if groups seem not to be functioning well, their membership may need to be changed or a whole-class discussion held to remind students of the purpose of peer response. Yet, in the long view, peer response is one of the most valuable experiences students can have, for it provides a way for them to internalize the standards of a writing program while also making them more responsible for their own success in writing.

Developmental Evaluation

Providing the kind of response to student writing that has been suggested thus far requires that teachers have a clear developmental model in mind when they look at their students' writing. No single ideal measure exists for this purpose, but one of the most promising efforts is the Crediton Project. A team of researchers located at the University School of Education at Exeter and working with teachers in schools at Crediton, Devon, England, chose to focus on student writing produced by 11-year-olds and 15-year-olds (Wilkinson, 1986). Since the project's purpose was to focus on the writers' development, conventional grading systems were quickly rejected. The approach to the writing had to be as comprehensive as possible, "looking at the quality of the thought, of the feeling, and of the moral stance manifested in the writing, as well as at the style" (Wilkinson, 1986, p. 14). From the study emerged developmental models that were categorized as Cognitive, Affective, Moral, and Stylistic. Each of these categories was described on a continuum from basic to complex. A summary of each follows:

> *Cognitive:* Students begin with a world that shows few differences among instances—a series of events, each equally important in the mind of the writer—and gradually move toward a view of the world that contains generalities and abstractions and differentiation among events or ideas.
>
> *Affective:* Students begin by acknowledging that other people are present, then move to acknowledging that people have unique qualities, usually by beginning to describe their actions or give their words. Feelings and thoughts of others are considered next. Then analytical or interpretive comments on behavior and character appear, which are

followed by fully developed characterization and finally by the ability to see people and interactions in extended contexts.

Moral: Students start by having no sense of rules, a kind of lawlessness. This, in turn, makes way for rule by giving and receiving from others. Finally, a sense of making independent judgments—a kind of self-rule—emerges.

Stylistic: Students begin with the simple, literal declarative sentence. Features such as structure, cohesion, verbal competence, syntax, reader awareness, and language appropriateness gradually go through modifications, moving toward a growing sophistication.

Two examples from the Crediton study show how these models of development might be identified in students' writing (Wilkinson, Barnsley, Hanna, & Swan, 1983). Peter is 7 years old and provides the following sample of autobiographical writing:

> I got up from bed and in front of me was loads of parcels I opending them, And there was a England football kit. A ball a pair of football boots I was ever so happy. Then I went down stairs and their was a huge dinner on the table then I rember it was my birthday I had a nother suprise as well my anty came round for tea and she gave me three pounds and we had a tea party. I was ever to good that night so my mum let me stay up and watch match of the day then I went to bed that was the happest day of my life. (Wilkinson, 1986, p. 16)

In the Cognitive category, Peter's writing is basically *descriptive,* describing a series of facts and events in chronology. In the Affective category, the writing shows strong egocentricism with a statement about the needs of the self. Others in this case are seen only as contributors to the self's satisfaction: "Mum" provides comfort and rewards; "anty" provides three pounds, and so forth. There is little development of the *physical environment,* and *reality,* or the human condition, in Peter's view, is considered to be under one's control as long as one is "good." In the Moral category, Peter's thinking reflects a fairly low level: Virtue is rewarded, but wrongdoers are punished.

Moving to an examination of the Stylistics of the passage, it becomes evident that the *organization* is basic but complete, with strong emphasis on chronology. Simple connectives such as "and," "but," "as well," and "so," provide the *cohesion,* while simple sentences, or the appearance of simple sentences, provides the *syntactical* structure. In the *lexis* category, Peter has few adjectives or adverbs; instead, there are signals of a developmental stage in word use. Peter relies heavily on multipurpose words, especially universal verbs such as "be," "have," "got," and "go," but these carry no shades of meaning at this stage. In fact, words at this stage rarely have more than a single connotation, and that connotation arises directly from the context in which the words were learned; that is, dinner as midday meal versus dinner as an evening meal. Peter makes little attempt to interest the *reader* in his day, although words such as "rembering" and "suprise" may relieve the listing effect slightly and suggest a developing sense of *appropriateness* in writing. Still, the overall effect is one closer to speech than writing.

By looking at a sample of similar writing done by Pauline, 1 year older than Peter, and applying the same criteria, the reader can discern some differences.

> I had just moved into a new house. I had no friends my sister was only about 4 years old I looked for some friends but I couldn't find any. Then I heard a noise someone was bouncing on a matrue then I looked over the wall and there I found somebody I said who are you? what is your name? she said the same to me it was my old friend I knew in play school (she is in this school now) she is called nicola Thorn. We played skipping until it was time for me to go in. I had my tea and I watched the television and I went to bed I said to myself I think that was the happiest day of my life. Nicola has been one of my Greatest friends right from that day. And she sometimes breaks with me but she soon comes running to me when she is my friend again. (Wilkinson, 1986, p. 17)

Pauline provides a sample of descriptive narrative, but, more significantly, she also interprets and explains, accounting for her isolation. At the end of the piece she implies a possible generalization in her comment about friendship: Friendship can withstand shocks. Pauline acknowledges the importance of Nicola to her happiness and suggests that she may be ready for a more objective view of her relationship ("I said to myself . . . "). She also provides much more information about herself, suggesting awareness of the needs of others. She displays some sense of interaction with her *environment*, but exhibits a more advanced sense of *reality* than Peter does by acknowledging that life has some unpleasantness (people get lonely, quarrel, etc.), but she does not connect these conditions with any *moral* perceptions.

Her *organization* reflects a movement from chronology to narrative. Where chronology's purpose is to provide an almost relentless march of events, narrative calls for selection and development of the unusual or the significant. Pauline shows a growing sensitivity for the reader's needs by providing necessary background and by bringing us up to the present. Over all, however, there remains a strong emphasis on speech features rather than those of writing. Note, for example, the use of asides—"(she is in this school now)." The *lexis* shows more variety than Peter's does, particularly in verb choice ("bouncing," "heard," "played skipping"), and the *syntax* reflects greater variation in sentence structure.

Examining student writing from the perspective suggested by the Crediton Project takes time and cannot be done with each piece of writing. But if teachers accept this new perspective, then they also must accept the premise that children's writing cannot be evaluated on the basis of an adult model. Therefore, classroom teachers would do well to pay more attention to the developmental signals in students' writing and base their instructional decisions, as well as their evaluation of student progress, on such evidence. When writing is approached this way, diagnosis and treatment, as well as evaluation, become inextricably joined and help students understand where they are as well as where they can aspire to be. In all cases the emphasis remains formative.

A successful formative evaluation system for the classroom, then, encompasses an understanding of the composing process and the developmental stages of young writers, a strong diagnostic component, and a method of response that incorporates both teacher and peer evaluation. Such a system should be set up with care, and the system should be continually evaluated for its effectiveness and how it relates to other systems for monitoring students' reading development. Since students move back and forth between reading and writing activities, having compatible systems of evaluation for the two areas is important. As student needs and abilities change, so should the system to accommodate growth as it occurs. With the framework for such a system in place, classroom teachers should never lack evidence of where their students are in their writing or reading development.

Evaluating the Program

Identifying where students are in their development leads to individualization and growth. But the teacher, as well as administrators and parents, will want to know the overall effect a particular writing program may be having at certain grade levels or across grade levels. Gathering the information necessary for what is called *summative evaluation* requires a different approach from that practiced with formative evaluation.

Within the last 7 to 10 years, there has been a marked increase in competency assessments. McCready and Melton (1981) reported that over 40 states now use some form of competency assessment for writing and the number of individual districts requiring writing assessments appears to be on the rise. One positive outcome of this emphasis may be more attention to reading/writing activities in the classroom; however, if the emphasis leads only to teaching for tests, the overall impact on students will be negative.

The findings reported in *Becoming a Nation of Readers* (Anderson, Hiebert, Scott, & Wilkinson, 1985) suggest that children already spend huge amounts of their class time practicing for competency assessments. This practice time is often classified as instruction in reading or writing, but its main purpose is nothing other than rehearsal for the state or district competency tests. Ruth (1987) pointed out that "instead of learning how to read and write, students are having to master the genre of the test question" (p. 757).

Students focus on learning the formats of test items, being accurate within set time limits, and responding to material with little relevance to their own interests or needs. Time taken to test or prepare for tests is wasted when the same time could be devoted to instruction with an integrated evaluation process. The primary goal in any program assessment or evaluation, therefore, should be student learning, not percentile increases.

Standardized examinations rob teachers and students of instructional time; writing samples do not, if they are built into the regular sequence of reading/writing assignments in a program. For that reason, they are favored by writing teachers and have come to be well supported by research as valid measures of a writing program's effectiveness (McCaig, 1981; Myers, 1980). Knowing this, a growing number of districts are incorporating writing samples into their assessment plans. However, these samples are not evaluated in the sense of regular writing assignments; instead, they are scored—in most cases by using either holistic, primary trait, or analytical methods. Each method has particular characteristics that yield slightly different types of information and require slightly different scoring arrangements.

Holistic Scoring

The holistic method has gained considerable favor because it is seen as measuring the full ability to communicate through writing. The holistic approach is also sometimes called *general impression* or *impressionistic* because raters quickly read each paper and place it in rank order from strongest to weakest, not singling out any one item as better or worse than another but treating the writing as a whole. Such an approach may suggest possibilities for wide discrepancies among raters, but as Hillerich (1985) pointed out, reliability can be enhanced in "proportion to (1) the speed with which the papers are read, (2) similarity of the background of the raters, (3) use of anchor papers for comparison, and (4) the averaging of the ratings of at least two raters" (p. 235).

Myers (1980) and McCaig (1981) have provided detailed explanations of how to set up a holistic scoring system for either a school or a district. These guidelines could also be used by teachers in their own classrooms. The main ingredient for a successful holistic scoring program is a group of teachers who are willing to spend time discussing what they look for in a piece of writing. After some common agreement has been reached on features, or what is commonly called a *scoring rubric*, teachers are asked to read and rate a trial sample of papers to determine how much agreement can be reached. Myers (1980) suggested using an even number of rating categories such as 1 to 4 or 1 to 6 to avoid having papers "dumped" in the middle rating. For most groups, a four-category scale seems to work best, since the more categories there are, the more preciseness is necessary from the raters. Without considerable practice, reaching that degree of precision can become time consuming, and the effort required does not seem to justify the result. Rubrics can be quite complex (see Greenhalgh & Townsend, 1981) or fairly simple (see Figure 11.1).

After an initial reading, the raters compare their rankings of papers. The discussion centers on reasons for differences in ratings, and an attempt is made to resolve wide variations in rankings. Eventually, anchor or range marker papers are selected by consensus for each rating category; in many cases, a high and a low paper within each category are identified. Then the raters read another set of papers, using the anchor papers as benchmarks for rating the new papers. The raters again compare rankings, discuss differences, and perhaps adjust anchor papers slightly. This process continues until the raters show consistency in their rankings as a group. At that point, the reading begins in earnest, with occasional breaks to check on consistency.

Each paper receives a reading by at least two different raters; the sum of the two ratings is averaged and the paper placed appropriately; if there is a wide variation in the ratings, a third reader can be assigned and the two closest rankings are used. Duke (1985), and Mellon (1975) have reported interrater reliability correlations as high as .70 to .80 when the holistic approach is used correctly. Although the process may sound time consuming, once readers are familiar with the agreed-upon categories and have participated in the selection of range markers, the readings go rapidly, since no marking or written commentary is necessary. The one caution is that all papers must be of the same mode and stem from the same assignment. The results are valid only for the particular group of papers scored.

Holistic scoring provides a way for teachers to compare performance within a class, across classes, or throughout a school or district. The method does not provide individual diagnostic information, but it offers useful data for tracking changes in performance of large groups and providing a fast, yet reliable, way of determining the effectiveness of a writing program, especially if pre- and postassessments are done.

FIGURE 11.1 1–4 Holistic Scale

1: The writer offers nothing related to the topic aside from perhaps a single sentence or a paragraph of an idea from a recognized source.

2: The writer offers several sentences or approximations (run-ons) related to the topic but lacks organization; suggests random thinking in places; lacks a clear sense of structure.

3: The writer offers a number of sentences clearly related to the topic; demonstrates a sense of beginning and ending; provides some specific examples that support the topic. The writer provides a sense of a complete message.

4: The writer displays the same characteristics as item 3 on the scale, but also demonstrates originality of wording and ideas and/or has a more polished writing style; suggests a personality behind the writing.

Primary Trait Scoring

The National Assessment of Educational Progress (Mellon, 1975) has used primary trait scoring with consistent success in its various nationwide assessments of student writing. The method differs from impressionistic scoring in several ways and requires more careful preparation and scoring. Primary trait scoring relies heavily on the careful design of a writing assignment that specifies topic, purpose, and audience and that calls for the presence of a particular trait such as description or narration. Once the writing task has been developed (and preferably field-tested on an appropriate student population), a detailed scoring guide, called a *rubric*, must be developed. This rubric identifies the particular elements that must be present in the writing for evaluation. The rubric is then tested on a sampling of papers written for the assignment and is refined as necessary. After the rubric has been tested, readers are trained in its use in much the same fashion as for impressionistic readings. The procedures from this point on are parallel, including the double readings, the averaging of scores, and so forth.

One of the writing prompts used by the National Assessment of Educational Progress in 1974 with children ages 9, 13, and 17 called for use of primary trait scoring. The scoring guide used with this exercise appears in Figure 11.2. The prompt provided students with a printed photograph of five children playing on an overturned rowboat and the following directions:

> Look carefully at the picture. These kids are having fun jumping on the overturned boat. Imagine you are one of the children in the picture. Or, if you wish, imagine that you are someone standing nearby watching the children. Tell what is going on as she or he would tell it. Write as if you were telling this to a good friend, in a way that expresses strong feelings. Help your friend FEEL the experience too. (Lloyd-Jones, 1977, p. 48)

Results from such a scoring do not yield a great deal of useful diagnostic information, although some teachers have begun to use the primary trait approach as a basis for identifying particular problems students may have with a certain mode of writing. Basically, however, primary trait scoring reveals how well a group of students write in a particular mode. Like impressionistic scoring, therefore, the method is appropriate only for determining how effectively a particular form of writing has been taught in a program. A series of primary trait scoring exercises, done over the span of a year, could yield some interesting data about differences or similarities in performance as students move from one writing mode to another. Using such data, teachers could then adjust their programs to provide more practice in modes with which students seem to have the greatest difficulty.

FIGURE 11.2 Primary Trait Scoring Guide

Entire Exercise

0 Makes no response; gives sentence fragments.
1 Is scorable.
2 Is illegible or illiterate.
3 Does not refer to picture at all.
9 I don't know.

Use of Dialogue

0 Does not use dialogue in the story.
1 Gives direct quote from one person in the story. The one person may talk more than once. When in doubt whether two statements are made by the same person or different people, code 1. A direct quote of a thought counts. Can be in hypothetical tense.
2 Gives direct quote from two or more persons in the story.

Point of View

0 Point of view cannot be determined, or does not control point of view.
1 Point of view is consistently one of the five children. Include "If I were one of the children . . ." and recalling participation as one of the children.
2 Point of view is consistently one of an observer. When an observer joins the children in the play, the point of view is still "2" because the observer makes a sixth person playing. Include papers with minimal evidence even when difficult to tell which point of view is being taken.

Tense

0 Writer cannot determine time, or does not control tense. (One wrong tense places paper in this category, except drowned in the present.)
1 Uses present tense. Past tense may also be present if not part of the "main line" of the story.
2 Uses past tense. If a past tense description is acceptable brought up to present, code as "past." Sometimes the present is used to create a frame for past events. Code this as past, since the actual description is in the past.
3 Uses hypothetical time. Papers written entirely in the "if I were in the boat" or "If I were there, I would." These papers often include future references such as "when I get on the boat I will." If part is hypothetical and the rest past or present and tense is controlled, code present or past. If introduction, up to two sentences, is only part in past or present, then code hypothetical.

Note: From Lloyd-Jones, R. (1977). Primary trait scoring. In C. Cooper & L. Odell (Eds.), *Evaluating writing* (pp. 47–53). Copyright © 1977 by the National Council of Teachers of English. Reprinted by permission of the publisher.

Analytical Scoring

One of the earliest large-scale assessment methods for rating writing samples was developed by Diedrich (1974). From his approach has evolved the analytical scale, which falls between the impressionistic and the primary trait in terms of its degree of difficulty and format. Like primary trait scoring, analytical scoring requires identification of particular elements of writing expected to be found in effective pieces. When these are agreed upon, they are placed into a rubric much like the one shown in Figure 11.3.

Surveying such a rubric reveals what most experienced writing teachers would agree ought to appear in effective writing. The particular labels may vary from group to group, but considerable agreement emerges from such discussions. A group of teachers will find that just the discussions alone of what constitutes an effective piece of writing will help tremendously in clarifying the goals of a writing program, not to mention leading to greater consistency in evaluation throughout the school. Time should be provided, however, for teachers to develop a rubric that they find acceptable. Presenting a rubric designed by someone else will tend to lead to needless debate. Teachers need to feel they have a stake in the evaluation process, and by generating their own criteria for effective writing they will be more committed to the assessment and it will more closely reflect the student population being evaluated. Since learning to write effectively is a developmental process, teachers need to adjust their expectations for the grade levels being evaluated.

Once the analysis of effective writing has been done, the resulting rubric should be tried out by the raters on some sample papers; any necessary modifications in the criteria can then be made. When agreement emerges, the full-scale reading begins. Although it may appear that having so many features will slow the reading, most readers find, after some practice with the analytical scale, that it does not impede their reading. However, sufficient discussion and examination of representative papers should occur so that all readers share the same general view for each feature. Some groups do not use the ranking numbers at all but continue to use range markers representing broad categories. Others may find that they want to use an overall score compiled from the numbers so that they can track more closely which features are handled well and which are weak. Regardless of the approach, consistency in application and reporting is the main concern.

None of these approaches is fool proof. They are subject to the decisions of a group of readers who may or may not agree with another group of readers from a different school or program. Factors such as handwriting, word choice, length, even topic, can influence the ratings. However, the alternative of norm-referenced tests provides information only about individual elements of writing. With careful attention to training teachers, setting realistic tasks for students, and monitoring the scoring, useful, reliable, and

FIGURE 11.3 Sample Analytic Scoring Rubric

Organization

1 Clear organization is absent; is unclear, confusing.
2 Is somewhat disjointed; is not always related to topic.
3 Demonstrates thought, stays with main idea; has order.
4 Is well organized; expands main idea; has good transitions.

Sentence Structure and Word Choice

1 Any semblance of sentence structure is absent; uses highly general vocabulary.
2 Has mostly sentence fragments, run-ons or connected with "and"; mostly general vocabulary.
3 Sentences are complete but lacking in variety and development; uses more precise vocabulary but occasionally misuses wording.
4 Sentences are complete and show variety in type; effective selection of words.

Flavor

1 Is dull, uninteresting.
2 Is imitative of models, but clear.
3 Personal examples, some originality are present; shows interest in subject, but cannot sustain it.
4 Shows sense of real person behind piece; uses language originally and effectively; uses effective, concrete examples.

Fluency

1 0–20 words.
2 21–50 words.
3 51–80 words.
4 81 or more words.

Mechanics

1 Has so many errors as to be unreadable.
2 Shows frequent erratic punctuation, capitalization, and spelling.
3 Has reduced number of errors, which do not interfere with meaning.
4 Has virtually no errors.

valid measures of large-group writing performance can be produced. Such assessments provide teachers, administrators, parents, and even students with a reasonable basis for comparisons about the effectiveness of writing instruction and their writing program.

Reporting Results

At some point in any system of evaluating writing, the time comes when a public reporting of the results is necessary. If the teacher has been using formative evaluation on a regular basis as outlined in this chapter, then the public accounting should not present difficulties. But providing feedback to students and parents on the development of writing skills should not focus solely on assigning letter grades or percentages to writing performance. Any symbol or percentage means little unless supported by clear, specific responses that provide the student or parent with a basis for interpretation.

The groundwork for reporting results should be laid at the beginning of the school year, not at the end. Teachers who intend to use the writing process and stress formative evaluation should alert parents to this by means of either a letter home explaining the goals of the program or a presentation for parents at a PTA meeting. Some schools have developed brief booklets that explain their reading/writing program and the evaluation process. The booklets contain nontechnical explanations of the measures to be used and provide sample anchor papers and teacher comments.

All schools have a regular reporting schedule already in place based on the usual marking periods. If the teacher establishes a portfolio system to track the writing done by students, the report issued at the end of each marking period should be easy to compile. These student portfolios range in complexity from having a writing folder for each student in which are placed all drafts of written work to having the more complex ones suggested by Newman (1982) and Hillerich (1985) that include forms for keeping track of various error patterns in the students' work, a series of conferencing notes, and the actual writing done. Portfolios have a number of other uses besides providing evidence for reporting. For example, students find the portfolios useful for keeping track of their own progress; they can date their drafts, and, if the portfolios are kept in a certain place in the classroom, each student has ready access to his or her work without worrying about losing it. The portfolio also becomes a useful resource during conferences between student and teacher because quick reviews of progress up to a certain point are possible. Teachers also like the portfolios because students can easily locate pieces to work on in workshops or to use as a basis for other language skill lessons. Of course, the portfolios are always available as a reference during parent/teacher conferences.

The portfolios serve another important function. By keeping their work in progress on file, students have ample opportunity to revise it. The teacher also can postpone grading individual pieces and can concentrate on more helpful formative evaluation during the writing process. Each marking period, students can select from their portfolios the two or three pieces they believe represent their best work for the period. These are polished and then submitted for a writing grade. Contrary to popular belief, students do not need grades on every piece of work in order to continue to improve. As was suggested previously in this chapter, if formative evaluation in the form of conferencing, written comments, and peer response occurs regularly, students will know where they are in their development. The A, B, or C that goes on a paper tells far less to the student, and students quickly learn this.

Reporting program evaluation and the particular level of achievement for each student within the program should be handled in two ways. First, actual public reports of grade- or school-level achievement should be done with a clear explanation of the evaluation process and its limitations. Efforts also should be made to include a variety of data in the reports on students to provide a true reflection of their development. Cooper (1975) and Straw (1981) have outlined useful systems of evaluation that can result in a variety of data that show student growth in various aspects of writing skill but avoid grading students against each other. Such systems help to educate the public to the importance of seeing evaluations in a broader context than just single performance on a single test. Second, teachers should base their summative reports to students and parents on what the student actually has done in the program, not on some outside standard. Again, the portfolio provides a much better basis for assessment than any single test. Among the questions about a student's performance teachers might want to consider in summative evaluations are the following:

- What subjects and modes of writing has the student undertaken and what do these suggest about the student's development?
- What signs of stylistic development appear in the writing?
- What indications of increased fluency appear in the writing?
- What features of syntax and punctuation does the student seem to understand?
- What understanding of structural features (beginnings, endings, chronology, narrative, etc.) does the student seem to have?
- What evidence of revision and self-evaluation appears in the student's writing?

SUMMARY

McCaig (1981) observed that "if the right time for learning is not seized in a child's developmental history, the omission may be irreparable. Many students who do not learn to compose in the elementary grades may never learn to write competently" (p. 92). But if teachers have developed their diagnostic skills and have identified the developmental stages of the writers with whom they work, evaluation of any kind should be demonstrably easier and more precise. After all, the signs of progress along the way tell more about instruction and its effect on students than any single final performance. If teachers provide systematic evaluation of both a formative and summative nature to students as an integrated part of reading/writing programs, they should note demonstrable improvement in students' writing performance.

FOLLOW-UP QUESTIONS AND ACTIVITIES

1. Recall some of your own writing experiences at an early age. How did teachers respond to your writing? What effect did these responses have on your willingness to write?
2. Based on your reading in this chapter, how would you now define *evaluation* as it is used in relation to writing?
3. What are some of the different ways to conference with students about their writing?
4. What are the different stages students experience in their development as writers? How are these stages recognized?
5. Select two pieces of student writing. Evaluate one fully, marking all errors and writing extensive comments. Respond to the second piece selectively, identifying the major problem and focusing all your comments on that area. Now compare the appearance of the two papers and answer the following questions:
   a. If you were a student, which paper might cause you to approach revision more positively?
   b. In the first paper, how will the student know which problems are most serious and where he or she ought to begin revising?
6. Write a short piece on any subject of your choosing; then find several people to form a response group. Ask them to listen to your piece and then to respond. Analyze the kinds of comments you receive and how you feel about them. From this experience, formulate some guidelines for how you would like students to respond in peer groups. If possible, test your guidelines' effectiveness.

ADDITIONAL READINGS

Chall, J. S., & Jacobs, V. A. (1983). Writing and reading in the elementary grades: Developmental trends among low SES children. *Language Arts, 60*, 617–626.

Duke, C. R. (1975). The student-centered conference and the writing process. *English Journal, 64*, 44–47.

Graves, D. H., & Giacobbe, M. E. (1982). Research update: Questions for teachers who wonder if their writers change. *Language Arts, 59*, 495–502.

McDonell, G. M., & Osburn, E. B. (1980). Beginning writing: Watching it develop. *Language Arts, 57*, 310–314.

Newkirk, T. (1985). The hedgehog or the fox: The dilemma of writing development. *Language Arts, 62,* 593–603.

Russell, C. (1983). Putting research into practice: Conferencing with young writers. *Language Arts, 60,* 333–340.

REFERENCES

Anderson, R. C., Hiebert, E. H., Scott, J. A., & Wilkinson, A. G. (1985). *Becoming a nation of readers: The report of the Commission on Reading.* Champaign, IL: Center for the Study of Reading.

Bissex, G. (1980). *Guys at work: A child learns to write and read.* Cambridge, MA: Harvard University Press.

Calkins, L. (1986). *The art of teaching writing.* Exeter, NH: Heinemann.

Cooper, C. (1975). Measuring growth in writing. *English Journal, 64,* 111–120.

Diedrich, P. B. (1974). *Measuring growth in English.* Urbana, IL: National Council of Teachers of English.

Duke, C. R. (1985). Developing a writing assessment of candidates for admission to teacher education. *Journal of Teacher Education, 36,* 7–11.

Graves, D. H. (1983). *Writing: Teachers and children at work.* Exeter, NH: Heinemann.

Greenhalgh, C., & Townsend, D. (1981). Evaluating students' writing holistically: An alternative approach. *Language Arts, 58,* 811–821.

Hillerich, R. L. (1985). *Teaching children to write K–8.* Englewood Cliffs, NJ: Prentice-Hall.

Jackson, B. (1965). *English versus examination.* London: Chatto and Windus.

Lagana, J. R. (1972). *The development, implementation, and evaluation of a model for teaching composition which utilizes individualized learning and peer grouping.* Unpublished doctoral dissertation, University of Pittsburgh.

Lloyd-Jones, R. (1977). Primary trait scoring. In C. R. Cooper & L. Odell (Eds.), *Evaluating writing* (pp. 33–68). Urbana, IL: National Council of Teachers of English.

McCaig, R. A. (1981). A district-wide plan for the evaluation of student writing. In S. Haley-James (Ed.), *Perspectives on writing in grades 1–8* (pp. 73–92). Urbana, IL: National Council of Teachers of English.

McCready, M., & Melton, V. S. (1981, December). *Feasibility of assessing writing using multiple assessment techniques.* (Research Report No. NIEG-80-0195). Ruston: Louisiana Tech University, College of Education.

Meeks, L. (1986). *Developing the internal editor: Peer revision in a third grade class.* Unpublished doctoral dissertation, Arizona State University.

Mellon, J. C. (1975). *National assessment of the teaching of English.* Urbana, IL: National Council of Teachers of English.

Myers, M. (1980). *A procedure for writing assessment and holistic scoring.* Urbana, IL: National Council of Teachers of English.

Newman, R. E. (1982). *Reading, writing, and self-esteem.* Englewood Cliffs, NJ: Prentice-Hall.

Peacock, C. (1986). *Teaching writing.* London: Croon Helm.

Protherough, R. (1983). *Encouraging writing.* London: Methuen.

Ruth, L. (1987). Reading children's writing. *The Reading Teacher, 40,* 756–760.

Straw, S. B. (1981). Assessment and evaluation in written composition: A commonsense perspective. In V. Froese & S. B. Straw (Eds.), *Research in the language arts: Language and schooling* (pp. 181–202). Baltimore: University Park Press.

Wilkinson, A. (1986). *The quality of writing.* Milton Keynes, England: Open University Press.

Wilkinson, A., Barnsley, G., Hanna, P., & Swan, M. (1983). More comprehensive assessment of writing development. *Language Arts, 60,* 871–881.

PART THREE

Effective Organization and Management of the Classroom Reading Program

Part Three deals with issues related to effective management and organization of the classroom reading program. Chapter 12 presents an overview of the organizational decisions that the effective teacher must consider in order to cope with the realities of individualizing instruction in the classroom. Chapters 13 and 14 provide suggestions for planning effective reading lessons. Chapter 13 deals with effective use of basal readers, while Chapter 14 discusses elements of a well-planned reading lesson. Adapting reading instruction to the special needs of students is the topic of Chapter 15. Chapter 16 concludes Part Three with information on and suggestions for involving parents and volunteers in the classroom reading program.

12

Organizing for Effective Reading Instruction

WINNIE R. HUEBSCH

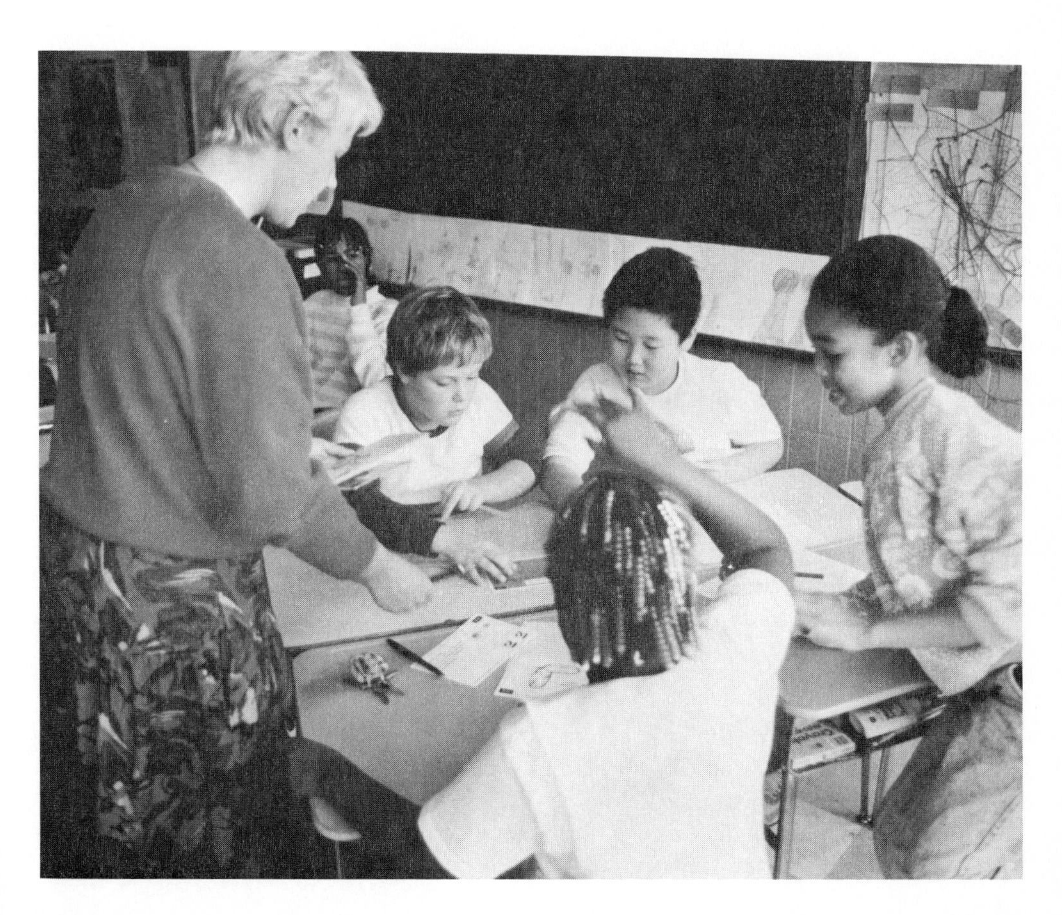

THERE ARE MANY factors that effective teachers must consider as they begin to organize their reading program. In Chapter 12, Winnie R. Huebsch discusses what instructional programs are most appropriate for reading and writing and what organizational approaches might best contribute to student growth in these areas. She first provides a discussion of the characteristics of well-organized teachers and classrooms. She then points out that recent research suggests that direct instruction by the teacher with small groups of children is effective. However, she cautions that this approach is not without its concerns, and she advocates that effective teachers be flexible both in the types of instruction they provide and the ways they group children for instruction.

An overview of four different approaches to organizing students for instruction are provided, along with a discussion of how effective teachers might arrange the classroom environment to best facilitate the selected grouping plans. The chapter concludes with an overview of the importance of selection and use of instructional materials and a record-keeping program.

STUDY QUESTIONS

1. What constitutes an effectively organized classroom? Think of those classrooms from your own school experience that appeared to you to be the most conducive to learning.
2. What teacher behaviors are necessary for running a classroom smoothly?
3. Were you instructed in reading with a basal reading series? Were you grouped for reading instruction? What memories do you have of that experience?
4. What different ways are there to group children for reading instruction? How can children's ability levels, interest levels, and ability to concentrate influence your grouping practice?
5. What form of room arrangement appeals most to you?

Teachers are the prime movers in organizing the environment in which learning takes place. Our planning and daily instruction influences the classroom environment in so many ways that any evaluation of students becomes an evaluation of ourselves and of the management and organization we bring to the learning environment. Seeing ourselves reflected in the classroom environment and in the varied responses of the children entrusted to our care helps us to better understand the nature of language learning, reading, and writing and also allows us to become more aware of the influence *we* have on that learning process.

This chapter considers several factors that contribute to an effectively organized classroom. We know that effective teachers conceptualize and organize for classroom instruction, maintain orderly environments, select materials thoughtfully, and arrange the physical nature of the room in such a way as to make the environment conducive to learning. An effectively organized classroom makes provisions for the uniqueness, individual capabilities, and learning needs of all students. Therefore, an effective teacher is aware of the crucial factors that can, and often do, influence a child's performance in reading.

Characteristics of an Effectively Organized Classroom

Managing for classroom instruction is a many-faceted concept that defies a precise definition. The main purpose of effective management is to enhance and enliven the learning potential of children by manipulating certain aspects of the schooling process. While there is a great deal of literature on classroom management, a review of recent research appears to suggest that, although teachers differ considerably in the ways they organize their classrooms for reading instruction, students generally continue to spend more time on their own with workbooks and worksheets than in group instruction (Otto, Wolf, & Eldridge, 1984). However, the results of these management effectiveness studies do suggest that teachers' management decisions affect student performance. Therefore, we should be aware of the characteristics of *effective classrooms* that enhance the reading and learning environment. What follows is a discussion of the characteristics of the educational setting and teacher behaviors that are essential to providing students with effective learning experiences.

Instructional Setting

Mangiere (1980) noted the following characteristics of effective instructional settings:

- Individual differences of children are recognized and valued, and provisions are made to accommodate those differences.
- Ongoing and comprehensive diagnosis occurs in order to determine a student's reading strengths and weaknesses.
- Both immediate planning and long-range planning for effective reading instruction take place regularly.

- The "nonteaching conditions" of the educational setting are employed to their maximum potential.
- Instructional procedures that will produce optimal reading achievement for all children in the classroom are used.
- Evaluation is conducted in a continuous, ongoing, and thorough manner and is integral to the process of teaching and learning.

The effectively organized classroom makes provisions for the diverse reading, writing, and language capabilities of each child. The thoughtful teacher acts as facilitator of the learning process, providing an emotional and physical environment that is conducive to risk taking and literacy learning. The nonteaching conditions of the educational setting, such as the child's emotional and social growth, are considered as thoughtfully as the academics involved. Most important, children are valued for the knowledge they bring to the learning process.

Teacher Behaviors

We all have had occasion to reflect on that certain teacher in our educational career who seemed to involve us in the creative process to such a degree that the class remained actively engaged and happily involved in the learning process. It may be one of the reasons we chose to join the teaching profession, for model teachers have tremendous impact on their students. Kounin (1970) found that the following six teacher behaviors were positively correlated with student work involvement and freedom from disruption:

1. *Withitness:* the ability of a teacher to be aware of what is going on in all parts of the classroom (the old "eyes in back of the head" syndrome).
2. *Overlapping:* the ability to do two or more things at the same time.
3. *Smoothness:* the ability to end one activity and move directly to another without destroying the rhythm of the classroom and the ability to deal with minor management problems effectively.
4. *Momentum:* the ability to maintain the pace during an activity and make quick and efficient transitions.
5. *Accountability:* the awareness of the response performance of all students in the group, making sure that all students participate and that there is corrective feedback, if necessary.
6. *Alerting:* the ability to keep all students attentive to the task at hand.

These behaviors are exhibited by the most effective teachers, because their time is not wasted during class transitions, the lesson moves efficiently, the learning environment is positive, and children remain productively engaged in the learning process. Rosenshine & Stevens (1984) noted that the indicators of effective instruction include the *amount of content covered, academic engaged time,* and *student error rate.* They maintained that higher achievement in school is directly related to briskly paced lessons that cover more content, students who display on-task behaviors, and performance that results in a low error rate for young students. Therefore, it appears that the most effectively managed classrooms reflect a warm, productive atmosphere in which both children and teachers actively, purposefully, and enthusiastically engage in literacy learning.

The very best teachers are reflective in the analysis of their performance, respecting all members of the learning community. They use their knowledge of the physical and emotional needs of their students to make informed judgments about instruction. Teacher behavior and attitude strongly set the tone of the instructional setting.

Approaches to Reading Instruction

Direct Instruction

Research has noted that most reading comprehension instruction involves assessment (Durkin, 1978–1979), with teachers asking the majority of questions and telling students whether or not their answers are correct. Durkin noted that specific instruction directed toward helping a student learn a rule of process for aiding in reading comprehension occurred less than 1% of the time during the typical reading lesson. How, then, can teachers best enhance the learning process, improve student involvement, and promote comprehension development and literacy learning in order to have the most effective classroom possible for reading instruction? Several researchers (Berliner, 1981; Rosenshine & Stevens, 1984; Samuels, 1981) have suggested that direct instruction in reading is most beneficial.

These scholars maintain that students who receive instruction from a teacher consistently do better on reading achievement tests than those who are expected to learn on their own. They also suggest that rapid-paced, teacher-directed, small-group instruction is more efficient than one-to-one instruction and allows for better supervision than large-group instruction. The direct instruction model provides for instruction, guided practice, feedback, and independent practice. Chapter 14 provides guidelines for effectively employing many of these suggestions.

According to Rosenshine and Stevens

> Investigators have found that 1) students who receive much of their instruction from the teacher do better than those expected to learn on their own or from each other and 2) students learn to read most efficiently when teachers use systematic instruction, monitor student responses, and give students feedback about their performance. (p. 746)

However, Goodman, Goodman, and Hood (1989) have questioned whether achievement tests accurately reflect the reading and learning process, pointedly challenging the direct instruction model. They have challenged the notion of behavioral objectives, mastery learning, and narrow curricula and criticized the standardized, multiple-choice reading tests commonly used to measure achievement in reading. They maintain that these tests are contrived, confining, and controlling and reduce reading and writing to trivial, decontextualized, and abstract skills.

Depending on the nature of the instructional situation and the sense of personal responsibility and ability levels of the individual students, direct instruction varies in its effectiveness. The apparent key to the effectiveness of direct instruction is not that teachers consistently prefer either large- or small-group instruction in reading or choose to use prepackaged published materials, but that they remain *flexible* in their formation and use of reading/learning groups. According to Vacca, Vacca, and Gove (1987):

> If our purpose is to increase gains in achievement test scores . . . students may perform slightly better on these tests with direct or traditional teaching. If our purpose is to develop creativity and problem-solving or to improve students' attitudes, independence, and curiosity, students may do somewhat better with less traditional teaching. (p. 418)

Direct instruction, while applauded by some teachers and rejected by others, is strongly associated with most traditional basal reading programs currently used in the majority of elementary school classrooms in the United States, although these reading materials may be used in many diversified ways. Otto, Wolf, and Eldridge (1984) noted that basal series are characterized by their comprehensiveness. The typical series structures a total curriculum for teaching reading in kindergarten through grade 6 and provides all the necessary materials (readers, workbooks, worksheets, and reinforcement activities) needed for carrying out reading instruction. (Chapter 13 offers a detailed discussion of effective basal reading instruction.)

Advocates of basal series claim that children benefit from a systematic and comprehensive organization of the curriculum. Critics claim that these series promote and encourage lock step group instruction, denying the children access to natural literacy events (Otto, Wolf, & Eldridge, 1984). In spite of the diversity of opinions of traditional basal reading series, in actuality the vast majority of school districts have adopted them as part of their formal reading program, and many individual classroom teachers have chosen to use certain portions of these prepackaged curricula during at least some portion of their reading instructional time. Given these considerations, it is appropriate to discuss how to use these reading and learning tools most effectively. The use of basal readers is strongly associated with the practice of grouping.

Grouping

One of the most commonly observed phenomena in the elementary school setting is the traditional reading group. Many of us remember these groups from our own school experiences. Daily reading circles of low, average, or high ability levels often gathered for "round-robin" oral reading from basal readers. Some may have stronger memories of them than others, remembering with a chill the child who struggled so valiantly in the group but was unable to perform and became increasingly frustrated and unmotivated. It must be noted that while there are distinct benefits to certain grouping practices, grouping for expediency's sake can be harmful. Grouping children solely by reading level does *not* account for variations in learning rate and for the wide range of specific reading proficiencies that are typical within most elementary classrooms.

Homogeneous grouping is achieved when students are brought together who are more nearly alike than other students in the population. The stated purpose of homogeneous grouping is to facilitate planning and instruction in order to accommodate students' individual needs and allow them to experience learning with other students who have similar characteristics. Homogeneous grouping may be done within the classroom or without regard for grade placement, much as secondary school departmentalization is handled.

For example, many teachers choose to group children according to reading ability level, dividing the classroom into three instructional reading groups. While one group works with the teacher on oral reading, story discussion, or word analysis skills, the other two groups work independently on seatwork or reinforcement activities of some kind. Many teachers find that homogeneous grouping relieves the pressures of continuous classroom management. However, recent studies show that the practice of tracking students in this way appears to actually *depress* the achievement of students assigned to low groups. These students are given fewer and poorer opportunities to learn than their more advanced peers. Kulik and Kulik (1982) reviewed 52 studies of homogeneous grouping and found the following:

- Grouping generally has little effect on student achievement.
- Students in high ability groups benefit more in relation to achievement gains than those assigned to low ability groups.
- Ability grouping has only trivial effects on the achievement of average and below average children.

Heterogeneous grouping is intended to facilitate individualization by eliminating some of the most common constraints of the traditional self-contained elementary classroom. Heterogeneous grouping allows for a mixture of ability, interest, or discussion levels among students, allowing children of high and low ability to interact freely and learn from the experiences and knowledge each has to offer the other. Discussion and interaction can be powerful tools for exploring new concepts and ideas, which are so necessary for true literacy learning. With heterogeneous grouping, peers can provide models of speaking, listening, reading, and writing from which the lowest and highest ability students can benefit. Such grouping demands a wide range of reading and writing materials, as well as respect for the individual learning needs and styles of every child in the group, regardless of ability. It also demands insightfulness and organizational ability on the part of the teacher.

Recent research appears to indicate that heterogeneous grouping provides more leadership opportunities, tolerance for the uniqueness of individuals, and positive role models for children of low ability than does homogeneous grouping (Wisconsin Department of Education, 1986). Students are allowed to progress at their own rate when the conventional ability grouping situation is eliminated and replaced with a more flexible learning environment. Heterogeneous grouping, combined with individualization of instruction whenever possible, appears to be effective in meeting the needs of children's inquisitive minds. O'Donnell and Moore (1980) summarized the research and literature on grouping as follows:

1. Homogeneous grouping has not been demonstrated to be an effective method for raising the reading achievement levels of students.
2. Ability grouping tends to result in the "hardening" of the categories, especially among low-achieving students.
3. Interaction among students of different achievement levels tends to stimulate low-achieving students positively.
4. Criteria for forming groups have to be carefully examined.
5. Grouping plans should include an examination of the strengths and weaknesses within groups.

Individualized Instruction

At the opposite end of most schemes of curriculum management is *individualized reading instruction.* Here, the emphasis is on self-discovery, self-selection of reading/learning materials, and self-pacing by the student. Reading activities often flow spontaneously from topics under discussion, which have been identified by students as relevant and personally meaningful. Self-selection of materials is an integral part of such a program. There is an integrative approach to reading and language arts instruction wherein listening, speaking, reading, and writing are treated as mutually supportive and are often combined during instructional time. In some instances, small groups may be convened; however, group structure is often temporary and flexible, changing as the learning needs or instructional demands change. More often, students work on their own. The basic characteristics of individualized reading instruction are as follows:

- Joint teacher and student diagnosis.
- Joint teacher and student prescription for improvement.
- Student selection of goals, learning materials, activities, and instructional aids.
- Self-pacing and self-leveling.
- Objectives and prescriptions based on student interest.
- Stress on student creativity. (O'Donnell & Moore, 1980)

Teachers *can* structure an individualized reading and learning environment, but it requires a bit of dexterity. Beginning readers appear to need more teacher direction than older students, and they are not as capable of prolonged independent work. However, a wide variety of and easy access to materials *and* an opportunity to use these materials independently seem to enhance this form of reading instruction. Student interest and learning centers in the classroom also facilitate this kind of instruction. Consequently, classroom arrangement is essential to an effectively run individualized reading program.

Whole Language Instruction

Whole language instruction is a grassroots movement among teachers, motivated in part by a positive view of the teaching and learning experience and a new understanding of language development and learning (Goodman, Goodman, & Hood, 1989). It involves an integration of oral and written language with conceptual learning; that is, whole language instruction believes that the individual learns to read and write while reading and writing to learn new concepts. Whole language instruction has its roots in New Zealand and Australia and has only recently been adopted as an instructional philosophy by many teachers in the United States. Teachers who use this approach have rebelled against traditional reading textbooks, behavioral objectives, and standardized test measures, believing them to be artificially contrived and not representative of the true learning process.

Whole class instruction is often employed, using a language experience model for reading instruction (Hall, 1981), and small-group instruction emphasizes the process writing model for writing instruction (Graves, 1983). Children are then encouraged to work in small interest or activity groups to apply the processes of reading and writing to meaningful situations. The major focus of the approach is as follows:

1. Reading and writing are viewed as processes, rather than an accumulation of small skills.
2. Children are asked to respond to the largest units of meaning first, as in whole selections, and only after this immersion are they asked to

respond to smaller units of meaning such as the word, sentence, or paragraph.

3. Traditional scope-and-sequence-of-skills orientations to reading instruction are viewed as inappropriate to whole language instruction, which prefers to introduce skills within the framework of meaningful reading situations and only as needed.
4. The language arts are integrated meaningfully and purposefully.
5. Assessment is holistic, focusing on the *process* rather than merely on the product. Interaction, observation, and analysis are employed. (Goodman, 1986; Goodman, Goodman, & Hood, 1989; Harp, 1988)

While whole language instruction is relatively new to many classrooms in the United States, it is becoming an increasingly popular method of instruction, demanding a flexible grouping and learning environment. The environment is viewed as critical to effective learning. Consequently, room organization plays a major role in the whole language approach.

Room Organization

Regardless of what type of grouping arrangement you choose to use with your students or your personal preference for whole class or small group instruction, a room organization that reflects the true nature of the teaching/learning process in your classroom is essential. One of the most important things a teacher must do is create a warm, accepting, and risk-free environment in which children can blossom as learners. Unfortunately, these environments do not appear by magic. Individual classrooms come with unique characteristics—chalkboards and bulletin boards, sinks (or lack of them), desks or tables for students and teacher, shelves, dividers, closets, and wall space. We are often given these items on the first day of school, rather than having the opportunity to select what we want. What we choose to do with them and how we choose to arrange them promotes or hinders our effectiveness.

Spatial arrangements are important in the classroom. Some activities are quiet; others noisy. Some activities require children to be near particular materials or shelves and to engage in independent or group activities. Room arrangement plays an important role in the effectiveness of these activities. Classrooms that focus on individualization or whole language concepts are often noisier than traditional classrooms. Rugs are useful in absorbing some of the sound made during noisy activities. Attractive, cozy reading corners or learning center areas, out of the way of direct traffic areas, help create a risk-free environment that promotes independent learning/thinking activities. Desks may be moved into groups of two or four, providing for more movement space within the room. Dividers may be used to help the child who has a tendency to become easily distracted. As you set up your classroom, be mindful of the traffic patterns that will promote the greatest access to materials and self-expression without hindering the activities of others within the classroom.

Learning centers or *stations* are one way of organizing to individualize instruction, reflecting a compromise between the traditionally structured classroom environment and the disenchantment resulting from too-noisy or undirected classroom atmospheres. The purpose of the learning center is to create a classroom environment conducive to individualized reading instruction and to increase the opportunity for students to become involved in activities that are self-directive and thought provoking (Tierney, Readance, & Dishner, 1985). An area is set aside for a particular focus, and students have easy access to the materials available in that area. Listening stations with tape recorders and headsets; writing areas with access to pencils, paper, scissors, crayons, and tape; reading centers with an abundance and rich variety of material available at the child's independent reading level; science and mathematics centers with hands-on activities—all promote the individualization of instruction and learning. Dividers may be used to partition learning centers off from other learning areas, if necessary. While room organization varies according to the availability of materials and nature of instruction, the diagrams shown in Figures 12.1 and 12.2 provide a useful framework for classroom organization possibilities.

The environmental elements of sound, light, and temperature must be considered as well as the design of the classroom (Carbo, Dunn, & Dunn, 1986). Give some consideration to the artificial lighting design. Is it efficient? Can modifications be made, if necessary? Children may be adversely affected by an environment that is either too bright or too dim. Sound bothers some children as well. Give consideration to the sound elements within your classroom and the hall patterns outside of it. Are the distractible children seated near the doorway? If so, it may be better to provide them an area with fewer distractions. Finally, room temperature can affect young children. An environment that is overly warm promotes drowsiness and inattention. Give proper attention to the heating elements in the room, allowing fresh air in as often as possible.

Materials

Children respond well to educational materials that fit their needs and draw them naturally into the learning process. A lack of proper materials for instruction can limit effectiveness, but creative teachers are able to fit available instructional materials to the perceived needs of their students and do not let the materials control the learning process. A materials-driven curricu-

FIGURE 12.1 Sample Room Arrangement

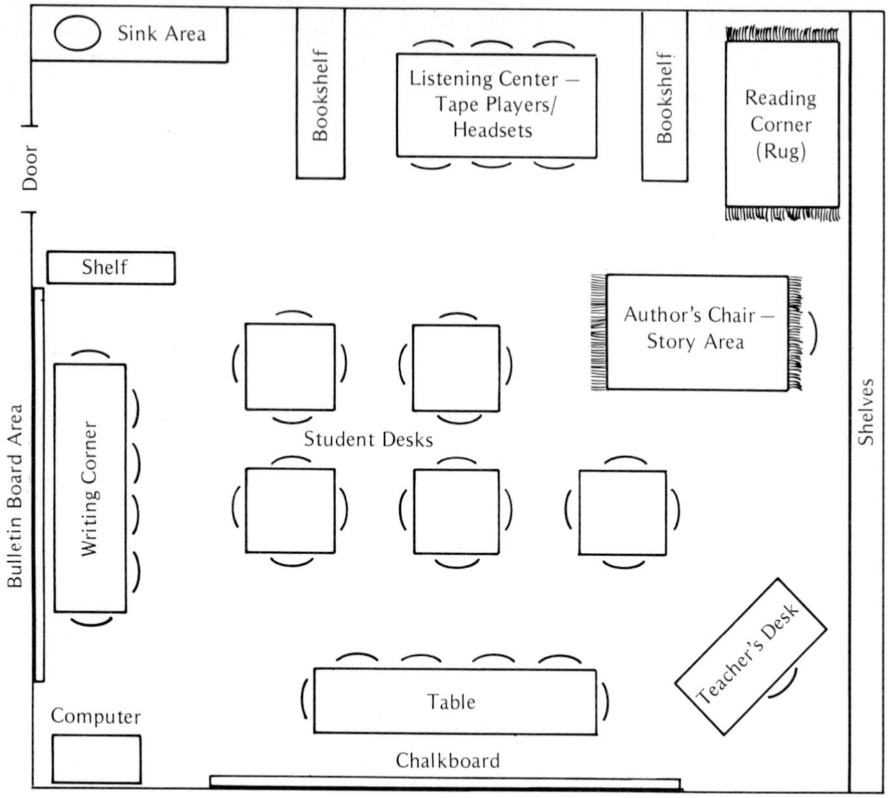

lum often does not serve the best interests of the child. While basal reading materials and worksheets may have their place, teachers often overemphasize these prepackaged materials, not taking into consideration the uniqueness of the individual. Remember that these are instructional tools and they vary in their usefulness. Let the needs and interests of the children in your classroom determine your choice of instructional materials.

The computer is a useful tool for revision during the writing process, and children appear to enjoy the immediacy of response that it affords. Computer-assisted instruction has its benefits, and access to one is recommended.

The materials listed in Table 12.1 are suggested for an integrated reading/language arts primary or intermediate classroom. As you can see from the suggested materials, children are encouraged to interact with print freely. Provide space for and unlimited access to these materials in order to maximize their potential.

FIGURE 12.2 Sample Room Arrangement

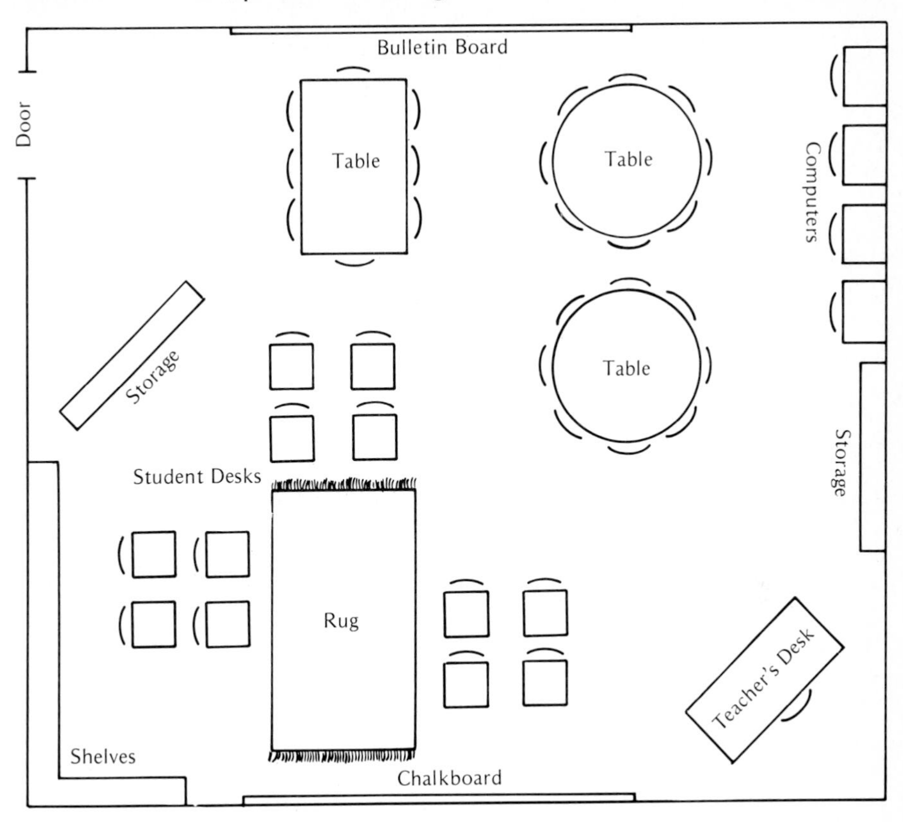

TABLE 12.1 Materials for an Integrated Curriculum

Reading	*Language*	*Writing*
Trade books	Tape recorders	Construction paper
Big books	Headphones	Scissors/tape
Pattern/predictable books	Cassettes	Glue/paste
Chart stands/chart paper	Room dividers	Writing paper
Rug/pillows	Recorded stories	Folders/journals
Multiple copies of several books	Writing paper	Pencils/markers
Magazines/newspapers	Pencils/markers	Computers
Mystery/humor books	Computers	Typewriter
Writing paper		
Pencils/markers		
Basal reading series (used selectively)		

Record Keeping and Assessment

To avoid becoming overwhelmed by uninterpreted observations of student performance, teachers need an organizational system that facilitates assessment of the major components of their reading program and recording of student growth or other significant findings (Memory, 1980). As discussed in Chapters 9 and 11, assessment should be an *ongoing* process. Individual records and portfolios on students' performance help in establishing the overall organizational plan. Record keeping should focus on daily and long-term performance (observed both objectively and subjectively). Records may be kept on skill/strategy needs, materials used, test scores, and recommendations for future instructional placement. As you evaluate student reading/writing performance, be mindful of the following good record-keeping procedures:

- Record keeping should be integrated with diagnosis, prescriptive planning, and assessment, as well as with the materials and activities used in instruction.
- Students should be allowed to participate in maintaining records, checking their own work, recording their results, and commenting on their performance. (Memory, 1980)

A good reading program includes much more than managed skills instruction. It may be best to keep a notebook or file cards to record subjective data, as well as a record book for those instructional activities that *can* be graded.

SUMMARY

When organizing for reading instruction, it is best to begin by considering your own reading philosophy before setting up the physical organization of your classroom. Consider as well the elements of effective classrooms: provision for individual differences, ongoing and comprehensive diagnosis, appropriate planning, consideration of the social and emotional needs of the students, appropriate instructional procedures, and appropriate evaluation techniques. Be mindful of teacher behaviors that are associated with high-quality education: "withitness," ability to overlap, smoothness, momentum, accountability, and alerting. How successful you are depends to a great extent on your ability to readjust the learning environment as needed.

Consider how you might best organize your students for reading instruction. Would they benefit most from direct instruction, homogeneous grouping, heterogeneous grouping, individualized reading instruction, or immersion in whole language experiences? Only after these considerations are addressed should you plan the physical arrangement of your classroom. Provide an environment that is supportive to the learning goals you have set out to achieve, and allow your students access to a wide variety of instructional materials. Be both objective and subjective in your evaluation of student performance, for not all reading behaviors are easily tested on skill sheets or reading achievement tests. Keep thorough and ongoing records that have links to diagnosis, planning, and evaluation, and allow your students to participate in the evaluation of their own performance.

Finally, be mindful of the following saying:

Instruct me—I forget.
Show me—I remember.
Involve me—I understand! (Anonymous)

FOLLOW-UP QUESTIONS AND ACTIVITIES

1. What constitutes an effective instructional environment? What teacher behaviors are most associated with productive learning?
2. The children in your classroom this year range in reading ability level from preprimer to grade 3. How would you provide reading instruction for the varying needs of these children? What kind of grouping arrangement would be most suitable for your purposes? Discuss your instructional plan with two or three other class members.
3. The school district has given you two standard basal reading series and accompanying workbooks as the backbone of your reading program. One series is designed to address the needs of average and above-average readers, the other the needs of low-achieving students. Unfortunately, neither basal series appears to adequately address the needs of your students. The school district demands accountability. How would you rectify this situation? Consider materials, time allotment, evaluation procedures, and the social and emotional needs of your students.
4. You have been given a classroom with 25 desks, 2 tables, 2 bookcases, and a long shelf. The room is quite small. You wish to organize for individualized or whole language instruction. How would you organize the physical environment? Draw up a room plan that would accommodate this form of reading instruction. Discuss your plan with two or three other class members.

ADDITIONAL READINGS

Carbo, M., Dunn, R., & Dunn, K. (1986). *Teaching students to read through their individual learning styles.* Englewood Cliffs, NJ: Prentice-Hall.

Goodman, K. (1986). *What's whole in whole language?* Portsmouth, NH: Heinemann.

Goodman, K., Goodman, Y., & Hood, W. (1989). *The whole language evaluation book.* Portsmouth, NH: Heinemann.

Graves, D. (1983). *Writing: Teachers and children at work.* Portsmouth, NH: Heinemann.

Lapp, D. (Ed.). (1980). *Making reading possible through effective classroom management.* Newark, DE: International Reading Association.

REFERENCES

Berliner, D. C. (1981). Academic learning time and reading achievement. In J. Guthrie (Ed.), *Comprehension and teaching: Research reviews* (pp. 203–226). Newark, DE: International Reading Association.

Carbo, M., Dunn, R., & Dunn, K. (1986). *Teaching children to read through their individual learning styles.* Englewood Cliffs, NJ: Prentice-Hall.

Durkin, D. (1978–1979). What classroom observations reveal about reading comprehension instruction. *Reading Research Quarterly, 14,* 481–538.

Goodman, K. (1986). *What's whole in whole language?* Portsmouth, NH: Heinemann.

Goodman, K., Goodman, Y., & Hood, W. (1989). *The whole language evaluation book.* Portsmouth, NH: Heinemann.

Graves, D. (1983). *Writing: Teachers and children at work.* Portsmouth, NH: Heinemann.

Hall, M. (1981). *Teaching reading as a language experience.* Columbus, OH: Merrill.

Harp, B. (1988). When you do whole language instruction, how will you keep track of reading and writing skills? *The Reading Teacher,* 42(2), 160–161.

Kounin, J. S. (1970). *Discipline and group management in classrooms.* New York: Holt, Rinehart & Winston.

Kulik, C., & Kulik, K. (1982). Effects of ability grouping on secondary school students: A meta-analysis of evaluation findings. *American Educational Research Journal, 19,* 415–428.

Mangiere, J. N. (1980). Characteristics of an effectively organized classroom. In D. Lapp (Ed.), *Making reading possible through effective classroom management* (pp. 10–26). Newark, DE: International Reading Association.

Memory, D. (1980). Record keeping for effective reading instruction. In D. Lapp (Ed.), *Making reading possible through effective classroom management* (pp. 146–185). Newark, DE: International Reading Association.

O'Donnell, M. P., & Moore, B. (1980). Eliminating common stumbling blocks to organizational change. In D. Lapp (Ed.), *Making reading possible through effective classroom management* (pp. 186–215). Newark, DE: International Reading Association.

Otto, W., Wolf, A., & Eldridge, R. (1984). Managing instruction. In P. D. Pearson (Ed.), *Handbook of reading research* (pp. 799–828). New York: Longman.

Rosenshine, B., & Stevens, R. (1984). Classroom instruction in reading. In P. D. Pearson (Ed.), *Handbook of reading research* (pp. 745–798). New York: Longman.

Samuels, J. S. (1981). Characteristics of exemplary reading programs. In J. Guthrie (Ed.), *Comprehension and teaching: Research reviews* (pp. 255–273). Newark, DE: International Reading Association.

Tierney, R., Readance, J. E., & Dishner, E. K. (1985). *Reading strategies and practices.* Boston: Allyn and Bacon.

Vacca, J. L., Vacca, R. T., & Gove, M. K. (1987). *Reading and learning to read.* Boston: Little, Brown.

Wisconsin Department of Public Instruction. (1986). *A guide to curriculum planning in English language arts.* Madison: Author.

13

Understanding and Using Basal Readers Effectively

D. RAY REUTZEL

ALTHOUGH BASAL READERS are the dominant form of reading instruction used in elementary schools, they have long been criticized on many counts. For example, they are said to contain unnatural sentence patterns and constrained vocabulary usage; they do not provide for different learning modes; they are not representative of the cultural diversity within our society; they promote the usage of rigid grouping and tracking practices; they do not provide for individual needs by requiring all students to do all accompanying skill and worksheet pages; they do not actually provide skill development opportunities for students; and the content is boring and unrealistic.

In this chapter, Ray Reutzel provides an overview of basal reading series. He discusses both the strengths and weaknesses a teacher must be aware of when using these instructional materials, contending that teachers must be aware of common shortcomings in such materials if they are to provide activities to overcome such concerns. He then discusses and provides an example of a standard basal reader directed reading lesson. Several strategies that the effective teacher can use to extend and enrich the use of basal readers are covered. The chapter concludes with a discussion of reconciled reading lessons; extending the basal reader with story maps and language experience activities; suggestions for oral reading activities; effective use of questions; and finally, an in-depth discussion of skill development concerns.

STUDY QUESTIONS

1. What are the major components of a basal reading series?
2. Name five strengths and weaknesses of basal readers.
3. What are the parts of a directed reading lesson?
4. How does one teach a reconciled reading lesson?
5. Describe five ways to improve questioning.

Basal readers have played an integral role in reading instruction in the United States for over a century. Today's basal readers have descended from a long ancestry of basal readers, beginning with the famous *McGuffey Eclectic Readers* introduced in the 1830s by William H. McGuffey (Bohning, 1986). In a 1977 national survey, the Educational Products Information Exchange (EPIE) reported that 94% of U.S. teachers use commercially developed basal materials for reading instruction. Because of the widespread and pervasive use of basal readers as the core for providing fundamental reading instruction (Shannon, 1983), it is imperative for preservice and inservice teachers to learn to use these readers with judgment and skill.

This chapter provides information necessary for making informed instructional decisions about how, when, and why to use basal readers for reading instruction and presents effective procedures to improve and enrich basal reader instruction.

Overview of the Basal Reading Program

A basal reading program is "a comprehensive, integrated set of books, workbooks, teacher's manuals, and other materials for developmental reading instruction . . . " (Harris & Hodges, 1981, pp. 30–31). In short, a basal reading program is a set of commercially prepared and sequenced materials for providing reading instruction in elementary and middle schools.

Program Components

Basal series are usually composed of a set of core materials including the student's text; the teacher's manual; the student's and teacher's workbooks; supplemental practice exercises and enrichment activities (usually both of these are in the form of ditto masters); and skill, end-of-unit, or end-of-book tests. Other supplemental materials are available at additional cost (e.g., filmstrips, picture cards, picture with letter cards, letter cards, word cards, large charts, additional ditto sheet masters, and classroom trade book libraries). Since many teachers have access to only the core components of the basal reading program, this discussion will be confined to those materials.

Teacher's Manual

Perhaps the most important part of the basal reading program is the teacher's manual (TM). Within its pages there are usually three important features. First, the TM contains the scope and sequence of the particular basal reading program. A scope and sequence describes in detail the range of concepts and skills to be taught in the basal program, as well as the order in which the concepts and skills are to be presented. The second major feature is a reduced version of the student's text, and the third feature is a suggested lesson plan for the teacher. It is important for administrators, novices, and experienced teachers alike to realize that the TM is a tool to be used discriminatingly, not a script to be followed rigidly. Teachers should not allow the TM to dictate the reading program. Rather, they should decide what is and what is not appropriate in the TM for use with a particular group of children.

Student's Basal Text

The student's text contains an anthology of stories and other selections. Some stories have been created expressly for the student's basal reader, and others have been adapted from children's trade books. Along with an attempt to include high-quality literature in contemporary basal readers, publishers often go to great lengths to provide equally high-quality artwork and illustrations. Interspersed throughout the student's text are poetry selections, jokes, riddles, puzzles, informational essays, and special skill and/or concept lessons. Some basal texts contain questions children should be able to answer after reading the stories. Upper-level basal readers often contain a glossary of words that students can refer to when decoding new words or looking up the meaning of new words in the text. A hallmark of basal reader stories is their carefully controlled vocabulary and text difficulty, which allow for the introduction of a predetermined number of unfamiliar words in each new story.

In recent years, readability formulas have been applied to basal reader stories to control for reading difficulty. Typically, readability formulas measure the difficulty level of a text by counting the letters or number of syllables in a word and the number of words in each sentence. Shortening sentences and reducing word size by using simpler words in place of longer ones renders a text less difficult to read when text difficulty is gauged by readability formulas. However, research by Pearson (1974) has challenged the concept that shorter sentences are easier to read. Short, choppy sentences tend to be more difficult to comprehend because explicit connecting or sequencing words such as *because, and, so, then, before,* and *after* are deleted from the text and consequently need to be inferred by the reader. In addition, the twin practices of controlling vocabulary and readability have been criticized because shortening words and sentences tends to distort the meaning of the stories, resulting in senseless or poorly written texts (Armbruster, 1984).

Workbooks

Perhaps the most often used part of any basal reader series is the workbook (Durkin, 1984; Mason, 1983; Osborn, 1985). Workbooks provide a means for students to practice skills independently. They often contain practice exercises for reviewing previously taught reading skills as well as those currently being taught. In this way, workbooks serve a dual function of practice and review.

Research reveals that students spend up to 70% of the time allocated for reading instruction in independent practice or completing worksheets such as those found in workbooks (Anderson, Hiebert, Scott, & Wilkinson, 1985), while less than 10% of reading instructional time is devoted to silent reading. Based on these findings, it seems clear that workbooks have been misused and overused in classrooms. Workbooks are not the same thing as real reading; they tend to break reading into subskills. However, when teachers judiciously select exercises to support instruction already provided, workbooks can provide students with valuable practice and feedback on reading skills. Moreover, completed workbook exercises can provide teachers with critical evaluative information on the effectiveness of instruction as well as diagnostic information on the quality of students' learning. In short, workbooks can be a valuable resource when used correctly and a debilitating deterrent to students' reading progress when overused or misused.

Production of Basal Readers

Basal readers are produced by several large publishing houses owned by corporations such as Xerox and Gulf+Western. The production of a basal reader is supervised by a managing editor with the assistance of a senior author, a figure who is known and respected as a reading expert. Basal reading programs are typically known by the names of the publishing houses that produce them, for example, the Allyn and Bacon, Houghton Mifflin, or Ginn basal reading series. Minor revisions of basal readers occur every few years. Major revision cycles occur every 5 or 6 years and are usually slated for completion during the same year Texas and California consider basal readers for statewide adoption. As a result, Texas and California textbook adoption committees clearly exert more influence on the content and quality of new basal readers than do states that do not adopt them on a statewide basis. In reading circles, it is often said that "as California and Texas go, so goes the nation."

Strengths and Weaknesses of Basal Readers

Since basal readers are used in over 90% of classrooms in the United States, most teachers will inevitably have occasion to make use of this approach to reading instruction (Zintz & Maggart, 1984). In order to make instructional decisions about how, when, and why to use the basal approach, teachers must know its strengths and weaknesses. Figure 13.1 lists some common advantages and disadvantages of the basal approach. Clearly, basal readers possess certain positive qualities that contribute to their continuing popularity in the classroom. Publishers are also attempting to correct many of their shortcomings as newer editions are published.

Although they are popular, basal readers are not without significant deficiencies. Narrative selections in students' texts have been criticized repeatedly in the past two decades. They tend to be repetitive and boring, employing language that is well below the oral language abilities of the children and unlike the spoken language with which they are familiar. Stories have been criticized for their lack of literary worth and for failing to deal with children's real-life concerns and values.

Expository selections tend to be geared toward the lowest common denominator, containing little real content. This practice prompted an article

FIGURE 13.1 Advantages and Disadvantages of Basal Readers

Advantages

- A hierarchically sequenced curriculum of skill instruction is provided. Skills instruction is arranged to provide for both initial instruction and a systematic review of skills taught.
- A continuous arrangement of instruction from grade to grade is supplied.
- To save teachers' time, a completely prepared set of stories, instructional directions and activities, instructional practice materials, and assessment and management devices is available.
- Stories are arranged in a sequence of ascending difficulty as measured by readability formulas and controlled vocabulary.
- Reading skills are gradually introduced.
- Teachers are provided explicit lesson plans.
- Students are exposed to a variety of literacy genres in basals.
- Organization and structure of basals are helpful to beginning teachers just learning about the reading curriculum.
- Organization and structure offer reassurance to administrators and school patrons that reading skills are being taught.
- Primers usually feature the same characters in many stories, giving children a feeling of familiarity and confidence.

Limitations

- Vocabulary control often renders story content dull and repetitious.
- Skill instruction is rarely applied in or related to comprehending the story content.
- The basal lesson design in teachers' manuals very often fails to relate one part of the lesson, e.g., vocabulary introduction, to subsequent parts of the reading lesson, e.g., story comprehension discussion.
- Stories often do not relate to students' interests.
- The format of basals is often less appealing than the format of trade books.
- Special interest group censorship leads to stories that contain little real subject matter content, deal with few real-life applications, or present societal or ethical content for appropriate living.
- The application of readability formulas to text selections results in stories and text features that are void of content and inconsiderate of the reader's need to understand.
- Teachers' manuals seldom contain useful directions on *how* to teach reading comprehension.
- A rigid adherence to the basal leaves little room for teacher creativity and decision making.
- The grading or leveling of basal readers promotes the use of traditional ability or achievement groups in classrooms.
- Management demands of the basal program can become so time consuming that little time remains for students to self-select their reading materials.
- Use of the basal reader approach has traditionally been associated with the use of "round robin" reading. Such a practice is encouraged by insisting that all children simultaneously attend to the same selection while another child reads orally.

in *The Reading Teacher* entitled "Basal reading texts: What's in them to comprehend?" (1984). Much of the criticism surrounding the stories found in the students' readers can be traced to publishers' efforts to fit story content into the straightjacket of readability formulas. However, publishers should not take the blame alone for the use of readability formulas in developing basal stories. Well-meaning but uninformed textbook adoption committees have pressured publishers into using readability formulas to measure reading difficulty.

Basal readers have also been criticized for poorly representing societal groups and concerns, and today, basals are being assailed for poor instructional design and content. Durkin (1981) found that many teachers' manuals contained an abundance of questions and evaluative activities that were mislabeled as instructional activities. What was labeled as instruction often was found to be nothing more than an assessment exercise. Despite these limitations, basals should not be discarded (McCallum, 1988). Figure 13.2 provides a checklist of important elements educators should consider in judging the relative strengths and weaknesses of basal series. Only after teachers are sufficiently well informed can they act to correct or adjust the use of these texts to benefit their students.

Finally, basal readers were never intended to displace the teacher's instructional decision making in the classroom or to supplant opportunities for students to read a wide variety of text materials. Rather, basal readers were intended to be an instructional resource to help teachers provide basic, sequenced reading instruction for a wide range of student abilities.

Teacher-Directed Reading

Most basal readers employ a lesson structure commonly known as the *directed reading activity* (DRA) or the *directed reading lesson* (DRL). Emmett Betts first introduced the DRA in 1946. Since that time, it has become the standard approach for structuring reading lessons in basal readers. As discussed in Chapter 6, the DRA is also appropriate for content area reading lessons. The DRA can be divided into the following seven steps:

1. *Background building.* This involves the teacher and students in a discussion of the topic and unfamiliar concepts to be encountered in the story. Beck (1986b) encouraged teachers to focus discussion on the central problem or critical concept necessary for understanding the story. The intent of this part of the DRA is to provide the necessary knowledge to facilitate students' comprehension of the story content.
2. *Preteaching unfamiliar vocabulary.* Since comprehension of a story depends on knowledge of the meaning of specific unfamiliar words, this part of the DRA involves activities designed to help students

FIGURE 13.2 Quick Checklist for Evaluating Basal Readers

Rate each basal series from 1 to 5 on the following points:
1 = Excellent, 2 = Better Than Average, 3 = Average, 4 = Worse Than Average, 5 = Unsatisfactory

Scope and sequence is easy to follow and understand.	1 2 3 4 5
Reading skills relate to the stories and reading.	1 2 3 4 5
Has high-quality literature selections.	1 2 3 4 5
Reading lessons make use of all language arts skills.	1 2 3 4 5
Stories appear interesting for the age group.	1 2 3 4 5
Teacher's manual provides ideas on how to teach.	1 2 3 4 5
Reading selections represent a variety of genres.	1 2 3 4 5
Program encourages sustained reading and writing.	1 2 3 4 5
Tests measure important reading skills.	1 2 3 4 5
Book is durable and attractive.	1 2 3 4 5
Reading lessons include ideas on how to extend stories to other curricular areas.	1 2 3 4 5
Nonfictional material is accurate and current.	1 2 3 4 5
Students' basal contains helpful guides, references, and study tips.	1 2 3 4 5

understand how the word or words will be used in the context of the story.

3. *Introducing and setting the purpose for reading.* To provide a motivation and purpose for reading the story, this part of the lesson centers on reading the story title and subtitle(s) and looking at the pictures to predict the plot and outcome of the story. Along with generating predictions from the titles and pictures, the teacher sets the purpose for reading by directing students to read for a particular purpose (e.g., to answer questions or to compare and contrast characters in the story). These activities provide the framework for guiding students toward purposeful reading.
4. *Guided reading.* During this part of the lesson, students read to answer questions or to confirm predictions based on the previous lesson activities. Most teachers' manuals state that guided reading should be silent reading. However, some teachers, especially teachers of beginning readers, have students read the stories orally to make sure they are pronouncing the words correctly.

5. *Story discussion.* After the children finish reading the story, a discussion ensues that focuses on answering questions about the story content. Questions for conducting this part of the DRA are found interspersed throughout the story and following the story in the teacher's manual.
6. *Skill instruction and practice.* This part of the DRA focuses on developing skills in three areas of the reading curriculum: decoding, vocabulary, and comprehension. Separate skill lessons follow on selected subskills from each of these areas. After instruction, students practice the skills in workbooks and on ditto sheets.
7. *Enrichment activities.* These activities are designed to focus on and extend the story content and skill instruction. During this time, students are encouraged to go beyond the content of the story or skill lessons to pursue related personal interests, topics, and skills.

Sample Lesson: A Directed Reading Activity for First or Second Grade

The children will be reading "The Little Red Hen." The following are suggestions that might be found in a teacher's manual.

Building Background The teacher carefully reflects on the central message of the story. Children should be led to understand that one cannot expect to get something for nothing. Children could be asked to brainstorm what the phrase "getting something for nothing" means. After brainstorming, the teacher could explain that "getting something for nothing" means expecting to get something and not having worked to earn it.

Preteaching Unfamiliar Vocabulary Words such as *cottage, gossip, vain, wheat, thresh,* and *mill* will be discussed and read in a sentence-level context that is congruent with the meanings these words represent in the story. The teacher might also point out that wheat is threshed and then ground into flour and that people use flour to make bread.

Introducing the Story and Setting the Purposes for Reading During this part of the DRA, the teacher focuses the children's purposes for reading the story. This is usually accomplished by asking questions. The teacher might say, read this story to find out what happens to the Little Red Hen and how she teaches her friends a lesson.

Guided Silent Reading The teacher writes the purposes for reading on the chalkboard. This will remind the children what to watch for as they read. The teacher can freely move about the room at this time to help children who are having difficulties. Also, the teacher might stop occasionally and ask a child a question or two to assess understanding.

Story Discussion After the children have completed the reading of the story, the teacher asks them questions. Often, the children will return to the story to document their answers in response to the teacher's questions. The discussion is designed to help them understand the relationship between the main idea and the details in the story and make connections between the story and their own experiences. During this time, the teacher can ask students to orally reread portions of the story to assess their word recognition abilities as well as comprehension of the story.

Skill Instruction Following the reading of the story, most teachers' manuals contain several lessons focusing on reading skills. Decoding, vocabulary, and comprehension are the skill areas usually taught. After each lesson is presented, skill application is provided in the workbook. Children usually complete several workbook pages and worksheets in which recently taught skills are applied for the first time and skills previously taught are reviewed.

Enrichment Activities The children reread "The Little Red Hen" as a group and decide to make the story into a play. They divide into groups to make the story into a play script, design costumes, produce the stage background, select music, and work out the general details of play production. The play is practiced and performed for students in the class. Children from other classrooms might also be invited to come and see the play.

The directed reading activity provides teachers with a useful framework for presenting structured reading lessons. By using the DRA, teachers can build background in preparation for reading, introduce unfamiliar vocabulary words to facilitate decoding, motivate children to read, assess reading comprehension, teach new reading skills, and extend language and learning after reading. Used well, the DRA is a valuable resource for teaching children to read.

Extending and Enriching the Basal Lesson

Although the DRA is useful, it is not without distinct weaknesses in practice. A quick look at basal teachers' manuals reveals a heavy emphasis on evaluation after reading (Durkin, 1981), not on comprehension instruction before reading. Beck (1986a) indicated that if a choice between the prereading and postreading parts of the reading lesson were necessary, she should definitely choose the prereading activities. Recent research has emphasized the importance of the prereading phase of the reading lesson to build, modify, or enhance the readers' background knowledge and experience in preparation for successful reading (Durkin, 1984).

Research on schema theory, a theory about how prior knowledge and experiences act to facilitate the acquisition of new knowledge, has clearly punctuated the importance of teaching students how to comprehend before reading rather than fixing up misunderstandings after reading. Durkin (1984), in an observation of classroom teachers' use of basal teachers' manuals, found that "none of these teachers reviewed or developed background information. At a time when the significance of world knowledge (background knowledge and experiences) is receiving widespread attention, the omission was unexpected" (p. 737).

The reason why teachers do not build background for reading is that very little substantive information is provided in their teachers' manuals on how to go about it. One remedy to this problem is the use of the reconciled reading lesson (RRL). This involves shifting the emphasis from evaluation after reading to instruction before reading.

Reconciled Reading Lesson

Using the RRL involves reversing the traditional basal lesson sequence to improve readers' comprehension (Reutzel, 1985a). Teachers begin the lesson by turning to the last section of the reading lesson in the teachers' manual, often labeled "Enrichment Activities" or "Language Extension Activities." The activities suggested in this part of the lesson are often excellent for building background knowledge and discussing unfamiliar concepts or vocabulary. For example, in one major basal reader a lesson on a story entitled "Where Do Animals Live?" suggested making arrangements with a local veterinarian or naturalist to speak to the class about animals and their homes. Another activity involved taking children on a nature hike around the school or a local park while looking for signs of animal homes. These activities would be more appropriately used for background building to facilitate children's comprehension of the story before reading than as enrichment after reading.

The second modification proposed to the basal lesson in the RRL centers on the placement of skill instruction. Teachers should teach reading skills prior to and related to the stories rather than after reading. Such a practice helps children understand that reading skills are to be applied during their reading of the story. The comprehension skills to be taught in the reading lesson just mentioned is "identifying details in a story." The teacher's manual instructs the teacher to write a four-line story on the chalkboard and ask the children to identify the details, whereas it seems much more pertinent to teach this skill as it applies to the story of "Where Do Animals Live?".

Another skill lesson associated with this story dealt with teaching children the consonant blends, *sn, sm,* and *sc.* A quick glance over the text of the story reveals that not a single word in the story begins with or even contains one of these consonant blends. Basal lessons seldom relate their skill instruction to the stories the children will later be expected to read (Reutzel & Daines, 1987). Because of this, teachers should be prepared to make explicit the relationship between the skills their students are to learn and how these skills can be applied as they read the story.

If the story does not lend itself to the concepts to be learned, then teachers must adapt instruction to the story. For example, "Where Do Animals Live?" used other consonant blends that could have been taught and applied while reading the story. Instructional decisions such as these are characteristics of effective teachers.

The third modification to the basal program in the reconciled reading lesson involves discussion of the story through guided questioning. While the typical organization of the DRA provides for discussion of the story through questions *after* reading the story, the RRL makes guided questioning, discussion, and prediction an integral part of the *prereading* phase of the reading lesson. Children are encouraged to make predictions about the questions and read to confirm their predictions. Such a practice helps them focus their attention during reading and provides a purposeful framework for reading.

The remainder of the RRL is brief. Students read the story. Postreading activities are aimed at assessing whether or not the students understood the story and applied the reading skills taught to understand the story. Did the students comprehend the story? How well did they predict answers to the prequestions? Did they revise their predictions as a result of reading the story? Do they understand the meanings of the new vocabulary words as they were used in the context of the story? To support the use of the RRL to enhance the basal program, Prince (1986) reported that after using the RRL, students' comprehension and recall of text were significantly greater than with the traditional DRA.

Semantic Webbing or Story Mapping

Similar to the semantic maps discussed in Chapter 3, story maps or semantic webs are graphic displays for representing the relationships among concepts, characters, and events in text. Maps can be organized to highlight particular text organizations such as cause and effect and sequential lists of events, and they can be used to compare or contrast text structures. Story maps help teachers and students perceive relationships, organize their thoughts, and better recall both narrative and expository text. As a result, teachers provide more focused and coherent instruction and students focus their efforts on comprehension more effectively (Reutzel, 1985b). Story maps have been shown to improve students' reading comprehension significantly, especially for readers who are disabled (Sinatra, Stahle-Gemake, & Berg, 1984).

To construct a story map, the teacher begins by writing a summary list of the main idea, major events, and major characters in the story. Next, the teacher places the main idea or major question in the center of the web or map, and draws enough ties projecting out symmetrically from the center circle to accommodate the major events and characters in the summary list. The major concepts in the circles are then attached to these ties in clockwise sequence around the center circle. Finally, minor events or concepts (details) are entered in clockwise sequence around the circles containing major events or concepts in the story map. Figure 13.3 presents an example of a story map.

The teacher places a copy of the story map on the board or overhead projector and tells the children they will be reading a new story that day. Next, the children are told the title of the story to be read while the teacher points to the map. The teacher asks a series of questions that will lead the students through the story map, dealing with setting, characters, time, initiating event(s), attempts, and outcomes. The students can use the map as a means for answering these questions. After the children read the story, the story map becomes a focus for discussion. Another story map portraying in detail the attempt and outcome may be produced through group discussion.

An extension of story maps that has also proved useful is the cloze story map (CSM), which replaces every fifth concept or event in a story map with a blank concept shape (see Figure 13.4). During the prereading part of the reading lesson, students predict information that has been deleted from the map and enter their own predictions in a personal-sized map. They then read to confirm their predictions. If the text reveals information contrary to the reader's predictions, then the reader changes his or her predictions on the personal map. The CSM helps students monitor their own comprehension as they read (Reutzel, 1986a, 1986b). After reading, the CSM provides a focal point for discussing the important elements of the text and a framework for remembering what they read. The questions the teacher asks after reading should not be trivial. Rather, they should be guided by the story map to focus on the major concepts or events in the text for optimal effectiveness. Sadow (1982) suggested the following five generic questions teachers can ask about a story based on story maps or webs:

1. Where and when did the events in the story take place and who was involved in them? (*setting*)
2. What started the chain of events in the story? (*initiating event*)
3. What was the main character's reaction to this event? (*reaction*)
4. What did the main character do about it? (*action: goals and attempts*)
5. What happened as a result of what the main character did? (*consequences or outcome*) (p. 520)

Teachers can use story maps or webs to plan reading instruction, guide prereading or introductory activities, more carefully focus pre- and postreading questions, and evaluate students' learning from narrative and expository texts. Students can use maps or webs to help them relate new concepts to their own experiences, summarize their memory of text, and focus their efforts on comprehension of major and important minor ideas in text during reading.

FIGURE 13.3 Example of Story Map

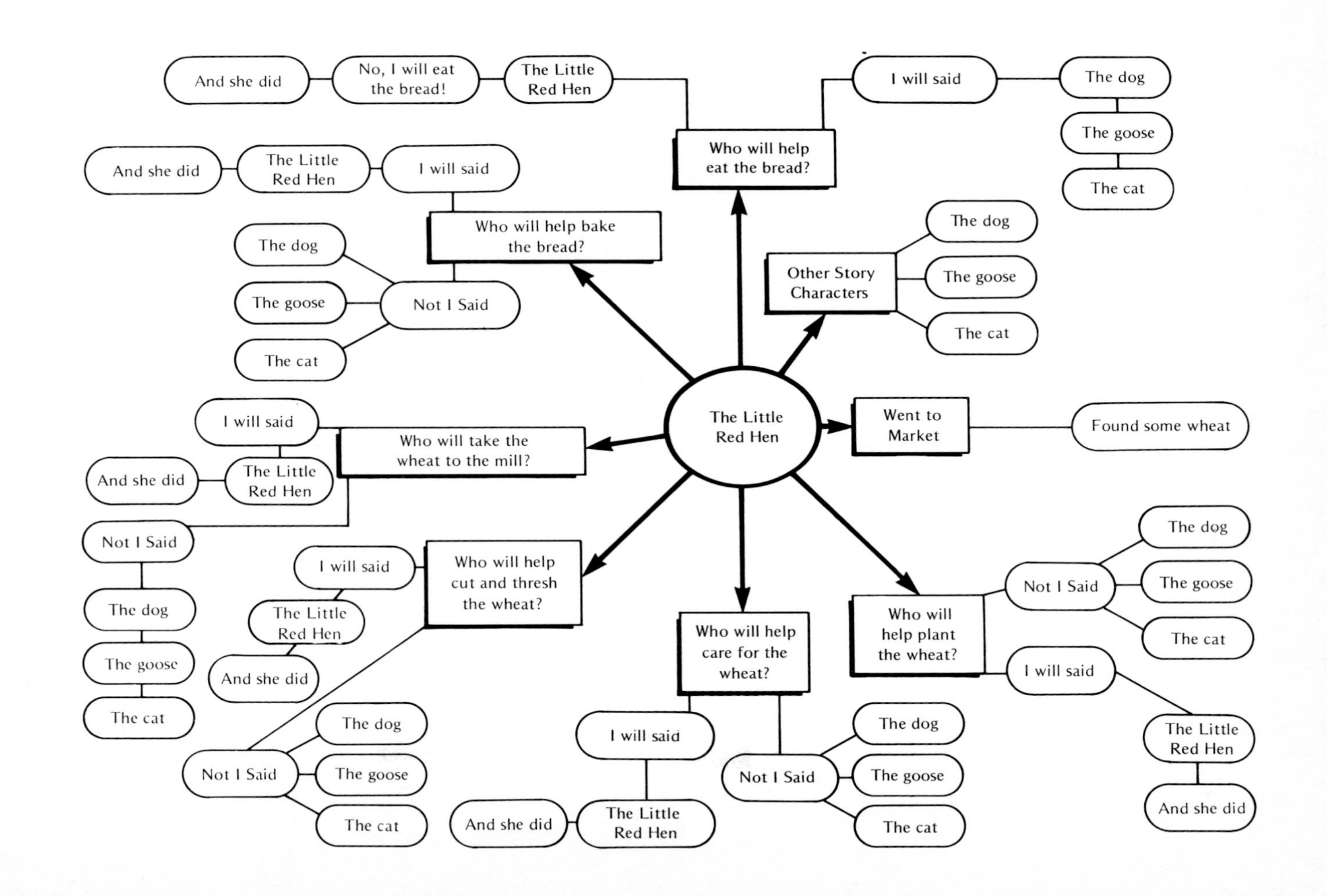

FIGURE 13.4 Example of Cloze Story Map

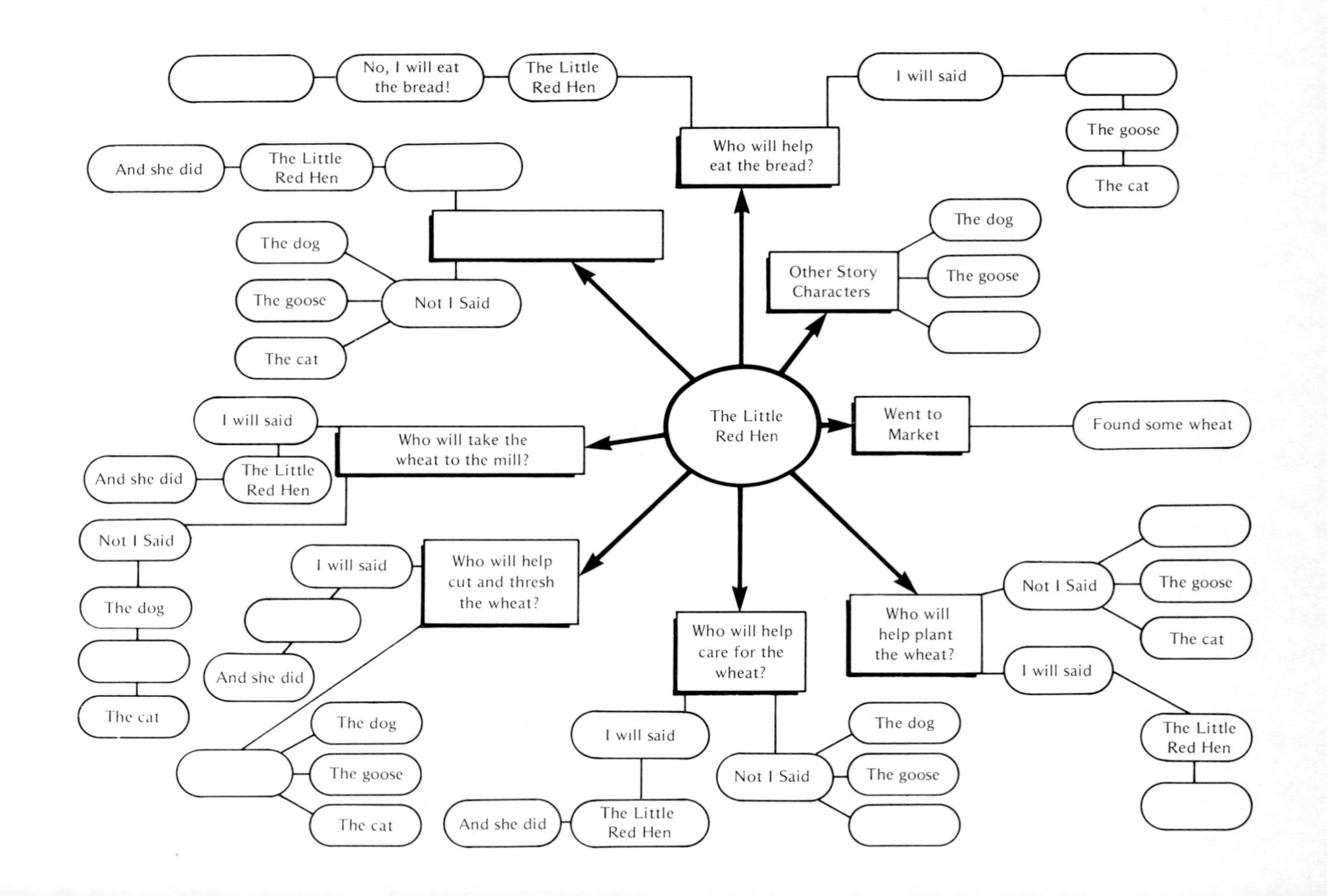

The Language Experience Approach

The language experience approach (LEA) consists of using children's oral language and experiences to create personalized reading materials. These materials often take the form of a dictated chart describing a group experience, a small book that has been dictated to an adult scribe by an individual child, or a box of personal or important sight words chosen by children. Although dictated stories and charts have been used by some teachers in the primary grades to motivate children's reading, many teachers do not use the LEA for two reasons. First, they feel obligated to use the basal reader as the core component of reading instruction. Second, they may not know how to integrate this approach to reading instruction with the basal program. Jones and Nessel (1985) described how the LEA can be integrated with the basal approach to extend the use of both types of lesson.

The basic steps in obtaining dictated language experience stories are as follows:

1. Through science experiments, unique or interesting objects, activities or field trips, the teacher provides students with a stimulus that invites student participation.
2. Through discussion with the teacher and other students, the students develop concepts and experiences through observations and talking.
3. Children dictate to the teacher an account of the experience or activity. This dictation is usually recorded on large chart paper or posterboard while the teacher and children read what is written.
4. The teacher reads the dictated account back to the children. Next, with teacher help, the students read the account with the teacher. The dictated story becomes the basis for phonics, structural analysis, and context usage lessons as well as a review of basic sight or key words over the next few days.
5. Students read other books on related topics. They often reread the dictated story alone or in small groups during the day.
6. Learning from reading is reinforced with activities employing the other language skills, writing and listening activities, promoting general communication growth. (Jones & Nessel, 1985, p. 18)

To integrate this approach with the basal program, Jones and Nessel recommended that an experience be constructed to complement the basal story. For example, for the basal story "Stone Soup," the teacher could make stone soup and have the children eat the soup prior to reading the story. After eating, the children could describe how the soup tasted and what they thought the ingredients were for preparing stone soup. They might even like to try to dictate a predicted recipe for making stone soup. This account and the recipe could be recorded on the chart or on smaller paper for the children to reread during the next few days. Words from the LEA dictated account could be placed on word cards for practice as a means of acquiring and maintaining a sight vocabulary. Usually, many of the words in the children's dictated stories will be the same words that will appear in the basal story. Thus, new or old vocabulary terms will have been introduced or reviewed prior to reading the basal story. After reading the basal story, another story could be dictated using words from both the original dictated story or recipe and the basal, thus providing more opportunities to practice skills and sight words. Finally, skill instruction could be taught using the dictated stories to show children how reading skills can be applied to help them read a story. Using dictated stories and experiences is a useful way to build students' background in preparation for reading to enhance reading comprehension. While such LEA activities need not be done with every story in a basal series, they should be done often enough that students clearly understand the relationships among speaking, listening, reading, and writing.

Oral Reading

Oral reading is often an integral part of basal reading lessons. Pearson and Fielding (1982) emphasized that oral reading can help children comprehend what they read by placing attention on the rhythm, tempo, and melody of written language. Wood (1983) recommended a set of oral reading variations called *four-way oral reading.* After the students read a story or selection silently in preparation for oral reading, the teacher tells them they will be called on randomly to read, rather than in a predetermined sequence as in "round-robin" reading. Children may be called on to read aloud individually, in pairs, or in groups. In the first oral reading variation recommended by Wood, a pair of students reads aloud in unison and the teacher provides help with difficult words. The second variation uses choral reading. Everyone in the group reads in unison until the teacher indicates a stopping point. The third variation employs a technique called *imitative reading.* The teacher reads a sentence or two aloud and tells the children to read the sentences back just as he or she read them. In essence, the children echo the sentence reading of the teacher. Finally, children can become involved in *mumble reading,* the fourth oral reading variation. This is defined as reading aloud quietly or mumbling.

These four oral reading strategies can be used to add variety to the reading of any story or text. For example, a teacher might begin the reading of a selection by having several pairs of students read a paragraph or two each. Next, the teacher could have the entire group read the next few paragraphs in chorus. After that, the students might be asked to read a few sentences echoing the teacher's reading. And finally, the students might mumble read individually to the end of the story. An important fact to remember is that oral reading is performance. These oral reading variations provide a psychological safety net for students when they read aloud, thus eliminating or at least reducing the risk of public failure and embarrassment generally associated with solo oral reading in the round-robin reading circle.

Effective Questioning

Asking questions is an integral part of teaching a basal reading lesson. However, asking *effective* questions requires considerable knowledge and skill on the part of the teacher. A cursory review of any basal reader lesson reveals far too many questions of a literal/factual level, questions inappropriately placed in the sequence of the reading lesson, and questions that do not help children build a framework for remembering. Durkin (1978–1979) has pointed to the fact that questions are often more evaluative than instructive in nature.

It is important to know that the quality, quantity, and sequence of questions asked can affect the quality of instruction as well as the quality and quantity of students' comprehension. Consequently, teachers must know how to use questioning as an effective instructional tool. Questioning can be improved by attending to several principles supported by research on effective questioning.

Prequestions versus Postquestions

It is important to know when to ask a particular question during a reading lesson. If questions are asked prior to reading, they serve to restrict reading to a search for the answers. However, if it is critical for a student to know a specific bit of information, then prequestions will direct the student's attention toward locating that information during reading (Tierney & Cunningham, 1984). Questions asked after reading can prompt students' recall, thereby leading to a more cohesive remembrance of the text. Prequestions restrict and focus attention, while postquestions cause students to review and return to the text. Teacher questioning should be consistent with this principle and the objectives of instruction.

Reciprocal Questioning

Questioning should not be one-way. Students should be encouraged to ask as well as answer questions. In fact, the central goal of teacher questioning should be to encourage students to generate their own questions about a text. Teachers can encourage students to generate questions through a process known as *reciprocal questioning* (Manzo, 1969). The lesson begins with the teacher reading a sentence in a basal story, closing the book, and answering any questions students ask about the sentence in the basal story. Next, the roles are reversed. The students read a sentence from the basal story, close their books, and answer questions the teacher asks. Next, the teacher asks the students to predict the events and outcome of the basal story and makes a list of their predictions. The students then read the basal story to confirm their predictions. After reading, the teacher leads a discussion in which the original predictions are reconsidered, confirmed, or corrected.

Wait Time

With the current emphasis on pacing and content coverage in the teacher effectiveness literature, teachers may be tempted to embrace a "faster is better" questioning strategy. In 1974, Rowe investigated the pacing of teacher questioning during science lessons. Her primary unit of observation centered on the length of time interval between the time a teacher asked a question and then expected a response, redirected the question to another student, or rephrased the original question. Rowe found that the average teacher wait time was only .9 seconds. On the other hand, when teachers allowed at least a 3-second wait time, both teacher questioning behaviors and student answering behaviors improved appreciably.

Improved teacher questioning behaviors included asking fewer but higher quality questions; teachers were more flexible in their assessment of student responses considered acceptable; and teachers' expectations of certain students were positively affected by the increased wait time. Student answers were also positively affected by the increased wait time. Shy and slow students were willing to try to answer more questions; student answers to questions were more elaborate; and students evidenced greater confidence in their answers as reflected in their vocal inflection. Knowing that a wait time of 3 seconds can positively affect both teacher questions and student answers, teachers should make every effort to observe this principle.

Choral Response to Questions

During the typical reading lesson, students respond one at a time to teacher questions. But what would happen to students' question-answering behavior if every child could respond to every question? First of all, students could become more actively involved in answering questions. Second, teachers could observe the correctness of *all* student responses in lieu of sampling only a selected few. Third, shy students could answer questions without having to risk becoming the focus of attention. These few benefits alone should be enough to motivate teachers toward more frequent use of choral response methods in questioning.

Hopkins (1979) recommended several ways teachers can make use of whole group response methods. For word recognition, students could be given Yes/No cards to respond to questions asked about words. For example, the teacher might show the children the word *monkey* on a card and ask, "Is this word the word *mouse*?" True/False cards could be used to assess students' comprehension of various aspects of the text; for example, "Goldilocks liked Father Bear's bed. True or false?" Stick puppets could be used to answer questions about story characters. An extension of Hopkins's (1979) ideas includes the use of lap-sized chalkboards or magic slates that can be erased and reused for answering questions in choral arrangements.

Both teachers and students are benefited by techniques of choral response to questioning. Teachers receive more feedback about students' learning from text, and students become more actively engaged in the reading lesson. However, high-quality questioning takes planning, preparation, creativity, intelligence, and patience. Without these ingredients, questioning becomes just another form of testing rather than teaching. Conversely, with careful planning and modeling, as well as effective involvement of students during questioning, both teachers and students will reap the benefits of greater motivation, attention, and comprehension during reading lessons.

Teaching Skills from the Basal Reader

For many years, basal teachers' manuals have been used as the primary resource for providing reading skill instruction. Recently, researchers have found that these manuals provide little structure and rationale for helping teachers provide effective skill instruction. In fact, teachers themselves rate skill lesson directives in teachers' manuals as only moderately helpful (Bacharach & Alexander, 1986).

Durkin (1981) found that comprehension skill lessons in teachers' manuals were more evaluative in nature than instructional. Because basal manuals provide little help for teaching effective skill lessons, teachers often resort to a practice Durkin labeled "mentioning and assigning" (1981, p. 524). *Mentioning* is defined as saying just enough about a skill or concept to assign a worksheet. In fact, recent reports indicate that skill instruction in many classrooms generally consists of teachers assigning and monitoring students' completion of commercially developed worksheets (Anderson, Hiebert, Scott, & Wilkinson, 1985).

In direct instruction, the teacher is central to and actively involved in the teaching act, taking an active role in explaining, modeling, or demonstrating how something can be learned. Over the course of the lessons, the teacher gradually turns over responsibility for learning completely to the students. Blanton, Moorman, and Wood (1986) have recommended the application of a direct instruction or teacher-directed model to basal skill lessons to improve reading skill instruction. Researchers such as Anderson, Evertson, and Brophy (1979), Good (1979), Rupley and Blair (1978), and Stevens and

Rosenshine (1981) have established strong connections between student achievement and the use of direct instruction procedures.

Durkin (1978) defined *comprehension instruction* as the teacher's engaging in modeling, demonstrating, explaining, and defining how to comprehend a text. Pearson (1985) exhorted teachers to assume the role of "sharers of secrets, coconspirators, coaches, and cheerleaders" (p. 736) and provide students with guided practice and substantive feedback. (Chapter 14 provides additional information about planning and conducting effective reading lessons.)

Hunter's (1984) model can serve as an effective framework for designing direct, explicit instruction in skill lessons in reading. The steps involved in using the Hunter model are summarized in Figure 13.5.

To help teachers use direct instruction to plan and present basal skill instruction, Reutzel and Cooter (1988) have presented a sample lesson on the comprehension skill of "getting the sequence." This skill was chosen because many teachers find it particularly difficult to teach.

Sample Lesson: Getting the Sequence

Anticipatory Set The lesson begins with a discussion of several real-world situations in which getting the sequence is of critical importance such as using recipes, working mathematics problems, assembling a bike, and so forth. Children can be asked whether they can recall a time when they failed to follow the correct order and the consequences that resulted. This is done to make critical ties between the skill taught and the individual backgrounds of the children.

Objective and Input Next, the students are informed that the objective for the lesson is "getting the sequence." Getting the sequence is defined as the ability to recount the order of events that occur in a story or in life.

The lesson input begins with a piece of text shown to the entire group on an overhead projector. Texts in which magic tricks are described serve well to demonstrate sequence of events. For example, children can be shown the water glass trick by filling a glass of water, putting a heavy piece of paper over the glass, turning it over, and observing that the water remains in the glass without touching the paper. After this demonstration, a discussion of the written directions for the water glass trick ensues. Emphasis is placed on locating sequence signal words by pointing out the words (vocabulary) in our language that often signal sequence (e.g., *before, after, next, first, second, then*). Then the teacher sequences the directions on a timeline. To test the correctness of the sequence, several children can be invited to come forward and, by following the sequence of directions, perform the trick. This helps students immediately monitor their construction of the sequence of events leading up to the successful completion of the water glass trick.

FIGURE 13.5 Direct Instruction Skill Plan for Teaching Reading Skill Lessons

ANTICIPATORY SET

Relate the reading skill to be taught to the children's experiential backgrounds.

OBJECTIVE AND INPUT

Inform students about which reading skill they will be learning.

Give students a purpose for learning the reading skill.

MODELING

Demonstrate how one learns and applies the reading skill.

PURPOSE-SETTING AND GUIDED APPLICATION

Prepare the students to apply the reading skill
in
reading the basal story
or
in a real-life situation.

INDEPENDENT PRACTICE

Students apply the reading skill
in
reading the basal.

CHECKING FOR UNDERSTANDING

Understanding of the reading skill is checked throughout the lesson.

REAL-LIFE APPLICATION

ASSESSMENT

Modeling The role of the teacher during this stage of the lesson is to model the desired reading and thinking behaviors pertaining to the skill lesson. This usually means that a "think-aloud" process is used whereby the teacher discusses and demonstrates the application of his or her mental strategies to determine the sequence for the children. It is crucial for the teacher to select an example for modeling that closely parallels the story to be read by the students during subsequent stages of the reading lesson.

Another text passage can be placed onto the overhead projector that deals with hot air ballooning. The teacher reads the passage aloud to the class and lists the important elements of the text related to hot air ballooning on the chalkboard. As these elements are ordered and reordered, the teacher thinks aloud for the class so that the students are allowed to witness the logical processes and verification strategies used to successfully complete the task.

Once the modeling process is completed, the teacher's steps for determining the sequence of hot air ballooning are recorded on the chalkboard. Students ask questions afterwards, and they will frequently offer alternatives in logic that can bring them to the same conclusions. When the teacher is reasonably certain that the students have grasped the essential elements of the skill, the lesson proceeds.

Guided Practice The purpose of guided practice is to supervise the application of the skill or concept being taught and verify whether or not the children have understood it. Another reading selection is chosen that closely parallels those previously used; this time, the selection is on how to assemble a bicycle. To begin, the teacher conducts a discussion about unfamiliar vocabulary and background information in preparation for reading the passage. After previewing the title of the story, surveying pictures, and reading any subheadings, the teacher asks the students to close their books and think about the necessary sequence for successfully constructing a bicycle based on their limited knowledge of the story. Next, the children make their predictions, then read the story silently. If the predictions are incorrect, the children are instructed to revise them on their own to match the passage information. When students feel they have successfully noted the correct sequence, the summary is presented to the teacher for final evaluation.

Checking for Understanding A pervasive element in direct instruction is checking for understanding. Teachers should continually assess student understanding throughout the instructional sequence and be prepared for reteaching activities as necessary. The most crucial checkpoints seem to be after modeling, guided practice, and independent practice.

Purpose Setting and Independent Practice The purpose of independent practice is to verify whether or not the children have understood the skill or concept being taught and can apply it to their reading without additional teacher assistance. At this point in the lesson, teachers also can assign worksheets to individual students for practice and application, to help make explicit the relationship between the skill instructed and its application to reading the story or text. During independent practice, the teacher does not intervene until the assignment has been completed by the student(s).

Assessment To evaluate the effect of instruction, a test from other selected texts or passages can be assigned to assess the skill of getting the sequence. Informal observations of the students' performance during real-life application projects can also be used to assess student learning.

The lesson structure presented in the sample lesson can be applied to any skill in the basal reader. The lesson was not intended to be a script to be followed without variation and innovation on the part of the teacher. Teachers must decide which parts of the direct instruction lesson model are appropriate for their students, but as they plan and implement instruction, the direct instruction lesson model presented here can be of help in structuring and contextualizing reading skill instruction.

SUMMARY

This chapter has provided information for making informed instructional decisions about how, why, and when to use the basal reader to provide reading instruction. In addition, various ways to adapt and enrich basal reading lessons to both improve and add variety to reading instruction have been discussed. Since basal readers will continue to exert a major influence on reading instruction, teachers should take the time to become well acquainted with the series used in their school districts. Chapter 14 provides suggestions on how to develop and refine skills for planning and conducting effective reading lessons.

FOLLOW-UP QUESTIONS AND ACTIVITIES

1. How would you describe the use of reciprocal questioning?
2. Find a story in a basal reader. Using the teacher's manual as a guide, write a lesson plan to teach a directed reading activity (DRA). If time and circumstances permit, teach this lesson to a group of children in the public schools. Write a short paragraph on the experience. If circumstances do not permit teaching your DRA to children, teach it to a group of your peers. Ask them for evaluative comments regarding your lesson plan and presentation.
3. Locate a lesson in a basal teacher's manual. Using the information presented in this chapter, design a reconciled reading lesson (RRL). If possible, teach your RRL to a group of children or your peers.
4. Decide on a story for which you would like to create a story map or cloze story map. Following the directions outlined in the chapter,

create a story map. For the best experience, the map should be integrated into the regular DRA, or it can be used in conjunction with the RRL to teach a reading lesson to a group of children or peers.

5. Plan a reading lesson in which you integrate the language experience approach into the DRA. Teach this lesson to a group of younger readers if possible. Keep a log of your experiences.
6. Try reading a basal reader selection with a group of children or peers using one of the oral reading variations recommended in the chapter. Over a period of time, introduce the other three recommended variations and record the students' reactions. Did these techniques add variety?
7. Visit a local classroom and ask to observe a teacher during the reading period. Take note of the number and types of pre- and postquestions the teacher asks. How many children are involved in responding to the teacher's questions? Does the teacher encourage children to ask as well as answer questions? How much wait time does the teacher allow after asking questions? Keep notes of your observations. What did the teacher do well? What could the teacher do to improve her questioning? How will this knowledge help you conduct discussions of basal stories during reading lessons more effectively?
8. Plan and teach a reading skill lesson to a group of children or a group of your peers. You may also wish to evaluate several reading skill lessons in basal teachers' manuals against the criteria outlined in the chapter. Do these lessons provide you with information on how to teach rather than test? If not, how could you improve upon the lesson to teach rather than test?

ADDITIONAL READINGS

Anderson, R. C., Hiebert, E. F., Scott, J. A., & Wilkinson, I. A. G. (1985). *Becoming a nation of readers: The report of the Commission on Reading.* Washington, DC: National Institute of Education.

Applebee, A. N., Langer, J. A., & Mullis, I. V. S. (1988). *Who reads best?* Princeton, NJ: Educational Testing Service.

Aukerman, R. C. (1981). *The basal reader approach to reading.* New York: Wiley.

Aukerman, R. C. (1984). *Approaches to beginning reading.* New York: Wiley.

Goodman, K. S., Shannon, P., Freeman, Y. S., & Murphy, S. (1988). *Report card on basal readers.* New York: Owen.

REFERENCES

Anderson, L., Evertson, C., & Brophy, J. (1979). An experimental study of effective teaching in first-grade reading groups. *Elementary School Journal, 79,* 193–222.

Anderson, R. C., Hiebert, E. F., Scott, J. A., & Wilkinson, I. A. G. (1985). *Becoming a nation of readers: The report of the Commission on Reading*. Washington, DC: National Institute of Education.

Armbruster, B. (1984). The problem of inconsiderate text. In G. Duffy, L. Roehler, & J. Mason (Eds.), *Comprehension instruction: Perspectives and suggestions* (pp. 202–217). New York: Longman.

Bacharach, N., & Alexander, P. (1986). Basal reader manuals: What do teachers think of them and how do they use them? *Reading Psychology*, 7(3), 163–182.

Basal reading texts: What's in them to comprehend? (1984). *The Reading Teacher, 38*, 194–195.

Beck, I. (1986a, January). *Setting the stage for comprehension*. Paper presented at the meeting of the Seventh Rocky Mountain IRA Regional Conference, Colorado Springs, CO.

Beck, I. (1986b). Using research on reading. *Educational Leadership, 43*, 13–15.

Betts, E. (1946). *Foundations of American reading instruction*. New York: American Book.

Blanton, W. E., Moorman, G. B., and Wood, K. D. (1986). A model of direct instruction applied to the basal skills lesson. *The Reading Teacher, 40*, 299–304.

Bohning, G. (1986). The McGuffey Eclectic Readers: 1836–1986. *The Reading Teacher, 40*, 263–269.

Durkin, D. (1978–1979). What classroom observations reveal about reading comprehension instruction. *Reading Research Quarterly, 14*, 481–533.

Durkin, D. (1981). Reading comprehension instruction in five basal reader series. *Reading Research Quarterly, 16*, 515–544.

Durkin, D. (1984). Is there a match between what elementary teachers do and what basal reader manuals recommend? *The Reading Teacher, 37*, 734–744.

Education Product Information Exchange. (1977). *Report on a national study of the nature and the quality of instructional materials most used by teachers and learners*. (Tech. Rep. No. 76). New York: EPIE Institute.

Good, T. (1979). Teacher effectiveness in the elementary schools: What we know about it now. *Journal of Teacher Education*, 30(1), 52–64.

Harris, T. L., & Hodges, R. E. (1981). *A dictionary of reading and related terms*. Newark, DE: International Reading Association.

Hopkins, C. (1979). Using every-pupil response techniques in reading instruction. *The Reading Teacher, 33*, 173–175.

Hunter, M. (1984). Knowing, teaching, supervising. In P. L. Hosford (Ed.), *Using what we know about teaching* (pp. 169–192). Alexandria, VA: Association for Supervision and Curriculum Development.

Jones, M. B., & Nessel, D. D. (1985). Enhancing the curriculum with experience stories. *The Reading Teacher, 39*, 18–23.

McCallum, R. D. (1988). Don't throw the basals out with the bath water. *The Reading Teacher, 39*, 204–209.

Manzo, A. V. (1969). The request procedure. *Journal of Reading, 13*, 123–126.

Mason, J. (1983). An examination of reading instruction in third and fourth grades. *The Reading Teacher, 36*, 906–913.

Osborn, J. (1985). Workbooks: Counting, matching, and judging. In J. Osborn, P. T. Wilson, & R. C. Anderson (Eds.), *Reading education: Foundations for a literate America* (pp. 11–28). Lexington, MA: Lexington Books/D.C. Heath.

Pearson, P. D. (1974). The effects of grammatical complexity on children's comprehension, recall, and conception of certain semantic relations. *Reading Research Quarterly*, 10(2), 155–192.

Pearson, P. D. (1985). Changing the face of reading comprehension instruction. *The Reading Teacher, 38,* 724–738.

Pearson, P. D., & Fielding, L. (1982). Research update: Listening comprehension. *Language Arts, 59,* 617–629.

Prince, A. (1986, October). *Comparison of a reconciled reading lesson with the traditional reading lesson.* Paper presented at the meeting of the College Reading Association, Knoxville, TN.

Reutzel, D. R. (1985a). Reconciling schema theory and the basal reading lesson. *The Reading Teacher, 39,* 194–197.

Reutzel, D. R. (1985b). Story maps improve comprehension. *The Reading Teacher, 38,* 400–405.

Reutzel, D. R. (1986a). Clozing in on comprehension: The cloze story map. *The Reading Teacher, 39,* 524–529.

Reutzel, D. R. (1986b). Investigating a synthesized comprehension instructional strategy: The cloze story map. *The Journal of Educational Research, 79,* 343–349.

Reutzel, D. R., & Cooter, R. B. (1988). *Research implications for improving basal reader instruction. Reading Horizons, 28,* 208–216.

Reutzel, D. R., & Daines, D. (1987). The text-relatedness of reading lessons in seven basal reading series. *Reading Research and Instruction, 27,* 26–35.

Rowe, M. B. (1974). Wait-time and rewards as instructional variables. Their influence on language, logic, and fate control: Part One—Wait-time. *Journal of Research in Science Teaching, 11,* 81–94.

Rupley, W. H., & Blair, T. R. (1978). Teacher effectiveness in reading instruction. *The Reading Teacher, 31,* 970–973.

Sadow, M. W. (1982). The use of story grammar in the design of questions. *The Reading Teacher, 35,* 518–523.

Shannon, P. (1983). The use of commercial reading materials in American elementary schools. *Reading Research Quarterly, 19*(1), 68–85.

Sinatra, G. C., Stahl-Gemake, J., & Berg, D. N. (1984). Improving reading comprehension of disabled readers through semantic mapping. *The Reading Teacher, 38,* 22–29.

Stevens, R., & Rosenshine, B. (1981). Advances in research on teaching. *Exceptional Education Quarterly, 2,* 1–9.

Tierney, R. J., & Cunningham, J. W. (1984). Research on teaching reading comprehension. In P. D. Pearson (Ed.), *Reading Research Handbook,* New York: Longman.

Wood, K. D. (1983). A variation on an old theme: 4-way oral reading. *The Reading Teacher, 37,* 38–41.

Zintz, M. V., & Maggart, Z. R. (1984). *The reading process: The teacher and the learner* (4th ed.). Dubuque, IA: William C. Brown.

14

Planning and Conducting Effective Reading Lessons

BETH ANN HERRMANN

IN RESPONSE TO the criticism that basal readers are used ineffectively by many teachers, Chapter 13 offered some guidelines for more effective use of this widely employed instructional tool. Another common criticism of basal readers is that they do not provide suggestions for teaching reading skills and strategies; instead they merely provide practice and reinforcement of reading skills. In this chapter, Beth Ann Herrmann discusses what teachers need to consider in developing effective reading lessons to use not only with basal reading sources but also other instructional texts.

After a brief discussion of the importance of developing well-conceived instructional objectives for reading lessons, Herrmann presents a five-step plan for teachers to consider when planning indirect instruction. She goes on to provide an outline of the steps that three direct instructional lessons would include. Two of these lessons are used for developing process outcomes: strategy instruction for developing mental-processing outcomes and reciprocal teaching for developing text-processing outcomes. The third type of direct instruction covered is the directed reading lesson, which is used for developing content outcomes.

Herrmann provides specific examples of reading lessons that are based on the steps of each procedure discussed in the chapter. Since the instructional materials teachers rely on the most are often seriously deficient in providing specific suggestions for instruction, it is imperative that effective teachers understand how to develop and conduct well-planned lessons on their own.

STUDY QUESTIONS

1. How is direct instruction different from indirect instruction?
2. What are the planning decisions you would make when planning an indirect instruction lesson and a direct instruction lesson?
3. What is the teacher's role in direct explanation, reciprocal teaching, and the directed reading activity?
4. How does teacher modeling in direct explanation differ from teacher modeling in reciprocal teaching and the directed reading activity?

Developing Worthwhile Lesson Objectives

Effective reading instruction does not occur accidentally or haphazardly; it is goal directed and intentional. Hence, the most important thing you will do when planning reading instruction is develop worthwhile instructional objectives that guide decision making when planning and conducting reading lessons.

Developing worthwhile instructional objectives involves much more than scribbling a note in a lesson plan book or developing a mental script of what you want students to do. It involves serious decision making. For each lesson, you must develop a complete statement of what should be learned, why it is important for students to learn it, and conditions under which it should be used. Developing such objectives will enable you to plan and conduct focused reading instruction that ensures that students are accomplishing worthwhile goals.

You must make two major decisions when developing instructional objectives. First, decide on the specific outcome of the lesson so you know what the students are to accomplish and why it is important for them to accomplish it. The effectiveness of your outcome decisions will depend on the answers to two important questions:

1. What will the students be able to do at the end of the lesson?
2. Why is it important for them to be able to do this?

Second, decide on reading situations in which the desired outcome will be used. An example of a well-written statement of a lesson outcome is, "The student will learn how to use a context clue strategy to figure out hard words in print that are causing comprehension difficulties."

Indirect Instruction

Indirect instruction is used primarily for developing attitude outcomes such as a positive response to reading and a conceptual understanding that reading is a worthwhile, purposeful activity. (See Chapter 17 for further discussion of how to enhance positive attitudes toward reading.) You will use indirect instruction primarily in large-group settings, but occasionally you will want to use it with small collaborative (heterogeneous) groups or in learning centers.

The teacher's role as facilitator is crucial in indirect instruction lessons, since objectives are achieved through teacher-guided student interaction with the environment. Hence, indirect instruction is usually activity centered, with an activity/discussion/activity format.

The effectiveness of your indirect instruction lessons will be closely tied to the care with which you make decisions about the lesson during the planning phase. Begin by developing worthwhile lesson objectives. Then carefully decide which activities and discussion procedures to include and how to summarize and evaluate the lesson.

Planning Indirect Instruction

In planning indirect instruction lessons, decisions must be made about objectives and the environment, both of which must be structured so that students interpret the lesson tasks in ways that lead them to specific attitude outcomes. The following five-step decision making process is helpful when planning an indirect instruction lesson:

Step One: Decide on the lesson outcome. Decide what the students will learn, why it is important for them to learn it, and how to state the outcome as a lesson objective. For example, suppose your students are experiencing difficulty with reading and writing tasks because they do not understand how reading and writing are related. You want their reading and writing performances to improve, but you also want them to develop an appreciation for the connections between reading and writing. A sample objective for such a lesson would be, "The students will develop an understanding of relationships between reading and writing that will lead to improved performance and an appreciation for reading and writing connections."

Step Two: Decide on the opening activity. After you have stated the lesson objective, decide on an opening activity that will motivate the students to want to achieve the desired outcome. Decide on materials you will need and the procedure that will be followed when introducing and involving students in the activity. For example, for the reading and writing lesson described in step one, helping the students write their own endings to a story would be a good opening activity.

Step Three: Develop discussion procedures. Once you have decided on the opening activity, decide on procedures for discussing the activity once it is completed. Decide how you will involve the students in the discussion. For example, a good way to involve the students in the activity described in step two would be to ask them to read and discuss their story endings.

Step Four: Decide on a follow-up activity. Decide on a second activity that the students will complete immediately following the discussion of the opening activity. The second activity further develops the desired outcome. For example, a good follow-up activity in the reading and writing lesson would be for students to brainstorm how reading and writing are connected.

Step Five: Design a summary and evaluation. Decide how you will summarize what has been accomplished in the lesson and how you will evaluate whether or not the outcome has been achieved. For example, in the reading and writing lesson, the teacher would summarize the students' ideas about reading and writing connections.

Conducting Indirect Instruction

After carefully planning the indirect instruction, you are now ready to conduct the lesson. Use the following five-step procedure:

Step One: Explain the objective. Explicitly describe the outcome of the lesson—what the students will learn and why it is important for them to learn it, as illustrated in the following lesson excerpt:

> T: I've been watching how you complete many of our reading and writing tasks, and I've noticed that many of you think of these tasks as separate activities. I think you are having a problem with some of these tasks because you do not see the relationship between reading and writing. Today we're going to work on an activity that will help you better understand reading and writing connections.

Step Two: Introduce the opening activity. Introduce and involve the students in the opening activity, as illustrated in the following excerpt:

> T: I'm going to read the beginning of a story. I want you to listen carefully because you're going to write your own ending to the story. [The teacher reads the story and asks the students to independently write their own ending. While the students are working the teacher provides necessary individual assistance.]

Step Three: Discuss the opening activity. Involve the students in a discussion of the completed opening activity. Note how the teacher involves the students in a discussion about their story endings in the following lesson excerpt:

> T: Glen, will you read us the story ending you wrote? [Glen reads his ending.] Thank you Glen. Let's talk about Glen's ending for a minute. What do you think is the best part of his ending?

Step Four: Explain the follow-up activity. Introduce, explain, and involve students in the second activity as illustrated in the following lesson excerpt:

> T: Now there's something else I want you to work on this morning. I'm going to put you in groups of three, and I want you to brainstorm lots of ways that reading and writing are con-

nected. Think about the activity we just completed. That will help you. In about 15 minutes, I'll ask one person from each group to share your ideas.

Step Five: Summarize and evaluate the lesson. Summarize the lesson activities and what has been learned. Evaluate whether or not the intended outcome has been achieved. Notice how the teacher closes the lesson in the following lesson excerpt:

> T: I am pleased with the ideas you have come up with today. Let me summarize some of your ideas about how reading and writing are connected. Many of you said that it is important to spell correctly, not only for spelling tests, but also when we write stories, because if we spell incorrectly it will be difficult for us, as authors, to get our message across to the reader. You also said that what can be written can be read and that both reading and writing are important ways to communicate our ideas to other people. [The teacher closes the lesson by reading the real ending to the story.]

Direct Instruction

Direct instruction also may be used to develop attitude outcomes, but its primary use is to develop process and content outcomes. (See Chapters 4 and 6 for further discussion of process and content outcomes.) The teacher's role in direct instruction involves much more than simply being a facilitator. Direct instruction relies heavily on teacher/student interactions. Instruction may be task centered or activity centered, but in both situations the teacher directs the lesson with a conscious effort to explain and model new information and shape students' understandings of specific lesson outcomes. Direct instruction lessons are almost always conducted in small groups formed on the basis of ability.

Different types of direct instruction are used to focus on different types of outcomes. For example, direct explanation is particularly useful for developing mental reasoning processes associated with effective reading (e.g., how to use context clues as an aid to word identification). Reciprocal teaching and the directed reading activity (DRA), on the other hand, are useful for developing an understanding of content as well as process.

Direct Explanation

One way to help students understand how the reading process works and how to construct meaning from text is to provide direct explanation of specific reading strategies (Duffy & Roehler, 1989; Duffy, Roehler, & Putnam, 1987; Duffy, Roehler, & Rackliffe, 1986). The teacher's role as information giver and mediator is crucial in direct explanation. The teacher explains and models reasoning processes associated with specific reading strategies and, on an ongoing basis, directly shapes students' understandings of these processes by re-explaining and/or re-modeling.

In a typical basal reader lesson, direct explanation occurs before students read a selection, and it focuses on reasoning processes used to monitor comprehension and reasoning processes associated with "fix-it" strategies that are used when a comprehension breakdown occurs.

Direct explanation is a complex and difficult two-phase task that includes being an information giver (directly and explicitly explaining and modeling how to use reading strategies) and a mediator (shaping students' understandings of reasoning processes associated with these strategies). Your success depends on how well you make several planning decisions.

Planning a Direct Explanation Lesson

Use the following eight-step decision making process when planning a direct explanation lesson segment:

Step One: Decide on the outcome. Decide which strategy to teach, why it is important for the students to learn it, and when the students will need to use it. State the outcome as an instructional objective. For example, suppose your students frequently experience difficulty understanding what they read because they have trouble figuring out difficult words. You want them to learn how to apply reasoning processes associated with using context clues. A sample objective for such a lesson segment would be, "The students will be able to use a context clue strategy to figure out hard words in recreational and content area materials."

Step Two: Conduct a task analysis. Decide on the reasoning processes associated with the strategy. Ask yourself these questions:

- What is the outcome I am after? What do I want the students to be able to do?
- What mental sequence do I want the students to follow when using this strategy?

The result of the task analysis is a reasoning process consisting of certain steps and a sequence that students use as a starting point when trying to use the strategy to make sense out of text. For example, a sequenced set of reasoning processes that are employed when using context clues to figure out unknown words in print includes (a) thinking about what is already known about the topic; while at the same time (b) examining the context for syntactic or meaning relationships that might give clues as to what the unknown word is; (c) predicting what the word might be; and (d) testing predicted words to see whether or not they make sense.

Step Three: Select text examples. Collect several text examples you can use when explaining and modeling reasoning processes associated with the strategy as well as text examples the students can use to practice using the strategy. Make sure you select enough examples, and make sure they all are appropriate for the strategy you plan to teach. For example, a short selection from a content area textbook would be a useful piece of material for explaining and modeling how to use the context clue strategy. Several short selections from a variety of recreational texts such as library books would be useful student practice material.

Step Four: Assess basal textbook manual suggestions. Assess the suggestions provided in the teacher's basal textbook manual for (a) a description of the strategy, (b) an indication of the usefulness of the strategy, and (c) directions for how to use the strategy. Disregard suggestions that do not help you explain and model reasoning processes. For example, suppose the teachers' manual suggests that you teach context clues by having students complete a fill-in-the-blank activity. While such a suggestion may be useful as a follow-up activity, it does not focus on explaining or modeling reasoning processes associated with using context clues. Therefore, the suggestion should be disregarded as an introductory activity.

Step Five: Plan introductory comments. Decide what you will say to introduce the strategy. Your introduction should include a statement of what will be learned, why it is important, and when it will be used. For example, introductory comments for the context clue lesson would focus on the usefulness of the strategy for figuring out difficult words.

Step Six: Plan a modeling sequence. Decide what you will say and do when modeling how to use the strategy. Practice thinking aloud as you use the strategy. For example, a modeling sequence for the context clue lesson would reveal to students the invisible reasoning processes used to figure out difficult words.

Step Seven: Assess the basal text selection. Scrutinize the basal text selection for opportunities to use the strategy. For example, identify difficult words in the story.

Step Eight: Decide on mediation strategies. Although shaping students' understanding is spontaneous and involves making ongoing "in-flight" decisions that cannot be planned for in advance, anticipate the kinds of problems you think your students will have in learning when and how to use the strategy. Decide how you will re-explain and/or re-model the strategy if necessary, and select appropriate analogies that may be used to clarify misunderstandings. For example, if you think your students might have difficulty understanding how to use the context clue strategy because they are used to using phonics knowledge only for word pronunciation, then you will need to figure out a way to re-explain and illustrate the usefulness of context clues.

Conducting Basal Reader Lessons That Include Direct Explanation

Use the following eight-step procedure when conducting basal reader lessons that include a direct explanation lesson segment:

Step One: Introduce the selection and the strategy. First, activate the students' prior knowledge of the story content by discussing the title and/or pictures and asking students to share experiences that relate to the topic. Second, explain in detail what strategy will be taught, why it is important, and when it will be used. Use difficult story parts to demonstrate the usefulness of the strategy and activate students' prior knowledge about the strategy. For example, notice how the teacher introduces the selection and a context clue strategy in the following lesson excerpt:

> T: Today we are going to read a story about a birthday party. How many of you have been to a birthday party? [Students respond.] Look at this picture of the boy in our story. His name is Russ. What is Russ doing in this picture? [Students respond.] That's right, he is blowing out the candles on his cake. Let's read the title of our story together. [Reading] "The Birthday Surprise." Very good. Now there's something I want you to know about this story. There are some hard words in the story that might give you some trouble. Here's one right here [shows students]. Before we read our story today I'm going to teach you a strategy for figuring out these hard words so that when you come to them in the story you will be able to figure them out yourselves.

Step Two: Model. First, think aloud to model when the strategy should be used. Read aloud from one of the text examples and pretend to have trouble comprehending the material. Verbalize exactly what is causing the comprehension breakdown, and explain that when such problems occur it is time for the strategy to be used, as illustrated in the following excerpt:

> T: OK. I want you to watch me closely to see how I know when to use this strategy and how I go about using it. I'm going to read part of our story to you, and I'm going to pretend that I don't know a hard word. Watch what I do when that happens. [The teacher reads and pretends to have trouble with a hard word.] Hmmm. I don't know that word, let me skip it and keep going. Maybe I won't need to know it. [The teacher continues reading and pretends that a comprehension breakdown has occurred.] Oh, now I'm really in trouble. Not knowing that big

word back here is making me get confused. [Addressing the students] I want you to understand that right now is when I should use our strategy, because I've stopped understanding what I am reading.

Second, think aloud to model how reasoning processes associated with the strategy are used to repair the comprehension breakdown. The trick is to make visible the invisible reasoning process, as illustrated in the following lesson excerpt:

T: OK. I'm in trouble now because of this hard word. Watch what I do to figure out what it is. [The teacher re-reads the sentence that contains the word.] Hmmm. I don't get any hints from the sentence. I'm going to have to do more than just re-read the sentence. Let me think a minute. I know something about birthday parties. My son just had a birthday party, and he blew out the candles on his cake just like Russ did in the story. But when John tried to blow out his candles they didn't go out, because we tricked him with phoney candles that don't go out when you blow them. Let me read this part of the story again and think about what I already know. I'll also try to sound the first letter of the word when I get to it. [The teacher re-reads the sentence again and sounds the first letter of the unknown word] . . . but Russ' candles didn't go out because they were /f/ . . . fake! The candles were fake. Let me see if that makes sense now.

Step Three: Shape students' understanding. Immediately after you model when and how to use the strategy, check how the students have restructured the instructional information. Ask them to tell or show you when and how to use the strategy. Listen carefully as the students respond, because your job is to figure out how well they understand the reasoning processes associated with the strategy. If the students understand when and how to use the strategy, provide supportive feedback for using the process correctly and move to the next phase of the lesson. However, if some of the students do not understand when and/or how to use the strategy, re-explain, re-model, provide an analogy, or otherwise clear up misunderstandings.

Shaping students' understanding is an ongoing process that occurs over a number of trials, sometimes over a period of several class sessions. It is possible that on several occasions the strategy lesson will end shortly after the modeling segment and begin again the following day. After several opportunities to shape students' understanding, explain that you expect them to try to use the strategy even though they are still learning it. Notice how the teacher attempts to shape students' understanding of the strategy in the following lesson excerpt:

T: Now I want to give you all a chance to show me what I did when I used the strategy. John, let's start with you. Can you show me how to use the strategy to figure out this hard word in this sentence?

S: Well, I would go back and read the sentence again.

T: OK, Jerry, remember when I just re-read the sentence? I didn't get much help until I did something else. Do you remember what I was thinking about when I re-read my sentence?

S: How to sound out the word?

T: No, Jerry. That comes later. There's something else you should do first. Watch me use our strategy again with this sentence. The rest of you help me if you can. [At this point in the lesson, the teacher re-models how to use the strategy, eliciting assistance from the students. Immediately following the re-modeling, she checks to see how Jerry restructured the additional instructional information by asking him to tell her what she did. This process is continued until Jerry has a better understanding of the strategy.]

Step Four: Set purposes for reading. Share the title and the pictures once again, and ask the students to predict what they think the story will be about. Jot down a few predictions (including any of your own) on the chalkboard. Remind the students that there are some parts of the story that may give them trouble, and if that happens they are to try to use the strategy they are learning, as illustrated in the following lesson excerpt:

T: Now we are going to read the story about Russ's birthday party. I want you to look again at the title of our story and some of the pictures [shows title and pictures]. What do you think this story will be about? [The students respond, and the teacher writes a few predictions on the chalkboard.] OK. That's good thinking. Now I want you to remember that there are hard words in this story, and when you come up against one I want you to try to use our strategy. I'll help you if you need it.

Step Five: Guide silent reading. Tell the students how far you would like them to read and what you expect them to do when they finish. As the students are reading, continue shaping individual students' understanding of the strategy by modeling and/or re-explaining or clarifying how to use the strategy.

Step Six: Discuss the story and strategy use. Lead a discussion by asking questions about the use of the strategy and the content of the story. If time permits, ask one or two students to describe how they used the strategy while reading. Shape students' understanding of the content and strategy by assisting those who had trouble answering questions about the story or explaining how to use the strategy, as illustrated in the following lesson excerpt:

> T: OK. Let's look again at the guesses we made about what would happen in the story. Johnny, you said you thought Russ would get a bicycle for his birthday. Did you find out anything about that when you read? [Student responds.] [The teacher continues a discussion of each prediction, erasing those that are untrue.] Ralph, I noticed you trying to use our strategy while you were reading silently. Can you show us which word was giving you trouble and how you used the strategy?

Step Seven: Close the lesson. Close the lesson by asking the students to summarize what happened in the story and how the strategy was used to improve their understanding of the story. As a final closing statement, explain other times the strategy can be used (expository text, newspaper, etc.). Notice how the teacher closes the lesson in the following lesson excerpt:

> T: Let me summarize what we learned from our story and strategy today. First, we learned that Russ got faked out by some phoney candles, didn't we? We also learned that he did not get everything for his birthday that he was expecting and that he got some things that he was not expecting to get. You also learned how to use a strategy for figuring out hard words. That strategy will work for you in other things you read, too, so I want you to try to use it this afternoon when we read our social studies. I'll be asking some of you to show me how to use it with that book.

Step Eight: Provide applications. Provide opportunities for the students to practice using the strategy on their own, as illustrated in the following lesson excerpt:

> T: I'm going to work with the Gremlin group now, so I want you to be working quietly at your seats. You already have your board work to finish, but I also want you to work on this worksheet about our strategy. [The teacher gives the students a fill-in-the-blank worksheet. The students are to fill in the blanks with a word that makes sense and then explain how they used the context clue strategy to help them figure out which word to use. It should be noted that this activity is not

the same thing as using contextual analysis when we read. However, this activity helps students approach the use of contextual aids.]

Reciprocal Teaching

Reciprocal teaching was discussed in Chapter 6 as a way to enhance students' interaction with content area reading material. A further discussion of this teaching strategy is provided here as one way to help students—especially those who are academically marginal—understand and learn from text (Brown & Palincsar, 1986; Palincsar, 1986; Palincsar & Brown, 1984). Reciprocal teaching is an interactive procedure whereby the teacher and the students collaborate in the joint construction of text meaning. Lessons focus on four comprehension-fostering and -monitoring activities believed to be used by expert readers: generating questions, summarizing, predicting, and clarifying (Brown & Lawton, 1985).

The reciprocal teaching procedure is a form of expert scaffolding (Bruner, 1978; Cazden, 1979) in which students and teachers share responsibility for learning and refining the four comprehension activities. *Expert scaffolding* refers to a procedure by which an expert (a teacher, a peer, a parent, a master craftsman) provides supporting context in which students can gradually acquire skills. As the expert, the teacher initially takes on the major responsibility for the group's activity. Novices are encouraged to watch and participate before taking their turn as discussion leader. The teacher models and explains, relinquishing part of the task to the novices only at the level they are capable of negotiating at any particular point in time. Increasingly, as the novices become more competent, the teacher increases the demands, requiring participation at a slightly more challenging level.

The basic reciprocal teaching procedure is simple. A teacher and a group of students take turns leading a dialogue concerning a section of text they are jointly attempting to read and understand. The dialogue includes spontaneous discussion of the four main comprehension-fostering activities: summarizing, questioning, clarifying, and predicting. The discussion leader (first the teacher, then the students) leads the group through the four activities, monitoring each group member's performance as a means of helping that student understand the meaning of the text, critically evaluate the author's message, remember the content, and apply newfound knowledge flexibly and creatively. The learner observes the leader during the demonstration of the activities, develops a conceptual framework for the activities before actually attempting to lead them, and follows the leader's example by assuming the role of the leader. All of the activities are embedded in the context of natural dialogue between student and teacher that takes place during the actual task of reading with a clear goal of deriving meaning from the text.

As a form of expert scaffolding, reciprocal teaching involves continuous trial and error on the part of the student coupled with continuous adjustment on the part of the teacher. Through interactions with the teacher and more knowledgeable peers, each student is led to perform at increasingly more mature levels. Sometimes this progress is fast, sometimes slow, but regardless of its pace, the teacher provides an opportunity for each student to respond at a slightly more challenging level.

Planning a Reciprocal Teaching Lesson

Planning a reciprocal teaching lesson is a two-phase process. Become familiar with the text to be taught by following this five-step procedure:

Step One: Study the text. Identify text segments that will be taught.

Step Two: Plan possible questions. Identify salient questions in the text and generate additional questions about the material.

Step Three: Plan possible predictions. General possible predictions about each segment of the text.

Step Four: Prepare possible summaries. Underline summarizing sentences and generate possible summaries for each segment of the text.

Step Five: Identify possible sources of confusion. Circle difficult vocabulary and/or concepts.

Next, make several diagnostic decisions about the students who will participate in the lesson. First, evaluate the students' general reading abilities. Second, decide what kind of overall support they will need. Third, evaluate more specifically the students' abilities to generate text questions, summarize, predict, and clarify, and decide what kind of support they will need to participate in and eventually lead each of these activities. Fourth, decide what activities the students already use when reading and what needs to be done to help them learn from the text.

Conducting a Reciprocal Teaching Lesson

As indicated earlier, there is a certain structure to the reciprocal teaching lesson (e.g., the use of dialogue to instruct the four activities), but there also is plenty of opportunity for teacher decision making relative to specific content and direction of the lesson. Generally, the following six-step procedure is followed:

Step One: Elicit predictions. Read the title of the story and elicit predictions from the students as to what they expect or would like to learn from the story. Summarize the group's predictions and, if appropriate, add a few of your own. Notice how the lesson begins in the following excerpt:

T: What is the title of our new passage?

S: The Miracle of Butterflies.

T: Right. What is the miracle of butterflies? Just in your own words, what would you predict this is going to be about?

S: How butterflies fly?

T: So the miracle might be that they fly.

S: How butterflies fly?

T: Oh, that's a good prediction!

S: What they do.

S: What season they come out, like summer.

T: OK. Those are some excellent predictions. Let's begin . . . .

Step Two: Read a story segment. Read a small portion of the text aloud, paragraph by paragraph.

Step Three: Generate questions. Ask a question about the information contained in the story. Invite the group to answer the question and invite individual group members to share additional questions generated while reading the story, as illustrated in the following excerpt:

T: My question is: [Modeling] What have the people of Butterfly City, USA, done to protect the butterflies?

S: They made a law making it illegal.

T: To do what? You are right, Quinton.

S: To kill butterflies.

T: Exactly. Good answer.

Step Four: Summarize. Summarize what has been read by identifying the gist of the segment, and explain how you arrived at this summary. Invite the group to comment on the summary. Notice how the teacher summarizes in the following excerpt:

T: [Modeling] My summary is that this is about the migration of the monarch butterflies. I thought of that summary because they [the authors] introduced the story with a good topic sentence. That was a good clue. Do you have anything that should be added to my summary?

Step Five: Discuss/clarify. Lead a discussion to clarify any words or ideas that are unclear or confusing to the students. Notice how the teacher clarifies an unclear meaning in the following excerpt:

T: Let me ask you something here. Is there an unclear meaning in this paragraph?

S: Yes. Where it says [reading] . . . scrawls in wavy light.

T: Now, does the sun ever write a message in the sky?

S: No.

T: No. What is the author doing here?

S: Making up the whole thing in his mind.

T: Good. It doesn't really happen, but the author is using this expression to say that the sun sends us a message, and that is that it can be used as an energy source. But certainly you will never look at the sky and see a message written by the sun.

Step Six: Elicit predictions. Signal preparation to move on to the next portion of the text by eliciting and making predictions regarding upcoming content. Select a student to be the next teacher.

At any point in the lesson when a student has trouble participating in any one of the comprehension activities, modify the student's level of participation in the discussion by adjusting the task demand, as illustrated in the following excerpt:

T: OK. Let's try for another question. Let me read a part of this again. [The teacher reads the second paragraph again.]

S: I never heard that before.

T: Can you think of a question? [Pause.]

S: I know. They can see themselves.

T: Hmm. You could ask a question about that sentence, couldn't you? Start the question with "How."

S: How can the . . .

T: aquanauts . . .

S: see themselves in the mirror?

T: OK. That's close. You answered your own question. What is the mirror?

S: The water.

T: So you might ask, "How could the aquanauts see themselves?" or "What was the water like?" Let's go on now.

The Directed Reading Activity

The directed reading activity (DRA) is a problem-solving approach to reading that is used to guide the reading of basal stories or content area material. The DRA is appropriate for use with homogeneous ability groups of 8 to 12 students. The primary purpose of the DRA is to help students understand the content of what they read. The teacher sets purposes for reading, guides silent reading, and checks achievement of purposes. Skill development occurs after a selection has been read. When students have difficulty understanding content, the teacher focuses on the topic, the author's purpose, and specific information contained in the selection.

Planning a Directed Reading Activity

Use the following eight-step planning procedure when planning a directed reading lesson:

Step One: Evaluate the selection on the basis of interest and content. Decide whether or not the basal selection or chapter to be read is worth reading. If you decide that it is not worth reading, evaluate the next selection or chapter.

Step Two: Develop an objective. Identify specific reasons why a selection or chapter is worth reading and develop an objective describing these reasons.

Step Three: Analyze the selection. Analyze the selection and decide what the students need to know about various knowledge sources (words, topic, purpose, and text structure) that will be used to get meaning from the text.

Step Four: Select stopping points. Analyze the selection again and, on the basis of text difficulty, decide whether the selection will be read in its entirety at once or in segments. If you decide that the students should read the selection in segments, select appropriate stopping points for each segment.

Step Five: Evaluate/develop questions. Evaluate text questions provided in the teacher's manual and decide whether or not they are worth asking. If necessary, develop additional questions to include in the discussion of the content.

Step Six: Prepare skill development activities. Evaluate the teacher's manual suggestions for the text (including workbook pages) and decide which paper-and-pencil tasks or seatwork activities to use as learning aids to ensure that students understand the content.

Step Seven: Sequence the lesson. Decide the sequence of the lesson and what will be said in the lesson.

Step Eight: Select lesson evaluation techniques. Decide how you will evaluate whether or not students have learned the content.

Conducting a DRA Lesson

Use the following seven-step process when conducting a DRA lesson:

Step One: Introduce the lesson. The purpose of the introduction is to get the students ready for the lesson, so it is important to (a) review relevant information the group has previously learned, read about, or experienced; (b) present key new vocabulary terms; (c) introduce the author, setting, or situation of the selection; (d) preview or survey the selection in order to find out about its overall format, topic, or subject; (e) stimulate interest in the selection; and (f) motivate the students so that they will want to read the selection. Notice the teacher's introduction in the following excerpt:

> T: Today we're going to read a story about turtles. The title of our story is [reading] "A Safe Place for Turtles." How many of you have ever had a turtle for a pet? [The students respond, and some of the students' experiences are discussed.] OK. Let's talk a minute about some hard words in this story. [The teacher writes three or four vocabulary words on the chalkboard, pronounces them, and briefly discusses each one.] I think you're really going to like this story today, because something pretty remarkable happens to the turtle in our story.

Step Two: Set specific purposes for reading. Give the students a specific question to read for or elicit from them reasons why they want to read the selection. List a few purposes on the chalkboard. Notice how the teacher sets purposes for reading in the following excerpt:

> T: I think I want to read this story to find out where some safe places for turtles are. Griffen, why do you want to read this story?
>
> S: I want to know what happens to the turtle.
>
> T: OK. That's a good reason for reading the story. Laura, how about you?

Step Three: Guide silent reading. Direct the students to read to the first stopping point, and tell them what you expect them to do when they finish reading (e.g., close their books, put their heads down). While the students are reading, observe them and record symptoms of reading difficulties.

Step Four: Check achievement of purposes. When all of the students have completed the silent reading, check achievement of purposes by repeating the purpose questions and asking students to read aloud sections of the text that answer the questions. Discuss these answers with the class. Notice how the teacher checks achievement of purposes in the following excerpt:

> T: Let's see what we have learned so far. Griffen, you said you wanted to find out what happened to the turtle in our story. Did you find out yet?
>
> S: Yeah.
>
> T: OK. Find the part of the story where it tells us what happened to the turtle and read it out loud to us. The rest of you try to find it, too.

Step Five: Continue the lesson. Repeat steps two through four until the entire selection has been read.

Step Six: Summarize and evaluate. Summarize what has been done, what new knowledge has been acquired, what skills have been reviewed or presented, and how the day's activities relate to what has previously been done in class and/or will be done later. Evaluate whether or not the lesson is a success. Notice how the teacher summarizes and evaluates the lesson in the following excerpt:

> T: You all did such a good job today. We learned lots of new things about turtles, didn't we? We already knew something about what turtles eat from the science chapter we read yesterday, but today we learned something about where turtles go to hide and be safe. I want you to think about that later today as we continue with our science chapter, because I think that information will come in handy.

Step Seven: Direct skill development activities. Assign seatwork and other pencil-and-paper activities.

SUMMARY

Planning and conducting effective reading lessons is a crucial organizational step that begins with developing worthwhile lesson objectives. Lesson objectives are important because they guide decision making when planning and conducting reading lessons. A good objective includes a clear statement of what will be learned, why it is important, and reading situations in which the desired outcome will be used.

This chapter explained how to plan and conduct indirect instruction lessons for developing attitude outcomes, direct explanation lesson segments for developing process outcomes, and reciprocal teaching lessons and the directed reading activity for developing content outcomes. These types of instruction are similar in that all are interactive, all are used with basal selections or content area text chapters, and all take place within the context of regular reading instruction. The lessons differ greatly, however, in the type of outcomes they achieve and in the role the teacher plays. Figure 14.1 summarizes similarities and differences between these three types of instruction. You will use all three at different times to achieve different objectives, but regardless of the type of instruction you decide to use, you must first

FIGURE 14.1 Comparing Direct Explanation, Reciprocal Teaching, and the Directed Reading Activity

Similarities

All three require face-to-face teacher-student interaction.

All three may be used with stories or expository prose.

All three take place during regular reading instruction.

Differences

	Direct Explanation	*Reciprocal Teaching*	*Directed Reading Activity*
Goals:	Teaches reasoning processes used by strategic readers. (Lessons show students how to construct meaning from text.)	Deals with text content and how to study and learn from text. (Lessons focus on questioning, summarizing, predicting, and clarifying text content.)	Teaches specific text content. (Lessons focus on concepts and topics included in a selection or chapter.)
Role of Modeling:	The teacher makes visible the invisible reasoning processes. (Thoughts about mental processes are verbalized.)	The teacher demonstrates procedures expert readers follow to study and learn from text.	The teacher demonstrates setting purposes for reading.
Teacher Responses:	When students misunderstand reasoning processes, the teacher re-explains, re-models, and clarifies by eliciting student feedback and providing more elaboration.	When students have difficulty generating questions, summarizing, predicting, or clarifying, the teacher lowers the task demand.	When students have difficulty understanding text content, the teacher clarifies by asking questions and/or discussing specific aspects of the selection or chapter.

develop a good lesson plan. A well-constructed lesson plan ensures that the lesson will accomplish much more than simply filling up instructional time.

FOLLOW-UP QUESTIONS AND ACTIVITIES

1. Write two instructional objectives for an indirect instruction lesson. Then plan a 20-minute lesson for second-, fourth-, or sixth-graders.
2. Conduct a task analysis to figure out the reasoning processes associated with constructing main ideas. Then select text materials for modeling the reasoning processes and show the class how to use the main idea strategy you have developed.
3. Study the basal reader teacher's manual suggestions for teaching prefixes and suffixes. Figure out how to modify the suggestions to include a focus on reasoning processes associated with using prefixes and suffixes to figure out hard words. Explain your modifications to the class.
4. Using a basal reader selection, plan and teach a reciprocal teaching lesson or a directed reading activity.

ADDITIONAL READINGS

Estes, T. H., & Vaughn, J. L. (1985). *Reading and learning in the content-area classroom.* Boston: Allyn and Bacon.

Jones, B. F., Palincsar, A. S., Ogle, D. S., & Carr, E. G. (Eds.). (1987). *Strategic teaching and learning: Cognitive instruction in content areas.* Alexandria, VA: Association for Supervision and Curriculum Development.

McNeil, J. D. (1987). *Reading comprehension: New directions for classroom practice* (2nd ed.). Glenview, IL: Scott, Foresman.

Vacca, R. T., & Vacca, J. (1989). Content-area reading. Glenview, IL: Scott, Foresman.

Winograd, P. N., Wixson, K. K., & Lipson, M. Y. (Eds.). (1989). *Improving basal reading and instruction.* New York: Teachers College Press.

REFERENCES

Brown, A., & Lawton, S. (1985). [An analysis of on-line study strategies for learning from texts]. Unpublished raw data.

Brown, A., & Palincsar, A. S. (1986). *Guided, cooperative learning and individual knowledge acquisition.* (Report No. 372). Cambridge, MA: Bolt, Beranek, and Newman; Urbana: University of Illinois, Center for the Study of Reading. (ERIC Document Reproduction Service No. ED 270 738)

Bruner, J. (1978). The role of dialogue in language acquisition. In A. Sinclair, R. J. Jarvella, & W. J. M. Levelt (Eds.), *The child's conception of language* (pp. 241–256). Berlin: Springer-Verlag.

Cazden, C. (1979). Peekaboo as an instructional model: Discourse development at home and at school. In *Papers and reports on child language development* (No. 17, pp. 1–19). Palo Alto, CA: Department of Linguistics, Stanford University.

Duffy, G., & Roehler, L. (1989). *Improving classroom reading instruction: A decision making approach.* New York: Random House.

Duffy, G., Roehler, L., & Putnam, J. (1987). Putting the teacher in control: Instructional decision making and basal text books. *Elementary School Journal, 87,* 357–366.

Duffy, G., Roehler, L., & Rackliffe, G. (1986). How teachers' instructional talk influences students' understanding of lesson content. *Elementary School Journal, 87*(3), 3–16.

Palincsar, A. (1986). The role of dialogue in providing scaffolded instruction. *Educational Psychologist, 21*(1 & 2), 73–98.

Palincsar, A., & Brown, A. (1984). Reciprocal teaching of comprehension-fostering and comprehension-monitoring activities. *Cognition and Instruction, 1,* 117–175.

15

Adapting Reading Instruction for Students with Special Needs

SHARON KOSSACK

ONE OF THE MAJOR concerns of effective teachers is meeting the special needs of the exceptional students in their classrooms. While many teachers may have assistance in working with children who have special needs, they must still be able to recognize and work with students who have a wide range of abilities. In Chapter 15, Sharon Kossack addresses the difficult problem of organizing and managing reading instruction for students with diverse strengths and weaknesses.

She first discusses the range of student ability that might be found in a classroom and suggests how the classroom teacher must adapt reading instruction accordingly. Kossack goes on to discuss the instructional concerns of students with special needs for whom teachers should make adaptations in their instructional programs.

The heart of the chapter is its discussion of the characteristics of the types of students with special needs whom teachers are most likely to have in their classrooms and suggestions for adjustments that must be made in order to meet those needs.

STUDY QUESTIONS

1. What range of reading levels can a teacher expect to encounter? Will all fifth-graders be reading at a fifth-grade level?
2. After they are diagnosed and correctly placed at a comfortable reading level, will all children progress at the same pace? Should reading groups remain static through later grades?
3. What types of learners with special needs can the classroom teacher expect to teach?
4. What are the learning difficulties of various types of students with special needs?
5. What adaptations can the classroom teacher apply to meet the needs of learners with special needs?

Teachers teach *children*, not books. And because children differ (in appearance, ability, language development, learning rate, and mode of learning), effective reading instruction adapts to learner needs and differences.

Students with special needs read significantly *below* or *above* grade placement levels when given traditional classroom instruction. Their performances deviate from those of their agemates because of low intellectual capacity, a variety of learning disabilities, socioeconomic deprivation, limited

English proficiency, or high intelligence. The deviation is high enough that standard group assessments and prescriptions do not foster adequate growth in reading; they require special assessment and instructional adaptation.

Public Law 94-142, The Education for All Handicapped Children Act of 1975, mandates that appropriate instruction be given to all children in the least restrictive environment possible (Richek, List, & Lerner, 1983). Since "least restrictive environment" is frequently legally interpreted as "the regular classroom," regular elementary school teachers *must* now accommodate children with special needs who are able to function in a classroom. All teachers must become knowledgeable about the adaptations needed to provide effective reading instruction for these special students.

Resources for Helping Students with Special Needs

As classroom teachers begin to provide for students' special needs, various resources must be tapped. A variety of special services are available to assist classroom teachers in assessment, instruction, and programming. In working with students with special needs, two approaches are generally taken: pullout programs and mainstreaming.

Pullout Programs

Government funding has been provided for special classrooms for youngsters whose disabilities are severe enough to warrant special class placement. Many schools have full-day programs for students with severe disabilities, for example. However, more often, part-day classes are offered to meet special needs—classes such as Chapter I (a compensatory education program for disadvantaged students funded by the federal government), English for speakers of other languages (ESOL), or speech, which students attend during a brief period during the academic day. Many educators are concerned about the fragmentation of instruction (with resource and regular classroom teachers teaching different skills and concepts) and segregation felt by learners in pullout programs.

Mainstreaming

To avoid the sense of fragmentation and segregation, resource teachers have been provided in many schools to diagnose, provide demonstrations, team teach, tutor in class, access materials and services, and/or suggest programming to regular class teachers. These resource teachers provide extended input to regular class teachers who are planning educational adjustment for learners with special needs, giving them the decided advantage of shared responsibility and a wider base of professionalism brought to solving learners' problems.

Classroom teachers rarely make the decisions regarding the manner in which services are provided, but they do have responsibilities to learners with special needs. These are to identify and appropriately refer students who need special assistance in reading and to identify available resources that can assist in diagnosis, educational planning, and prescription for these students. These resources might be outside the school system, as, for example, the Shriner's service to youngsters with physical handicaps or the Lion's Club's provision of free glasses.

Relating Instructional Adaptations to Specific Conditions

When teaching reading, the classroom teacher must adjust each child's instruction to a comfortable instructional reading level, use skill strengths to ameliorate skill deficiencies, and expect reasonable progress based on the child's reading *capacity*. This will require materials beyond those assigned for the grade level. Therefore, the first adaptive skill needed by classroom teachers is to know the range of expected reading levels for a given grade level so that materials can be selected that will span the ability levels of the students in a class.

With current placement practices, some people erroneously assume that all students are capable of learning at grade-placement level. It would not be logical to expect that all the children in a class wear the same size shoe; yet many teachers assume that all students in a given grade have achieved the same level of reading proficiency, and they assign a single textbook to all. It is just as illogical to expect all the children in a class to *read* at the same level as it is to expect them all to wear the same size shoe. It is important to avoid overestimating or underestimating abilities when teaching reading. Teachers must assess each child's reading level and teach new concepts at a comfortable instructional level. Normally, this is done with reading screening devices such as the informal reading inventory (IRI) discussed in Chapter 9.

Avoiding Mistaken Assumptions

Many teachers make mistaken assumptions about classroom reading screenings, especially as they apply to special learners. Some of the most common are described in the following paragraphs.

Spurious Deficiencies

Some skills diagnosed as deficient may not, in fact, be missing for some special learners. For example, students with limited English proficiency (LEP) may understand comprehension processes such as sequencing or main idea but not be able to apply them to English or express themselves well enough to demonstrate mastery. Some dialectically different children may understand a vocabulary idea but use another term for it (e.g., "peep eye" for "peeking").

Inappropriate Expectation of Progress

After students have been placed in groups based on a diagnosis, it is unwise to assume that they will maintain the same rates of progress. Within a group, students with LEP often show rapid gains in contrast to slow learners, whose achievement will be a fraction of the gain of average students. Thus, reading groups established in September may show drastic differences in achievement by December. Reading groups are not static.

Underexpectation

Students who are gifted may be underplaced, since their instructional reading levels may be at grade level—which is perceived as normal—when in fact they should be perceived as remedial because they are *capable* of reading at a much higher level. Thus, it is imperative that assessments be adjusted based on learner differences and that the results be compared to the level at which a student is *capable* of reading, *not to grade-level placement,* to detect actual reading skill deficiencies.

Grade-level placements are not descriptive of ability; they are somewhat arbitrary, age-defined placements. How does a teacher know where a child *should* be functioning in reading so as to avoid over- or underplacing and unrealistic expectations of progress?

Estimating Reading Expectancy

The level at which a learner is presently capable of functioning is called a *reading expectancy.* Reading educators can use the Bond, Tinker, Wasson, and Wasson (1989) conversion of intelligence test scores to estimate a child's potential for reading:

$$\left[\frac{\text{IQ}}{100} \times \text{Years Completed in School}\right] + 1.0 = \text{Reading Expectancy}$$

Thus, a fifth-grader who has completed 4 years of school (if never retained), with an IQ of 50, would be expected to read at a third-grade level. Another fifth-grader, with an IQ of 100 and never retained, would be expected to read at a fifth-grade level. A gifted fifth-grader, with an IQ of 150, would be expected to read at a seventh-grade level.

This expectancy level makes a good yardstick to gauge whether or not special adaptations need to be prescribed. If a student is placed in reading material at an expectancy level appropriate to his or her ability, minimal additional adjustments need be made. However, if the student's current reading level is below expectancy, adaptations may be in order. Grade-level placement does not factor into this comparison. It is entirely possible for a fifth-grader who is reading on a third-grade level to be placed appropriately, as in the case of the slow learner. Conversely, it is not at all likely that a fifth-grade student with an IQ of 150 is reading to capacity (i.e., expectancy) if placed in a fifth-grade basal. Corrections need to be made to assure that this student will progress to capacity. Appropriate placement is the first adaptation needed for *all* children, but especially for students with special needs.

From this contrast, it is apparent that a fifth-grade classroom would be expected to include children with quite a range of reading abilities (from third to seventh grade, using the examples just cited). It should also be clear that a wide range of materials will be needed at every other grade level as well. A fourth-grade classroom will need materials below, at, and above fourth-grade level to meet the diverse needs of fourth-graders. Therefore, a second adaptive skill needed by classroom teachers is the ability to estimate the range of materials that will be needed when preparing for instruction, based on students' abilities.

Predicting Range of Abilities

At any grade level it is reasonable to expect that there will be a wide range of reading abilities. The range of abilities in an average classroom is approximately two-thirds the chronological age of the students (Bond, et al., 1989). Thus, a third-grade class has readers ranging in ability from .3 (preprimer) to 5.7; a fifth-grade class from 1.6 (first reader) to eighth-grade level. (See Figures 15.1 and 15.2.) Why does this range occur?

FIGURE 15.1 Computation of Range of Abilities for a Fifth-grade Class

Expected Classroom Range (R) = ⅔ (Chronological Age)

For a fifth-grade class, the range is computed as follows:

$$\text{Chronological Age} = (5.2 + \text{Grade Level})$$

$$R = 2\left[\frac{5.2 + 5}{3}\right]$$

$$R = 2\left[\frac{10.2}{3}\right] = 2\ (3.4) = 6.8$$

The range of abilities is 6.8 years; that is, there will likely be some students in this class reading at a 1.6 level and others reading at an 8.0 level. Materials must be gathered accordingly.

FIGURE 15.2 Expected Range of Reading Abilities by Grade Level

Range Formula Conversion Chart

Gr	Span	Range	
		Low	High
K	3.4	–K	1.7
1	4.2	–K	3.1
2	4.8	–K	4.4
3	5.4	–K	5.7
4	6.2	.9	7.1
5	6.8	1.6	8.4
6	7.4	2.3	9.7
7	8.2	2.9	11.1
8	8.8	3.6	12.4
9	9.4	4.3	13.7
10	10.2	4.9	15.1
11	10.8	5.6	16.4
12	11.4	6.3	17.7

A wide range of abilities should be expected, since not all students function at the same intellectual level or have the same motivations to learn, backgrounds, or aptitudes. Figure 15.3 illustrates the effect of such differences. A child with an average IQ (and no socioeconomic interferences) would be expected to master a year's worth of reading for every year in school, as compared to a child with much higher IQ (who would be expected to develop reading skills at a more accelerated level) or a child with a much lower IQ (who would proceed at a much slower rate and might never be able to achieve levels of reading available to the child with an average IQ).

Observe the distance between the lines of projected achievement as these students progress through the years (Figure 15.3). In first grade, the difference between the low achiever and the gifted student is relatively small compared to their differences in fourth grade. With proper instruction, these differences will become more and more divergent as this class moves into high school. This is to be expected, because the sharper students learn more and their achievement levels diverge from those of the students of lower ability, who continually fall behind the "norm." Thus, if teachers do a good job of challenging gifted students and meeting the needs of slower learners, it is to be expected that the range of abilities will *increase* as the grades progress, with the largest divergence occurring at the junior and senior high school levels (see Figure 15.4). The teacher's task, then, is to adjust a prescribed curriculum to meet the widely divergent skills and abilities of the students so that each child can perform to his or her greatest capability.

FIGURE 15.3 Reading Progress by Ability

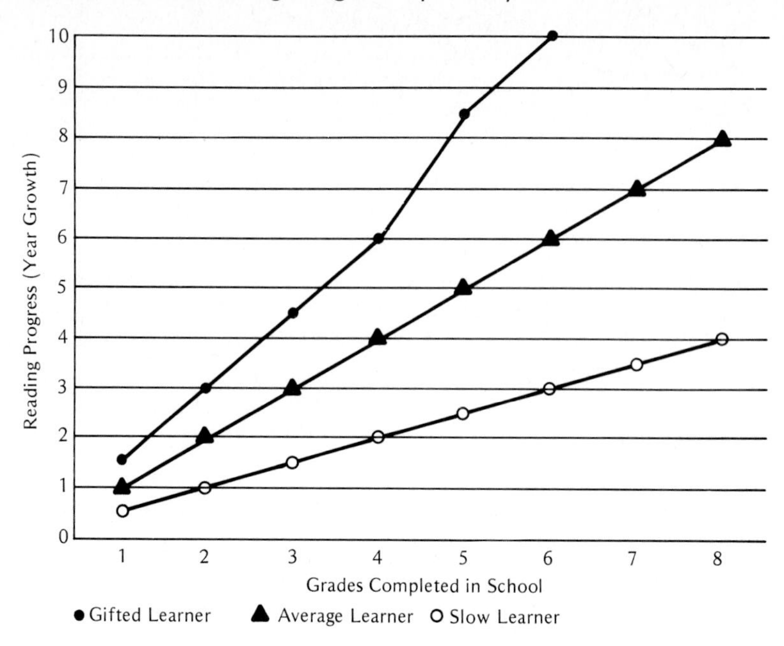

FIGURE 15.4 Increase in Range of Reading Levels with Grade-Level Increase

Reading Levels

Grade	Span	K	1	2	3	4	5	6	7	8	9	10	11	12	Col
K	3.4	•													
1	4.2		•												
2	4.8			•											
3	5.4				•										
4	6.2					•									
5	6.8						•								
6	7.4							•							
7	8.2								•						
8	8.8									•					
9	9.4										•				
10	10.2											•			
11	10.8												•		
12	11.4													•	

This range of abilities is an important concept for two reasons. First, every classroom teacher needs to approach instructional planning *expecting* to teach a wide variety of levels. That is, adaptation should be perceived as normal. Second, teachers need to be able to predict the range of levels needed for this adaptation so that enough materials can be provided to meet the needs of an increasingly diverse student population.

Given the data presented in Figures 15.1 and 15.2, a fifth-grade teacher must prepare materials spanning almost 7 years of reading levels. This range would be expected to be half above and half below the fifth-grade level, which suggests that materials need to be adjusted so that they can teach fifth-grade concepts to students reading at second-, third-, fourth-, fifth-, sixth-, seventh-, and eighth-grade levels. Naturally, the upper and lower levels of this range are shifted higher or lower depending on the school, even though the range (i.e., the difference between the lowest and highest levels) tends to remain about the same. Urban schools in low socioeconomic areas may have a downward shift (i.e., lower lows and lower highs), whereas schools in affluent areas would probably experience an upward shift.

Instructional Adjustments for Students with Special Needs

Most school systems provide self-contained classes for some students with severe special needs. Therefore, most regular class teachers do not have the challenge of working with children who are severely retarded, some who have severe physical handicaps or severe learning disabilities, and many children who are gifted. This section suggests techniques teachers can use to deal with mainstreamed students who are slow learners, have learning disabilities, have auditory or visual impairments, are disadvantaged, or have limited English proficiency.

Students Who Are Slow Learners

A teacher may think, with frustration, "M. is a real problem. I teach and teach and teach, but nothing seems to stick."

A child with a low IQ (below 70) may be working to capacity—and thus *not* be *remedial*—but frustrate conscientious teachers because poor performance does not improve. The expectancy formula suggests that a fifth-grader with an IQ of 70, never retained, should be reading at a 3.8 grade level. Placement in a fifth-grade reader would be detrimental. The student needs instruction in a 3.5-level basal. (It is important to note that the 3.8 expectancy estimate may be inflated, because learners with mental retardation seem to hit a plateau above which they do not function. This varies from not being able to read at all, as in the case of severe to profound retardation, to functioning maximally at a third- to fourth-grade reading level, depending on intelligence level.)

Since students with mental functioning below the level required to adapt to the regular classroom routine (those classified as educable, trainable, and custodial) are placed in special classes, the regular class teacher will expect to deal with students described as having borderline retardation, that is, students with IQs of 70 to 80 (Stoodt, 1989). These students are not considered retarded but are often described as "slow learners," which gives teachers expectations for their progress that may be unrealistic. The term *slow learner* leads the educator to assume that if the student is given a particular task enough times it can be mastered. However, since there will be levels of reading and specific reading skills these children will be unable to attain, there must be a process of determining what academic skills *must* be mastered to enhance everyday living, leisure, and employment skills.

It is important to note that there are a disproportionate number of male, minority, LEP, and disadvantaged children who are mislabeled as retarded, unfairly penalized by cultural and linguistic interference on tests of intelligence and ability (Ovando & Collier, 1985). Teachers must show extreme care in attaching labels to students, since these labels have a perverse tendency to remain with students and predispose others to view them as retarded when, in fact, they may not be.

Students who are slow learners need realistic, concrete skill presentation. Teachers are well advised to use manipulatives such as templates, models, and realia and to involve all of the students' senses in learning. Active, tactile learning is encouraged, as with finger plays or puppets, and learning that is transferred to real-life contexts is more likely to be retained than learning that is restricted to the academic setting.

These students have difficulty remembering what is learned, so *overlearning*—providing opportunities to repeat practice in interesting ways such as tape recorded rereadings, games, and choral readings—is a key strategy.

A short attention span is often characteristic of children who are slow learners; it necessitates short-range objectives in which teacher and learner proceed in small steps, dealing with short activities in which the pace is changed often. The careful lesson planning discussed in Chapter 14 is essential if teachers are to be effective with these students.

Many teachers observe that these students will remain on task, showing some understanding of the activity, with direct supervision, but they are likely to cease work when asked to work independently. This phenomenon is partly due to their tendency toward distractibility. Cooperative learning, in which students are grouped for interactive tasks, eases this problem. Aides or older learners from upper grades can also be used to focus the learning of dependent learners. Teachers report that timed practice, with tangible rewards for on-task focus and progress, is effective with many such students. ("Oh, look! You got two more done in a minute than last time! Aren't you proud of your concentration? Here's a star to celebrate!") Time spent in helping a child who is a slow learner concentrate is time well spent, because study skills are being established that will benefit the child later. Consider providing a study area, perhaps with a boxed in study carrel, that removes the child from things others are doing that might be distracting.

Children who are slow learners are aware of the achievement of others and are easily discouraged when they experience repeated failure. They need a sense of achievement. Teachers can record progress on charts, giving tangible rewards such as stars, raisins, pretzels, certificates, tickets that can be exchanged for erasers, stickers, or pencils.

Because it is so difficult for them to learn new things, these students may seem rigid and resistant to change. Games were suggested as a motivator for repeated practice, but teachers should consider reusing games with simple convertible formats so that the learners are only focusing on the skill practice, not being required to learn new game procedures. This convertible format is also useful with other classroom tasks. With a similar, set, structured schedule for day-to-day work, these learners can take comfort in consistency.

Students with Learning Disabilities

A teacher may think, with frustration, "R. is a puzzle. Easy tasks are beyond understanding, but other things may come easily. Difficult tasks cause such extreme frustration that I think R. will give up."

Children with learning disabilities (LD), who may appear quite able in some tasks but do other activities very poorly, generally have an average to above average IQ but work below capacity, showing severe highs and lows in performance. For example, a child with LD may have an IQ of 110. Using the fifth-grade analogy, this child (perhaps retained once) would be expected to be reading at a 6.5 level but is not.

There persists a great deal of confusion about this classification of student, since the definition and placement widely vary from school system to school system. The National Advisory Committee on Handicapped Children (1968) proposed the following definition as cited in Collins-Cheek (1989):

> Children with special learning disabilities exhibit a disorder in one or more of the basic psychological processes involved in understanding or in using spoken or written language. These may be manifested in disorders of listening, thinking, talking, reading, writing, spelling, or arithmetic. They include conditions which have been referred to as perceptual handicaps, brain injury, minimal brain dysfunction, dyslexia, developmental aphasia, etc. They do not include learning problems which are due primarily to visual, hearing, or motor handicaps, to mental retardation, emotional disturbance, or environmental disadvantage. (p. 393)

Learning disabilities affect almost 20% of the student population. In fact, undiagnosed learning disabilities may be the basic factor in the poor performance and misbehavior of underachievers, students with discipline problems, and dropouts. Identification of the characteristics of children with LD is extremely difficult, because each child manifests a different combination and level of problems. All show achievement levels at wide variance to projected levels of performance based on average or above average intelligence.

It is difficult to suggest direct prescriptions based on specific needs when speaking of children with LD, because they are more dissimilar than similar, often suffering multiple disabilities. However, at the risk of oversimplification, here are some predominant characteristics of mainstreamed children with LD and instructional adaptations teachers have found to be effective with them.

The child with LD may appear easily distractible and resistant to new or changed tasks. This may seem to indicate that the child is not listening, is unable to follow directions, or is too disorganized to complete a task. When giving directions for a learning task, a teacher should speak slowly and distinctly, using short, precise sentences. Directions should be limited to two or three tasks, and the child should repeat back the steps required to complete the task. These can be written on the blackboard for later reference. Then, the teacher should model the task *and* step through it once more *with* the child before asking the child to do it independently. When introducing a new idea, the teacher should give many examples (preferably using ideas that are *known* to the child).

Children with LD are often easily drawn off task. Teachers often describe these children as lacking concentration enough to complete a task. The teacher must set realistic, achievable task goals for such a student. It is helpful to do this cooperatively with the student as a means of building student "ownership" of the activity. The number and complexity of tasks can be increased gradually as the student's accuracy and confidence build with repeated success and persistence is encouraged.

Compounding the problem of underachievement, the child may have an unrealistic self-appraisal. Students with LD tend to lack confidence, and they often do not work to capacity. When challenged, they have a tendency to react adversely (become angry, cry, or refuse to do the task). If the teacher sets achievable goals in short assignments; works from the child's strengths to overcome weaknesses; models procedures or otherwise focuses the child's attention on the effective procedure; presents tasks in a format in which the child can function; and rewards effort and improvement with progress charts, logs, or other means of highlighting progress, the child will gradually develop a more positive self-image. It is important that this knowledge of progress be linked to the task in a timely manner; otherwise, it will not be effective in building persistence and self-image. The teacher may wish to consider using self-checking tasks so this immediacy of feedback is built in to the task itself.

Sometimes the student's inattention and frustration can be offset with the use of motivating, realistic, relevant, concrete contexts or materials that are at least one level below where the student is functioning. The low level allows the student to focus on the skill unhampered by the difficulty of the context.

The child with LD may have a tendency toward overactivity, so the importance of using games; movement; and concrete, manipulative materials cannot be overemphasized. This child needs to be involved in active learning.

Many teachers speak of inconsistency when talking of children who have learning disabilities, using phrases such as "does very well one day, poorly the next." Part of the reason for this is the student's need for overlearning. The teacher must make sure students with learning disabilities are given appropriate learning procedures. These students need to use all modes of learning (visual, auditory, kinesthetic, and tactile) whenever possible. Many opportunities should be provided for practice, reinforcement, and review. The teacher should emphasize points of transfer; for example, syllabication learned in the morning can be applied to social studies and science words in the afternoon.

Students with Auditory Impairments

Since the strength of this type of student is *not* aural, the teacher must be sure that he or she is in clear view of the student when giving oral input and must speak slowly and clearly, giving visual emphasis to key points (e.g., by writing key ideas on a chalkboard or assignment sheet). Teachers should work actively with these students to encourage them to ask for visual clarification and secure confirmation ("Would you write that down for me?" "This is what I understand you to say . . . . Is that accurate?"). In this way, teachers can impart to these students some effective interactive skills that will enhance future dealings with people who may not know how to adjust for their disability.

Since this type of child does not learn well by listening, the teacher should try to build concepts by using objects, pictures, books, movies, filmstrips, or other visual media. Bright markers, crayons, highlighters, sticky-backed notes, brightly colored letters, and other devices give visual emphasis.

Since phonics may present a problem for learners with auditory impairments, teachers should emphasize a more visual delivery by using the following techniques:

- Introduce words as a visual unit (e.g., sight vocabulary, whole word learning).
- Emphasize the visual image of a word by having students trace the word, associating the sound with the image.
- Move the visual image into the child's memory by tracing it on the child's palm while emphasizing the letter-sound associations and asking the child to say the word as a whole after the tracing.
- Trace the word on the child's back, allowing the child to guess the identity of the word.

Phonics should be avoided as the only approach to teaching word attack skills. (See Chapter 2 for other suggestions on building word identification skills.). Sound–symbol associations should be approached by linking them initially with words from a bank of words the child knows and then changing one phonic element at a time (e.g., *band* becomes *hand, sand,* then *bland, stand*). These changes are easier to grasp if they are made in the initial position first (e.g., *man, fan, can*), then the final position (e.g., *at, as, am*), and finally in the medial position (e.g., *hat, hit, hot, hut*).

Children with auditory difficulties will often also have speech problems such as immature speech, so speech therapists are a potential resource. As a child learns difficult speech sounds, the speech therapist can be enlisted to associate the appropriate letter sound with it.

Language experience lessons are oral dictations by the students combined with written versions recorded on overhead transparencies or chart paper. They are an effective method of working with students with auditory impairments at any grade level and in any subject.

Tunes, rhythms, and poetry may present problems for this type of student. Associating them with pictures, words, or phrases that provide vivid visual images can enhance retention. Oral reading may also present persistent problems. To overcome this, teachers can rely on suggestions offered in Chapter 13 for helping children to read orally in groups. In decoding unknown words, the teacher should stress the use of context clues (definition/synonym, antonym, example, mood/tone/experience). Words that give persistent difficulty can be highlighted or underlined to provide added visual emphasis.

Students with Visual Impairments

Since children with visual impairments do not learn well by sight (whole word) methods, it is a good idea to try using phonics-based approaches in which students look at a word, close their eyes, and say the word out loud (subvocalize), blending the sounds "aloud in their heads." These children will often confuse words, numbers, and letters, especially those that are shaped similarly. The following techniques can help overcome this difficulty:

- Have the child trace the letters in clay, on a blackboard, on construction paper, or in sand, sounding the word as it is traced.
- Stress visual discrimination by having the child assemble the word, sounding it as it is built out of individual alphabet letters.
- Have the child track the word or letter in a paragraph, pronouncing it when it is identified.

These techniques will prove particularly helpful when the child must deal with irregularly spelled words (e.g., *laugh*) that *must* be learned by sight.

Tape recorders or read-aloud materials are particularly useful for teaching a quantity of material. The teacher can have other children record the passage and allow the learner to listen for the information. For word study, the Language Master (an adaptation of a tape recorder) is useful. Lecture, class discussion, teacher talk, and other oral presentations are also particularly helpful with this disability.

Not only do children with visual impairments have difficulty gathering information visually, but they may have difficulty performing visually as well. That is, handwriting may present a problem that could be overcome by allowing them to present information via tape recording, recitation, or discussion instead. This will also be necessary during testing.

Students with Socioeconomic Disadvantages

A teacher may say in frustration, "J. doesn't understand *how* to learn. There is so much that is not understood because it has never been experienced: color/letter names, places, things. School must be an unfamiliar, overwhelming experience!"

There are whole classes of students in urban and rural schools who do not perform to the levels met in suburban schools. Parents and teachers alike are concerned that these students are not receiving equitable educational opportunities.

In many large urban and rural school systems, there are schools characterized by large percentages of failing students, dropouts, and demoralized teachers. Unfortunately, frustrated educators tend to view these schools and students as deficient. Teachers indicate that they lack sufficient materials, administrative support, and parent involvement. In their frustration, they say that the children lack such essentials as appropriate background, language, and concepts (Stoodt, 1989), when, in fact, there are also positive factors on which to build student success.

Active, student-involved tasks are needed by learners with socioeconomic disadvantages. Many of these students have a tendency to react well to physical and tactile tasks, learning through drawing, role playing, language experience, magnetic boards, tachistoscopes, puppets, or other media that involve visual, auditory, tactile, and kinesthetic modes. Teachers should try to organize tasks so that every child can respond. For example, when asking a question, the teacher can let all children respond with thumbs up for "yes" or thumbs down for "no." "Simon Says" or other listening activities can help develop listening skills.

Since many disadvantaged youngsters lack basic concepts and experiences, teachers should provide concrete objects, pictures, or perhaps field trips to build the concepts necessary for lessons. These students may be deprived of more than information. They tend not to be school wise, and so must be actively taught the process of performing school tasks (e.g., classroom behavior, test taking, notetaking, outlining, and other study skills, as discussed in Chapter 5). They may not receive active academic encouragement from home, and so teachers must provide time and an area for study to offset overcrowded, noisy home conditions. By observing students' approaches to study, teachers can suggest effective adaptations. For example, alternatives to pencil-and-paper tests (e.g., orally presented tests) might allow students a better opportunity to show what they have learned.

Many of these students do not see the relevance of school and, in fact, may be influenced by negative attitudes toward school held by their families and friends. Teachers should make learning realistic, related to areas that are important to them such as jobs, food, cars, or clothes, and present information via active, interesting channels such as games and competitions. Highly interesting, active instruction may not alleviate student misbehavior, however, so it must be paired with class rules that are generated by the students. This tends to assure student "ownership" of behavior guidelines. In addition to anti-intellectualism, poor learning skills, and misbehavior, repeated failure tends to cause students from disadvantaged backgrounds to have low academic self-esteem. Teachers must encourage, support, and reinforce their efforts, behaving toward them as if they were highly intelligent students who are having temporary difficulty. Concepts to be learned should be related to what is familiar in their backgrounds. (See the discussion of schema theory, mapping, and language experience presented in other chapters.) Students should be encouraged to record new words or ideas in a "Hip Dictionary" in which they define terms in their own informal language.

Since many of these students may come from cultures that respect masculine contexts, teachers should stress sports, adventure, science, science fiction, and the world of work. Since many of these students are very socially oriented, allowing them to work in cooperative but structured groups may prove quite effective. Learning centers, projects, a buddy system, peer tutors, paired reading, and group games provide such a format for learning. Music can be used to build concepts, word knowledge, comprehension, and language skills while lowering the anxiety associated with learning for many of these students.

Students with Limited English Proficiency

A teacher might complain, "M. can't speak English, and it is never spoken in the home. Since I don't speak Spanish, I don't know how I can be expected to teach a Spanish child. How will M. ever understand enough to read?"

Millions of learners who have limited English proficiency are presenting an instructional challenge in our schools. Expectancy formulas cannot be applied to them, since evaluation in English would be inappropriate and resources may not be available to assess in the native language. How do teachers cope?

The total number of students coming from non-English-language backgrounds was estimated to be 3.8 million in 1976 and is expected to increase to 5.1 million by the year 2000 (Ovando & Collier, 1985). Over half of the primary-age children in this estimate were born in the United States, but 63% of these children come from Spanish-speaking homes. Another 14% of this group come from homes in which Asian languages are spoken.

Instructional Difficulties

Since the language of instruction in the United States is predominantly English, these students can be expected to experience difficulties in learning to read because of the mismatch in syntax (word order), phonology (word sounds), and vocabulary (between English and their home language). For example, in Spanish "the red pen" is expressed "la pluma roja" (the pen red), a reversal of English word order. Phonology also varies greatly from language to language. For example, Spanish uses many more inflected verb forms and has no final blends. Spanish words do not begin with the /s/ sound. As Hispanic students attempt to pronounce English words that begin with the letter *s*, they will match their pronunciation to the closest version of /s/ in Spanish, adding a short /e/. For example, "stop" becomes "estop," "special" becomes "especial," and "star" becomes "estar." These are not mistakes in pronunciation, but merely the child's attempt to approximate what is heard with what is *most like it* in the child's primary language.

English vowel sounds give LEP learners particular difficulty. Spanish has only one sound associated to each vowel letter, whereas English has a variety of sounds associated with each vowel. Consider, for example, the various sounds associated with the vowel letter *a* in *apple, hand, about, are* and *ate* or the vowel *o* in the word *tomorrow*. Learners whose primary language is French or Spanish will have difficulty hearing the /oo/ in *hood*. Much auditory discrimination practice in which the sound differences are hyperaccentuated (stressed in the word context) will be needed before they will be able to distinguish and produce these sounds. Initial attempts to produce them will result in pronunciations that derive from sound patterns of the home language.

In spite of these differences, students who are transferring from romance languages to English have a far easier job than those who are not used to the Roman alphabet. Students whose home language is Vietnamese, Chinese, Russian, or another nonromance language must concomitantly master new letter forms, word constructions, sound systems, and vocabulary.

Listings of the various language sound differences are available from the National Clearinghouse for Bilingual Education, 1555 Wilson Boulevard, Suite 605, Rosslyn, Virginia 22209 (800-336-4560).

Vocabulary

Naturally, a student learning a new language has thousands of different vocabulary terms to master. In learning these new terms, unexpected interference occurs. There are some word forms (false cognates) that *appear* to have the same meaning in both languages but do not: for example, *carpeta*

Interference also comes from other language differences, such as where stress is placed. Students whose home language is characterized by equal stress will not hear the low-stress elements in English (e.g., prepositions, adjectives, articles) and thus will omit them in their speech (e.g., "He farmer?"). Temporary stress should be placed on these words during direct study.

There will be some points of assistance in the form of *cognates*—words that have a structure, sound, and meaning similar to the accompanying words in the home language. For example, *telephono* in Spanish is *telephone* in English. However, it is important to beware of *false cognates*—words that seem as though they are the same but in fact are not (e.g., *lectura* is not a *lecture*).

Since skills, concepts, *and* language must be learned, the learning pace of students with LEP will be slower at first, and they will require more repetition than their peers whose first language is English.

Some students whose home language forms are closely associated with the phonetic and structural forms of English will be excellent oral readers. With these students, teachers need to focus consistently on meaning, since flawless oral reading without comprehension is not desirable. Meaning must be stressed at all times in reading instruction as a means of avoiding this problem.

Teachers are also sometimes misled by students who have excellent "street English," not understanding that good oral English may not be sufficient for academic achievement (Cummins, 1980). Therefore, it is crucial to make sure that these students have a clear understanding of subject area vocabulary and concepts.

As readers with LEP progress, there seems to be a pattern of difficulty with inferential and critical levels of questioning. Often this results from the emphasis on pronunciation and the absence of higher-order questions. Teachers must build meaning in all areas of instruction, with emphasis on higher orders of thinking in spite of language limitations.

When students with LEP take tests, their scores may be deflated due to linguistic or cultural bias or because they are unable to process language to the degree required on timed tests. Teachers may wish to use dual native language/English testing or factor in a percentage of the errors due to a "language factor" in their scoring so that results more accurately reflect these students' actual ability. In any case, a teacher is wise to avoid placing undue trust in any test measure of this type of learner.

SUMMARY

Classroom teachers are responsible for teaching students with wide and varied abilities, including students who are slow learners, mainstreamed students who have learning disabilities, learners from disadvantaged socioeconomic backgrounds, and learners for whom English is a second language. Care must be taken when diagnosing, placing, and prescribing for these learners with special needs. It should be clear that groups of youngsters with the same grade placement and similar reading levels may, in fact, have very different instructional needs, abilities, and expectancies for achievement. The teacher who truly understands the concept of reading expectancy will avoid pushing a child who is a slow learner and will work to challenge a learner who is gifted. Knowledge of the range-of-achievement formula will enable the teacher to gather appropriate levels and types of materials to foster effective learning for the spans of abilities found in the average classroom.

Of the learners discussed in this chapter, those who have severe mental retardation or learning disabilities and those who are gifted will probably be removed to special programs. Nevertheless, it is important for classroom teachers to know the characteristics of these learners in order to refer them appropriately for screening and special placement. Most classroom teachers will have direct responsibility for adjusting the instructional programs for learners who are slow or disadvantaged, and those with limited English proficiency.

This chapter described a number of the characteristics of these learners, along with suggestions for techniques that might prove effective when instructing them. These suggestions are only a beginning. It is essential that teachers be flexible and creative in discovering what adjustments meet the needs of individual learners.

FOLLOW-UP QUESTIONS AND ACTIVITIES

1. Will all fifth-graders be reading at a fifth-grade level? What range of reading levels can a teacher at each grade expect to encounter? Calculate these, then compare the spans of expected reading achievement with the actual reading scores of classrooms of children in some of the local public schools. Try to get a variety of types of schools (i.e., advantaged, urban, etc.). How do the spans differ across these types of schools? Interview some of the local classroom teachers. Ask them to list the highest and lowest expected reading achievement levels in the grades they teach. Compare these levels to the chart shown in Figure 15.2. How accurate were the teachers in their predictions?
2. Once diagnosed and correctly placed at a comfortable reading level, will all children progress at the same pace? Should reading groups formed in the primary grades remain static through later grades? Interview some of the teachers in the local schools and ask them how they

place their students in groups. If diagnosis is used, ask whether or not rediagnosis (or continuous diagnosis) is done.

3. What types of learners with special needs can the classroom teacher expect to teach? What is the classroom teacher's responsibility to these students? Interview the school psychologist in a local school. Inquire about the procedures for referral and the services available in the local school system for students with special needs.
4. What are some of the characteristics of the various types of students with special needs? Ask to observe in a special education classroom (e.g., gifted, LD, ESOL/LEP). Using a list of characteristics as an observational checklist, watch a class for a few hours, checking off the characteristics you observed. Using the observations you recorded, mentally prescribe instructional adjustments to accommodate each of the characteristics. What adaptations can the classroom teacher apply to effectively help learners with special needs?

ADDITIONAL READINGS

Chamot, A. U. (1981, May). *Applications of second language acquisition to the bilingual classroom.* Paper presented at the International Bilingual Bicultural Education Conference of the National Association for Bilingual Education, Boston, MA.

Hargis, C. H. (1982). *Teaching reading to handicapped children.* Denver: Love Publishing.

Hart, V. (1980). *Mainstreaming children with special needs.* New York: Longman.

Labuda, M. (Ed.). (1985). *Creative reading for gifted learners: A design for excellence.* Newark, DE: International Reading Association.

Schon, I. (1982). Recent outstanding books for young readers from Spanish-speaking countries. *The Reading Teacher, 36,* 206–209.

Seitz, V. (1977). *Social class and ethnic group differences in learning to read.* Newark, DE: International Reading Association.

Tway, E. (1981). The gifted child in literature. *Language Arts, 57,* 14–20.

REFERENCES

Bond, G. L., Tinker, M. A., Wasson, B. B., & Wasson, J. B. (1989). *Reading difficulties: Their diagnosis and correction.* Englewood Cliffs, NJ: Prentice-Hall.

Collins-Cheek, M. D., & Cheek, E. H. (1989). *Diagnostic-prescriptive reading instruction: A guide for classroom teachers* (3rd ed.). Dubuque, IA: William C. Brown.

Cummins, J. (1980). The construct of language proficiency in bilingual education. In J. E. Alatis (Ed.), *Current issues in bilingual education* (Georgetown University Round Table on Languages and Linguistics, pp. 81–103). Washington, DC: Georgetown University Press.

Ovando, C., & Collier, V. (1985). *Bilingual and ESL classrooms.* New York: McGraw-Hill.

Richek, M. A., List, L. K., & Lerner, J. W. (1983). *Reading problems: Assessment and teaching strategies*. Englewood Cliffs, NJ: Prentice-Hall.

Stoodt, B. D. (1989). *Reading instruction* (2nd ed.). Philadelphia: Harper & Row.

16

Using Parents, Partners, and Volunteers

NICHOLAS P. CRISCUOLO

CHAPTER 15 DISCUSSED the wide range of reading abilities and student needs that the effective teacher is likely to find in any classroom. With this in mind, it becomes apparent that extra help in the reading program would be beneficial. In an effort to meet this concern, and in recognition of growing citizen concern and commitment to education, educators will want to consider using volunteers in their reading programs. In this chapter, Nicholas Criscuolo provides information to increase our understanding of how parents, partners, and volunteers can help the school provide an effective tutorial program for students who need extra help in reading. He also offers suggestions for tapping community resources and using volunteers to assist the classroom teacher in the reading program.

In the first part of the chapter, the general objectives of a well-conceived tutorial program are discussed. Criscuolo goes on to offer guidelines in such key areas as recruitment and screening of volunteers, recruitment of students into the tutorial program, training of tutors, and the important aspects of what makes for a good tutorial experience for students. The chapter concludes with a discussion of a variety of tasks, responsibilities, and opportunities for volunteers, partners, and parents to become involved in the operation of the schools in a manner that is of direct benefit to classroom teachers.

STUDY QUESTIONS

1. What can teachers do to capitalize on parents' interest in the reading achievement of their children?
2. What are the key components of an effective volunteer program?
3. What kinds of activities can volunteers provide in the classroom reading program?
4. How can the use of volunteers contribute to more public support for education?

The number of parents, partners, and volunteers working in school reading programs is rapidly increasing. This can be attributed to two factors: scarcity of funds and increased emphasis on citizen participation and involvement in the schools. The volunteer movement long ago passed the stage in which it was viewed with suspicion and even hostility by teachers. Volunteers do not replace teachers; they merely expand services to children.

Involving parents, partners, and volunteers in the reading process is a

Editor's Note: Nicholas Criscuolo passed away when this textbook was in production. He is greatly missed by reading educators.

worthwhile endeavor because it allows them to see firsthand what the schools are doing to develop literacy among children. Participation is also worthwhile because it gives parents, partners, and volunteers an opportunity to have input and make a contribution to the development of literacy. Maximum input leads to maximum support for the schools and increases the public's confidence in public education.

Classroom teachers understand the value of using volunteer tutors to help them in their daily work. Despite grouping procedures that help teachers individualize instruction, there are still children in many classrooms who need extra assistance in reading. Teachers do as much as they can for these children, but the use of tutors is a great aid to busy teachers who have students who need reinforcement of reading skills.

It has been estimated that about one-third of all elementary school students can be considered poor readers. The problem of learning to read becomes more complex as a youngster advances in the grades. Problems accumulate, and often the student develops a negative attitude toward reading.

An effective tutorial program can do much to reduce the number of disabled readers. It is not wise to wait until a youngster is in the upper elementary grades to initiate such a program. If it is structured properly, primary grade children will also benefit from a well-designed tutorial program.

A Parent/Teacher Partnership

Parents are extremely interested in the reading achievement of their children. They want to know what they can do at home to reinforce important reading skills. Parents are the child's first teachers, and they serve as role models for their children's behavior—especially as it applies to reading. Building a literate, supportive atmosphere in the home can do a great deal to nurture the child's attitudes and enthusiasm for reading.

Wise classroom teachers capitalize on the interests of parents in the reading program. During parent/teacher conferences, they can offer concrete, specific ways for parents to help their children in reading. The teacher/parent approach can yield good results and serve to form a strong home/school partnership.

Some parents are willing to come to school for several hours during the week to assist the classroom teacher. Parents can help catalog books in the library, run off dittos for use by the children, monitor children in the cafeteria and on the playground, and carry out a host of other activities.

The most desirable and meaningful way teachers can make use of the interests and talents of parents is to involve them directly in the reading program by using them as volunteer tutors for individual or small-group assistance. Busy classroom teachers often do not have time to sit with children while they pronounce words from their word banks or use them in sentences. Teachers often do not have enough hours in the school day to sit with a small group of children playing a game that gives the children practice in developing basic sight vocabulary. It is also difficult to find time to listen to children read orally each day or to take young children's dictation for language experience stories.

Parents, with some training and supervision by the classroom teacher, can engage in these activities. Many parents (as well as other interested citizens) are willing to serve as volunteer tutors, and classroom teachers must seize upon their willingness and plan a tutorial program that will not only improve children's reading ability but also enlarge the scope of services offered to children as they sharpen and enrich their reading skills.

Tapping the Resources of the Community

Before discussing specific aspects of a tutorial reading program, it is important to discuss the community and the resources it offers to the schools.

Classroom teachers should recognize the importance of the community and extend the reading program beyond the four walls of the classroom. The community provides a wealth of opportunities for children to put their reading skills to good use. If the reading program is to be truly comprehensive, it must involve the community. The following paragraphs discuss some ways to achieve this goal.

Pride of book ownership can be fostered through book drives to solicit usable books for children. This can be done under the auspices of the school's Parent/Teacher Association (PTA). Enough books can be collected to give each youngster at least one book to read and then keep to add to his or her personal home library. This volunteer effort can help children form a lifelong reading habit.

Local business firms and organizations can be solicited by the classroom teacher in a book drive. Employees can deposit usable children's trade books in receptacles placed in various locations throughout the city or town. Enough books can be collected to give each teacher a set to enlarge the classroom library and foster the habit of reading for pleasure among the children in the class. Some of these books can also be used by parents and partners in the tutorial reading program.

Authors of children's books live in every community. When asked by a classroom teacher, they are often willing to meet with children to talk about how they get ideas for books and other aspects of their writing efforts. They may even leave copies of the books they have written. These books will be read eagerly by the children. Authors are a free community resource, readily available to increase youngsters' interest in reading.

Objectives of a Tutorial Reading Program

There are many facets to reading instruction. In addition to the classroom teaching provided, many opportunities must be given to youngsters to apply the skills and strategies learned. In many instances, this requires individual or small-group sessions in which a youngster can engage in meaningful activities that reinforce these reading skills.

A reading program that permits individual or small-group instruction and reinforcement in an atmosphere free from tension serves such a goal. The effective teacher ensures that the tutorial program takes into account each child's instructional level and, more specifically, areas of strengths and weaknesses in the reading process. Thus, a good tutorial reading program is one in which the teacher determines specific areas of weaknesses by diagnostic means and provides opportunities to remedy those weaknesses.

The activities of a tutorial reading program must be paced to sustain interest. Since participation in a tutorial reading program is often voluntary, an integral part of such a program is the pleasure the youngster derives from participating in it. Therefore, in addition to the remediation of specific weaknesses, careful attention must be given to selecting materials that cap-

FIGURE 16.1 Specific Classroom Objectives of a Tutorial Reading Program

1. Determine specific areas of weakness and provide opportunities to remedy such deficiencies.
2. Reinforce reading skills and offer opportunities to apply these skills to the reading task.
3. Provide individual or small-group instruction in a pleasurable atmosphere.
4. Build a strong partnership among the classroom teachers, parents, and volunteers in order to increase a youngster's desire to read.
5. Encourage creative expression of ideas related to reading in an informal atmosphere.
6. Develop the youngster's interest in engaging in recreational reading.
7. Extend and enrich reading skills and experiences.
8. Offer fresh approaches to skill development through the use of varied techniques and materials.
9. Assist in the full personal development of the child by means of vicarious experiences through reading.
10. Build good habits and attitudes toward reading.
11. Establish an appreciation of the value of reading as an essential skill in the acquisition of knowledge.
12. Develop a meaningful relationship between classroom activities and the tutorial program.
13. Establish rapport and contact by means of the pupil-tutor relationship.
14. Allow for continuous evaluation of pupil progress through records, testing, and inventories.
15. Encourage classroom teacher involvement in a successful reading program.

ture the youngster's imagination and interest and enrich experiences in reading.

Figure 16.1 outlines the specific objectives of an effective tutorial reading program.

Distinction between Remedial and Tutorial Programs

Techniques for remediation in reading are often the same for remedial programs and tutorial programs. The essential differences appear to be in recruitment, the time at which the program is offered, and the number of children in each group. Whereas remedial reading is usually offered during the school day by someone certified in the reading field, this may not be so in the tutoring program. Most often the tutor will be a parent or volunteer with or without a college background who has taken few or no courses in reading instruction. The program may take place during the school day or after school. In many cases, a tutoring program is held on an informal individual or team basis.

Tutorial Program Components

Recruitment

A tutoring program should be of service to as many children as possible. It should serve youngsters whose discrepancy between potential and actual achievement in reading, as discussed in Chapter 15, is such that immediate attention is warranted. However, since two prime objectives of a tutorial program are to reinforce reading skills and to increase a desire to read by offering experiences that complement the reading process, youngsters who have reading disabilities due to low intellectual ability but display a genuine interest in attending the program should also be given consideration. In addition, there will be occasions on which any child, regardless of reading ability, can benefit from a personal interaction with a caring tutor.

Individual tutorial assistance is desirable but not always possible; tutorial help may have to be given in small groups. The size of each group will vary according to the number of participants, as well as the facilities available, but the number of participants should be kept small. Four children often constitute a workable number; it allows the tutor to offer whole-group instruction economically, yet it can easily be broken down into groups of two children as well as lend itself to various individualized approaches.

The first step in the recruitment of pupils is to ask the classroom teacher to compile a list of pupils who need additional help in reading. The names of children who express an interest in participating in the program for enrichment purposes should also be listed. The teacher should emphasize from the beginning that only those children who are able to attend the full weekly sessions will be considered. The lists will provide a basis for screening. It is important that parents be notified of their children's acceptance in the program so that they will not only be aware of their responsibilities but also offer cooperation and support. Consultation with the reading specialist who services the particular school is an excellent procedure.

Tutors can come from many sources. They can be college students, city employees, senior citizens, and other community members who can devote a few hours a week to serve as volunteer tutors. Older children can also tutor younger children at the school. Most of the tutors, however, will be parents who have a vested interest in the reading achievement of children and are willing to tutor children other than their own at the school. Generally speaking, parents have proved to be reliable and dependable tutors.

Number and Length of Sessions

In order to ensure maximum efficiency, tutoring sessions should be held at least twice a week. This gives sequence to the program and permits a chance to reinforce reading skills. Three sessions per week will produce a tutoring program of depth. Perhaps all children in the tutoring program can attend two of the three sessions, while those who have deep-rooted problems or express a keen desire to attend the program can attend the third session. At least 1 hour per session is the desirable length for older children; less for younger children.

Tutor Training

Volunteers may possess the enthusiasm and understanding necessary for a good tutoring program, but most likely they will need training in the use of worthwhile techniques. Leadership for such a training program can come from the classroom teacher or a member of a specialized service group.

The training program should not be a lengthy one, but it should discuss successful techniques and strategies. The use of technical jargon should be avoided, since this will only serve to confuse the parent or other prospective volunteer. Ongoing supervision of volunteers, partners, and parent tutors can be provided by the classroom teacher and the school's reading specialist working in tandem.

Screening

The initial step in the screening of children for tutorial reading is the administration of a standardized reading test, which preferably has alternate forms and is fairly easy to administer and score. (Chapter 10 provides a detailed discussion of the appropriate use of standardized tests.) Pretest and posttest scores will help to determine a youngster's overall growth in the program; however, this growth cannot be totally attributed to the tutorial reading program since the youngster is still receiving classroom instruction in addition to being tutored in reading. Diagnostic tests that measure specific strengths and weaknesses, such as the Stanford Diagnostic Test (Psychological Corporation, 1984), are worthwhile, as are informal skills checklists developed by classroom teachers and administered on an individual basis.

As discussed in Chapter 9, the child's actual instructional reading level can be determined by the administration of an informal reading inventory by the teacher or reading specialist. This information is valuable, because the tutor can take the child's instructional reading level into account to recommend material for supplementary reading and independent projects. This helps the tutor provide suitable material for the child to read.

Determining Interests

The questionnaire shown in Figure 16.2 can also be given at the first session. This is important because it will help the tutor determine pupil interests. The questions can be adjusted to the age level of the student. With young children, the inventory can be administered as an interview. (Chapter 17 offers additional suggestions for assessing reading interests and attitudes.)

Setting the Scene

Reading is a highly personal experience that can offer much satisfaction to the pupil. It should be fun and interesting, as well as relevant to the pupil's personal needs. In the group experience of school, it is not always possible to stimulate this aspect of reading, since classes may be large and the materials used for instruction may fail to capture the reader's interest. A tutoring program, geared to individual or small-group needs in an atmosphere of informality, serves the important function of helping children see how reading can be a pleasurable and worthwhile experience while improving their reading skills at the same time.

In the beginning part of the program, the tutor should find out as much as possible about the tutee. After administering the interest inventory, the first step might be to have the student make an autobiography. A young child can compile it from photographs or draw some pictures that tell about himself or herself. Autobiographical sketches can also be written by older pupils. The information on each child should be kept in a folder with samples of the youngster's work. The sketches will also provide a good basis for individual conferences between tutor and pupil. Undoubtedly, the pupil has formed some attitudes about reading, and, because he or she has experienced failure in learning to read, these attitudes may be negative. The parent or

FIGURE 16.2 Interest Inventory

The purpose of these questions is to find out what kinds of things boys and girls your age like or dislike.

1. Tell me what things do you like to do most in your spare time?

   a. ______________________________

   b. ______________________________

   c. ______________________________

2. How many books do you look at or read each week? ______________
3. What famous person would you most like to be? ______________
4. What magazines do you sometimes look at or read?

   a. ______________________________

   b. ______________________________

   c. ______________________________

5. How many books have you looked at or read in the past 3 weeks? ______________
6. If you had $1,000, what would you do with it?

   a. ______________________________

   b. ______________________________

   c. ______________________________

7. How many hours a week do you spend watching television? ______________
8. What are your favorite television programs?

   a. ______________________________

   b. ______________________________

   c. ______________________________

9. Tell me *three* of the following things you like to do best.

watching television	playing games	going on trips
reading	visiting your friends	making things

10. Tell me which of the following kinds of stories you like or dislike:

science	nature	flying
love	fighting	adventure
how to make things	spy	romance
animals	travel	history
sports	war	biography
humorous	make believe	true

volunteer should feel free to discuss these attitudes openly and be a willing listener to the pupil's thoughts about reading. The tutor should not, however, spend time trying to analyze or probe too deeply, since the essential task is to provide assistance in reading.

Procedures

Skill deficiencies and problems in reading are many and varied. However, there are some important points that the tutor should consider when working with the children enrolled in the tutoring program.

1. *Silent reading precedes oral reading.* The student should always have an opportunity to read material silently before doing so orally. The tutor should watch for lip movements, regressions in eye movements, and inattentiveness during silent reading. (See Chapter 13 for additional suggestions in this area.)
2. *Oral reading is a gauge for word recognition.* It is by listening to oral reading that basic reading difficulties can be ascertained. The student should be able to read clearly and fluently, with proper phrasing, good enunciation, and expression. Such signs as fingerpointing, hesitations, substitutions, omissions, faulty phrasing, and unsuitability of reading material can be determined by means of oral reading. Various types of dramatization, poetry reading, choral reading, and reading dialogue with the tutor will help improve oral reading ability. (See Chapter 9 for additional information in this area.)
3. *Reading is a thought-getting process.* The tutor should never lose sight of this fact. Comprehension should be emphasized at all levels, and the child should always be checked on his or her understanding and retention of material read. Questions should be varied so that the youngster is able to answer inferential as well as factual questions. Comprehension will be improved if motivating questions are asked prior to silent reading so that the tutee is engaging in purposeful reading. (See Chapter 4 for additional suggestions in this area.)
4. *Reading should be related to other activities.* The tutor must encourage all activities that grow out of the student's reading and express involvement in it. In art, for instance, the pupil can make posters, murals, puppets, and book jackets. In writing, the pupil can write creative stories and character sketches, and in drama the student can act out stories found to be particularly interesting. Trips will also broaden and enrich experiences in reading. Reading should not become an isolated skill but should serve as a valuable tool as it relates to other experiences. (See Chapters 7 and 8 for additional suggestions in this area.)

The tutor must be actively involved in helping the pupils acquire basic reading skills. Too often, tutoring sessions consist of little more than distributing materials to children and identifying words for them. There is little justification for such a practice, since the size of the group is so small. By means of active participation, the tutor acts as a stimulus to the tutee, who is encouraged to engage fully in the program's activities designed to enhance reading ability.

Due to the fact that the tutoring program is so well suited to meet individual needs, problems related to discipline are minimal. If a youngster evinces disruptive behavior, however, it might be advantageous for him or her to remain for a reading game followed by a free-reading period. The pupil should be allowed to remain for this part of the session and then be dismissed. A conference should first be scheduled with the tutor, classroom teacher, and principal of the school in which the program is operating to discuss the situation. Perhaps a flexible plan could be worked out whereby the pupil, if he or she continues to be a disruptive influence on the other children, might be shifted to another group. In any event, every effort should be made by the tutor to arouse the child's interest so that the pupil will exert effort and retain enthusiasm during each session.

Materials

Selection and use of appropriate reading materials constitute an important phase of the tutorial program. The materials should be the type that motivate the child to learn essential reading skills. Basal reading materials should, for the most part, be avoided, since these are used in the classroom. The child may have already experienced difficulties with such reading materials and may even associate failure with them. Also, duplication of effort may occur if basal reading materials are used in the tutorial program, and this should be avoided.

There are many effective materials that can be used in the tutorial program. Many of them have a game aspect that captures interest and stimulates the student to learn. Many of these materials consist of reading games, booklets, trade books, and worksheets that reinforce reading skills already introduced by the teacher. Many of them should be of the high-interest, low-vocabulary-difficulty type. The classroom teacher and/or reading specialist can recommend appropriate materials for use by the parent or volunteer.

In addition to commercially prepared materials, there are many materials that can be constructed by the tutor for use with a particular group of children. Tutoring provides an excellent venue for putting creative and imaginative talents to use.

If the tutoring program is to be complete, many opportunities for free reading should be given. Time should be set aside during each session for the

FIGURE 16.3 Independent Reading Record

Name ______________________ School ____________________ Grade __________

	Title of Book	Author	Publisher	Rating
1.				
2.				
3.				
4.				
5.				

Key to rating: Excellent = 1; Good = 2; Fair = 3; Poor = 4

youngsters to do some voluntary reading, discuss stories and books they have read, and write about or illustrate books they enjoyed.

There are many books on today's market that, because of interesting plot and reduced vocabulary load, appeal to youngsters. There are many publications that list reading levels, interest levels, and brief synopses of books. These can be examined before selecting books for the youngsters enrolled in the tutoring program.

Long reports on books read should be avoided. Some brief record, however, should be kept on the number and type of books read in the tutoring program. In addition to the pertinent data regarding the book, a chance for the pupil to critically evaluate each book is a worthwhile procedure. Chapter 18 provides additional suggestions for encouraging recreational reading. An example of a record of books read independently is shown in Figure 16.3.

Additional Uses of Parents, Partners, and Volunteers

Volunteers, partners, and parents are invaluable resources for the schools. There are a variety of tasks, responsibilities, and opportunities for them to become involved in the operation of the schools that are of direct benefit to classroom teachers. These activities, however, should be conducted under the classroom teacher's supervision.

In addition to working in tutorial programs, volunteers, partners, and parents can assist classroom teachers by telling and reading stories to children. Reading aloud to children is one of the most worthwhile activities volunteers can perform for them. Children love to be read to and hear the sounds and flow of language and follow the adventures and exploits of favorite story characters. Classroom teachers can select the stories and books to be read by volunteers and parents.

Children also love to share the stories and books they read. Volunteers can assist by serving as story partners. They can listen as children read portions of books and stories aloud. On occasion, a volunteer can read aloud a few sentences from a book or story and then have the child read aloud the next few sentences or paragraphs to the story partner. The volunteers and the youngster can then engage in a discussion of the entire story or book, talking about plot, story characters, and the illustrations.

These resource people can follow up on storytelling activities by conducting arts and crafts projects related to themes, plots, and characters contained in the books read. For example, one natural activity is to help children construct stick or paper-bag puppets of story characters. Another is to use media to depict scenes from storybooks. These types of activities that volunteers can do with groups of children can provide opportunities for the teacher to spend extra time with students who are in need of additional assistance.

Volunteers, partners, and parents can also assist in making materials for the classroom teacher's use. They can make letter or word wheels from paper plates to reinforce letter or sound recognition, as well as puzzles constructed by cutting pictures into various shapes and pasting them onto cardboard for the children to put together.

Under the teacher's supervision, volunteers can prepare dittos and skillsheets that reinforce reading and language arts skills already introduced. They can also correct seatwork. In some cases, a volunteer who speaks the language of a non-English-speaking student, as discussed in Chapter 15, can provide valuable assistance in helping that child adjust to the new language demands of the classroom.

Guidelines for Working with Volunteers

In working with volunteer reading tutors, the following guidelines will prove helpful to teachers and administrators:

1. All volunteers must make a commitment to attend all training and tutoring sessions.
2. All volunteers are interviewed, but there are no age or educational requirements beyond a high school diploma.
3. Volunteers are placed only in schools where the teachers and principals are receptive and only at the request of a teacher.
4. Each tutor is assigned to children in the same classroom so that the tutor can work with one teacher and one grade level. Too many tutees and a wide span of grade levels assigned to one tutor defeat the purpose of a volunteer tutoring program in reading.
5. Each tutor is expected to have an initial conference with the

teacher. The volunteer also observes the teacher giving a reading lesson.

6. Each child tutored is tested, and test results are shared with the tutor.
7. Volunteers do not take students out of their regular reading classes. Tutors supplement and reinforce; they do not replace regular or special class work.
8. A daily log is kept by the volunteer for each student, noting the skills covered, materials used, and an evaluation of progress.
9. A weekly conference between the volunteer and teacher is recommended. Communication is stressed in every aspect of the tutor's work.
10. The practice of plying the tutee with candy or little gifts should be avoided. This is a condescending and objectionable practice.
11. Feedback sessions, conducted by the reading teacher, should be held periodically for all tutors. Tutors can ask questions and share experiences at the sessions. Feedback sessions are valuable because they minimize the feeling held by some tutors that they are "suspended in space."

SUMMARY

The essence of a good tutorial program is that it capitalizes on what the pupil does *not* know, not on what is already known. Discovering specific weaknesses and then taking steps to reinforce the needed skills is a basic precept of an effective tutoring program in reading. The process of evaluation, therefore, must be given top priority.

The process of learning is built upon (a) the use of varying and interesting techniques and procedures; (b) the use of a variety of effective materials that focus on meaning; and (c) continuous evaluation, reevaluation, and pursuant recommendations.

Recent cutbacks in Chapter I and other funds have resulted in reducing the amount of professional reading help provided for children who desperately need it. Using parents, partners, and volunteers can restore this help so that children can become proficient, competent readers.

FOLLOW-UP QUESTIONS AND ACTIVITIES

1. How would you explain to a PTA group why their volunteer efforts are important to the success of the school reading program?
2. Develop a list of activities that you believe volunteers could perform in the classroom that would enhance the reading program.

3. Think of as many places as you can in your community that you might contact for possible volunteers to help in your reading program.
4. Discuss activities or projects that volunteers could perform outside of school that would enhance the school's and classroom's reading program.

ADDITIONAL READINGS

Becker, S. (1986). What you should know about tutoring centers. *Instructor, 95,* 88–90.

Burd, J. S. (1978). New program for retired teachers. *School and Community, 64,* 26–27.

dePillis, S. (1982). Recruit grandpeople as volunteer tutors. *American School Board Journal, 169,* 28–30.

Ellis, D., & Preston, F. W. (1984). Enhancing beginning reading using wordless picture books in a cross-age tutoring program. *The Reading Teacher, 37,* 692–698.

Massey, J., & Myers, J. D. (1975). Volunteer mothers as tutors in the classroom. *Journal of Research and Development in Education, 8,* 54–63.

McCuaig, S. M. (1985). Large scale unbudgeted elementary school tutorial programs. *Educational Leadership, 32,* 331–334.

Meyer, V., Keefe, D., & Bauer, G. (1986). Some basic principles of the reading process required of literacy volunteers. *Journal of Reading, 29,* 544–548.

Rauch, S., & Sanacore, J. (1985). *Handbook for the volunteer tutor* (2nd ed.). Newark, DE: International Reading Association.

Rice, E. M. (1984). Tutor and child. *Language Arts, 61,* 18–23.

Ring, B. C. (1980). Training adult tutors for your classroom. *Academic Therapy, 15,* 415–419.

Sleisenger, L., & Lancaster, J. (1979). *Guidebook for the volunteer reading tutor.* Thorofare, NJ: C. B. Slack.

PART FOUR

Increasing Positive Attitudes: Reading and the Affective Domain

Part Four examines aspects of the reading program that will enhance students' attitudes toward reading. Emphasis is placed on the development of students' motivation to read, interest in reading, and desire to read—in other words, the affective component of reading instruction. Chapter 17 discusses the concern teachers must give to their own actions, the materials, and the use of instructional activities in their reading programs if they are to promote positive attitudes in students toward reading. Chapter 18 suggests ways to help teachers establish voluntary or recreational reading programs in their classrooms. Chapter 19 concludes this section with a discussion of how newspapers can be used in the classroom reading program to promote interest and motivation.

17

Developing Positive Attitudes toward Reading

RICHARD J. SMITH

IN CHAPTER 17, Richard Smith discusses the importance of children's reading attitudes and habits and suggests that effective teachers consider these as important as skill development in reading instruction. Smith suggests that the reading attitudes and habits that students develop are the results of the kinds and quality of reading experiences they have in school. He argues that it is not concrete rewards that produce positive attitudes toward reading; it is the individuals who serve as good reading models and the pleasurable reading experiences they provide.

Smith provides practical suggestions and information on three factors related to teaching reading that have impact on both skill and attitude development. First, there is the teacher factor. Smith explains that teachers are influential for good or bad in the attitudes their students develop and offers suggestions to help make their influence a more positive one. He then discusses the materials factor, suggesting that while materials play less of a role than teachers, they are important in forming students' attitudes and must be given careful consideration. Finally, he looks at the instructional factor, presenting guidelines for providing instructional activities that enhance, rather than detract from, the development of positive reading attitudes and habits.

STUDY QUESTIONS

1. What is an attitude?
2. Why is attention to attitude development important for the teacher of reading?
3. What can teachers do to build positive attitudes toward reading?
4. How do instructional materials promote positive or negative attitudes toward reading?
5. How can teachers measure their students' attitudes toward reading?

The story is told of a language arts teacher who taught a novel so well that her students determined never to read another one. The moral, of course, is that students' affective development is as important as their cognitive development in reading. Students who complete their skills development exercises accurately and score well on reading achievement tests, but avoid rather than seek out reading experiences, have been poorly served by their instructional programs.

An attitude is a predisposition to move toward or away from a particular subject, in this case reading. Alexander (1983) pointed out that "both attitude and motivation are prerequisites to actual reading. If a child has a positive attitude toward books, and is motivated (will act), he will want to pick up material to read" (p. 6). Obviously, teachers at all academic levels must be mindful of the attitudes their students are developing toward reading as well as their skills development

Duffy and Roehler discussed "attitude outcomes" as a major goal of reading instruction (1986, p. 27).

> To control the reading process students must have a concept of what reading is and must feel that reading is an activity worth pursuing. A student who has an incomplete or erroneous concept of reading or who perceives reading negatively is unlikely to gain control of the reading process and use it purposefully. (p. 29)

They emphasized the importance of the kind and quality of reading experiences students have in school as determinants of the attitudes and habits they develop. The emphasis in this chapter is essentially the same: Positive attitudes toward reading are developed not so much by extrinsic reinforcers as by intrinsic reinforcement. That is, smiling faces on papers, grades on report cards, free pizzas, money donated to worthy causes, and other rewards for pages read are probably not as powerful attitude determinants as are good models and pleasant reading experiences in and out of school. The extrinsic reinforcers may get students started with reading, but the pleasure they get from reading is the factor that keeps them coming back.

This chapter offers teachers some practical information and suggestions for teaching reading so that students' skills and attitude development are both well served. The following attitude development factors are discussed: (a) the teacher factor, (b) the materials factor, and (c) the instructional activities factor.

The Teacher Factor

Next to family members, teachers are probably the most important people in students' lives with regard to the kinds of attitudes they develop toward reading. Teachers can maintain the positive attitudes some students bring from their home situations, make positive the neutral attitudes others bring, and reverse the negative attitudes still others bring. On the other side of the coin, teachers can change positive and neutral attitudes to negative ones and negative attitudes to even more negative ones. Teachers are a powerful force for good or bad in the attitudes their students develop toward reading. It is unlikely that the attitudes of many, if any, students remain unaffected by their teachers.

While it would be impossible to discuss all of the ways teachers influence attitudes toward reading, the following suggestions may be helpful.

Assess Your Own Attitude toward Reading

The reading habits of teachers are important to the attitudes their students develop toward reading. It is difficult for salespeople to sell products they do not use. Teachers who read show their enthusiasm for reading in many ways. They know the pleasure the material they are reading is giving them, and they are eager for their students to have similar pleasures.

Smith and Johnson (1980) offered the reading attitude inventory for teachers that is shown in Figure 17.1. Those who tend to disagree or strongly disagree with the inventory items would be in a poor position to advocate reading to their students.

Teachers who have never cultivated or who have lost the reading habit should discipline themselves to spend 15 to 30 minutes daily reading as a professional responsibility. Teachers who have done this report benefits not only to their students, but to themselves as well. They also report the tendency to increase their daily reading time period, not out of a sense of duty but rather because of the enjoyment they receive from their recreational reading (R. J. Smith, personal survey, 1988).

Assess Students' Attitudes toward Reading

Teachers, administrators, and parents go to some length to assess students' skill development in reading. End-of-unit tests in basal series, standardized reading achievement tests, diagnostic reading tests, skillbook exercises, and other assessment measures are administered, scored, and duly reported, all in the interest of students' cognitive growth. Yet attitudes are, for the most part, unmeasured, except for the subjective observations teachers make.

Students' attitudes toward reading should be measured on a regular basis in all classrooms, certainly not after every assignment, but after every four or five. They should be measured with regard to reading instruction and with regard to reading assignments in the content areas. They should also be measured to ascertain the effects of writing, oral discussion, and other reading-related activities on students' affective responses to assigned reading. Doing a distasteful book report has been known to take the shine off a book that might, without the report requirement, have been read and enjoyed. Too many distasteful reading and/or reading-related experiences can cause students to develop negative attitudes toward reading in general.

Students' attitudes toward reading selections and follow-up activities can be measured simply and straightforwardly. A simple procedure to use with primary-grade students is to have them respond "yes" or "no" or point to a smiling or frowning face in response to simple statements such as "I liked that story."

Older students may be asked to mark their feelings about a story or activity on a simple scale such as the one shown in Figure 17.2.

FIGURE 17.1 Reading Attitude Inventory for Teachers and Prospective Teachers

1. As a leisure-time activity, I value reading highly.

 _____ Strongly Agree

 _____ Agree

 _____ Disagree

 _____ Strongly Disagree

2. I look forward to doing the reading that I feel is important for a teacher to do.

 _____ Strongly Agree

 _____ Agree

 _____ Disagree

 _____ Strongly Disagree

3. If someone insisted that I do only what I wanted to do for an entire day, I would spend some of that day reading.

 _____ Strongly Agree

 _____ Agree

 _____ Disagree

 _____ Strongly Disagree

4. One reason I value teaching as a profession is that I have an opportunity to share my love for reading with my students.

 _____ Strongly Agree

 _____ Agree

 _____ Disagree

 _____ Strongly Disagree

5. I think I will be distressed and perhaps a bit angry with my students who clearly do not enjoy reading.

 _____ Strongly Agree

 _____ Agree

 _____ Disagree

 _____ Strongly Disagree

FIGURE 17.1 *Continued*

6. People who know me well, know that I enjoy reading.

_____ Strongly Agree

_____ Agree

_____ Disagree

_____ Strongly Disagree

Note: From Smith, R., & Johnson, D. (1980). *Teaching children to read* (pp. 372–373). Reading, MA: Addison-Wesley.

Number equivalents can be assigned to quantify students' responses as shown in Figure 17.3.

Responses can be obtained to as many statements as desired with a range and mean score calculated for individual students over several stories, textbook chapters, and/or reading-related activities. The same can be done for the class as a whole to give teachers a broader picture of their students' affective responses to reading assignments.

Teachers of upper-grade students may want to use a scale that is somewhat more sophisticated such as the one shown in Figure 17.4. The more complex scale includes both positively and negatively worded items with opportunities for students to respond on a five-point scale from "Strongly Agree" to "Strongly Disagree." Note that there are an equal number of negative and positive items on the scale. Note also the reversed scoring scheme for the positive and negative items.

Since the items are all constructed to assess pleasure or displeasure, a consistent scorer would mark "Strongly Agree" for the positive items and "Strongly Disagree" for the negative items if she or he thoroughly enjoyed the material read. A student who was thoroughly displeased with the material would mark the items in reverse. Given the point values for each response, then, students who thoroughly enjoyed the material would score 30 and students who were thoroughly displeased would score 6. Students whose attitudes were not so strong in either direction would score somewhere

FIGURE 17.2 Simple Attitude Scale

I enjoyed this story.

Very Much — Some — Not at all

|____|____|____|____|

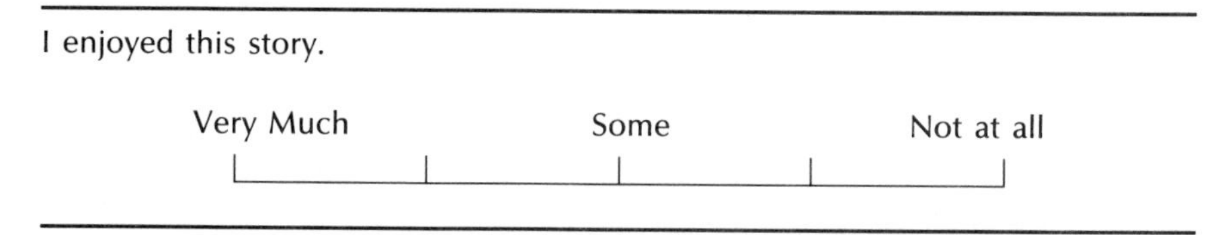

FIGURE 17.3 Number-equivalent Scale

I enjoyed this story.

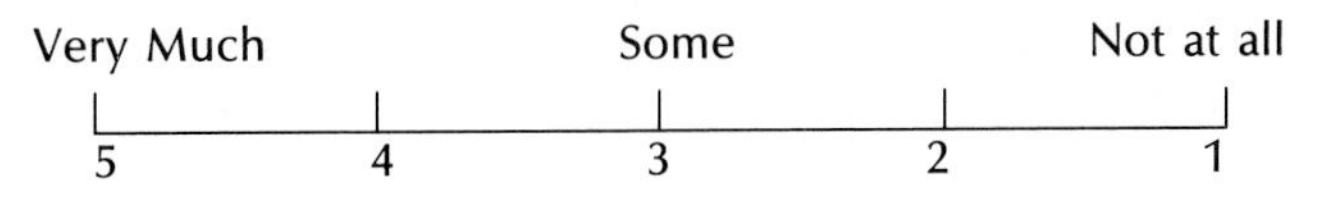

between 6 and 30. For example, a student with a neutral feeling toward the material would score 15.

Certainly teachers should assess students' developing attitudes toward reading in subjective ways as well as with more formal measures. Observing students' recreational reading habits, their familiarity with newspapers and

FIGURE 17.4 More Sophisticated Attitude Scale for Upper-grade Students

This is a good chapter.

_5_ Strongly Agree

_4_ Agree

_3_ Undecided

_2_ Disagree

_1_ Strongly Disagree

This chapter is boring.

_5_ Strongly Agree

_4_ Agree

_3_ Undecided

_2_ Disagree

_1_ Strongly Disagree

I hated reading this chapter.

This chapter was fun to read.

What a dumb chapter.

Great chapter.

magazines, their discussions about reading selections, the questions they ask about reading materials, and other behaviors can tell teachers a great deal about the kinds of attitudes they are developing toward reading. Students' informal behavior with regard to reading should reflect pleasure and enjoyment in the reading act. Obviously, teachers should not be expected to provide only material students enjoy. Nor should they be expected to please all students with the same selection. However, frequent or widespread displeasure with reading selections and/or reading-related activities is a symptom of a program that is more likely to produce negative than positive attitudes toward reading. Such a program is in need of modification.

Read Aloud to Students

Students of all ages enjoy being read to by their teachers. As Durkin (1989) put it, "Because children enjoy being read to—assuming appropriate material is selected and presented effectively—teachers at all grade levels should allow time for reading to students on a regular basis" (p. 27).

In the early grades, teachers should probably read to their students daily. They should read material that appeals to them and their students—stories, poems, newspaper articles, excerpts from novels, or entire novels, one part each day. Teachers in the later grades should read every day as well, also from material they and their students both find appealing. Many students recall their teachers' reading to them as one of their most enjoyable school experiences.

Tell Students about Your Leisure-Time Reading

The teacher as a model of positive attitudes toward reading is not a new idea. In 1956, Wendell Johnson wrote that

> Reading is something we do, not so much with our eyes, as such, as with our knowledge and interests and enthusiasm, our hatreds and fondnesses and fears, our evaluations in all their forms and aspects. Because this is so, a fondness for reading is something that a child acquires in much the same way as he catches a cold—by being effectively exposed to someone who already has it. (p. 123)

Students enjoy hearing their teachers talk about magazine articles, newspaper articles, and other materials of shorter length, as well as novels or longer selections. Regardless of what they are reading, teachers, by sharing it with their students, are communicating their enthusiasm for reading as a leisure-time activity.

Teachers might be guided by the student survey shown in Figure 17.5 as they model for their students. Hopefully, students would respond to the

FIGURE 17.5 Student Survey

1. My teacher reads
   a. a lot.
   b. a little.
   c. Don't know.
2. My teacher enjoys reading.
   a. Yes.
   b. No.
   c. Don't know.
3. What kind of reading does your teacher do for fun?
4. I like to hear my teacher talk about his or her reading.
   a. Yes.
   b. No.
   c. He/she never talks about it.
5. I have received good ideas about things to read from listening to my teacher.
   a. Yes.
   b. No.
6. If I wanted a suggestion for something good to read, I would ask my teacher.
   a. Yes.
   b. Maybe.
   c. No.

survey in a way that indicates that their teachers are acting as good reading models and thereby playing a positive role in their development of attitudes toward reading.

Provide Class Time for Students to Tell about Their Reading

Students can, if given the opportunity, do a good job of selling a book they are enjoying, or have enjoyed, to other students. Providing time for volunteers to talk briefly about books they are reading or have read can have a powerful influence on the reading attitudes and habits of other students.

One approach is to require all students to have some reading material to talk about once or twice a week. At the appointed time, certain students can be asked to tell the class what they are reading or the class can be divided into small conversation groups to share recreational reading experiences. Smith (1986) offered the type of questions shown in Figure 17.6 to help students discuss stories they have read. These questions are open-ended and cannot be judged as correct or incorrect, and they are focused on students' personal responses to the material.

FIGURE 17.6 Questions to Guide Reading Discussions

1. Were there any characters in this story that you especially liked?
2. Were there any characters you especially disliked?
3. Did you find anything humorous in this story?
4. Did you ever feel sad, worried, or frightened while you were reading this story?
5. Were you surprised at anything that happend in this story?
6. Were there any parts of this story that were especially interesting or exciting to you?
7. Did you get a mental picture from this story that you especially enjoyed or disliked?
8. Were there any parts of this story that were boring to read?
9. Did you find yourself wondering about the author while you were reading or after you finished the story? For example, was this written by a man or a woman? How old is the author? Where does the author live? Where did the author get the idea for this story?
10. If authors of stories received awards for the following categories, for which awards would you nominate the author of this story?
    a. Creating characters that are real-to-life.
    b. Developing exciting plots.
    c. Giving readers vivid mental images.
    d. Writing stories that maintain readers' interest.
    e. Writing humor.
    f. Bringing out readers' emotions.
    g. Other.
11. All things considered, how would you rate this story on the following scale:

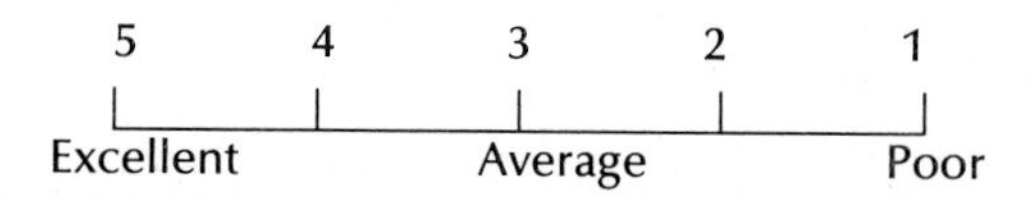

Note: From Smith, R. (1986). A guide for examining personal responses to stories. *Middle School Journal, 17*(2), 21–22.

Provide School Time for Reading

Students cannot develop positive attitudes toward reading (or skills for that matter) if they do not read. Therefore, getting them into interesting materials at school in the hope that what is begun at school will be continued out of school is a promising practice. Many teachers have reported improved student reading habits because of Uninterrupted Sustained Silent Reading (USSR), Drop Everything And Read (DEAR), or other programs that essentially provide school time for silent reading of self-selected materials. Chapter 18 provides a detailed discussion of ways to provide time for in-class reading.

Do Not Neglect Skills Instruction

Having the skills necessary to read interesting material is requisite to developing positive attitudes toward reading. Suffice it to say that attitude development objectives cannot be attained in a reading program that does not also have a strong skill development program.

The Materials Factor

Authors, as well as teachers, play an important role in the kinds of attitudes students develop toward reading. For materials to elicit positive affective responses from student readers, they must present well-drawn characters, engaging plots, descriptions that induce mental images, and other characteristics of high-quality writing whether it be in story, essay, poetry, or some other literary form. However, it is unlikely that materials play as important a role in students' attitude development as teachers play. In this regard, Mangrum and Forgan (1979) pointed out that

> the relationships you develop with your students, not the materials you use with them, will make major differences in their attitudes toward school and reading. Students cannot have meaningful relationships with materials, even if praise is built into materials as found in many audiovisual programs. There is no replacement for the rapport between student and teacher. (p. 54)

Ascertain Students' Interests

It stands to reason that students who are given material of interest to them will develop more positive attitudes toward reading than those who are not. As discussed in Chapter 16, simple interest inventories may be helpful in determining students' current interests, and they should be used. However, they are most effective if they are constructed by a teacher for his or her students. Figure 17.7 gives an example of such an inventory.

These inventories should be updated and administered every month or so. They should alert students to what is available and should contain explicit suggestions for students' reading based on the teacher's knowledge of his or her students' likely interests and the materials available to them.

Another approach for discovering students' reading interests, which is probably as effective as a written inventory, is to hold periodic class discussions about what students are reading or would enjoy reading. If the school librarian is present for these discussions, she or he can recommend material to satisfy expressed interests on the spot.

FIGURE 17.7 Sample Interest Inventory

1. About how much time each week will you spend in out-of-class reading?

 _____ 1 hour

 _____ 2 hours

 _____ 3 hours

 _____ More than 3 hours

2. We have some good biographies of successful black people in the library. Would you like to look them over?

 _____ Yes

 _____ Maybe

 _____ No

3. A magazine called *Cricket* is in our library. It has a lot of short stories and informational articles. Would you like to look at it?

 _____ Yes

 _____ Maybe

 _____ No

Provide Variety

Sometimes students develop an interest in a topic, a particular literary genre, or a certain kind of reading material. When this happens, they should be allowed to pursue their preference until they are satisfied. Trying to change their preference before it is satisfied is likely to result in more negative than positive attitudes toward reading. Most adult readers have become hooked on an author and read as many of his or her books as they can find, sometimes to the point of overdose. In time, however, reading preferences change, so it is unwise for teachers to risk the development of negative attitudes toward reading for the sake of developing well rounded readers. Students have plenty of time to become well rounded.

Although reading variety need not be forced, it is important to have a variety of materials available to students. Just as some students become narrowly focused at times, others look for a broader focus. Reading materials come in so many varieties it is reasonable to expect there is something out there for everyone. Students for whom short stories fall out of favor can be introduced to poems, essays, or biographies. Menus, classified advertisements, newspaper articles, new car brochures, cereal boxes, magazines, and other materials not typically considered part of the school reading program should be used to "hook" reluctant readers and give variety to avid readers who are getting bored with the usual fare.

Pay Attention to Difficulty

Trying to read a book that is too difficult for the reader's skill development is almost certain to result in negative attitudes toward reading. As discussed in Chapter 9, teachers must understand that there are three different difficulty levels for reading materials: the frustration level, the instructional level, and the independent level. Materials at the independent level can be read comfortably without assistance and those at the instructional level can be read with teacher assistance, but those at the frustration level cannot be read even with teacher assistance and should not be assigned.

However, one point should be made with regard to the difficulty of reading material and the development of attitudes toward reading. That point has been articulated well by Hunt (1970):

> One phenomenon which contradicts the validity of the reading levels theory is readily observed. It is the case of the high-interest book and the low-powered reader. Every observant teacher has seen the highly motivated reader engrossed in a book which for him is obviously of considerable difficulty. But because interest and involvement are high, he persists in the pursuit of ideas and he gets some.
>
> Certainly in such instances the reader does not get all the ideas, not even all important ideas, but he does get enough to sustain his interest. If oral reading renditions were required, his performance would be catastrophic; the material would be classified as well beyond the frustration level. However, when he has chosen the material to read because of personal interest, he can break many of the barriers. Strong interest can frequently cause the reader to transcend not only his independent but also his so-called instructional level. Such is the power of self-motivation. (p. 147)

The Instructional Activities Factor

Instructional activities are the third factor involved in direction and intensity of the attitudes students develop toward reading.

As Figure 17.8 indicates, the three factors discussed in this chapter do not function as separate entities. They are characterized more by their interdependence than by their independence. Consequently, some of the preceding discussion might be placed here as appropriately; for example, the questions for helping students discuss stories they have read (Smith, 1986).

An important point regarding the effect of reading-related activities on students' attitudes toward reading is that teachers should strive to assign

FIGURE 17.8
Interdependence of Attitude Factors

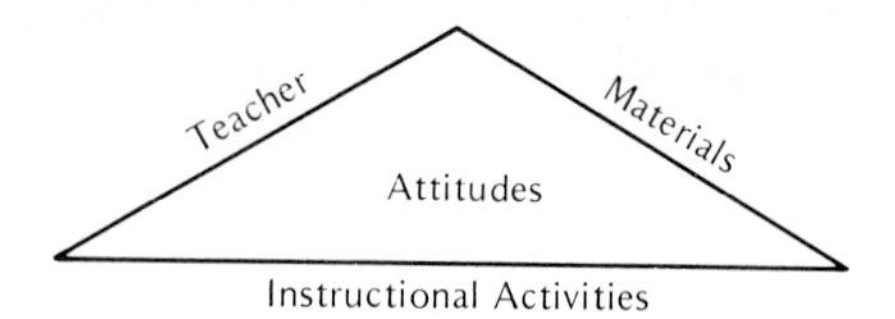

activities that enhance, rather than detract from, a reading experience. Fear of giving a book report in front of the class might cause a student to view the book in a negative light, and too many books viewed negatively can foster a negative attitude toward reading in general.

Integrate Reading and Writing Activities Carefully

In a study of the effects of integrating reading and writing on high- and low-ability fourth-grade readers' attitudes toward a reading selection, Smith and Hansen (1976) concluded that

> since attitudes toward the story were not affected positively or negatively by the writing task . . . it appears that teachers may integrate reading and writing without detracting from pupils' enjoyment of reading selections if they use good judgment in constructing the tasks. (p. 244)

While it may seem that attitudes are not in danger of being affected negatively by integrating reading and writing, Smith and Hansen did qualify their findings by saying "if they use good judgment in constructing the tasks." This qualification was based on their finding that both high- and low-ability readers had more negative attitudes toward the writing tasks than toward the reading tasks. The nature of the writing task is important. In general, in constructing reading-related writing tasks, teachers are well advised to provide the following:

1. Tasks that allow for student choices (e.g., Complete one of the three writing tasks below).
2. Tasks that encourage speculation (e.g., Extend this story by writing an addition to it. Tell what happened next).
3. Tasks that request personal feelings (e.g., Do you feel people should be allowed to keep wild animals as pets? Write an essay explaining your point of view).
4. Tasks that solicit evaluation (e.g., Write a letter to the author of this story. Tell her whether you did or did not enjoy it and why. You may want to include some suggestions on how it could be improved).

5. Tasks that elicit responses that can be judged as reasonable, but not necessarily as correct or incorrect.

These guidelines are derived from the author's experience and not from research findings. They should be viewed only as suggestions. Chapters 7 and 8 offer additional suggestions for integrating reading and writing.

Encourage Mental Imagery

Again in the experience of the author, encouraging students to form mental images as they read seems to enhance their attitude toward the selection. The first essential for inducing mental imagery is a selection that has good potential for image production. Most writing has imaging potential, but some selections or passages in selections have more than others. The following passage has considerable potential for the inducement of mental images:

> Manuel was daydreaming on the couch in his family's living room. The television was on, but his thoughts were far away from the 10:00 P.M. news. He was belting out a homer with the bases loaded in the bottom of the ninth.
>
> Suddenly, Bandito, who was on the other side of the room, growled and moved closer to Manuel. Manuel tensed and listened for whatever it was that had awakened Bandito. He felt cold under the flannel shirt that had been keeping him warm just seconds earlier.
>
> There was a strange sound coming from the bedroom he shared with Joseph, his baby brother. The sound was not coming from Joseph's crib. Manuel had all of those sounds memorized from other times he had babysat while his mother worked the late shift.
>
> Manuel's hand slid off the couch and felt for the baseball bat he always kept nearby, just in case.
>
> His hand clenched the handle of the bat, and he lifted himself from the couch. Bandito growled again. Outside, a bus pulled away from the curb.
>
> Manuel moved to the side of the living room that was opposite Joseph's and his bedroom. He could see the nightlight behind the mostly closed bedroom door. Tomorrow's weather was coming from the TV set, but Manuel wasn't hearing it. He felt his feet move toward the bedroom door.

One activity for inducing mental imagery is to place passages with good imagery potential in the context of a television production. Television is a medium students are familiar with and toward which they generally have positive attitudes.

The teacher either reads the passage (which should not be longer than three or four paragraphs) to the students or asks them to read it silently, trying to get pictures of the scene in their minds. Then the teacher asks them to read the passage again with the following conditions and questions in mind:

> Pretend this is a scene from a script for television and you are the director of that script.
>
> 1. Describe the actor you would want to play the part of Manuel (age, size, general appearance).
> 2. Describe how you would dress Manuel (shirt, pants, shoes, colors).
> 3. Describe the dog you would select for Bandito (breed, size, colors, general appearance).
> 4. What camera close-ups would you want for this scene? What distance shots?
> 5. Make a list of sounds the audience should hear during this scene.
> 6. Would you use background music during this scene? If so, for what parts? Describe the music you would use (fast, slow, scary, peppy, sad).

After the students have completed the questions, the teacher may choose to have them share their answers in a whole-class discussion, or may divide them into groups of three or four to share. Another variation is to have the students work in pairs or small groups to make decisions about the answers to the questions.

Provide Activities to Foster Attitude Changes

The preceding discussion emphasized the importance of engaging students in activities that allow them to make choices, write and speak from a personal viewpoint, and engage in higher-level or divergent thinking behaviors, all without the intimidation of being correct or incorrect. The following is a list of activities that conform to those principles. They are included here to acquaint teachers with the wide variety of instructional activities that can be designed with an eye toward attitudinal development as well as skills development. Unlike the suggestions given previously, which are more general in nature and well suited for typical school reading materials, some of the following suggestions apply to materials that may not be part of the typical basal reading program. They have been used successfully to change the attitudes of students who have decided that reading is not for them.

1. Take a shopping trip through a department store catalog. If you had $500 to spend, what would you buy?
2. Read a restaurant menu. What would you order? Describe the

"perfect meal." Make up your own restaurant and design a menu for it (e.g., "Root-Beer World," "Spinach Heaven").

3. Use the TV section from a newspaper. Plan a weekly viewing schedule for a person your age. If you were allowed to watch only one show per day, which would you choose?
4. Read several cereal boxes. Compare ingredients and notice box designs. Make up a cereal and design a box for it. Write a radio commercial for your cereal.
5. Read the comics section of a Sunday newspaper. Use the pictures and write your own captions.
6. Read old birthday or other greeting cards. Make a collection of your favorites. Create your own cards and greetings.
7. Read the used automobile advertisements in the classified section of a newspaper. Which car would you buy? Do the same for new cars.
8. Look through several books of riddles. Read those you enjoy most to a friend.
9. Using pictures from the sports section of the newspaper, make a scrapbook of your favorite sport.
10. Check the weather report in a newspaper and chart the temperatures for a month.
11. Cut out pictures of food from magazines. Label each one and write about your favorite. Create an imaginary dessert and tell all the things you would put in it.
12. Get free travel brochures from a travel agency. Plan your ideal vacation.
13. Read several magazines from your school library. Decide which one you like best. Create a plan for a new magazine for students in your school.

SUMMARY

Attitude development should be an important objective of all school reading programs. Students who can read but choose not to are not well served by print.

Teachers, instructional materials, and instructional activities have the potential for fostering either positive or negative attitudes toward reading. Teachers should examine their own behavior, the materials they make available to students, and the reading-related activities they assign to determine whether they are forces for positive or negative attitude development.

The key to attitude development lies more in intrinsic reinforcement (i.e., personal satisfaction and enjoyment) than in extrinsic reinforcement (i.e., prizes, grades, praise). Therefore, the job of teachers with regard to the development of attitudes toward reading is to design reading programs that give students personal pleasure along with skills mastery.

FOLLOW-UP QUESTIONS AND ACTIVITIES

1. Discuss your personal reading habits as they have changed through the years with others in the class.
2. What effect do you think television has on the reading habits of children? How about adults?
3. Which of the suggestions made in this chapter do you plan to implement in your teaching? Which do you feel you are unlikely to implement? Explain your reasons.
4. Make a list of reasons for including positive attitude development as a major reading program goal for all elementary teachers.

ADDITIONAL READINGS

Duffy, G. G., & Roehler, L. R. (1989). *Improving classroom reading instruction: A decision-making approach* (2nd ed.). New York: Random House.

Durkin, D. (1989). *Teaching them to read* (2nd ed.). Newton, MA: Allyn and Bacon.

Fredericks, A. D. (1982). Developing positive reading attitudes. *The Reading Teacher,* 35, 38–40.

Heathington, B. S., & Alexander, J. E. (1984). Do classroom teachers emphasize attitudes toward reading? *The Reading Teacher,* 37, 484–488.

Zintz, M. V., & Maggart, Z. R. (1989). *The reading process: The teacher and the learner* (5th ed.). Dubuque, IA: William C. Brown.

REFERENCES

Alexander, J. E. (1983). *Teaching reading* (3rd ed.). Glenview, IL: Scott, Foresman.

Duffy, G. G., & Roehler, L. R. (1986). *Improving classroom reading instruction: A decision-making approach.* New York: Random House.

Durkin, D. (1989). *Teaching them to read* (5th ed.). Boston: Allyn and Bacon.

Hunt, L. C., Jr. (1970). The effect of self-selection, interest and motivation upon independent, instructional and frustration levels. *The Reading Teacher,* 24, 146–151, 158.

Johnson, W. (1956). *Your most enchanted listener.* New York: Harper & Row.

Mangrum, C. T., & Forgan, H. W. (1979). *Developing competencies in teaching reading.* Columbus, OH: Merrill.

Smith, R. J. (1986). A guide for examining personal responses to stories. *Middle School Journal, 17*(2), 21–22.

Smith, R. J., & Hansen, L. H. (1976). Integrating reading and writing: Effects on children's attitudes. *The Elementary School Journal, 76,* 238–245.

Smith, R. J., & Johnson, D. D. (1980). *Teaching children to read.* Reading, MA: Addison-Wesley.

18

Initiating the Classroom Recreational Reading Program

DIXIE LEE SPIEGEL

ONE OF THE GOALS of an effective teacher is to help children become skillful readers. However, as discussed in Chapter 17, the attitudes and habits that children develop toward reading are equally important. Effective teachers must provide opportunities for children to develop a lifelong desire to read. To acquire the reading habit, children must become familiar with a variety of reading materials.

In Chapter 18, Dixie Spiegel suggests that the best way for children to become familiar with various reading materials is through a well-organized recreational reading program. She provides suggestions for classroom teachers on how they can establish recreational reading programs for their students and ways to promote children's interest in books and a desire to read in school and at home. Spiegel explains how teachers can organize their classroom environment for a recreational reading program, prepare their students for participation in the program, get the recreational program started, enlist the cooperation of parents, and secure the support of their principals.

Of special interest are the sections on management suggestions for student participation in the program and ideas for gaining parents' cooperation and support in the recreational reading of their children.

STUDY QUESTIONS

1. What is a classroom recreational reading program?
2. Why is it important to have such a program in a classroom?
3. How might a teacher go about organizing his or her classroom for a recreational reading program?
4. How might the teacher prepare the children for a recreational reading program?
5. How might the teacher actually get the program started?
6. What are some ways in which the teacher can gain the support of parents and the principal for the program?

Why spend so much time trying to teach children to read, especially if they are reluctant to learn? Certainly the reason is not that they will then be able to read basal readers, although many children seem to see that as the purpose. Basal readers or any other commercial reading programs are a means to an end. That end is to develop an individual who can read and wants to read. "Can read" means that the person is able to decode and comprehend printed material well enough to meet his or her needs, whether figuring out how to make a cake, keeping up with the news of the world, escaping from reality for a while, or finding out what kind of care tulip bulbs need. Educators have been doing a pretty good job lately in producing the "can read" individual (NAEP, 1981). Unfortunately, the "wants to read" aspect of this goal often remains elusive. There are many children who lack a strong desire to read. Most will read, most can read, but many will not choose to read voluntarily. Effective educators want children to learn to enjoy reading and seek it out as a major leisure-time activity.

Fortunately, one solution to creating a thirst for reading in children is simple: Let them read. Provide time, materials, and places for them to read, and then let them do it, with a minimum of interference. This simple solution is supported by the Report of the Commission on Reading. In this report, *Becoming a Nation of Readers,* the authors emphasize that "Children should spend more time in independent reading" (Anderson, Hiebert, Scott, & Wilkinson, 1985, p. 119). Children do not get enough practice with reading during the daily instructional program. Dramatic evidence of the power of "just reading" was presented by Anderson, Wilson, and Fielding (1986). They found that even 10 minutes of book reading a day outside of school had a significant impact on scores on standardized tests of reading comprehension.

This chapter describes a set of guidelines and procedures to help classroom teachers set up a voluntary or recreational reading program for students. These procedures will deal with organizing the classroom environment for a recreational reading program, preparing students and actually getting the program started, enlisting the cooperation of parents, and securing the support of the principal. But the first task for classroom teachers is to convince *themselves!*

Getting Rid of Guilt

It is 1:15 P.M. on Wednesday. Four of Ms. Filch's third-grade students are sprawled on their bellies in the middle of the floor. Two are lying on their backs with their heads supported by pillows, one is actually leaning against the teacher's desk, and one young fellow is under the science table. The other students are at their desks. No one is talking: not a student, not the teacher, not the aide. No one is even looking at anyone else—not even Ms. Filch. She is at her desk with her feet propped up on the bottom drawer, reading. She is not reading a text on how to teach science through the inquiry method, nor is she reading a pamphlet on using assertive discipline in the classroom. She is reading Judy Blume's latest novel. The aide is reading *Sports Illustrated.*

In walks the principal, Mr. Jones. Beckoning the teacher out into the hall, he says, "Ms. Filch, yesterday when I walked by your classroom at about this time you were not teaching. You were sitting here at your desk reading.

Today I find you not teaching again. Our school district does not pay you for reading. We pay you for teaching. Now get in there and *teach!*"

This is the crucial moment. If Ms. Filch is to have a successful recreational reading program, she must not feel even the slightest quiver of guilt. Rather, she must confidently explain the following points:

1. The children are doing recreational reading. This means that they, rather than the teacher, have chosen what they wish to read and that the teacher has provided them a sustained period of time in which to do that reading. This is sometimes called SSR (Sustained Silent Reading), USSR (Uninterrupted Sustained Silent Reading), and DEAR (Drop Everything And Read).
2. In this way, the children are practicing the skills Ms. Filch has taught them during class. They cannot practice these skills in any meaningful way through short worksheets that focus on single skills or by just reading basal stories that have been chopped up into segments.
3. Through recreational reading, the children are also expanding their meaning vocabularies (the set of words for which they have at least one meaning) and broadening their knowledge of the world and thus their experiential backgrounds.
4. Furthermore, the children are learning to enjoy reading because they are allowed to read whatever they wish and no one is going to quiz them about what they have read to prove that they did it.
5. Finally, Ms. Filch *is* teaching. She is teaching the students that reading is something that adults do voluntarily and even look forward to. She is serving as a role model. If she did not read at this time, but graded papers or worked with children who needed extra help instead, she would be distracting those who were reading. She is also teaching them that reading is important enough to be a regular part of every day's curriculum.

As a final clincher to her argument, Ms. Filch should invite the principal to come in tomorrow and teach the class about the joys of reading himself, reminding him to be sure to bring a good book!

The purpose of this little scenario is to help classroom teachers get rid of guilt. A well-functioning recreational reading program is so pleasant, so easy, and so rewarding that it almost seems like cheating to get paid for it. In addition, teachers feel guilty because there are children who do need individual guidance and it may feel like a waste of instructional time to sit there reading. However, these teachers *are* providing instruction. If classroom teachers do not give children time to read, the children do not get practice at school and they may not become fluent readers. If teachers do not model reading themselves, they are modeling something else—that reading is something teachers do not value as an activity for themselves. Classroom teachers may be doing as much for the development of children who can and will read during this period as they are during direct instruction.

Organizing the Environment

Organizing the environment for a recreational reading program means four things: creating a physical environment that makes voluntary reading easy and enticing; establishing a classroom ambiance that "invites children to read" (Spiegel, 1981, p. 51); making a lot of reading material readily accessible; and developing a minimal set of rules that promote, rather than restrict, reading.

Creating a Physical Environment

Children can do recreational reading anywhere, even sitting at their desks or under substandard lighting. However, there is some evidence (Morrow & Weinstein, 1982) that a more pleasant physical environment enhances a voluntary reading program. In an effort to entice more kindergarten children into literature experiences in classroom library corners, Morrow and Weinstein had teachers use the following guidelines (among others) for creating inviting environments:

- The library corners were in a quiet area of the classroom.
- These corners were visually and physically accessible. That is, the library corners were in places where children would notice them (not hidden behind a set of filing cabinets) and could get to them without bothering others or skirting furniture.
- A literature bulletin board or a display with books and related objects (such as stuffed animals) was set up.
- At least four children at a time could visit the corner.
- Some element of softness (e.g., pillows) was present in the corner.

Although these guidelines were specifically for literature centers and for kindergarten children, they are applicable for all efforts to promote voluntary reading in the classroom. Morrow and Weinstein (1982) found that creating such an environment was so successful that the mean number of children using each kindergarten literature corner as a free-choice activity changed from .28 children (in a classroom of about 20) per period to 5.75!

Establishing an Inviting Ambiance

Unfortunately, many children have to be enticed into recreational reading. They have to be drawn in by some sort of a siren song that sells them ahead of time on the enjoyment of reading and the excitement of getting lost between the pages of a book. Then, after they have experienced the pleasures and satisfactions of voluntary reading, many of them will eventually get "hooked." But first of all, the teacher has to get them reading. One important part of enticing children into voluntary reading is establishing a classroom ambiance or atmosphere in which reading is viewed as something pleasurable, painless, and worthwhile.

Part of the pleasurable aspect of recreational reading is the sense of "down time." The reader is alone with a book, drifting at his or her own pace down the Amazon, worrying about Peter Rabbit as he slips into Mr. MacGregor's garden, exploring the intricacies of electricity, or suffering the agonies of first love. But in order to experience this aspect of reading, the children need relatively large chunks of uninterrupted time. The amount of time will vary from grade level to grade level and even from class to class. It might be 5 minutes for a first-grade class in October and 20 minutes for sixth-graders by December. The basic premise remains constant, however: A person cannot really get into the suspended animation of reading if forced to "eat on the run," in little nibbles here and there and with lots of other activities competing for attention.

Reading does not have to be just a solitary act. The reader can also partake of the pleasures of sharing reading experiences by voluntarily discussing what has been read with a peer or the teacher. This shared community of knowledge and experiences will enhance the pleasure of reading and extend the pleasure beyond the reader's self.

The pleasurable ambiance of recreational reading centers around self-selection of reading material, self-pacing, and absence of accountability. Voluntary reading should mean that the children themselves choose what they will read and how fast they will move through the material. Except in extreme circumstances, there should be no well-meaning interference from the teacher to select more difficult books or read from a wider variety of genres. If a child wants to read the cornflakes box for the fourth day in a row, the teacher should maintain a hands-off policy. When children feel confident and ready to move on, they will.

The absence of accountability is one of the most important aspects of the pleasurable ambiance of recreational reading. If children are asked to be accountable for their reading, the implicit message is that they are not to be trusted. Furthermore, the message implies that one must be forced to do reading, that without accountability it would be natural to try to evade the activity. Recreational reading is not a time to perform and compete and be evaluated; it is a time to enjoy and savor and meet one's own needs.

Recreational reading must be seen as worthwhile in order to compete successfully with video games, dance class, and basketball. Children need to become enveloped in the wonder of the world of now and then and yet-to-be, the world of here and there and only-in-our-minds. They must become intrigued by what a person can learn and do and feel through reading. Reading must change their worlds in some way in order to be worth the time.

Making Reading Materials Accessible

Most people, if they are reluctant to do a task and the slightest impediment stands in the way, will use that impediment as an excuse to put off the task. Recreational reading has the same hazard. If a wide variety of fresh materials in a complete range of genres and levels is not readily accessible, many children will not read. Instead they will offer the excuses of "I've already read all the books," "There's nothing there I want to read," or "I'm tired of stories. I want to read real-life stuff." Both Powell (1966) and Morrow and Weinstein (1982) found that the more accessible reading materials were, the more recreational reading was done. Bissett (1969) found that children in classrooms with their own libraries read 50% more books than students without access to classroom libraries.

In order for a recreational reading program to function smoothly, children must have something to read ready at hand at all times. They may bring these materials from home or from the public library, but more commonly, they will find them at school. This means three things: First, the children must have free access to the school library so that they can exchange books at almost any time and can take out more than one book at a time. Nothing is more deflating than finding you really do not want to read the one book that you have! Second, reading material is not restricted to books. Children should be allowed to read whatever they wish—comics, newspapers, magazines, or even cereal boxes. Third, children need access to a classroom library that has a rotating collection of books that students in the class will find inviting. In order to have a fresh variety of books at all times, teachers can trade books with other teachers, haunt garage sales, involve the children in book clubs, and make deals with the public library. Subscriptions to children's magazines such as *Ranger Rick* and *National Geographic World* can ensure some fresh, up-to-date reading matter monthly. A rule of thumb might be to have, on the average, a turnover of 25% in the classroom library each month. The children themselves can be involved in the selection process, but the keys are variety and change. Stale books are no more likely to be ingested than stale pastries.

Developing Rules for Recreational Reading

Rule one is to have very few rules. Any rule that interferes in the least way with voluntary reading is a bad rule. This means that there should not be restrictive rules about how long a book can be checked out or how many books by one author a child can read or who can read what. All of the rules for recreational reading should facilitate reading.

There should be rules to ensure quiet times for reading, such as no extended conversations near a reader; no talking at all during sustained silent reading time, when everyone in the room is supposed to be reading; and no wandering aimlessly around the room during SSR. There should be rules to ensure access to reading materials, such as requiring a child to have something to read within reach at all times. When nearing the end of a book or beginning to suspect that the book is not just right, the child may be expected to have the alternate already picked out before SSR begins. These kinds of rules follow the spirit of recreational reading, enhancing its status as something a child would want to do rather than something that the child has to do and has to be coerced into doing.

Getting Started and Keeping Going

Children have to be convinced of the value of a recreational reading program, and they have to be eased into it. Teachers must have a plan for maintaining the program throughout the year and for finding ways to get a sense of how well the children are responding to the program.

Preparing the Students

Teachers should begin preparing their students by sharing their own purposes for such a program, explaining to the children what they hope the students will gain from the program. One procedure might be to make a list of the teacher's goals and post it. Next, in order to get them to become invested in this program, the teacher could have the children identify class goals for their recreational reading. Examples of these goals might be that as a class they will read an average of two books per month per student or that as a class they will read at least six different types of reading materials a month. These goals will help to establish ownership of the program and should be posted with the teacher's goals.

Finally, and perhaps not right at the beginning, each child should set one or two personal goals. These goals must be tailor-made for the individual, and they will point up the differences among children. These goals are not to be posted. It is important for them to be realistic and attainable. For example, an already avid reader who tends to read only fiction might set a goal of reading one nonfiction material a month. A reluctant and not too able reader might set a goal of reading at least four pages a day of *anything*. These goals should change as the children become more aware of themselves as readers and as their own needs, interests, and talents change.

The children should also be involved in setting up the rules for their program. The various needs of the program should be discussed, with special emphasis on relative quiet and access to books. Then the class might make up a tentative set of rules, with the understanding that these rules will be reviewed regularly to determine whether or not they are working, whether or not they are needed, and whether or not others must be added. The rule for rules is: Does it facilitate recreational reading?

Actually Beginning

The key word is s-l-o-w-l-y. Many children are not used to doing anything for a sustained period of time. Teachers should not expect their students to suddenly triple their attention spans. One kindergarten teacher set a wise example: A student rushed home one day and proudly announced, "We did recreational reading today for 30 . . . seconds!"

McCracken (1971) suggested a data-based approach to deciding how big a gulp of reading should be tried. He proposed that the teacher should decide on an amount of time that every child in the room should be able to sustain attention to reading. A timer is then set to that amount and placed unannounced in the teacher's desk. When the timer rings, the teacher looks up (for he or she, too, has been reading) and asks the class whether they wish to continue reading for awhile. If the consensus is that they would like to keep reading, the teacher notes how much total time has passed when about one-third of the children begin to get restless. For the next day, the timer is set for slightly less than that amount of time. It rings, the class decides, the teacher observes, and so on. In this way, the true limits are found without ever having a failing experience.

With a particularly reluctant class, the teacher might begin introducing the children to recreational reading by spending most of the period reading to them. Gradually, the proportion of time spent with the children reading themselves should be increased, until the teacher's reading aloud is relegated to an entirely separate part of the day. However, the teacher should read to the class every day, regardless of the age and reading ability of the students.

Some teachers may find it difficult to have a period of sustained silent reading each day. Especially in the intermediate and middle-school grades, the school day can be so fragmented that the teacher may feel that the students are never together as a class! But classroom teachers should try to have SSR at least twice a week. They should also remember that recreational reading in school does not *have* to be SSR; it does not have to be done as a whole group. Children should be expected to grab any chance for reading for pleasure that comes their way during the school day.

There is one wonderful opportunity for individual recreational reading that exists in most school programs every single day: independent seatwork time! Rather than deluging students with worksheets and workbook pages, a practice that has never been associated with improving reading achievement (Anderson et al., 1985), teachers might require that each child spend a substantial portion of independent seatwork time just reading. Then there should never be a child wandering up to the teacher in the middle of a reading group complaining that he or she has nothing to do.

Teachers who are concerned about giving up the reinforcement provided by some worksheets might make a deal with their students: If a child does one-half of a worksheet absolutely perfectly, the teacher will be convinced that the child does not need to do the other half. However, if the child misses even one item, it is obvious that more practice is needed. In this way children are more likely to do their best work, the teacher only has to grade half as much, and the children now have more free time to *read!*

Maintaining the Program

Although most teachers are not interested in playing "Let's Quiz the Kid" after every book a child has read, many teachers do want some low-key, unobtrusive way of gaining a sense of progress and on-task behavior during recreational reading. Book reports are not the answer! The golden opportunity to do a book report never motivated anyone to read. Most book reports can be done without reading the book anyway. Furthermore, it can often take longer to write the report than to do the reading. Worst of all, some children may avoid completing a book just to avoid writing the report, thus actually reading less than if they were left to their own natural inclinations.

The classroom teacher may wish to keep track in some way of the amount of reading individual children do. These records should be truly individualized and noncompetitive. The amount of effort it takes to read 5 pages may be more for one reader than the amount needed for another child to read 50. The teacher should negotiate with each child an amount of reading, either in time or number of pages, that both feel is a bit challenging but still fair. As the child finds it easier and easier to meet this criterion, the amount should be renegotiated with a spirit of celebration at the child's progress. When setting the amount of reading for beginning readers, it is important to remember that these beginners (regardless of age) must be given credit for picture books, listening to books on tape, and listening to someone read to them.

Keeping track of the number of books read is often too competitive, and it encourages children who could read longer books to whip through short ones in order to get more credit. It also penalizes the child who is a slower or less able reader. In recreational reading, the amount of effort is best measured in other ways.

Another way to get a sense of whether the children are growing from their voluntary reading is to encourage sharing—that is, *encourage,* not *require.* Children who wish to discuss what they have read or attempt to "sell" someone else on their book or author may announce that fact and seek an audience. Children may also share by preparing some sort of a visual presentation about their book—for example, making a book poster or decorating a part of a bulletin board to tell about what they have read. However, the sharing activity should take only a small fraction of the amount of time spent in the reading!

Children can also share in a more systematic way by sharing factual information gleaned from books, not just pleasurable feelings. Children might form interest groups so that several students who wish to learn more about kumquats pool their knowledge after a specified amount of time.

Jigsaw grouping (Aronson, Blaney, Sikes, Stephan, & Snapp, 1975) extends this information sharing to the whole class. For jigsaw grouping, each child is a member of an interest group. One group might be devoted to airplanes, another to Chinese food, a third to mythical monsters, a fourth to Brazil, and a fifth to kumquats. After each child has read about the common topic of his or her group, the group members pool their knowledge and decide what is important to be shared. Each child in the group then has the information from all of the other children, and this information has been sorted and sifted. Finally, the children from all the groups share with each other. To do this, a second round of groups is formed, with each new group having one airplane expert, one Chinese chef, one monster authority, and so on. Through jigsaw grouping, children learn interesting information about a wide variety of topics and may be stimulated to explore some of those topics themselves. In addition, they experience the satisfaction of sharing what they have read.

Usually, a recreational reading program will maintain itself with a minimum of attention from the teacher. The teacher only needs to ensure that lots of books are easily accessible, chunks of time are available for reading, and individuals who wish to share have that opportunity.

Enlisting the Cooperation of Parents

Unfortunately, many parents need to be convinced of the necessity of a recreational reading program. Morrow (1986) found that when parents were asked to rank comprehension, word identification skills, study skills, and voluntary reading for importance in reading instruction, voluntary reading was ranked as lowest. Furthermore, the parents' attitude toward recreational reading was significantly more negative than the attitude of teachers and principals, who also ranked voluntary reading lowest in priority. With this in mind, teachers should plan ways to enlist the cooperation of parents from the very beginning of a recreational reading program. (Chapter 16 offers many helpful suggestions for working with parents.)

Initial Contact

A combination of letters and personal contacts seems to be the best way to introduce parents to a recreational reading program. The classroom teacher might begin with a series of short letters that eases the parents into the idea, just as the teacher plans to ease the children into the program. A schedule should present the whole picture of the program in closely spaced but small bites of information. In that way, parents' questions about the program are likely to be answered quickly by successive newsletters, and concerns will not have time to grow. A schedule such as the following might be used:

> *Newsletter 1.* Explanation of what a recreational reading program is and how it will work in your class. Schedule of what information will be contained in subsequent newsletters.
>
> *Newsletter 2* (two days later). Rationale for having a recreational reading program, with emphasis on how it fits into the basic curriculum. Short statement of support from your principal and reading teacher.
>
> *Newsletter 3* (two days later). List of suggestions of ways parents can help support the program through their efforts at home.
>
> *Newsletter 4* (two days later). List of ways parents can volunteer their time in the classroom to support this program. (Spiegel, 1981, p. 58)

As a follow-up to these letters, parents might be invited to attend the next school visitation night accompanied by something to read for a 5-minute SSR period. (A wise teacher will have some emergency reading materials for parents who forget.)

Suggestions for Parental Support at Home

The most important way a parent can support a recreational reading program is to provide a "reading culture" (Cain, 1978) in the home. A reading culture involves having reading as a leisure-time activity for all family members and having materials to read available everywhere in the home. Morrow (1983) found that kindergarten children who had a high interest in reading were read to more at home, watched less television, and had more children's books in the home than children who had low interest. One especially interesting fact from this study was that every one of the high-interest children had books in their bedrooms, while only 16% of the low-interest children did. The low-interest children did have books available, but these materials were more likely to be kept in the playroom.

Morrow's research (1983) also emphasized the importance of reading to children in the home and having the parents serve as models of reading. Of the kindergarten children with high interest in reading, 76.8% were read to daily at home, whereas only 1.8% of the low-interest children were. Similarly, 78.6% of the high-interest children had mothers who spent some of their own leisure time reading, but only 28.1% of the low-interest children's mothers spent any leisure time in that way. For fathers, the figures were 60.7% for high-interest children and 15.8% for low-interest children.

In addition to modeling reading and reading to their children, parents can promote voluntary reading by encouraging their children to read by themselves. (Of course, "reading" can mean looking at picture books for beginners.) However, Cecil (1987) warned that too much encouragement may be detrimental: "Make reading time a 'treat'—not a 'treatment'" (p. 100). Many parents may appreciate specific guidelines from the teacher for amounts of time that their children should be expected to read at home. These guidelines should be tailored individually by the teacher for each child. For example, a child with a short attention span might do very well to read for 5 minutes, whereas a child in the same class who is capable of greater concentration but is just reluctant to read might be urged to read for 15 minutes. Parents might also like the idea of sharing the reading task with their children, with parent and child reading alternate pages.

Many parents are unsure of what their child should be reading. They might welcome lists of books or authors or series that their children would find appealing and with which they would be successful. Parents also might be given lists of local bookstores that handle children's books, suggested books to buy for holidays or birthdays, and local secondhand bookstores or flea markets where they can pick up inexpensive used children's books. Parents might also be reminded of that wonderful American institution, the garage sale.

Of course the least expensive source of books is the public library, but many parents do not regularly tap this wonderful resource. Morrow (1983) found that 37.5% of the high-interest kindergartners had their own library card, and 98.1% of them were taken to the library. By contrast, only 3.4% of the low-interest children had cards, and a mere 7.1% were taken to the library. To combat these discouraging statistics, some public libraries will allow teachers to distribute and collect applications for library cards. At the very least, parents should receive a map showing the location of the closest public library or bookmobile stop, the services offered, and the hours of operation.

One last way for parents to support recreational reading is through their involvement in organizations outside of the school. Many parents would like to help with the school's recreational reading program but are unable to come to the school to do this, because they work or because of child care or transportation problems. These parents might wish to ask their Sunday School class, fraternal organization, or even the business they work for to sponsor their child's program. Sponsorship could involve providing a class subscription to *Ranger Rick* for 1 year or supplying incentives such as tee-shirts or coupons for ice cream or pizza for children who meet their own reading goals. In this way the entire community can become involved in the school's program. Chapter 16 has many additional suggestions in this area.

Suggestions for Parental Support at School

There is a great deal that parents who are able to come to the school can do to support the program. Teachers should offer interested parents a wide variety of options, since some parents will not feel comfortable reading to the class because of their own limited reading skills or natural reticence. These options might include the following:

- Reading aloud to children (individuals, small groups, or the entire class).
- Listening to children read.
- Serving as a silent reading model.
- Taping books for children to listen to.
- Collecting or exchanging books for the classroom library.
- Taking orders for children's book clubs.
- Keeping the library corner organized and attractive.

Parents want to support their children's schools. It is up to teachers and principals to make opportunities available to them. Additional suggestions for involving parents as volunteers in the reading program are offered in Chapter 16.

Securing the Support of the Principal

The scenario described earlier in this chapter between Ms. Filch and her principal, Mr. Jones, never should have taken place. A teacher with any sense of self-preservation already would have alerted the principal that a recreational reading program was going on. In these days of checklists and accountability, principals are expected to have something to observe, and recreational reading at first glance does not provide many observable behaviors!

A wise teacher starts the recreational reading program not by preparing the children but by preparing the principal. This is the individual who will support the teacher with parents, central office staff, and even other teachers. However, the classroom teacher should not just breeze into the principal's office with a one-sentence explanation of this wonderful program. If recreational reading is to become an integral part of the curriculum, it must be as carefully presented and show as much evidence of thoughtful planning as any other curricular change. Therefore, the description of the proposed program should include a clear rationale for the program, a modest list of resources needed (including both time and materials), an honest assessment of what other changes in the classroom will result from adding recreational reading, and a request for the principal's support. The teacher might also ask that fire drills not be scheduled during SSR!

After the recreational reading program has begun working smoothly, the teacher might go back to the principal and invite him or her to become more directly involved. The principal might serve as a reading model during SSR, read to the class, or listen to children who wish to share their own reading. The principal might retrieve discarded books from central storage or the incinerator and place these books in classroom libraries. He or she might involve business leaders or fraternal organizations in supporting the school's program. The principal might support school-wide reading contests, book fairs or swaps, or a Book It! program. (This National Incentive Reading Program for children in grades 1 through 6 is sponsored by Pizza Hut. The program supplies rewards, including pizzas, for children who reach the reading goals set by their own teachers. Information about the program can be obtained by writing Book It! Program, P.O. Box 2999, Wichita, KS 67201 or calling 1-800-4-BOOK-IT.)

There are myriad ways the principal can help to make a recreational reading program a success, and most principals will welcome these opportunities.

SUMMARY

A recreational reading program is fun, easy, and important. Such a program provides children with crucial opportunities to practice real reading and to develop lifelong habits of choosing to read. A recreational reading program is not a frill; it is an essential part of any reading program. Try it. It may become your favorite part of the school day.

FOLLOW-UP QUESTIONS AND ACTIVITIES

1. List the goals of a basal reader series. (These can usually be found at the beginning of the teacher's manual.) Next to each goal, rate a recreational reading program as a means of reaching that goal. Use the following scale: 3 = more effective than the basal program for reaching this goal; 2 = about as effective; 1 = less effective. Be prepared to defend your answers.
2. Folk wisdom, the Puritan ethic, and fitness programs dictate "No pain, no gain." Respond to a parent, fellow teacher, or principal who urges you to require your students to read challenging books for their recreational reading.
3. Survey teachers in a local school about their attitudes toward and practices in using class time for recreational reading. Report the amount of time devoted to recreational reading, teachers' reasons for providing time, and teachers' reasons for not finding time for recreational reading.
4. Prepare a guide to your local library for parents interested in promoting voluntary reading with their children. Your guide might include a map of the location of the library; directions to the children's section; a blueprint of the children's section showing the location of easy

readers, picture books, nonfiction, and other types of literature; procedures for obtaining a library card; and the library's hours of operation. You might also wish to provide a list of authors or books that children in a particular grade level might enjoy reading or having read to them.

ADDITIONAL READINGS

Anderson, R. C., Wilson, P. T., & Fielding, L. G. (1986). *Growth in reading and how children spend their time outside of school* (Tech. Rep. No. 389). Urbana: University of Illinois, Center for the Study of Reading.

Cecil, N. L. (1987). *Teaching to the heart: An affective approach to reading instruction.* Salem, WI: Sheffield.

Cullinan, B. E. (Ed.). (1987). *Children's literature in the reading program.* Newark, DE: International Reading Association.

Morrow, L. M. (1985). *Promoting voluntary reading in school and home.* (Phi Delta Kappa Fastback No. 225). Bloomington, IN: Phi Delta Kappa.

Reed, A. J. S. (1987). *Comics to classics: A parent's guide to books for teens and preteens.* Newark, DE: International Reading Association.

Spiegel, D. L. (1981). *Reading for pleasure: Guidelines.* Newark, DE: International Reading Association.

REFERENCES

Anderson, R. C., Hiebert, E. H., Scott, J. A., & Wilkinson, I. A. G. (1985). *Becoming a nation of readers: The report of the Commission on Reading.* Washington, DC: National Institute of Education.

Anderson, R. C., Wilson, P. T., & Fielding, L. G. (1986). *Growth in reading and how children spend their time outside of school* (Tech. Rep. No. 389). Urbana: University of Illinois, Center for the Study of Reading.

Aronson, E., Blaney, N., Sikes, J., Stephan, C., & Snapp, M. (1975). The jigsaw route to learning and liking. *Psychology Today, 8,* 43–50.

Bissett, D. J. (1969). The amount and effect of recreational reading in selected fifth grade classes. *Dissertation Abstracts International, 30,* 5157A. (University Microfilms No. 70-10, 316)

Cain, M. A. (1978). Born to read: Making a reading culture. *Teacher, 95,* 64–66.

Cecil, N. L. (1987). *Teaching to the heart: An affective approach to reading instruction.* Salem, WI: Sheffield.

McCracken, R. A. (1971). Initiating sustained silent reading. *Journal of Reading, 41,* 521–524, 582–583.

Morrow, L. M. (1983). Home and school correlates of early interest in literature. *Journal of Educational Research, 76,* 221–230.

Morrow, L. M. (1986). Attitudes of teachers, principals, and parents toward promoting voluntary reading in the elementary schools. *Reading Research and Instruction, 25,* 116–130.

Morrow, L. M., & Weinstein, C. S. (1982). Increasing children's use of literature through program and physical design changes. *Elementary School Journal, 83,* 131–137.

National Assessment of Educational Progress. (1981, July). *Reading, thinking, and writing. Results from the 1979–1980 national assessment of reading and literature* (Report No. 11-L-35). Denver: Education Commission of the States.

Powell, W. R. (1966). Classroom libraries: Their frequency of use. *Elementary English, 43,* 395–397.

Spiegel, D. L. (1981). *Reading for pleasure: Guidelines.* Newark, DE: International Reading Association.

—19—

Using the Newspaper to Enhance Reading

BERNARD L. HAYES

THIS CHAPTER DISCUSSES the value of using the newspaper to promote the development and application of reading skills. The chapter suggests that the newspaper provides a realistic context for students to practice holistic application of reading skills in a variety of situations. The newspaper provides teachers an excellent opportunity to use materials that relate to the broad background of interests and abilities of the students in their classrooms. It is not only an excellent vehicle for teaching and expanding students' reading abilities and interests, but also an important source of information that students should be introduced to at an early age. Several reasons are given for why the newspaper is an excellent addition to the reading program, and suggestions are offered for introducing it into the classroom. The heart of the chapter consists of suggestions for reading activities using the newspaper to practice and apply a variety of reading skills.

STUDY QUESTIONS

1. Why use newspapers in the classroom reading program?
2. How would you introduce the newspaper into the classroom reading program?
3. What strategies are needed for reading the newspaper?
4. What content area subjects can be taught from the newspaper?

To help children understand the importance of learning to read, teachers must provide them with instructional materials that are relevant and interesting. They must also ensure that students can and will transfer what they learn from instructional materials to real-life reading situations. Effective teachers can be sure that they are addressing both of these concerns by providing supplemental activities for teaching reading skills through the daily newspaper. Any reading method is compatible with the newspaper because the newspaper provides high-interest content. Furthermore, the newspaper is an important resource that children should learn to use. Newspapers have a responsibility to ensure the public's right to know and to guard against secret governments; schools have a responsibility to prepare students to understand the issues involved in the maintenance of freedom of information. An early introduction to newspapers in reading instruction can greatly enhance students' understanding of the value of a free press. Perhaps most important, newspapers provide students with a means of assessing news, current events, and information about the so-called global village we all inhabit.

Newspapers can fit into any school's content area reading program. They are a current, constant source of information about events. Furthermore, they are suited to a wide range of reading abilities; almost every newspaper contains something that can be read by elementary and middle-school students. With their meaningful, interesting, and lively content, newspapers are a source of information that can be used for developing skills and strategies. Words related to social studies and science topics are found daily in newspapers. However, their most important value is that students meet these words in a context that clarifies and adds relevance to their meaning. Human-interest stories, reviews, opinion articles, and political cartoons show how the "facts" found in textbooks and encyclopedias are used by different people to influence others in their thinking. Certain newspaper sections, such as advertisements; radio, television, and movie schedules; the stock-market pages; and sports sections provide examples of the utility of mathematics skill in students' daily activities.

Several times in Chapters 17 and 18 newspapers were suggested as appropriate reading material for students. This chapter offers teachers some practical information and suggestions for teaching reading skills and strategies using the newspaper as the medium. The chapter presents a discussion of the advantages the newspaper has for teaching reading and suggestions for introducing the newspaper into the classroom reading program. It concludes with a listing of references and agencies that effective teachers may want to look into for additional information about using the newspaper in the classroom reading program.

Advantages of Using Newspapers to Teach Reading

Availability

Newspapers can be found in almost every community regardless of size or location. Based on figures from the American Newspaper Publishers Association (1984), the total daily newspaper circulation in the United States (not counting weekly newspapers) is over 61 million. On Sundays, nearly 55 million copies are printed. The estimated readership of weekly newspapers is 117 million people. In Canada, 5.5 million newspapers are circulated.

Low Cost

Teachers can get sets of newspapers for classroom use at half price or less from most newspaper publishers. This allows teachers to encourage students to underline, circle, clip, and take home copies for homework activities. Purchased once a week, a newspaper's different sections can be used on different days, and appropriate portions for different age and ability levels can be sent home for review or homework, making it an inexpensive and adaptable classroom teaching aid. For example, children in kindergarten through third grade might be asked to survey the newspaper for pictures that describe important events that are taking place in the community, while older students might be required to find information regarding a current event to be discussed in class.

Motivation

Newspapers work well because children are trying to be grown up and the newspaper is a grown-up thing. Children are less likely to be insulted or embarrassed when low-level skills are introduced and practiced in a newspaper context than when they are given low-level reading materials. Newspapers are widely read because they offer a variety of topics of high interest to everyone. This assures the teacher that students will always find some section of the newspaper that relates to their interests, whether it is the movies, the social page, the stockmarket section, the sports section, or any other part.

Relevance

The topics included in the newspaper deal with issues and concerns that students either are concerned with currently or are going to be concerned with in the future, such things as the energy crisis, nuclear proliferation, latest fashions, and political personalities. It is much more relevant to encounter reading skills in the context of their application to one's own world than in a textbook.

Current Information

Newspapers are published daily or weekly; therefore, they report current information and recent events. In contrast, textbook information is sometimes outdated before it gets into the classroom. Many reading series take 5 years to write and a couple of years to publish, and they are then adopted for use for the next 5 years. Teachers who are using basal series in their last year of adoption may be using materials reporting information that is 12 years old. Information from newspapers emphasizes and reinforces what students experience in their daily lives and on radio and television. This provides teachers with the advantage of using instructional materials in which students have background knowledge (they have heard the ideas and concepts before on the radio or television) and high interest (current information related to real issues and concerns), which in turn enhances effective reading.

Fostering Lifelong Interest in Reading and Learning

Students who have opportunities to become acquainted with newspapers in their classrooms are likely to remain newspaper readers for the rest of their lives. Using the newspaper is an effective way to enhance the application of skills and strategies (e.g., decoding, comprehension, critical reading, and study skills) to a resource that will continually aid students in gaining the information they need to be responsible citizens. Early introduction of the daily newspaper provides a means to promote lifelong reading and learning.

Bringing the Newspaper into the Classroom

The following suggestions can help teachers introduce the newspaper to their students effectively, setting the stage for its many uses. They are appropriate at any grade level.

1. Start out by holding a brainstorming session with students on the value of the newspaper. Encourage the students to develop the longest possible list of reasons for having a newspaper. Go over this list with them and discuss which reasons are the most important and why.
2. The students will get more information from and enjoy the newspaper more if they are familiar with it. Develop a sense of the newspaper's content. Have students work in small teams to list the different kinds of information found in a newspaper. This activity can be modified to meet the reading abilities of a wide range of students. Younger students can name the types of information while the teacher records them on the chalkboard or chart. Older students can make their own lists.
3. Newspapers are not easy materials for young students (K–2 level) to manipulate. Teachers should provide instruction and demonstrate how to refold the sections. Students will benefit from having their own paper for this activity.
4. After the newspaper has been introduced to students, hold a "scavenger hunt" to help them become more familiar with its content. Develop a list of required information for students to find in a certain period of time. Use of the index should be encouraged for this activity.
5. Encourage students to read the newspaper by providing them with a regular newspaper browsing time. This might be during a regular silent reading time or a short time set aside specifically for newspaper reading.
6. Involve students in a scanning or skimming game with the newspaper. Require them to find certain information, statements, or

words on a certain page or in a certain section. This game can be played as a team competition as well as with individuals. Explain to the students that *scanning* is searching for specific information while *skimming* is previewing the material to see what the features are and get an overview of the material.

7. Establish a newspaper center. Make activity cards or tasks to practice the skills and strategies related to specific reading objectives.

These suggestions can help in introducing the newspaper into the classroom; however there are some things to consider in preparing to implement a newspaper reading program. Teachers need to preview the issues and make choices about which articles, sections, and columns to use. Newspapers should not be used indiscriminately in class. There may be content that would not be appropriate in certain situations for classroom use.

Children's reading levels must be considered. Use of different sections of the newspaper should be based on children's reading ability rather than grade level. For example, less able readers or younger children can organize photographs, comic strips, or movie titles by major categories, while more able readers or older students can be required to match headlines to articles. Both of these activities stress the skill of finding the main idea at different reading levels. The effective teacher will need to match the reading ability of students with the reading demands of the activity.

Finally, teachers should have specific objectives or goals in mind as they plan activities with the newspaper. Instructional time is too valuable not to have well-planned lessons leading toward the development of specific skills, strategies, abilities, and attitudes in children.

Newspaper Activities That Enhance Reading

The following activities are examples of how effective teachers can use the newspaper in their classroom reading program.

Using the Comics

The comics sections of the newspaper is probably a favorite of a large number of newspaper subscribers, young and old alike, and it is one of the newspaper's first attractions for children. Teachers should be aware of the conceptual levels of the different comic strips and the maturation level of their students. Many popular adult comics such as "Peanuts" are loaded with satire and irony that may cause some less able students to miss their main ideas. The following activities all use newspaper comics to enhance children's reading skills in many different ways and at different levels of reading ability:

Sequencing comic strips: Select several simple comic strips and cut the frames apart. Number each frame on the back. Scramble the frames and ask individual students to arrange each strip in its correct sequence.

Describing comic characters: Ask some of the children to describe their favorite comic strip characters. Descriptions may include information about the character's home, family, age, profession, pets, and friends, as well as personality. Have other students try to guess what character is being described.

Creating comics: Remove the words from several comic strips. Ask the students to supply their own dialogue.

Replacing comics: Have the students circle pronouns in comics and indicate the name of the person, place, or thing represented.

Rewriting comic strips: Have the students rewrite a comic strip in narrative form, describing faces, setting and background, actions, and dialogue. Emphasize that each speaker's "balloon" is a direct quotation and that paragraphs change when there is a change of speaker.

Studying editorial cartoons: Have the students collect and learn the symbols representing different ideologies and/or countries, such as the following:

Uncle Sam—United States
Hammer and sickle—Russia or Communism
Donkey—Democratic Party
Elephant—Republican Party
Dove—Peace

Suggesting main ideas: In many cases comics have a central thought that is related to the reader in a few frames. Distribute strips to small groups of students and ask them to suggest a main idea. These resulting main ideas may vary between groups for some strips and will need to be discussed as to the relative merit of each.

Studying political cartoons: Have the students make a study of political cartoons, keeping the following questions in mind:

Which recent news story prompted the cartoon?
What is the cartoonist trying to say?
Is there an editorial that promotes the same or a different point of view on the topic?

Predicting comic strip outcomes: Many comic strips have continuous story lines (e.g., "Mary Worth"; "Rex Morgan, M.D.") or a weekly theme ("Doonesbury," "Garfield," "Peanuts"). Have students predict what might happen in the next day's strip.

Identifying cause and effect: Many times comic strip humor results from cause/effect situations. These situations are often predictable, resulting from universal conflicts between characters (e.g., husband–wife in "Blondie"; boss–employee in "Beetle Bailey"; teacher–student in "Peanuts"). Have students identify the people involved, the source of conflict (cause), and the result (effect). These examples of cause/effect situations in comics can be related to stories that students read.

Integrating Writing and Reading

The newspaper is an excellent medium for teachers to use for writing activities. The following activities can be designed to use with all age levels to develop skills and abilities that will have a positive influence on children's reading and writing:

Giving advice to world leaders: Ask the children to write an advice column (such as "Dear Abby") for leading political figures. Using information gained from reading the newspaper, they can pretend they are both the leaders and the columnist.

Creating a photo essay: Have children who have trouble with written or verbal communication create photo essays on a variety of subjects such as world peace, community helpers, sports, or society. With short captions, or no captions at all, a story can be told or an idea can be expressed using a series of news photos or illustrations from the newspaper.

Studying descriptive language: Using an assigned page or section of the newspaper, have the students make lists of descriptive words, metaphors, similes, personifications, hyperboles, and expressive verbs. Adding such words and expressions to their vocabulary can be helpful in increasing their reading and writing ability.

Practicing descriptive writing: Have the students write descriptions of facial expressions and body language that they see in news photos. Have them read their sentences aloud while the other students find the photo in the newspaper.

Trying out writing styles: Help students identify different writing styles that are used in newspapers by comparing and contrasting editorials, obituaries, feature articles, and sports stories. Students can try writing in these different styles.

Writing news stories: Have the children read or listen to a short news story and try to pick out the "5 W's": Who, What, When, Where, and Why. Discuss why the "5 W's" are important, and then practice writing news stories based on classroom experiences.

Writing movie reviews: Have the students read the movie or television reviews in the newspaper and then write a review of a television show or a movie they have seen.

Writing class news: Have the students pretend that they are reporters. They can interview each other and write news stories.

Writing letters to the editor: Have the students choose an issue discussed in a news story and decide where they stand on that issue and write a letter to the editor. The teacher will want to review the policy of the newspaper regarding letters to the editor. Newspapers are interested in young people's point of view, and the good letters have a good chance of being printed.

Using the Newspaper to Develop Main Idea

Detecting the main idea or central thought of a passage is basic to reading. Students need practice in stating the main ideas of selections in their own words or finding the main sentence in a newspaper article, which in many cases is the first sentence. Fortunately for teachers, the newspaper offers a realistic, interesting, and current context for practicing main ideas at many levels.

As discussed in Chapters 4 and 6, it is important to keep in mind that comprehension strategies must be taught, not just practiced. Many children might have little trouble with comprehension in their daily reading class, but fail to apply comprehension skills in real-life reading situations. Instruction should stress transfer of strategies and skills from easier levels (pictures and words) to more complex contexts (sentences and paragraphs). The newspaper provides the effective teacher with a realistic medium for making this transfer to multiple levels.

Using Pictures for Main Idea

Have the children select different comic strips for a linking idea (e.g., sports, family, animals, playing).

Using the sports section, have the children select news photos or artwork related to a main idea (e.g., tennis/squash/racquetball = sports played with a racquet; basketball/football/baseball = sports played with a ball).

Have the children identify the type of store depicted in a pictorial advertisement with the name removed (e.g., used car center/autoparts store/supermarket).

Using a pictorial advertisement, the child can select pairs of objects and challenge other children to identify the connecting idea (e.g., Saabs, BMWs, Fords = cars; apples, oranges, grapes = fruits).

Cut out news photos and fold back the captions. Ask the students to describe what makes the picture newsworthy.

Using Words

Have the students look for groups of words that should alert the reader to a coordinating idea or topic (e.g., won/defeated/blasted = the team won; import tax/labor cost/inflation = prices going higher).

Have the students select words from the comics that convey a central thought (e.g., Nancy, Blondie, Lucy = women; Garfield, Snoopy, Marmaduke = animals).

Use sections of the newspaper for central thought practice at the word level. Using the index, children can find which section relates to words that the teacher selects (e.g., Dallas, Cosby, and Family Ties can be found in the TV section; basketball, golf, and tennis can be found in the sports section).

Using word clusters clipped from advertisements in the newspaper, have the children identify a central thought. For example, beef, turkey, and sausage should suggest the central thought "meat" to children. Maytag, Hotpoint, and Frigidaire suggest household appliances.

Using Sentences

Have the students cut key sentences from news stories. For example, "Jones wins by narrow margin in Indiana" and "The new state senator's election was credited with her popularity in the large urban areas" would be connected with the main idea "election results," whereas "Smith's three-point basket with no time on the clock saved the game for the Wildcats" and "It was one of the biggest wins in Harris' career and will move him into an elite group of coaches with 500 or more wins" would be linked with the major idea of "basketball game."

Have the students link headlines by main ideas (e.g., "Big Win for Wildcats"/"Wildcats Go Wild"/"National Champions Go Wild" are all related to a basketball team winning the national championship; "Speed Week Roars In"/"Largest Crowds Ever See New Driver Take Pole Position" are related to auto racing).

Using Paragraphs

Have the students underline the major idea in each paragraph of a news story. Then have them generalize on the position of the major idea in news paragraphs.

Newspaper stories are good sources for teaching topic sentences. Have the students select stories and underline the topic sentence.

Guide the students to skim the material and circle the nouns. A review of the circled words will identify the person, place, or thing that occurred most frequently, which will suggest the main idea. The theme will likely be something that the noun did or that was done to it.

Have the students help create this activity by clipping stories that interest them. Then have them separate the story and headline. Put 8 to 10 stories in a folder and have groups of students work together to match headlines to the correct stories. Be careful to group stories that have headlines of equal column width, or students will match headlines to size instead of content. The students may also be asked to write their own headlines in this activity, rather than use the original.

Have the students sort articles by section of the paper, using the index as a guide, to build reference skills along with main idea.

Have the students analyze editorials and/or news stories by underlining facts that support the main idea. Have them classify these details as essential, important, helpful, minor, or unnecessary.

Have the students sort articles by location (local, state, regional, national, international) after identifying the dateline location or after circling "where" clues, to build geography skills as well as provide main idea practice.

Two news stories that vary greatly in their ideas can be clipped apart by sentences or paragraphs. Ask the students to sort the clippings by topic and suggest a title for the resulting sort.

Have the students choose an item from the newspaper about an event that has occurred locally, and summarize the item in no more than three sentences. Then discuss why they think the people in the article did what they did or reacted in the way the article reports.

Teaching Grammar through the Newspaper

Grammar is a subject that many teachers have trouble making interesting and relevant to students. However, it is a subject that is still included in many schools' curricula, and it is tested on many standardized tests. The newspaper is an excellent supplement to the language exercise books that many children dislike and cannot relate to real reading. The following activities can be helpful:

Pronouns: Ask the students to circle all the pronouns they find in a short news story. Then ask them to tell to whom each pronoun refers.

Adjectives: Have students look for an advertisement describing something they would like to have and determine which words describe the item for sale. Have them cut out or circle the words. Discuss how the advertisement would be different without adjectives. The children might create their own advertisements using adjectives.

In another activity, have the students find three pictures that illustrate the comparative nature of adjectives (e.g., sad, sadder, saddest) or have them look for examples of adjectives and classify them as positive, comparative, or superlative.

Conjunctions: Have the children cross out conjunctions in a news story and then read the story aloud. Ask what they notice about the smooth flow of the sentence?

Capitals: Have the students circle words that begin with a capital letter and explain why they are capitalized. Ask whether they can come up with any generalizations for capitalization.

Antonyms: For fun, have the students change adjectives in advertisements to their antonyms.

Plurals: Have the students find a news story of interest and circle all the words that mean "more than one." Ask them what word endings are usually used to make a word plural. Ask whether they can find any plural words that are exceptions.

Quotations: Have the children find examples of direct and indirect quotations and write who said each.

Possessives: Have the children look in the newspaper until they find a possessive noun. After the possessive noun has been identified, the students can determine ownership (e.g., "Tuesday's weather = the weather belonging to Tuesday).

Apostrophes: Have the children circle words in the newspaper that have apostrophes. When they have found at least 10, have them write the words in groups, with possessive words on the left side of the paper, contractions on the right. Have them check each other's work. Discuss the words that give problems.

S Endings: Have the students clip words that end with *s* and classify them as singular, plural, or possessive.

Types of Sentences: Have the students look through the newspaper for five examples each of declarative, imperative, and interrogative sentences.

Reading Activities for the Lower Grades

The following are activities that work well with young children who need practice in applying the basic skills and strategies of reading. The newspaper provides an interesting and realistic application of these important skills for young students.

The Alphabet: Have the children clip letters from headlines and advertisements until they have enough to complete the entire alphabet in upper and/or lower case. Paste the letters on paper and display them in the room.

Alphabet Book: Have the students clip out pictures that begin with each letter of the alphabet, paste them on sheets of paper, and make a book.

Names: Have the children clip letters from headlines or advertisements until they have the proper letters to spell their names. Have each child paste the letters on a piece of paper to spell his or her name.

Alphabet Scavenger Hunt: Have the students find a word that starts with "a" and circle it. Then have them find a word that starts with "b," circle it and connect the two words with a line. Have them continue until they have circled and connected words that start with each letter of the alphabet.

Initial Sound Recognition: Use advertisements containing illustrations to reinforce lessons on initial consonant sounds (e.g., "I see something in this ad that starts with the 't' sound. What is it?").

Confusing Consonants: Have the students underline newspaper words that begin with the following consonant sounds: *b/d, m/w,* and *p/g.* Work on one consonant at a time, and then switch to its "twin."

Word Hide and Seek: Select a word on a specific page of the newspaper and have the students ask "yes" or "no" questions to help them locate the word (e.g., Is the word in a headline? Is it a noun?).

Reading Activities for the Upper Grades

The following additional ideas can be used by effective teachers with the newspaper. The successful completion of these activities will enable students to expand their critical reading skills.

Have the students select a particular event in the newspaper that they can follow for at least a week. Examples might be a major sporting event or an important visit to the United States by a foreign leader.

Have the students select one news story of interest to them. Have them take facts from the story and rewrite it. They can make a list of new vocabulary words found in the story.

Have the students collect editorials for a week or more. For each story, have them underline the facts in one color and the opinions in another.

Have the students clip three news stories from the newspaper. Have them answer the following questions: (1) What is the purpose of the story: to persuade, to inform, to entertain, to form an opinion, or to interpret? (2) What key words and phrases are used to accomplish the purpose? (3) Is the story based on fact or opinion?

Ask the students to choose an item from the newspaper and write down the answers to the following questions, using no more than one sentence for each: *Who* was involved? *What* happened? *Where* did it happen? *When* did it happen? *Why* did it happen?

Choose an item from the newspaper about an event that has occurred locally. Ask the students to summarize the item in no more than three sentences. Then discuss why they think the people in the article reacted in the way the news story reports.

UNICEF means United Nations Children's Emergency Fund. Have the children read and find other initials that are commonly used in the newspaper. By reading the news story, they can find out what the initials stand for.

SUMMARY

If schools are successful, students will develop the skills necessary to read a wide range of materials. They will also develop the interest and motivation to read frequently on their own.

However, students need to be encouraged not only to read frequently, but also to read a variety of materials. Langer, Applebee, Mullis, and Foertsch (1990) reported that young children's reading is dominated by stories. Unfortunately, this is not unexpected since reading instruction, which constitutes a large portion of the reading that children do, relies largely on the use of the basal reader, which is story based. In the same report, substantial proportions of the students indicated that they rarely read in school from other materials such as newspapers, magazines, biographies, or even additional basic texts as supplemental material. In discussing this report, Phyllis Aldrich, chair of the reading committee of the governing board of the National Assessment of Educational Progress, stated that "the message for educators is that emphasis on a single basal reader at unchallenging levels might be hobbling children's ability to think. This report seems to indicate that we have underestimated our children's abilities, interests and willingness to work, and in the process we have short-changed them" (cited in "Reading Still Taught" [1990], p. 2).

By using newspapers in the classroom reading program, the effective teacher can not only help children learn to read, but also provide instructional materials that will encourage them to expand their reading horizons. Vocabulary, word-attack, and comprehension skills can be learned through the newspaper from primary grades through high school. Newspapers can be used for instruction in almost any area of the school curriculum.

Contemporary problems such as pollution, war, peace, hunger, space exploration, and economics are covered in the newspaper. This allows the teacher to provide materials of which the content is of vital interest to today's students, who often have great concerns about the world in which they live. In addition, the newspaper, with its "adult" status, does not belittle the less skilled older reader as might books written on a lower reading level.

FOLLOW-UP QUESTIONS AND ACTIVITIES

1. Contact your local newspaper for information about using the newspaper in the classroom.
2. Write the American Newspaper Publishers Association, Foundation for a free copy of *Bibliography: NIE Publications,* which annotates more than 100 NIE curriculum publications for students and teachers.

   ANPA, Foundation
   The Newspaper Center
   Box 17407
   Dulles International Airport
   Washington, DC 20041
3. Explain why newspapers are important to our form of government and how you might explain this to a classroom of fourth-grade students.
4. Discuss why newspapers may be a better reading material for fifth-grade students who are poor readers than remedial reading material provided by a textbook publisher.

ADDITIONAL READINGS

Bryant, J. R. (1988). Wacky wire service records capture students' interest. *Journal of Reading,* 32, 274–275.

Cheyney, A. B. (1984). *Teaching reading skills through the newspaper.* Newark, DE: International Reading Association.

Criscuolo, N. P., & Gallagher, S. A. (1989). Using the newspaper with disruptive students. *Journal of Reading,* 32, 440–443.

Hawks, G. (1988). Dollars & sense: The newspaper as an economic resource. *Journal of Reading,* 32, 166–167.

Kossack, S., & Sullivan, J. (1989). Newspaper activities for the second language student. *Journal of Reading,* 32, 740–742.

Patrie, J. (1988). Comprehensible text: The daily newspaper at the beginning level. *TESL Talk,* 18, 28–31.

Vail, C. O., Monda, L. E., & Koorland, M. A. (1989). Behavior disordered students use the news. *Journal of Reading,* 32, 364–365.

Wells, J., Reichbach, E., Kossack, S., & Dungey, J. (1987). Newspapers facilitate content area learning: Social studies. *Journal of Reading, 31,* 270–271.

REFERENCES

American Newspaper Publishers Association. (1984). *Teaching with the newspaper, 4*(1).

Langer, J. A., Applebee, A. N., Mullis, I. V. S., & Foertsch, M. A. (1990). *Learning to read in our nation's schools: Instruction and achievement in 1988 at grades 4, 8, and 12.* Princeton, NJ: Educational Testing Service.

Reading still taught the same old way, NAEP says. (1990, June 13). *Report on Education Research, 22*(12).

Author Index

H

I

J

K

L

M

N

O

P

R

S

T

Subject Index

Note: Page numbers followed by *f* indicate figures.

D

M

N

R

S

T

X